Crowding Out Fiscal Stimulus

John J. Heim

Crowding Out Fiscal Stimulus

Testing the Effectiveness of US Government Stimulus Programs

palgrave
macmillan

John J. Heim
University at Albany-SUNY
Albany, New York
USA

ISBN 978-3-319-45966-0 ISBN 978-3-319-45967-7 (eBook)
DOI 10.1007/978-3-319-45967-7

Library of Congress Control Number: 2016954261

Cover illustration: © Everett Collection Historical / Alamy

Printed on acid-free paper

This Palgrave Macmillan imprint is published by Springer Nature
The registered company is Springer International Publishing AG
The registered company address is: Gewerbestrasse 11, 6330 Cham, Switzerland

For
Sarah and Tom
J.B. and Jenn
Lindsay and Luke
Kelly and Casey
Scott and Ross

Executive Summary

Do deficit-financed government fiscal stimulus programs actually stimulate the economy? This study exhaustively tests a wide variety of different stimulus models, testing them in different time periods, and using different regression techniques in an attempt to answer this question. Fiscal stimulus programs examined include both those that cut taxes and those that increase government spending.

Most models that predict government deficits will stimulate the economy are Keynesian. A principal characteristic is that they are demand-driven. Each of their key structural equations indicate increases in demand will lead to increased supply (and employment), at least up to full employment of resources. Hence a deficit, which increases government demand by increasing government spending, or increases private demand by cutting taxes, stimulates the economy, according to stimulus theory.

In testing whether these stimulus programs actually work, we took care to test equations taken from the Keynesian model. This gives the stimulus effects of deficits, should they exist, the best possible chance of being verified empirically. 1960–2010 data on the US economy were used. A total of 228 models of the determinants of consumption, investment and the GDP were tested. These models differ in the variables included, the time period tested, the regression techniques used, the level of the economy when testing and the specific type of tax cut or spending stimulus used. Each model is reported in detail, with differences in each subsequent model compared to the last tested. Differences in results are compared as well. The work is lengthy, but necessarily so. Our goal was to test every conceivable model readers might feel stood a chance of showing positive stimulus effects. That way, whatever our results turned out to be, it would be difficult to argue we did not examine a wide enough breath of stimulus programs to give them a fair chance to show what they can do.

In theory, the effectiveness of stimulus programs can be curtailed by "crowd out". Crowd out theory suggests that whatever their stimulus effects, government deficits have the undesirable result of simultaneously reducing private spending, because funds normally borrowed by consumers and businesses must be used to fund the deficit. Reduced private borrowing in turn causes a reduction in consumer and business spending, offsetting the deficit's stimulus effects.

In testing to show crowd out effects, a deficit variable is added to each Keynesian consumption, investment or GDP model. This allows simultaneous testing of both Keynesian stimulus and crowd out effects. Each model shows stimulus and crowd out effects separately, and allows readers to directly calculate net effects of stimulus programs, for example, the effects of reductions in federal taxes on consumption spending, controlling for many other factors that affect consumer spending. Everybody acknowledges the possibility that crowd out, "if it occurs", can adversely affect stimulus programs. Rarely do people actually test to see if it does occur. This book's unique contribution is to *exhaustively* test to determine if it does occur, and if so, how serious a problem it is.

As alternatives to Keynesian models, we could have tested dynamic stochastic general equilibrium (DSGE) models, but these are models that typically contain assumptions about human behavior like perfect foresight and intertemporal utility maximization, that are designed to *infer from these assumed behavioral characteristics* that stimulus programs don't work in the long run. Similarly, we could have picked different combinations of five or six variables thought appropriate and tested VAR models. The problem here is that since VARs typically are not recognizable theoretical constructs, it is hard to know what your results mean. By comparison, we know what a Keynesian theoretical construct means, and if we slip a deficit variable into it and then test, the test will either show the variable statistically significant (crowd out matters) or not (crowd out doesn't matter), *controlling for all the other Keynesian influences.* In short, we will have a useful result, from a fair test, scientifically arrived at.

When examining how consumption or investment spending varies as deficits rise or fall, we control for the effect of business cycle variation on both government deficits and on private spending. This was necessary to unambiguously identify crowd out's effects. A declining economy alone can cause a growing deficit and simultaneously declining consumer and business spending, but that is a business cycle effect, not a crowd out effect in which the deficit *causes* the decline in private spending. Some argue it is only business cycle effects, not crowd out, which cause the negative relationship between deficits and private spending. They argue that without the stimulus programs, the observed decline in private spending associated with the deficit would have just been worse. The difference between this and the crowd out explanation has enormous political and economic implications for government's role in the economy.

Methodologically, extensive tests for endogeneity, stationarity and heteroskedasticity were undertaken. Testing was done in first differences, eliminating most non-stationarity and reducing multicollinearity problems by about half. Models explained 90–95 % of the yearly changes of consumption and investment during the 50-year period tested. Four different, though overlapping, time periods were tested. Findings were essentially the same for the 1950s and 1960s as for the 2001–10 decade, and for decades in between. Deficit results were also robust for moderate changes in the structure of the models tested. They were also generally robust to different regression techniques (OLS, strong and weak instrument 2SLS), and use of different strong 2SLS instruments. Hence, we feel our findings will be difficult to refute in reasonably well-constructed future models of how the Keynesian system works.

Our findings overwhelmingly indicate that as government deficits grow, creating observable stimulus effects, consumer and business spending declines due to crowd out, fully cancelling the stimulus effects (or worse). The offsetting decline in private spending appears due to "crowd out", that is, trying to finance both increased deficits and traditional private borrowing levels from a relatively unchanging sized pool of loanable funds.

This finding that stimulus programs do not work held in virtually all circumstances tested. The specific type of tax cut or government spending deficit did not matter, nor did it matter if we tested in recessions or normal economic times. Nor did it matter what particular decades since 1960 we tested, and, generally, it did not matter if we used one regression technique (OLS) versus another (2SLS) to do our analysis (though as a matter of good practice, where 2SLS is needed, it should be used). With rare exceptions, usually due to statistical problems like multicollinearity, none of these variations in the models we tested resulted in a net positive effect for tax cut or spending increase stimulus programs. In virtually all cases, results indicated crowd out fully, or more than fully, offset stimulus effects.

Examination of the 1981–83 recession period indicates the pool of loanable funds drops even faster in recessions than business and consumer loan demand. Hence, new deficit financing demands on the pool of loanable funds in recessions, if anything, cause even bigger crowd out problems than in normal times. The data examined support this conclusion.

The models from which we obtained these results also explain extremely well the behavior of consumption and investment during the 2007–09 economic crisis. Our econometric findings suggest that deficit-financed stimulus programs such as the 2009 Obama stimulus program have a substantial negative effect on the GDP, raising unemployment 2.26–2.94 % during the period they are in force. Deficits have this undesirable result because to fund them, funds normally borrowed by consumers and businesses are used. Reduced borrowing by consumers and businesses in turn causes a reduction in their spending, offsetting the deficit's stimulus effects.

Worse, "lumpiness" in borrowing tends to result in private spending reductions even greater than the stimulus' positive effects, leading stimulus programs to have a net negative impact on the economy. By lumpiness we mean the following: consumers who need to borrow $10,000 to buy a new car, but find that their bank can only lend them $9000 (because they lent the other $1000 to the government to finance a $1000 stimulus program), will not buy the car at all. This causes private spending to fall $10,000 from expected levels, a far greater drop than the stimulus can offset.

Chapter 16 provides a more detailed summary of findings and conclusions.

Preface

I left academic life in 1972, not to return until a quarter century later. When I returned, one of the most hotly contested issues of my youth, "Do Keynesian-type stimulus programs work?" was still unresolved. I was surprised because when I left academia, work in economics seemed more and more dominated by the new, econometrically based scientific method, rather than the older philosophical approach, i.e., mainly theoretical deductions derived from "self evident" truths about human and business behavior. I felt it would only be a matter of time before science provided an answer to the stimulus question. That did not occur.

My research interests in large-scale econometric modeling led me to try to develop and test a Keynesian-type model of the macroeconomy. For about six months, I kept trying to build and test simple Keynesian Cross and IS-LM models, and then extend the work to more complex models of the same type, but with no success. In empirical test after test, I kept coming up with the wrong sign on the government revenues variable: I was consistently getting positive signs, when Keynesian stimulus theory said I should be getting negative signs. Worse, I was having nearly as bad a problem with my government spending results. In more sophisticated models, test results for government spending were also giving me the wrong sign: negative instead of the positive sign Keynesian theory leads us to expect.

What to do? One thought was just scrap my Keynesian model testing program and move on to testing some other theory. This is clearly what many of my colleagues had done during the 1980s and 1990s when I was out of macroeconomics. What large-scale models remained were now DSGE-based.

This option, to me, seemed like throwing the baby out with the bath water. Despite the peculiar signs on the tax and government spending variables in my consumption and investment models, Keynesian models explained most of the variation in the economy over the past 50 years very well. They certainly did so better than DSGE models.

Hence, the better option seemed to be to try to find something that was missing from standard textbook Keynesian models that might clarify why in a Keynesian model that generally does a pretty good job of explaining economic behavior, results for fiscal policy variables were so at odds with Keynesian theory.

Endless numbers of variables were added and subtracted from the standard IS model, knowing that the "left out" variables problem, and the multicollinearity problem, can cause variables, for technical reasons, to have signs opposite of what theory would have us expect.

None seemed to cure the problem until we added the government deficit as a separate variable from the government spending and tax variables already in the model. The results clearly showed the expected stimulus effects of government spending and tax cuts Keynesian theory predicts, but the sign on the deficit variable (defined as government taxes minus government spending) was positive, indicating negative effects on the economy for tax cuts and positive effects for government spending cuts. When the two effects for taxes and government spending were added together, consolidating the two spending and two tax variables into one of each, and retesting, the net effect was to give both variables the wrong sign from the Keynesian perspective.

In reality, it just meant that there were two separate government spending and tax effects—the stimulus effects of deficits predicted by Keynesian theory, and the "crowd out" effects also caused by government deficits. Unfortunately, the crowd out is larger than the stimulus effect. This gives us the "perverse" signs on spending and tax variables when we force the two effects to be consolidated into one variable by only including one set of spending and tax variables in the model (i.e., by leaving the deficit variable out). This book includes test results for models that separately test for both the stimulus and crowd out effects. The tests find both effects occur whenever a stimulus program is enacted, that both stimulus and crowd out effects are statistically significant at high levels and that the crowd out effect dominates.

Albany, NY

John J. Heim

Acknowledgements

I am highly indebted to two distinguished econometricians, Kajal Lahiri and Terrence Kinal. Both provided extensive review comments and suggestions on an earlier draft, as well as continuing counsel along the way. They were a source of inspiration and without their involvement, especially Kajal Lahiri's, this book would not have been written.

Nor could the book have been written without the strong support of my wife, Sue. This book required two years' full-time work, and before that, considerable part-time work. The problems to be resolved required endless long hours at work, and it endlessly preoccupied my mind, even at home. Sue was always willing to make the sacrifices necessary to cope with all that.

Finally, I must acknowledge the secretarial assistance provided by Annemarie Hebert. She has helped pull together, duplicate and send out endless drafts of this work.

Contents

List of Tables

About the Author

John J. Heim has an MPA from Harvard University and a Ph.D. in Political Economy from SUNY Albany. He was Clinical Professor of Economics at Rensselaer Polytechnic Institute, Troy, NY, He joined RPI in 1997 after a career outside academia, and taught there for 15 years before retirement. He currently is Visiting Professor of Economics, SUNY Albany. He has published over 20 articles in the last nine years, and two books scheduled to be published in the next year, all of which attempt to strengthen the scientific base underlying macroeconomics. Dr. Heim also maintains an interest in engineering and In 2015 he was awarded a U.S. patent for an inexpensive renewable energy device that converts the power of water waves to electrical energy. In his early career, prior to joining RPI, he worked as an economics and econometrics consultant, a finance analyst in the NY State governor's office, he was Director of Fiscal and Budget Research for the minority party in the NY State Senate, and Commissioner of Administration and Finance for the city of Buffalo, NY. He also served as Assistant Executive Director of the Facilities Development Corporation, a public benefit corporation involved in construction management and real estate procurement. He also served as President of Heim Industries, Inc., which produced and marketed statistical software.

CHAPTER 1

Introduction

Over 30 years ago, Otto Eckstein, one of the world's most distinguished econometricians, noted the "crowd out" problem's impact on stimulus programs, though much debated, was "still" unresolved:

> Does fiscal policy work? Or does the financing of deficits "crowd out" private activity? This has been one of the more durable controversies in macroeconomic theory. (Eckstein 1983, p.35)

The most important unresolved question in macroeconomics over 30 years ago remains unresolved today. This reflects poorly on the macroeconomic science as a source of reliable macroeconomic guidance. The failure of macroeconomists to be able to answer what is perhaps the most important question asked of them, can only be an embarrassment to all economists.

By "crowd out" we mean the reduction in funds available to private borrowers from the existing pool of loanable funds that results when government borrows some of those available funds to finance deficits. This creates a problem for consumers and businesses who also wish to borrow from this pool of funds to supplement the purchasing power of their incomes; for example, consumers buy cars or businesses buy new machinery using borrowed money. Crowd out reduces the loanable funds available to private parties for such borrowing. When the private sector's ability to borrow is reduced by government borrowing from the same pool, it may reduce consumer and business spending that was to be financed out

J.J. Heim, *Crowding Out Fiscal Stimulus*,
DOI 10.1007/978-3-319-45967-7_1

of this borrowing. This may offset some or all of the stimulus effect of a government deficit. Evidence presented in Chaps. 5, 6, 7, 8, 10, 14 and 15 indicates it does.

While private borrowing does decline in recessionary periods, the decline in savings (loanable funds) may be as much or more than the decline in loan demand, since savings rise and fall with income. If so, government deficits during recessions will still have negative crowd out effects. Hence, one cannot say a priori that crowd out is less of a problem in recessions, when governments tend to deficit the most, than in good times. It is fundamentally an empirical question, depending on how fast savings have dropped relative to the demand for private loans. Flow of Funds evidence presented in Chap. 12 suggests savings drop as fast as or faster than private loan demand. If so, this means crowd out will be as much a problem in recessions as in more normal economic times.

Heim (2010) used a 23-equation structural econometric model of the US economy 1960–2000 to evaluate crowd out problems and the extent to which government deficits were related to reduced private consumer and investment spending. The results indicated that when a government deficit variable was added to standard Keynesian consumption and investment models, adjusting for a range of econometric issues, including endogeneity, stationarity, and so on, tests showed a highly statistically significant negative relationship between deficits and private spending. The study did not directly test the mechanism by which deficits seemed negatively related to consumer and investment spending. Hence, a number of explanations were possible, including the explanation that the findings simply measured normal business cycle effects which cause deficit growth and private spending declines to occur simultaneously in recessions. For "crowd out" to be the culprit, theory requires that reduced private borrowing, induced by government deficits, be the mechanism, and that the negative relationship occur even controlling for the effects of the business cycle. This paper attempts to test the crowd out hypothesis, controlling for changes in the business cycle.

The paper tests the crowd out mechanism hypothesis directly, testing to see if private *borrowing* is reduced by deficits as much as is spending. US Federal Reserve Flow of Funds data on borrowing 1960–2010 are used. It expands the data used in the 2010 study significantly, to include data through 2010, including the 2008 recession, and uses far more sophisticated tests of endogeneity and instrumental variable suitability than those used in the 2010 study.

Doing so, this paper examines

- whether the relationship exists between government deficits and private borrowing is negative, and whether borrowing and spending move in lock step.
- whether private borrowing is an *independent, additional* determinant of private spending, beyond income, interest rates, wealth, and so on. Total purchasing power, including access to borrowed funds, may be a better determinant of spending behavior than income alone. If so, constraints on borrowing clearly do affect private spending.
- whether crowd out is a factor in recessions, even if demand for borrowed funds drops.
- whether different types of tax cuts or government spending have different net crowd out effects.

CHAPTER 2

Theory of Crowd Out

2.1 Traditional (No-Crowd Out) Keynesian Stimulus Theory

2.1.1 *The Theory*

The standard Keynesian demand-driven structural model of the macroeconomy, though historically empirically successful in explaining a great deal of the economy's variation, does not normally include variables for crowd out in its consumption and investment equations. In such models, the impact of taxes and government spending are shown, and are derived from the GDP identity:

$$\text{GDP} = Y = C + I + G + (X - M) \tag{2.1}$$

where consumption might be given as a linear function of disposable income $(Y - T)$

$$C = \beta(Y - T) \tag{2.2}$$

which, when substituted into (2.1) gives

$$Y = \left(\frac{1}{1-\beta}\right)(-\beta T + I + G + (X - M)) \tag{2.3}$$

J.J. Heim, *Crowding Out Fiscal Stimulus*,
DOI 10.1007/978-3-319-45967-7_2

Notice the negative sign on the tax variable coefficient in standard stimulus—model mechanics.

The multiplier effects of ΔT and ΔG are:

$$\left(\frac{-\beta}{1-\beta}\right) \qquad \left(\frac{1}{1-\beta}\right) \tag{2.4}$$

Tax Multiplier Spending Multiplier

The clear expectation of standard model demand theory is that tax changes in are expected to be negatively related to the GDP, with a multiplier effect $-\beta/(1-\beta)$. Changes in government spending and net exports are related to GDP in the positive direction, with a multiplier effect $1/(1-\beta)$ and should when tested, have the same coefficients if the theory holds. The coefficient on changes in taxes should have a negative sign, indicating tax cuts would have a positive effect on GDP. In Chaps. 5–8 below, we will test these expected relationships to see if actual econometric estimates yield the predicted results for variables.

2.1.2 *Empirical Problems with Traditional Theory*

It is nearly impossible to get a negative sign on the tax variable in econometric tests, even in the simplest model, the so-called "Keynesian Cross", commonly used to instruct beginning economics students:

$$Y = f\ (T, G, \text{Investment}, X - M) \tag{2.5}$$

This means tax cut deficits depress the economy, not stimulate it.

Once we even slightly increase the sophistication of the model by replacing investment with its two most commonly cited determinants, the accelerator (ACC) and interest rates, for example,

$$Y = f\ (T, G, \text{ACC}, \text{Int Rate}, X - M) \tag{2.6}$$

all tests show the tax variable's sign to be both positive and statistically significant for this simple "IS" curve. In Table 2.1 below we show examples taken from 2SLS regression tests of these two models. All Keynesian models are tested using the best econometric methods: instruments for Hausman test—endogenous variables, Wald tests to avoid weak instruments and Sargan tests to ensure elimination of endogeneity in the instrumented

Table 2.1 Tests of simple Keynesian models for the stimulus effects of tax cuts

Model	*Tax coefficient (t-statistic)*
Keynesian Cross: $Y = f(T, G, \text{Inv(Total)}, X - M)$	+0.17 (2.2)
Simple IS Curve Model: $Y = f(T, G, \text{ACC}, \text{Int Rate}, X - M)$	+0.72 (3.4)
Sophisticated IS Curve Model: $Y = f(T, G,$ ACC, Int Rates, Dow Jones, Average Exch. Rate, Pop. Growth Rate, Prior Period M2 Growth, Consumer Confidence, Depreciation Allowances, Profits, $X)$	+0.49 (2.7)

models. Time trend variables were used to control serial correlation if needed. US data was used for 1960–2010.

In addition, in more sophisticated models, the sign of the government spending variable is also opposite what standard stimulus theory leads us to expect. Therefore, it tells us that spending deficits also depress the economy, not stimulate it. The same models were tested for other sample periods (1960–2000, 1970–2000 and 1970–2010) and generally provided the same results. Clearly, if even the simplest tests of standard stimulus theory variables consistently show deficits to have the wrong sign, it raises serious questions about the theoretical basis for government stimulus policy.

Despite these findings, it would seem excessive to throw out the whole of Keynesian demand-driven modeling theory based on these findings. Basic Keynesian theory empirically explains with uncanny accuracy much of the variance in consumption and investment over time. The determinants of these functions, when added together, constitute most of the IS function, a common statistical method of GDP determination. The inconsistency of some empirics with the theory may not necessarily be due to a fallacy in the theory itself (which would be an error of *commission*), so much as an error of *omission*: perhaps the standard stimulus model, though generally accurate, does not include a key variable which can offset the stimulus effects of deficits, namely, the explicit inclusion in tests (and theorizing) of the "crowd out" variable. If so, by adding the "crowd out" variable, a good model becomes even better at accurately explaining how the economy operates, albeit at the cost of reversing its earlier fiscal policy prescriptions.

2.2 Keynesian Stimulus Theory with Crowd out

To test the hypothesis that government deficits may reduce loanable funds available to finance consumer spending normally financed out of borrowed funds, the simplified consumption function used earlier must be modified to add the government deficit: the variable hypothesized to cause this crowd out: taxes minus government spending ($T - G$):

$$C = \beta\,(Y - T) + \lambda(T - G) \tag{2.7}$$

Lambda (λ) represents the marginal crowd out effect of the government deficit on consumer demand (spending). With this function, the simple Keynesian Cross model becomes

$$\begin{aligned} \text{GDP} = Y &= \beta\,(Y - T) + \lambda_1(T - G) + G + I + (X - M) \\ &= \left(\frac{1}{1-\beta}\right)\left((-\beta + \lambda_1)T + (1 - \lambda_1)G + I + (X - M)\right) \end{aligned} \tag{2.8}$$

From which we can easily see that the impact of a change in T or G on the GDP depends on the marginal crowd out effect (λ) as well as the marginal stimulus effect (β). The tax multiplier, showing the marginal impact of a change in taxes is now $(-\beta + \lambda_1)/(1 - \beta)$. The spending multiplier, showing the marginal impact of a change in government spending, is now $(1 - \lambda_1)/(1 - \beta)$. If the crowd out effect is greater than zero, *Both T and G net marginal stimulus effects will be smaller (in absolute terms) than they would have been without crowd out effects.*

We can expand this model to include effects of crowd out on investment spending. Assume a simple investment model in which investment is determined by only three variables: the accelerator (ACC), real interest rates (r) and access to credit, which varies with the government deficit ($T - G$).

$$I = \gamma(T - G) - \theta_1 r + \gamma\ \text{ACC} + \lambda_2(T - G) \tag{2.9}$$

where gamma (γ) indicates the marginal effect of crowd out (the government deficit) on investment spending, and (θ_1,θ_2) represents the marginal effects of real interest rates and the accelerator.

Replacing investment and consumption in the GDP identity with their hypothesized determinants, we obtain a typical Keynesian IS equation:

$$\text{GDP} = Y = \left(\frac{1}{1-\beta}\right)[(-\beta + \lambda_1 + \lambda_2)\,T + (1 - \lambda_1 - \lambda_2)\,G - \theta\,r$$
$$+ \gamma\,\text{ACC} + (X - M)] \tag{2.10}$$

In this IS equation, the normal stimulating impact of tax cuts on the GDP $(-\beta)$ is offset in part by the effects of deficit-induced changes in credit available to consumers and investors $(\lambda + \gamma)$. *Tax stimulus effects may switch from negative to positive if the crowd out effects* $(\lambda + \gamma)$ *are larger than the disposable income effect* $(-\beta)$. The effect of a change in government spending is also reduced per dollar of expenditure from just the stimulus effect (1) to that effect net of crowd out effects $(-\lambda - \gamma)$. Net stimulus effects may be reduced *or may even switch from positive to negative if crowd out effects exceed the stimulus effect.* The net exports stimulus effect (also 1) stays the same, now becoming relatively stronger relative to government spending or tax cuts. Results are shown in Table 2.2.

Simple extensions of this model allow for different effects of tax cut and spending increase deficits (see Chaps. 6 and 8), different effects during recession and non-recession periods (Chaps. 14 and 15), and different kinds of tax cuts or spending increases (Chaps. 3, p. 10; 5.12, p. 29; 10.3, p. 98 and 16, p. 116).

There are a number of theoretical reasons why λ_1 and λ_2 may leave the tax coefficient zero or positive, and the spending coefficient zero or negative. Discontinuities may cause private borrowing (and therefore spending) to decline more than the deficit has reduced loanable funds: a bank may only be able to lend a consumer part of what is need to buy a new car, but this reduces car spending by the whole amount. Also, in addition to the decline in private spending resulting from the stimulus, stimulus dollars may only be used to maintain previous spending levels among stimulus aid recipients. In

Table 2.2 Simple Keynesian mechanics with and without crowd out

	Without crowd out	*With crowd out*		*Without crowd out*	*With crowd out*
Tax coefficient	$(-\beta)$	$(-\beta+\lambda_1+\lambda_2)$	Government spending coefficient	1	$(1-\lambda_1-\lambda_2)$
Tax multiplier	$\frac{(-\beta)}{(1-\beta)}$	$\frac{(-\beta+\lambda_1+\lambda_2)}{(1-\beta)}$	Government spending multiplier	$\frac{(1)}{(1-\beta)}$	$\frac{(1-\lambda_1-\lambda_2)}{(1-\beta)}$

this case, the net effect of the stimulus is zero, since without the deficit, private spending out of borrowed money would not have declined, but private spending by stimulus recipients might have. Finally, evidence indicates that even holding income and economic conditions constant, private spending varies with availability of borrowing. Chapters 8.3, p. 88, 10.1, pp. 92–93 and 16, p. 123 present more detail on theory of crowd out.

CHAPTER 3

Literature Review

The validity of stimulus theory hangs heavily on whether deficits crowd out private borrowing, and therefore, private spending. We could find no serious scientific work directly testing the impact of deficits on private *borrowing*, and relatively little professional level work done testing the relationship between private spending and deficits, considering the policy importance of the topic. As noted earlier, Otto Eckstein, who fathered the 800-equation Data Resources, Inc. (DRI) large-scale macroeconomic model, noted the same problem 30 years ago:

Does fiscal policy work? Or does the financing of deficits "crowd out" private activity. This has been one of the more durable controversies in macroeconomic theory. (1983, p. 35)

3.1 Popular Press

The popular press is filled with seemingly endless discussion of crowd out effects when stimulus programs are proposed, typically based on the *assumptions,* not science, about whether crowd out does or does not work. A few typical examples include:

1. *Chan, S.* (*NY Times,* 2/7/10, p. A16): Chan noted the IMF had indicated that "rising government debt could crowd out private borrowing and raise interest rates for private borrowers, and slow down economic recovery."

J.J. Heim, *Crowding Out Fiscal Stimulus,*
DOI 10.1007/978-3-319-45967-7_3

2. *Barley, R.* (*Wall Street Journal*, 2/24/10 p. C14): Barley noted government bond buying by banks caused a crowd out problem, reducing loanable funds available to consumers and businesses.
3. Krugman (*New York Times*, 9/28/09) notes that in recessions, the accelerator effect is likely to dominate crowd out effects, leaving a net stimulus effect of government spending increases/tax cuts.

3.2 Professional Literature

3.2.1 General, Including Gale and Orszag

In the professional literature, most studies examining crowd out have principally been literature reviews of other studies.

Spencer and Yohe (1970) found in a review of studies over nearly 200 years, that the dominant view from all types of studies has been that government deficits cause crowding out.

Friedman (1978) is largely theoretical. He notes portfolio theory suggests the LM curve may shift in response to an IS shift due to a government deficit and that elasticity of substitution between bonds and stocks when interest rates rise (due to deficit borrowing) is key to whether crowd out (or crowd in) occurs: elasticities less than one lead to "crowd out"; greater than one: "crowd in". Therefore crowd out effects are indeterminate theoretically. Friedman's own empirical results, based on money demand models, were ambiguous.

Eckstein (1983, p. 37) indicated simulations using DRI's 800-equation large-scale structural econometric model showed that short-term effects of crowd out were positive, with multiplier effects of 0.6 to 1.6, depending on monetary accommodation, but long-term multiplier effects fall to 0–0.6 within 5 years due to the negative effects of inflation on prices and wages.

Gale and Orszag (2004) do include some empirical testing indicating crowd out may matter, but does not eliminate stimulus effects. Consumer demand was hypothesized to be a function of income defined as current and one period lagged Net National Product (NNP), government purchases, taxes, transfer payments, interest payments and the size of the government debt. Some models also added tax rate variables, and estimated state and federal taxes separately. Ordinary Least Squares (OLS) regression was used; the principal regressions tested models on data for 1954–92 or for 1954–2002, with markedly different results.

Specification: The consumption model tested is neither a VAR model nor structural, but has some structural components. It also includes variables that allow for testing both Ricardian and non-Ricardian hypotheses. There is the implication that anything left out is not necessary to control for, and doesn't influence key variables of interest (or perhaps is not available). Results were not robust to period sampled. For example, in the (1954–92) period sampled, neither taxes nor government spending had statistically significant stimulus effects on consumption. Crowd out may be the reason why, but this can only be a hypothesis, since crowd out requires a decline in private borrowing, and changes in borrowing associated with taxes or spending was not tested. Adding ten more years to the data set (1993–2002), shows tax cuts resulting in partial crowd out, with some statistically significant stimulus effects remaining. Lack of robustness for different time periods makes interpretation of either set of results difficult.

In a second set of tests on the longer 1954–2002 period, Orszag and Gale used separate tax variables for federal government compared to state and local government taxes. They found federal tax cuts having a statistically significant positive stimulus effect on consumption, while state and local tax cuts significantly related to reduced consumer spending. Tax rates for labor, when cut, stimulated consumption, but not tax rate cuts for capital. The only kind of government spending found to have a significant stimulus effect, was transfer payment spending (See Table 3, p. 135, col. 1 and 2). The percent of variance explained by the model is not given, but was probably substantial, since income variable, crowd out variables and a wealth variable are included as determinants. In structural studies cited below, these were found to be the major determinants of consumption, as were interest rates and exchange rates to a lesser extent. Gale and Orzag's 1956–2002 results for annual data (Table 3, col. 1) are shown below:

Table 3.1 Determinants of Consumption: β (Standard Error)

NNP_0	0.36 (.08)	$G_{Purchases}$	0.15 (0.15)	Gov't. $debt_{-1}$	−0.03 (−0.02)
NNP_{-1}	0.13 (.05)	$G_{Transfers}$	0.76 (0.29)	$Wealth_{-1}$	0.02 (0.01)
Federal taxes	−0.46 (−0.14)	$G_{Int.Paid}$	0.08 (0.31)	Tax $rate_{Capita(10)}$	1.03 (0.65)
S&L taxes	0.88 (0.49)	Retained $profits_0$	0.10 (0.16)	Tax $rate_{Labor(0)}$	−1.39 (−0.71)

Specification of the income variable in the model may have affected model results. We replaced the *gross* income variables (NNP and NNP_{-1}) used in Gale & Orzag's Table 2 and 3 with a representation of ***disposable*** income, (GDP—Total Taxes). Using first differenced data (not per capita) in a gross income model similar to Orszag & Gale's for roughly the same period of time, that is,

$$C = f(\text{NNP}, \ \text{NNP}_{-1}, T, G, \text{Real PR}, \ \text{DJAV}_{-1}) \qquad (3.1)$$

yielded tax results very similar to Orszag and Gale's panel 1: for 1960–92, insignificant T and G; but for 1960–2002, significant Tax effects {−0.23 ($t = 4.5$)}, but insignificant government spending effects.

Rerunning the same model with disposable income as the income variable instead of NNP yielded *statistically significant positively signed tax variables*; government spending remained insignificant. Interestingly, if we rerun the model using the NNP variable in disposable income fashion, that is, use (NNP-Taxes) and (NNP_{-1} − $Taxes_{-1}$), the tax variable stays positively signed and statistically significant, and government spending stays insignificant, suggesting Orszag and Gale may be getting negative signs on the tax variable coefficient because it isn't testing just the crowd out effect of tax cuts, but the net of the stimulus effect (the marginal propensity to consume - the mpc) and the crowd out effect, for example,

$$C = \beta(Y - T) + \lambda(T - G) = \beta Y + (-\beta + \lambda)T - \lambda G$$

where $(-\beta + \lambda)$ is the net marginal effect of a tax cut, after consideration of both its stimulus and crowd out effects. But this is not a refutation of the argument that crowd out makes a difference.

Using a gross income variable such as NNP can be faulted as failing the structural model requirement that the stimulus effects of tax cuts be shown as stemming from their effect on disposable income ($Y - T$), since you can't show the stimulus effect without a negative coefficient for the tax variable. The separate coefficients on ($Y - T$) and the deficit Tvariable in this study's alternate formulation of Gale and Orszag's model suggest a net negative coefficient is possible combining the two effects. This would give a net stimulus effect. (This does not include any crowd out effects the same tax cut may simultaneously have on investment, which ultimately have to be added in to determine the full net effect of stimulus and crowd out effects on GDP). Later in the study, it appears Gale and Orszag's Euler equation model (Table 5) also uses gross income and again leaves unclear what its tax effect estimates would have been if stimulus effects had been better separated.

3.2.1.1 Positive or Negative Stimulus Effects for Tax Cuts?

Orszag and Gale found positive stimulus effects for federal tax cuts, but negative stimulus effects for state and local tax cuts. They also found that the stimulus effects of government transfer spending was positive, but insignificant for all other types of government spending (goods, services and interest payments). Their work regarding these differential effects using OLS regression warrants further examination.

We have calculated OLS results for the differential effects of transfer payments and federal/state and local tax differences for the 1960–2010 period using this study's standard consumption and investment spending models, using either the unemployment rate or GDP lagged 3 periods to control for the business cycle's possible confounding of observed relationships between deficits and private spending. (The current period unemployment rate was multicollinear with taxes ($r = 0.78$); though including both variables increased explained variance in our findings below, the multicollinearity problem gave the wrong sign on the unemployment variable.) The results are shown below (variable definitions can be obtained from the text). The stimulus effect is given by the coefficient on the disposable income variable ($Y - T_T$) and the crowd out effects of taxes on consumption and investment spending are given as T_F, $T_{S\&L}$. Crowd out effects of government transfer payments compared to all other government spending are shown as G_{Trans}, G_{Other}. All models have passed the usual Hausman, Wald and Sargan tests, use Dickey–Fuller standard errors and are done in first differences to reduce stationarity and multicollinearity. Variable definitions are found at the beginning of Chap. 5.

Model 5.9b OLS estimates of the effects of one-variable crowd out on consumer demand W/O access to borrowing variable

(Unemployment lagged two periods used as business cycle control)

$$\underset{(t=)}{\Delta C_T} = \underset{(6.6)}{0.53\Delta(Y - T_T)} + \underset{(11.5)}{0.56\mathbf{\Delta}(T_F)} + \underset{(4.0)}{0.56\mathbf{\Delta}(T_{S\&L})}$$
$$-\underset{(-1.4)}{0.14\mathbf{\Delta}(\mathbf{G}_{Trans})} - \underset{(-4.5)}{.41\mathbf{\Delta}(\mathbf{G}_{Other})} - \underset{(-5.4)}{12.23\Delta PR}$$
$$+\underset{(4.8)}{.40\ \Delta DJ_{-2}} + \underset{(3.0)}{4.44\ \Delta XR_{AV}} - \underset{(-1.7)}{379.81\Delta POP_{16}}$$
$$+\underset{(2.9)}{0.013\Delta POP} + \underset{(1.8)}{0.60\Delta ICC_{-1}} + \underset{(4.1)}{43.49\Delta M2_{AV}}$$
$$+\underset{(2.5)}{0.11\mathbf{\Delta} C_{\mathbf{B}}} + \underset{(1.1)}{0.03\ \mathbf{\Delta} Y_{-3}} \quad R^2 = 95.2\% \quad D.W. = 1.8$$
$$MSE = 25.60 \tag{5.9b}$$

Parameter estimates and significance levels for taxes and non-transfer spending are robust changes in the business cycle control used or for the other time period tested (1960–2002). However, the transfer spending variable's sign fluctuates with the control and time period chosen, though remaining statistically insignificant.

Model 5.9c OLS estimates of the effects of one-variable crowd out on consumer demand W/O access to borrowing variable

(Unemployment lagged 0 periods used as business cycle control)

$$\underset{(t=)}{\Delta C_T} = \underset{(15.1)}{.55\Delta(Y - T_T)} + \underset{(12.0)}{.62\mathbf{\Delta}(T_F)} + \underset{(44.7)}{.66\mathbf{\Delta}(\mathbf{T}_{S\&L})}$$
$$-\underset{(-2.2)}{.26\mathbf{\Delta}(\mathbf{G}_{Trans})} - \underset{(-4.1)}{.38\mathbf{\Delta}(\mathbf{G}_{Other})} - \underset{(-5.5)}{10.10\Delta PR} + \underset{(5.5)}{.43\ \Delta DJ_{-2}}$$
$$+\underset{(2.4)}{3.47\ \Delta XR_{AV}} - \underset{(-1.6)}{336.42\Delta POP_{16}} + \underset{(2.7)}{.010\Delta POP}$$
$$+\underset{(2.7)}{.77\Delta ICC_{-1}} + \underset{(6.0)}{45.10\Delta M2_{AV}} + \underset{(2.9)}{.11\mathbf{\Delta C}_{\mathbf{B}2}} + \underset{(2.8)}{20.36\ \mathbf{\Delta UNEM}_{-0}}$$
$$R^2 = 95.7\% \quad D.W. = 1.9\ MSE = 24.20 \tag{5.9c}$$

Using the current unemployment rate as the business cycle control, all types of tax cuts or spending increase deficits are found to have statistically significant crowd out effects.

Model 8.2 OLS estimates of determinants of investment spending, using the unemployment rate as the business cycle control variable

$$\Delta I_T \underset{(t=)}{} = +.30\Delta(ACC) + .23\boldsymbol{\Delta}(\mathbf{T}_F) +) + .73\boldsymbol{\Delta}(\mathbf{T}_{S\&L})$$
$$(5.9) \quad (1.9) \quad (2.7)$$

$$-.30\boldsymbol{\Delta}(\mathbf{G}_{TR}) - .63\boldsymbol{\Delta}(\mathbf{G}_{Other}) + 1.40\Delta DEP + 2.97\Delta CAP_{-1}$$
$$(-2.5)) \quad (-4.7) \quad (3.9) \quad (1.2)$$

$$-2.80\Delta PR_{-2} - .51\Delta DJ_{-2} - .04\Delta PROF_{-2} + 6.44\Delta XR_{AV}$$
$$(-1.2) \quad (-3.9) \quad (0.4) \quad (4.1)$$

$$+.007\Delta POP - .03\,\boldsymbol{\Delta}(\mathbf{BOR}) - 18.09\,\Delta UNEM$$
$$(1.6) \quad (-0.7) \quad (-2.0)$$

$$R^2 = 95.3\% \quad D.W. = 1.9 \text{ MSE} = 28.55 \qquad (8.2)$$

Note: The estimated IS curve effect of a change in transfers spending on GDP would be

$$-.14\ (+) - .30 = -.44 \text{ point estimate } (t = -2.8^*)$$

*Calculating the *t*-statistic:

Assuming no covariance between the standard errors of both point estimates, we have

Standard errors = (−0.14/t = −1.4) = 0.1 = A for consumption effect; (−0.30/t = 2.5) = −0.12 = B for investment effect

Standard Error of −0.44 = √Var(A+B) = √(Var (A) + Var (B)) = √(a^2 + B^2) = √(0.01 + 0.0144) 0.156, which implies t = 0.44/0.156 = 2.8 for the combined crowd out effect of 0.44 in the IS equation

Coefficient and statistical significance results are robust to time period tested (1960–2002 or 2010) and business cycle control used (unemployment rate or GDP lagged three periods), except for the statistical significance of the federal tax variable, which fall to marginal significance (t = 1.4) for the 1960–2002 period when unemployment rate is used (but the sign stays positive).

These results indicate both government spending and tax cuts, in either form tested, have crowd out effects in models similar to Gale and Orszag's. Hence, we can see their findings are very sensitive to moderate changes in model specification.

Estimation Issues in the Orszag and Gale Study: To deal with stationarity issues, the regression was run in first differences, or first differences divided by NNP. Questions of endogeneity were not addressed, and OLS was used. If endogeneity is present, which seems likely between consumption and NNP, results could be distorted for failure to use instruments for the endogenous variables. Crowd out results are robust to the addition of variables representing tax rates to the basic model; robustness to other changes in model structure was not mentioned.

3.2.1.2 Gale and Orszag's Euler Equation Model

Orszag and Gale's Euler equation model produced strikingly similar results for the government spending, federal tax and state and local tax variables. The exact Euler model tested was very similar, though not identical to the non-Euler model above, and subject to the same problems regarding use of a disposable income variable. The principal difference between the Euler and non-Euler regression models was the replacement of NNP and NNP_{-1} with consumer's pre-tax income as the income variable (p.138–47). The data period used was the larger 1956–2002 set. Instruments appear to have been used for all right-side variables. There is no discussion of the instruments used as to whether they were strong or weak, or whether tests indicated they were successful in eliminating the endogeneity problem. Though there is switch in the income variable from NNP to gross income, it is not clear why disposable income wasn't used, since it is more theoretically appropriate. In our own consumption models, discussed below, the effect of using disposable income was to cause the tax variable to have a large positively signed and statistically significant effect (big crowd out effect). Using gross income reduced the effect to a small, positive and statistically insignificant amount. Hence, using disposable, not gross, income is critical to the results. Robustness of results for different sample periods for the Orszag and Gale's Euler model was not discussed.

3.2.2 VAR Models

Euler equation models are utility maximization models under conditions of perfect knowledge or conditions of uncertainty with known probability distributions, though some allowances can be made for a portion of the population behaving in more Keynesian "rule of thumb" manners, as Orszag/Gale's model shows. Euler equation models typically conclude intertemporal utility maximization requires consumption to follow a life cycle/permanent income hypothesis pattern, that is, $C_t = C_{t-1} = C_{t-2}$ for all t except for changes due to unforeseeable shocks to the system. See for example, Eckstein, (1983, p. 93, however he did not find such model good at explaining consumption variation, p. 113). This suggests VAR methods, which focus on spinning out the pattern over time of system responses to a shock or innovation are most appropriate for testing the effects of unforeseen deficit changes on consumption. However, Orszag and Gale's (2004) own findings showed that

> VAR based projections have been shown to be inferior to those produced by OMB and Data Resources, Inc. (p. 152)

The OMB and Data Resources, Inc. models referred to are similar to traditional, demand-driven Keynesian structural models, not VARs. This may explain why the Orszag/Gale study did not use a VAR model. Fair (1984) has also found VARs less useful for prediction than his more demand-driven structural models.

That said, VAR models are popular and their differences with structural models have been described as follows:

> A VAR is really a set of reduced form equations similar to what might be derived from a structural econometric model that relies heavily on economic theory. Such structural models make highly restrictive assumptions on the values of estimated parameters in their reduced form equations. These restrictions often take the form of exclusions of variables or lags of variables from these models. This in effect restricts the estimated parameters of these "excluded" variables to zero. This implies that these variables have no predictive or explanatory power in the model. A VAR, however, will include some of these variables, relying on a much less restrictive concept of economic theory as it applies to these reduced form equations. Data is then allowed to determine the contribution of variables instead of a priori economic structure. (Ford 1986)

To compare the differences with structural models, Ford notes the standard model for a simple structural model of supply and demand might be given as:

$$Q_{\text{Supplied}(t)} = f\left(P\ \text{Expected}_{(t)}, \text{Input prices}_{(t)}\right)$$
$$P_t = \ldots = f\left(Q_{(t)}, \text{ Disposable income}_{(t)}.\right)$$

whereas a VAR would estimate the current year values of each of the four explanatory variables (*Q*, *P*, Input *P*, Disposable Income) as a function of the past lagged values of all four of these variables (e.g., perhaps 6 lags). OLS would be used to estimate the current year values. The same explanatory variables—both exogenous and endogenous—would be used in four separate regressions to estimate current year values of *P*, *Q*, Input Prices and disposable income.

To these VARs are added shocks, and their effects on the variables allowed to spin themselves out over time dynamically.

Using a VAR methodology, Mountford and Uhlig (2008) found investment falls in response to both government spending increases *and tax increases* (the finding investment falls with rises in both variables is simultaneously inconsistent with both standard—model Keynesian stimulus theory and crowd out theory. No theoretical explanation is provided to explain the results). The VAR test specified consumption or investment as being a function of six lagged values of each of ten variables: GDP, *C*, *G*, taxes, real wages, private non-residential investment, adjusted reserves, the Producer Price Index (PPI) index and the GDP deflator. Notably, when cranked through the regression results, impulse responses to variables other than the GDP were constrained to what the authors considered appropriate signs for the variables involved, regardless of whether this was consistent with the regression results for the same variable and lag. Uhlig (2005) defends this as common practice in VAR modeling.

Mountford and Uhlig note their overall method was taken from Uhlig (2005), who in turn notes that his paper follows the general VAR strategy used by Sims (1972). Sims in turn notes that he is applying a variant of a (VAR) methodology developed by Granger (1969) as a way of determining whether one variable can explain ("cause") subsequent variation in another, better than the other can explain variation in the first, that is, Granger causality.

Basically, Granger's method was to regress a variable *Y* on lagged values of itself, and then re-regress *Y* on lagged values of itself and another variable *X*. If *X* explains variation in *Y* that *Y*'s own lagged values can't explain, *X* is said to "cause" *Y* (Sims, p. 44). If one finds that by reversing the procedure one cannot explain variation in *X* with *Y* when lagged values of *Y* are added to a regression with lagged values of *X*, then the causal relation between *X* and *Y* is determined as unidirectional from $X \rightarrow Y$.

Sims paper borrows the basic Granger notion of using lagged (and future) values of one variable (Money) to predict another (GDP) to resolve direction of causality problems associated with the St. Louis equation. His models typically use only the lags on one of these variables to predict contemporaneous values of the other. Subsequent authors gradually increased the number of explanatory variables for which numerous lagged values were used. Ford (1986) argued that the explanatory variables of the VAR should contain distributed lag formulations for all variables theory says are *important* determinants of the dependent variable(s), with a VAR for each using exactly the same explanatory variables and lags.

Uhlig (2005) notes that many researchers have used the VAR methodology of Sims (1972) to examine economic policy questions like the effect of money changes on the GDP. However, Uhlig notes that the actual VAR regression results are commonly considered as validating a policy conclusion only if the results *conform to general theoretical expectations as to what the results should look like*, and sometimes alter the signs of VAR-derived impulse response coefficients to achieve an expected or "consensus" result, e.g., interest rates should go up (or at least not down) when there is a monetary contraction (Uhlig, p. 383). In fact Uhlig's 2005 paper was about restricting coefficient sign effects of monetary contraction on three prices, non-borrowed reserves and the federal funds rate to ensure they entered into Impulse Response calculations only in ways a consensus of opinion says they should when he examined the effects of money contraction on the GDP.

Uhlig and Mountford's 2008 paper expands this restriction of allowable coefficient signs to ten variables when examining the effects of deficits on GDP, and then uses standard impulse response methodology to spin out the path GDP takes over time when tax cut or spending deficits are incurred. As noted, their results suggested both tax increases and spending increases result in some crowd out.

The issues to be evaluated when examining VAR results are fairly straight forward:

(1) Granger's definitions of causality may be other analysts' definition of correlation. If, for example, in the historic data, a portion of the variance in contemporaneous Y may not be explainable by some number of lags of Y (and if it was, the question of theoretical meaning of saying a variable is a function of its prior values remains), adding lags of X to the regression may explain variance. But if we do not know if theory stipulates Y is a function of its own past, we can't know if our finding is substantive, spurious or systemically non-causally correlated to the lagged variable. Adding X poses the same problem. If theory says Y or X are both just functions determined by lagged variables A, B and C, wouldn't interpreting results be more tractable and illuminating if we backward substituted and just estimated $Y = f(Y_{-1}) = f(A_{-1}, B_{-1}, C_{-1})$?

(2) Granger's (and Uhlig's) approach to determining causality may work for a two-variable case like the St. Louis equation, but how practical is it if there are, say, 15 variables in the economic system? Following the Ford/Minnesota approach, each would be represented on the right side of a VAR equation by some extensive number of lags, for example, eight lags. It takes more than 30 years of quarterly data just to get a positive number of degrees of freedom.
(3) It is not clear what the multiple past year distributed lags of the dependent variable (and other variables, often components of the dependent variables) *explains* about the determinants of change in the dependent variable; since the a priori lag formulations tend to be theoretically devoid of content, individual lags only having meaning if they are found significant.

It is hard to reconcile the approach with the spirit of the scientific method when the signs of empirical findings can be changed when evaluating policy implications of changes in policy variable determinants. For example, Uhlig (2005) notes

> "successful identification ... (in VAR models) ... needs to deliver results matching the conventional wisdom" ... (and notes) ... Leeper et al. (1996) explicitly appeal to the reasonableness of impulse responses as an "informal" identification criterion ... This paper proposes to push this idea all the way, and to identify the effects of monetary policy shocks by directly imposing sign restrictions on the impulse responses ... (reversing them if necessary to ensure there reasonableness). (pp. 383–4, comments in parenthesis inserted in the quotation added)

Uhlig and Mountford's (2008) paper is an extension of Uhlig (2005) paper:

> The identification method used in this paper is an extension of Uhlig (2005)'s agnostic identification method of imposing sign restrictions on impulse response functions. We extend this method to the identification of multiple fundamental shocks. More precisely, we identify a government revenue shock as well as a government spending shock by imposing sign restrictions on the fiscal variables themselves as well as imposing orthogonality to a generic business cycle shock and a monetary policy shock, which are also identified with sign restrictions. No sign restrictions are imposed on the responses of GDP, private consumption, private non-residential investment and real wages

> to fiscal policy shocks, and so the method remains agnostic with respect to the responses of the key variables of interest. (Mountford and Uhlig 2008, p. 1)

Methodologically, Uhlig and Mountford's paper tests the model using US quarterly data 1955–2000, in a ten-variable VAR with six lags.

Uhlig and Mountford's conclusions regarding deficit effects are that

- cutting deficits by tax increases cuts consumption,
- increasing deficits by government spending increases also cuts consumption.

These findings are partially in conformance with, and partially at odds with, both crowd out theory and Keynesian stimulus theory. They may be consistent with backward bending supply curve theory of tax increases effects on willingness to work, and therefore, ability to spend. This would reflect DSGE models of a real business cycle theory type. But there is nothing sufficiently structural about the VAR test to identify this as the causal mechanism, for example, an equation showing hours worked as a function of tax rates. (In the same sense, showing deficits inversely related to consumer spending does not show that *the mechanism* connecting the two is crowd out of consumer borrowing caused by the deficit. It may be some non-crowd out effect. To show crowd out, one must deficits reduce private borrowing, and that reduced consumer borrowing reduces consumer spending).

Earlier, Blanchard and Perrotti (2002) used a VAR model to obtain the same result for investment as Mountford and Uhlig (2008) when testing taxes and government spending, but more Keynesian results for total output, and non-Keynesian results for consumption. The a-theoretic nature of VAR makes it difficult to assess why, with consumption of 70 % of income (GDP), that changes in taxes or government spending should affect consumption one way, and total output (income) another.

There were some devices used in specifying the model which may have had a hand in significantly shaping the more conventional stimulus theory results obtained for the effects of tax increases on GDP (−), and the effects of spending increases on GDP (+). The basic VAR model used was

$$Y_t = A(L, q)Y_{t-1} + U_t$$

where $Y_t = (T_t, G_t, X_t)'$ is a three-dimensional vector in the logs of taxes, spending and GDP in real per capita terms. $U_t = (t_t, g_t, x_t)'$ is the corresponding vector of reduced form residuals which in general will have non-zero cross correlations. $A(L, q)$ is a four-quarter distributed polynomial that allows for the coefficients of each lag to depend on the particular quarter q that indexes the dependent variable (p. 4, NBER WP 7269, a 1999 version of 2002 Quarterly Journal of Economics (QJE) Paper).

The residuals vector components of U_t are further defined as (p. 5, NBER)

(1) $t_t = a_1 x_t + a_2 e_t^g + e_t^t$
(2) $g_t = b_1 x_t + b_2 e_t^t + e_t^g$
(3) $x_t = c_1 t_t + c_2 g_t + e_t^x$

The problem is that to identify c_1, in #3 regression of x on t and g, an instrument is used for t_t, namely,

$$t_t' = t_t - a_1 x_t = a_2 e_t^g + e_t^t$$

But in a period when GDP (x) is going up, this means that *by construction* the instrument used to value t_t for the same period may be going down. It is little wonder the regression coefficient for the relationship of decreases in t_t' to x_t is negative; every increase in x, ceteris paribus, causes t_t' to decline.

Similarly, the definition of g_t' as the instrument for g_t, that is,

$$g_t' = g_t - b_1 x_t = g_t \quad (\text{since } b_1 \text{ is assumed} = 0) = b_2 e_t^t + e_t^g$$

Furceri and Sousa (2009) examine 145 countries using a VAR methodology to determine if government spending as a percent of GDP varied systematically with private consumption and investment spending as a percent of GDP. They conclude the private spending is inversely related to government spending. The model tests dependent variables consumption and investment spending as a percent of GDP, against right-side determinants, including fixed effects variables for the individual countries, and the current and four lagged values of the government spending as a percent of GDP. While many of the government spending variables had statistically significant adverse effects, the lack of control for other structural variables makes it difficult to be sure the finding represents the crowd out effect, and does not perhaps occur because government spending is a good proxy for variables not controlled for. In addition, it is difficult to see how government spending as a percent of GDP can go up without the other components of GDP declining as a percent of GDP.

3.2.3 DSGE Models

DSGE models of consumption assume perfect knowledge of future earnings, investment opportunities, and so on, or that estimates follow known distributions, allowing consumers to be able to make consumption decisions now that will maximize lifetime utility. An Euler equation of the type

$$E_1 u'(c_2) = [(1+\varsigma)/(1+\rho)]\, u'(c_1)$$

Assuming the utility function is quadratic and $\rho = \varsigma$ utility maximization results in

$$E_1(c_2) = c_1 \quad \text{or} \quad c_2 = c_1 + \varepsilon$$

where ε is a random unforeseeable shock. This suggests consumption is a random walk, as introduced by Hall (1978).

Empirical work by Kuznets, Heim, Eckstein, Fair and Klein has found that rather than remain constant from year to year, real consumption varies consistently with changes in current year real income. This suggests a lack of the type of intertemporal foresight required for DSGE models, which typically use Life cycle or permanent income (average income over a long period) as the definition of income in the consumption function. DSGE allows growth in C due to technological progress, but this also results in a change in income. Though we did not review any literature testing random walk (implicitly testing DSGE models), others have and have claimed they have not been successful empirically:

> Controversy has arisen over using Euler equations to model consumption. Euler consumption equations have trouble explaining empirical data (Molana 1991). Attempting to test the Euler equations to model consumption in the United States has led some to reject the random walk hypothesis (Jaeger 2001) ... (taken from Wikipedia article entitled "Random walk model of consumption")

Barro and Redlick (2011) use a DSGE model to conclude that each dollar increase in government defense spending per capita has a positive effect on per capita income equal to \$0.68 per dollar of spending deficit incurred (1950–2006 data).

The model used is Barro and Redlick's (DSGE version of an) IS curve, that is, a curve which describes the determinants of the GDP. It appears to be missing a number of key determinants of GDP, namely, consumption, investment and net exports and taxes, and for this reason, only explains 48 % of the variance in GDP for the 56-year period. Considering the advances made in understanding macroeconomic mechanics since Keynes' time, this seems unduly low. Add the depression and World War II years to the sample, and government spending accounts for 75–82 % of the variance; include years back to 1917 and the model explains 66 %. Though increasing the R^2, neither of these time extensions addresses the possibility that omission of key explanatory variables from the model is resulting in distorted estimates of government spending's effects.

Because Barro and Redlick leave out of the right hand side of their version of the IS curve, both *C*&*I*'s determinants, and $(X - M)$, they end up not controlling for a raft of things that are highly positively multicollinear with *G*. Therefore, their *G* coefficient may pick up the collinear part of *C*&*I*'s effects, and becomes statistically significant (as would this author's if the author's IS equations dropped all the components of GDP except government spending). Barro and Redlick get a 0.68 coefficient on *G*, which is statistically significant and represents the per capita marginal effect of a change in government spending on the GDP. But putting other things in the model that covary with *G*, that is, the determinants of *C*, *I* and $(X-M)$, models described late in this paper get (−0.11) for this effect, results which are not statistically significantly different from zero.

In a more traditional IS model tested, −0.35 was obtained for this effect. If the model had GDP as a function of *G* only, more like Barro's and Redlick's model, the estimated "multiplier" effect, that is, the coefficient on the government spending variable, would have jumped dramatically from −0.35 to +1.63.

Raising further questions about the accuracy of Barro's +0.68 estimate is the fact that his R^2 is only 48 %. This author's experience has been that it is difficult to get robust marginal effect estimates out of any macro model that explains less than 80–85 % of the variance (and only then if all the major causal determinants are among the variables included in the model). If the $R^{2'}$ is lower than that, the smallest changes in model specification or period sampled may cause the marginal effect estimates to jump around, sometimes wildly. Low R^2s typically indicate you've failed to control for the effects of something important (i.e., left it out of the equation). If so, given the general collinearity problem in time series data, the left-out variable is probably somewhat correlated with some variables in the equation, thereby distorting marginal effect estimates for these variables.

We conclude Barro's estimates of what he describes as the government spending multiplier are probably higher and more statistically significant than they would be had the model contained all the key determinants of the GDP on the right hand side of the equation.

Finally, we note that Barro and Redlick's paper describes their regression estimates as "multiplier" effect estimates. This is only true in models where crowd out effects are assumed to be zero, leaving the implicit coefficient on the government spending variable (1) times the multiplier, as in the IS Eq. 2.10, repeated from above:

$$\text{GDP} = \text{Y} = \left(\frac{1}{1-\beta}\right)\left[\,(-\beta + \lambda_1 + \lambda_2)\,T + (1 - \lambda_1 - \lambda_2)\,G - \theta\, r + (X - M)\,\right] \tag{2.10}$$

Barro's and Redlick's coefficients are better described as multiplier effects net of crowd out. The actual mpc-based multiplier effect itself is likely to be larger if there are any crowd out effects offsetting the multiplier's stimulus effect.

Woodford (2011) also developed a DSGE model that shows that under assumptions made, the government spending multiplier is positive, and can be >1.0 if monetary policy is accommodating. However, this was a theoretical model only, and no empirical work was done to test the results.

> Woodford notes: "Much public discussion of this (government spending) issue has been based on old-fashioned models (both Keynesian and anti-Keynesian) that take little account of the role of intertemporal optimization and expectations in the determination of aggregate economic activity"

Part of the reason "old fashioned" models are used is that attempts to verify DSGE model assumptions and conclusions have not been successful Molana (1991), Jaeger (2001), Fair (2004), Heim (2008).

Kraay (2012) develops a slightly simplified version of the Barro and Redlick model which examines the effect of government spending on the GDP when it is financed by foreign borrowing from the World Bank.

Findings: Government spending in developing countries is positive, when spending is financed by foreign borrowing, but multiplier is less than 1.00: I.E., (+0.48). The model was tested using 2SLS, and is similar to Barro/Redlick:

$$\%\Delta GDP = f(\%\Delta G) \qquad \text{(Normalized, Decimal form of} \%\Delta)$$

Issues:

- Same issues as Barro and Redlick (2011) model discussed above
- Result surprising, since crowd out not a problem if deficits are financed by foreign borrowing, providing it does not come out of funds that would have been made available to the domestic country anyway.

3.2.4 *Structural Models*

Heim (2012a, b) developed models for estimating aggregate consumer and investment demand, using 1960–2000 data, based on the following structural determinants of demand (all in real terms).

Consumer Demand	**Investment Demand**
Disposable income ($Y - T_G$)	Accelerator ($Y_t - Y_{t-1}$)
Prime interest rate (PR)	Depreciation allowances (DEP)
Wealth (DJ_{-2})	Capacity utilization levels (CAP-1)
Exchange rate XRAV	Profits (Prof-2)
Population size (POP)	Prime interest rate (PR-2)
Population age composition (POP_{16})	Gov't. deficit ($T_G - G$)
Consumer confidence index (CCI_{-1})	
M2 (Esp. savings components) ($M2_{AV}$)	
Gov't. deficit ($T_G - G$)	

An attempt was made to include representatives of each type of variable found to be a determinant of consumption cited in an extensive search of the literature. Specific variables and lags used in each category, for example, "Interest Rates", were based on which variables considered required in consumption or investment functions on theoretical grounds, was found most systematically related to consumer or investment demand. The equations form part of a larger 30+ equation model of the US economy, though these papers focus principally on the regression results of testing these models on total consumer spending and borrowing, and total investment spending and borrowing. Testing the models on borrowing as well as spending was considered necessary to show that to the extent that private spending varied with the deficit, it could be determined whether the decline was systematically related to the decline in private borrowing (the stated cause of crowd out).

3.2.4.1 Estimation Issues

The extent to which adding crowd out variables to consumption or investment models increased explained variance, and was statistically significant was examined. 2SLS was used to estimate an instrument for disposable income in the consumption equation, and the accelerator in the investment equation. Remaining variables in each equation were used to construct the instruments used. Neither Hausman, Wald nor Sargan test results were cited in the papers, leaving unclear how effectively endogeneity issues were dealt with. Models were estimated in first differences to reduce stationarity, serial correlation and multicollinearity problems. Newey-West standard errors were used to address heterogeneity issues. The structural models explained 90 % or more of the variance in consumer and investment spending during the 1960–2000 period tested, though only about 60 % of the variance in borrowing. Durban Watson statistics indicated the serial correlation problem was adequately controlled for.

The results indicated deficits caused by both tax cuts and spending increases were systematically related to reductions in consumer and business borrowing, and that this occurred contemporaneously with declines in consumer and investment spending of equal magnitude, a result consistent with crowd out theory. Stimulus effects were completely crowded out. Point estimates of crowd out effects in recessions indicate slightly less crowd out than in normal times, but differences were statistically insignificant, indicating crowd out remains a significant problem even in recessions. Some typical results from Heim (2012b, p.11) are shown below, using Heim's (2012b) model numbers:

Model 29 Total consumption spending function with two-variable "average" crowd out

$$\underset{(t=)}{\Delta C_T} = \underset{(12.7)}{0.49\Delta(Y - T_G)} + \underset{(12.3)}{0.54\mathbf{\Delta T}} - \underset{(-3.6)}{0.75\,\mathbf{\Delta G}} - \underset{(6.5)}{10.75\Delta \mathrm{PR}}$$
$$+ \underset{(3.1)}{.63\,\Delta \mathrm{DJ}_{-2}} + \underset{(5.6)}{4.70\,\Delta \mathrm{XR}_{\mathrm{AV}}} - \underset{(-1.6)}{490.76\Delta \mathrm{POP}_{16}}$$
$$+ \underset{(4.7)}{0.01\Delta \mathrm{POP}} + \underset{(2.4)}{0.61\Delta \mathrm{ICC}_{-1}} + \underset{(5.8)}{34.41\Delta \mathrm{M2}_{\mathrm{AV}}}$$
$$R^2 = 96.4\% \quad \mathrm{D.W.} = 2.2 \tag{29}$$

Model 31 Total consumption borrowing function with two-variable "average" crowd out

$$\underset{(t=)}{\Delta C_B} = \underset{(3.9)}{0.36\Delta(Y - T_G)} + \underset{(1.9)}{0.42\mathbf{\Delta T}} - \underset{(-1.8)}{1.12\,\mathbf{\Delta G}} - \underset{(2.9)}{10.89\Delta \mathrm{PR}}$$
$$- \underset{(2.1)}{0.76\,\Delta \mathrm{DJ}_{-2}} + \underset{(3.4)}{9.19\,\Delta \mathrm{XR}_{\mathrm{AV}}} - \underset{(-0.3)}{217.35\Delta \mathrm{POP}_{16}}$$
$$- \underset{(-2.4)}{.01\Delta \mathrm{POP}} + \underset{(1.4)}{1.08\Delta \mathrm{ICC}_{-1}} + \underset{(0.7)}{25.36\Delta \mathrm{M2}_{\mathrm{AV}}}$$
$$R^2 = 65.5\%(31) \quad \mathrm{D.W.} = 1.8 \tag{31}$$

Model 28 Total investment spending function with two-variable "average" crowd out

$$\underset{(t=)}{\Delta \mathrm{I_T}} = + \underset{(6.6)}{.59\,\mathbf{\Delta T}} - \underset{(-4.9)}{.84\mathbf{\Delta G}} + \underset{(7.6)}{.28\Delta \mathrm{ACC}} + \underset{(1.0)}{.32\Delta \mathrm{DEP}}$$
$$+ \underset{(1.1)}{1.75\Delta \mathrm{CAP}_{-1}} - \underset{(-2.9)}{5.52\Delta \mathrm{r}_{-2}} + \underset{(0.4)}{.10\,\Delta \mathrm{DJ}_{-2}} + \underset{(1.9)}{.32\,\Delta \mathrm{PROF}_{-2}}$$
$$+ \underset{(4.9)}{5.70\Delta \mathrm{XR}_{\mathrm{AV0123}}} + \underset{(4.9)}{.01\Delta \mathrm{POP}}$$
$$\mathrm{R}^2 = .91 \mathrm{DW} = 2.6 \tag{28}$$

Model 30 Total investment borrowing function with two-variable "average" crowd out

$$\underset{(t=)}{\Delta I_B} = + \underset{(2.6)}{0.45\,\mathbf{\Delta T}} - \underset{(-2.6)}{1.41\mathbf{\Delta G}} + \underset{(1.4)}{0.14\Delta \mathrm{ACC}} + \underset{(1.3)}{1.56\Delta \mathrm{DEP}}$$
$$+ \underset{(0.8)}{3.33\Delta \mathrm{CAP}_{-1}} - \underset{(-1.5)}{8.77\Delta r_{-2}} - \underset{(-1.8)}{1.02\,\Delta \mathrm{DJ}_{-2}} + \underset{(1.3)}{0.57\,\Delta \mathrm{PROF}_{-2}}$$
$$+ \underset{(4.2)}{14.49\Delta \mathrm{XR}_{\mathrm{AV0123}}} + \underset{(0.1)}{0.001\Delta \mathrm{POP}}$$
$$R^2 = 0.62 \quad \mathrm{DW} = 1.9 \tag{30}$$

3.2.5 *Limitations of VAR, DSGE and Structural Models*

Structural: Structural models explain most variance, but do so using only a limited number of variables consistent with theory or past test results. Many are treated as "exogenous", or at least lagged, so as to allow for identification of the system. Sims' seminal study (1980) argues that it is very hard to define truly exogenous variables in the system; everything is fundamentally a function of some lagged value of everything else, so better to use a VAR methodology where each variable is specified as a general function of its own and all other variables past values, endogenous or exogenous. Specifying many lags in the model for each variable to be estimated allows for each variable to show its effects on others. Ford (1986) noted there should be a separate regression for each variable in the system, and each dependent variable is a function of itself and all other variables, with lags included.

VAR: Models appear a-theoretic, or minimally theoretic: sometimes hard to interpret results in economic terms, except by conjecture. Do not explain long-term variation as well as structural models (Fair 1984), (Orszag and Gale 2004). May require empirical results to be adjusted to achieve "commonly accepted" path effects, for example, negative effects of money growth on interest rates (Sims 2005).

Euler Equation (DSGE) models: DSGE models are constructed assuming consumption is based on (accurate) long-term notions of one's average income (Life Cycle/Permanent Income models). Hard to show long-term average income of either the rational expectations or adaptive expectations type explains current consumption as well as current income alone (Heim 2008). Others also had trouble reconciling empirical data with such models (Molina 1991), (Jaeger 2001). Intertemporal utility maximization assumed, and predicts constant levels of consumption each year (Eckstein 1983), except for increases attributable to technological progress, which raises income. This could be equivalent to saying it grows with (unanticipated) technological progress, if technological growth were unpredictable, but at the macro level it is not; it tends to be fairly constant over time, though occasionally there are divergences from the apparent long-term path.

Table 3.2 Government surplus/deficits 1960–2010 (Billions of 2005 Dollars)

1960	*$ 89.0*	*1970*	*$ −44.3*	*1980*	*$ −114.7*	*1990*	*$ −268.6*	*2000*	*$ 274.5*
1961	52.1	1971	−108.7	1981	−107.5	1991	−341.7	2001	29.0
1962	57.5	1972	−42.3	1982	−281.9	1992	−451.7	2002	−352.7
1963	80.4	1973	16.5	1983	−338.0	1993	−407.8	2003	−458.0
1964	51.9	1974	−20.0	1984	−276.6	1994	−299.6	2004	−410.2
1965	67.8	1975	−238.6	1985	−284.3	1995	−270.8	2005	−257.1
1966	66.5	1976	−152.0	1986	−310.7	1996	−168.2	2006	−145.6
1967	−14.7	1977	−101.3	1987	−238.8	1997	−31.4	2007	−212.1
1968	30.9	1978	−29.4	1988	−205.2	1998	104.7	2008	−595.0
1969	94.2	1979	−2.7	1989	−186.8	1999	177.2	2009	−1128.1
								2010	−1106.0

Source: *Economic Report of the President, 2011 and 2005.* Tables B7, B83

3.3 Real Government Deficits—The Historical Record

Table 2 below shows combined US real federal, state and local government budget surpluses and deficits. It shows a period generally characterized as one of government surpluses up until 1970, sizable deficits from 1970 until 1992, major reductions in the deficit 1992–97, surpluses 1998–2001, large deficits in the early 2000s, small in mid 2000s, and large since then (Table 3.2).

CHAPTER 4

Methodology

4.1 Data Used

1960–2010 data from the *Economic Report of the President* (2011 and 2002) and the *Flow of Funds Accounts* of the Federal Reserve (2011) were used to estimate the effects of a wide range of variables on consumption and investment spending and borrowing, including:

Consumption	Investment
Disposable income ($Y - T_T$)	Samuelson's accelerator (ACC)
Deficit variables ($T_T - G_{T\&I}$)	Deficit variables ($T_T - G_{T\&I}$)
Wealth (DJAV)	Depreciation allowances (DEP)
Interest rates (PR or r)	Interest rates (PR or r)
Exchange rates (XR_{AV})	Tobin's q (DJAV)
Consumer confidence (ICC)	Profits (PROF)
Population size (POP)	Exchange rates (XR_{AV})
Population age composition (POP_{16})	Population size (POP)
Money supply (M1 or M2)	

A substantial review of the economic literature found these variables, or representatives of them cited as the major determinants of consumer or investment demand. Hence, these variables were included in regressions as controls when testing the effects of crowd out for two reasons:

J.J. Heim, *Crowding Out Fiscal Stimulus*,
DOI 10.1007/978-3-319-45967-7_4

- To ensure crowd out was tested within a standard, generally accepted model of macroeconomic theory, that is, a model containing generally acknowledged determinants of consumption and investment.
- To ensure the effects of crowd out were not confounded with those of other determinants of consumption and investment left out of the test, with which crowd out might be correlated. This would distort estimates of the crowd out variable's (the government deficit) own effect.

Every model tested was one of these core "Keynesian" consumer or investment demand models, to which was added the deficit (crowd out) variable, since the key objective of this paper is to determine if crowd out (a deficit) offsets some or all of the stimulus effects of deficits predicted by Keynesian theory. The single deficit variable (government revenue-government spending $= T_T - G_{T\&I}$) was used first. The model was tested and the results for the deficit variable noted. Then one of the following three controls (GDP, GDP_{-3} or the unemployment rate) used to control for the state of the business cycle was added to the model, and the model was retested to see if, controlling for the business cycle, any change in the crowd out variable results was noted. This was repeated separately for each of the three business cycle controls. These eight consumption and investment tests were initially run in OLS. We then re-estimated them in weak instrument 2SLS (if the initial instrument tested was weak), then again in strong instrument 2SLS. This gave us 24 tests of the significance of the crowd out variable in Keynesian models. Results of each were noted.

Once this was done, these twenty-four tests were rerun adding a consumer borrowing variable (C_{B2}) or a business borrowing variable ($I_{B(-1)}$), giving us a total of 48 test results. After every test, the effects on the deficit variable were noted. Many of these 48 tests were repeated replacing the one-variable deficit with two separate deficit variables: the government revenue variable and the government spending variable, to determine if crowd out effects were different for tax cut deficits and spending deficits. These tests comprise the core of the paper. Additional tests were run using these models but testing for differences in crowd out effects in recessions and non-recessions, differences in types of tax cut or spending deficits. An additional 60 tests were made attempting to replicate initial results in three additional, different, though overlapping, time periods over the past 50 years. This brought the total number of tests to 228. Overwhelmingly they indicated that the crowd out effect of deficits is as real as the stimulus effect, and tend totally offset the stimulus effects.

The testing was exhaustive, but necessary, to ensure results could be considered definitive, that is, good quality science, and not "just another" of the many studies over the years testing for stimulus effects and getting different results. More often than not, those earlier studies involved testing just one or two models, noting the results, and rushing them off to a publisher. This is probably why after more than 60 years and tons of studies, we have not yet resolved the issue of whether deficits have a net positive stimulus effect. Hopefully this study will be seen as comprehensive and exhaustive enough to put the issue to rest.

4.2 Specifics of Methods Used

After identification of these variables in the literature, econometric testing was undertaken to determine the specific form and lag levels of these variables that were most systematically related to consumption and investment unless theory already provided answers to those questions. The general approach taken was to determine if theory held a variable to be a determinant (e.g., interest rates). If so, then it seemed reasonable to include the most appropriate form, (e.g., which interest rate? which lag level?). For that, the ones most systematically related to the dependent variable were selected. Generally, this means the form or lag of a variable that explains the most variance or has the highest t-statistic. Specific forms and lags used are detailed in the hypothesis testing sections of this paper, Chaps. 5, 6, 7, 8.

The principal scientific tool of analysis was Two Stage Least Squares regression (2SLS), applied to hypotheses concerning the structural nature of the consumption and investment functions. 2SLS was used since both consumption and investment spending are driven in part by income-related variables (disposable income, the accelerator, etc.), and hence are subject to simultaneous equations bias if ordinary regression techniques like OLS are used. 2SLS provides consistent estimates, and is commonly used to replace endogenous variables with highly correlated, but endogeneity—free instruments representing them. Hausman endogeneity tests were applied to all variables in the consumption and investment functions contemporaneous with the dependent variables (consumption spending and borrowing and investment spending and borrowing). Every time the model specification was changed, even slightly, all variables in the system were retested for Hausman endogeneity, since the second step in the Hausman process involves the respecified model. When simultaneity was found, all exogenous and lagged variables used in the consumption and investment functions were used as regression—weighted components of the instruments used to replace the endogenous variable. This approach to instrument construction when estimating structural models follows Hill, Griffiths & Lim (2011, pp. 452–53) and Pindyck & Rubinfeld (1991, p. 299).

Instruments were tested to determine if they were poor proxies having only limited correlation with the variables they replaced, using the Wald *F* or *t*-statistic weak instrument tests. If instruments initially developed were found weak, some of the many variables used to develop the instrument, but not found to be significant components of the instrument, were eliminated. Sometimes this was not enough, and additional variables were added to the instrument, usually other lagged values of exogenous or lagged variables in the model, or even lagged endogenous variables. Specific combinations of these techniques used with individual models varied from test to test and are discussed in the sections below as part of the discussion of each model's tests and test results. Hence, our potential endogeneity bias problem was resolved, and strong instrument results were obtained for all models, either in the form of *F*-statistics ≥ 10 for the whole instrument or $t \geq 3.3$ for at least one variable in the instrument, as per Wald criteria.

Sargan R^2 tests were then used to ensure the instruments judged strong (or at least adequate) had not, in the process of development, become endogenously related to consumption or investment.

Many earlier studies of the determinants of consumption and investment, some done decades ago, used only OLS, or if 2SLS was used, instruments were not necessarily tested for their strength. This raised the issue of how to compare the current study's results with the earlier studies, some done decades ago, before modern econometric methods were available, particularly if a difference in results was found. Though our findings are based on what strong instrument variants of 2SLS showed, we also present weak instrument and OLS findings testing the same structural model, for comparison. In this way, we have some information to use in assessing whether differences that might develop with earlier findings are fundamental, or just likely to be due to different techniques used. As it turns out, all three sets of results were remarkably similar for the models tested, particularly the OLS and strong instrument results.

Data were tested in first differences rather than levels to address non-stationarity (serial correlation) issues. In first differences, all consumption and investment function variables passed the Augmented Dickey—Fuller unit root tests, except the NYSE composite index, population size and population young/old ratio variables. However, all three proved cointegrated with the dependent variables in the models with which they were used. Hence, stationarity problems did not prove to be an issue.

Using first differences had two additional advantages: it resulted in major reductions in high multicollinearity pervasively found in time series data when used in levels. This increased considerably the stability of parameter estimates when changes were made to model specification.

Also, using first difference data strongly improved results of Durbin–Watson tests, as expected. Durbin–Watson tests were chosen to evaluate serial correlation as the most appropriate test for relatively small samples, such as ours, which involves 50 years of annual data (Hill, Griffiths & Lim, 2011, p. 355).

Newey West corrections to standard errors were used to avoid heteroskedasticity problems.

The validity of the argument that deficit-financed spending or tax cut programs stimulate the economy hangs on whether private sector borrowing is crowded out sufficiently by government borrowing to finance the deficit. Because of the importance of test results, robustness of crowd out findings obtained is critical. Much of this paper's testing is for robustness. We argue three types of robustness must be shown for any study results to qualify as good science. We also argue that a fourth is needed to show differences that occur when different regression methods are used, to provide a way of comparing studies from earlier times with modern results:

(1) Robustness over different time periods sampled. We test and report findings for the same models in four different sample periods: 1960–2010, 1960–2000, 1970–2000 and 1970–2010.
(2) Robustness of estimates when minor or moderate changes in model specification take place. This was done testing crowd out results two different ways: (1) with and without the borrowing variable. (2) Then, each of these two variants was subjected to four separate tests with one of three different business cycle phase control variables, and a fourth without any business cycle control.
(3) Robustness of results when different instruments were used in 2SLS models and
(4) Robustness of results to three different estimation techniques, using the same model: OLS, 2SLS strong instrument, 2SLS weak instrument.

For each hypothesis tested, the following results are reported:

regression coefficient,	Durbin–Watson statistic
t-statistic,	Standard error of the regression (mean square error)
R^2	R2

Throughout the paper, tests are based on 50 observations of data from the period 1960 to 2010. For all tests, *t*-statistics and their significance levels are

$$t = 2.7\ (1\%\text{level});\quad 2.0\ (5\%\text{level});\quad 1.8\ (7\%\text{level})$$
$$1.7\ (10\%\text{level});\quad 1.5\ (15\%\text{level});\quad 1.3\ (20\%\text{level})$$

Beside crowd out, another hypothesis tested is the "changes in the business cycle" hypothesis. This hypothesis asserts simultaneously increasing deficits and declining consumer/investment spending invariably occurs in economic downturns. That is, that the negative correlation may be caused by changes in the business cycle, not crowd out. This possibility was examined by testing each model separately with and without a business cycle control variable. Several different business cycle controls were tested, including current period real GDP, lagged real GDP and the unemployment rate. Each spending model was tested separately controlling for each of the three business cycle variables. A fourth model was tested without any business cycle control. Results for all four models are shown. The statistical significance of business cycle effects is noted. Also, differences in the crowd out variable's coefficient and statistical significance in models with and without business cycle controls was used to determine if some of what we were seeing as crowd out was really due to business cycle effects.

The current unemployment rate and the GDP, lagged three years, were the business cycle indicators found most systematically related to the deficit. Their effect on estimates of the deficit's impact, compared to the same models without these controls, are key to evaluating the Krugman thesis that declining phases of the business cycle, not crowd out, cause the decline in consumer/business spending observed to correlate with government deficit growth.

Model 4.1 Relationship of unemployment and lagged GDP to the deficit

$$\underset{(t=)}{\Delta(\text{Deficit})} = -\,103.51\,\underset{(-8.5)}{\Delta(\text{Unemployment Rate})} - 0.106\,\underset{(-2.2)}{\Delta\left(\text{GDP}_{\mathbf{Real}(-3)}\right)}$$

$$R^2 = 0.63 \qquad (4.1)$$

The three-year lagged GDP was the GDP variable most systematically related to deficit size. This suggests a growing GDP eventually triggers increases in government spending that outstrip the growth in tax revenue stemming from the GDP growth. The two-year lag was less statistically significant, and the one and one ad zero lagged values insignificant. Results are also presented using current period GDP for reference. Only the current period unemployment rate had a statistically significant relationship with the deficit, and it was far stronger than the GDP variable in explaining the deficit. Using the first-in stepwise regression procedure, the unemployment rate alone could account for 59 % of the variance; by comparison, three-year lagged GDP could only account for 8 %. However, the unemployment rate was very highly correlated with the government receipts variable ($r = -0.78$), enough for multicollinearity effects to reverse its expected negative sign in some regression tests, though its use did not alter much the estimated effect of deficits on private spending. Using lagged values of unemployment gave the right sign, but was not as statistically significantly related to deficit spending. Hence, they were not as adequate as controls for business cycle effects on the deficit.

Negative relationships between consumer spending and deficits do not directly indicate why they occur. Alternate causes, including crowd out, Ricardian Equivalence or the Krugman thesis about business cycle effects or the need for large deficits to get stimulus effects may be hypothesized.

To test the crowd out hypothesis, it is necessary to show that *private borrowing* as well as spending is negatively related to deficit growth, since the crowd out thesis is that financing the deficit reduces the pool of loanable funds available to private borrowers, and that this is what causes the decline in spending. In this study, tests of the deficit's relationship to consumer spending are followed immediately by tests of the relationship of the same deficits to consumer borrowing. The same approach was taken when testing investment spending and borrowing.

In the initial modeling of borrowing behavior, it was assumed that at least some of the variables that drive spending by consumers and business also drive their borrowing, so the determinants of borrowing tested are generally the same as for spending, with three changes:

- Real consumer or business borrowing rather than spending becomes the dependent variable.
- The growth of the savings components of the M2 money supply, real (M2–M1), was added to reflect the importance of saving as the essential determinant affecting the supply of loanable funds, compared to the M1 money supply. The non-M1 part of M2 was found more systematically related to borrowing than M1. This suggests how much people's savings in CDs, savings accounts and money market funds have more impact on the supply of loanable funds than how much M1 the Federal Reserve creates. In fact, generally, we were unable to find a statistically significant effect of M1 on the real economy, controlling adequately for other variables.
- The NYSE composite average lagged one period as a determinate of borrowing contributed far more to explanatory power than the two-period lagged version (which was far more important in the spending models), and hence, was used with the borrowing models. The two-lag version was used in spending models. For investment, some models use the zero lag, since the two lag seemed too correlated with current profits for the profits variable to be statistically significant.

Where conclusions require estimating impact on GDP, test results from the *C* and *I* equations are substituted into the GDP identity and the resulting Keynesian "IS" curve is examined. The IS curve was also estimated directly by regression of the explanatory variables in the consumption and investment equations, plus net exports, on the GDP. Results for crowd out variables are essentially the same.

4.3 Demand as a Function Purchasing Power, Not Just Income

If loanable funds that would normally be borrowed and spent by private users are instead borrowed by government to finance deficits, a reduction in private spending will result. Actual consumer or business spending is driven not only by income but also by access to loanable funds. The two together become the determinants of total consumer purchasing power and demand. Let

(C_B) = Net annual consumer borrowing = annual change in total consumer indebtedness (ΔC_{DEBT}). Consumer indebtedness data are taken from the Federal Reserve's Flow of Funds data.

(I_B) = Net annual business borrowing = annual change in business indebtedness (ΔI_{DEBT}). Business indebtedness data are taken from the Federal Reserve's Flow of Funds data.

where C_B and I_B are both given in real terms.

We want to test whether private demand is better explained by purchasing power (income plus borrowing power) than by income alone. We must also show that private borrowing as well as spending is negatively related to government deficits, controlling for other relevant variables. This is because it is the reduction in funds available to private parties to borrow when deficits occur that is the key mechanism through which crowd out theory works to reduce private spending. The hypotheses to be tested are

$$\Delta(\text{ consumer spending}) = f\Delta \text{Determinants of consumption, including borrowing and the deficit})$$

$$\Delta(\text{ consumer borrowing}) = f\Delta \text{ Determinants of consumption, including the deficit})$$

$$\Delta(\text{investment spending}) = f\ \Delta \text{ Determinants of investment, including borrowing and the deficit})$$

$$\Delta(\text{investment borrowing}) = f\Delta \text{ Determinants of investment, including the deficit})$$

In Chaps. 5, 6, 7, 8, these hypotheses are tested and results presented. In Chap. 5, the specific variables defined as determinants of consumer spending and borrowing are given. At the beginning of Chap. 6, the same is done for investment's determinants.

CHAPTER 5

Test Results: Consumer Spending and Borrowing Models (One-Variable Deficit)

In this chapter, we test using the single variable definition of crowd out, total government revenue minus total government spending, or ($T_T - G_{T\&I}$), to evaluate how crowd out affects consumer spending and borrowing. The two variables case, which tests for differences in crowd out effects when deficits are caused by tax cuts rather than spending increases, is tested in Chap. 7 below.

Section 5.1 tests 21 OLS models. The first nine OLS models, summarized in Section 5.1.1, find crowd out has a significant negative effect on consumption spending in all nine. Section 5.1.3 tests four OLS single variable crowd out models of consumer borrowing, and finds crowd out significantly affects consumer borrowing negatively in all of them.

Section 5.1.2 adds an additional eight OLS tests, four of consumption, and four of investment, to determine if some types of tax cut (federal vs. state and local) or spending deficit (goods and services vs. transfer payments) are immune from crowd out effects on consumption. For consumption, all four tests showed tax cut deficits, and spending on goods and services to have a negative effect, but only one showed spending on transfers to have a significant negative effect. For investment, all the spending deficits were found negatively related to investment, though three of the four tests of federal tax cuts had a marginally significant negative effect. Effects of different types of tax and spending deficits are examined further in Chap. 10 (Sect. 10.3) and Chap. 15.

Section 5.2 tests 25 2SLS one variable models of consumption. Section 5.2.1 tests 15 models of consumer spending, and finds crowd out

J.J. Heim, *Crowding Out Fiscal Stimulus*,
DOI 10.1007/978-3-319-45967-7_5

has statistically significant negative effects on spending in all of them. Section 5.2.2 tests 10 consumer borrowing models and finds crowd out has significant negative effects in seven of them. Two of the three not showing crowd out effects were methodologically deficient (weak instruments used).

Section 5.3 summarizes Sections 5.1 and 5.2 results. Sections 5.4 and 5.5 test eight spending models in four different, but overlapping periods of time (32 tests), and eight borrowing models in the same four time periods (32 tests). Crowd out is found to have a significant negative effect of consumer spending in all 32 tests, and a significant negative effect on borrowing in 22 of 32 tests.

Detailed analysis of each of these Chap. 5 tests is presented in the rest of the chapter.

The following variables are hypothesized to be determinants of consumer spending and are tested using a variety of regression techniques. Results of the tests are then compared for consistency.

C_T = real consumer goods and services

$(\Upsilon - T_T)$ = real disposable income, defined as GDP minus total government receipts, which yields numerical estimates very similar to Kuznet's "national income" definition in his landmark 1947 study of consumption/income relationships: $\Delta(\Upsilon - T_T) = 1.01\ \Delta(\text{National Income})$

$(T_T - G_{T\&I})$ = real government deficit: total receipts minus total expenditures on government consumption, Investment, transfers, interest and subsidies

PR = real prime interest rate defined as the nominal rate minus the average of the past two completed years inflation

DJ_{-2} = a measure of wealth (NYSE Composite Index), lagged two years

XR_{AV} = the real broad US exchange rate average for current and past three years (foreign currency per dollar)

POP_{16} = ratio of young (20–24) to old (65+) in population

POP = population size

ICC_{-1} = Index of Consumer Confidence (Conference Board measure), lagged one year

$M2_{AV}$ = real M2 money supply; average of second, third and fourth past years (Used to measure how fluctuations in the savings components of M2 over several years affect consumption.

Preliminary testing indicated M1 unrelated to consumption, explaining why $M2_{AV}$ yielded similar results to using $(M2-M1)_{AV}$).

$M2-M1$ = savings components of M2 for the current period

C_B = total net consumer borrowing (defined as annual change in consumer debt in current period)

Excluding the borrowing and the M2 variables, these variables represent the "standard" consumption model used in all our tests. The standard spending model also includes $M2_{AV}$, but not $(M2-M1)$. The standard borrowing model also uses $(M2-M1)$, but not $M2_{AV}$. The explanatory variables are used as controls when testing the relationship of the crowd out variable to consumer spending and borrowing. We vary the tests of crowd out by adding or subtracting the borrowing variable to the model, and by adding or subtracting business cycle control variables.

Current period values are typically, though not always, denoted without subscript; when subscripts are used, the current period is denoted "0"; other subscripts indicate periods lagged. These variables were found related to consumer spending in previous studies of consumption. Lags were determined by assessing which lag was most significantly related to consumption. Our approach to determining the right level of lag to use was that if theory said a variable was a determinant of consumption, then the lag that best demonstrated this relationship should be the lag used.

Some of the models tested, including the first model below, contain a measure of consumer borrowing as one of the explanatory variables. Consumer borrowing (net) is defined as the annual change in consumer debt (US Federal Reserve Flow of Funds Accounts, Table Z1, end of period data). This variable is used to test the hypothesis that consumer demand (spending) is a function of availability of borrowed funds as well as income, that is, that consumption spending is a function of *purchasing power, not just income alone.* Clearly, if access to credit affects consumer spending *independently* of its role as a way consumer demand driven by income, wealth and so on, is manifested, the variable will be found to have a positive, statistically significant regression coefficient in models in which the other determinants are well described.

Also included in most models is a variable controlling for the state of the economy each year 1960–2010. This is included to control for any possible Krugman business cycle effects which could reasonably be interpreted as causing negative deficit/consumer spending relationships in the same year, that is, for reasons having nothing to do with crowd out. By including a business cycle variable, we can control for business cycle effects on the deficit/consumer spending relationship when evaluating crowd out effects. Each model is tested using four different controls, or lack thereof: the current GDP, GDP-lagged three periods, the current period unemployment rate or using no control at all.

5.1 OLS Models

Results in Chap. 5 (Sect. 5.1) are estimated using OLS regression. As noted earlier, due to likely endogeneity issues, this method is probably less satisfactory than 2SLS, which we will use later to retest these same models, if necessary to eliminate potential simultaneous equations bias due to endogeneity. The OLS regressions provide a means of comparison with older studies. Many classic studies of consumption are older studies and used OLS. To the extent their results differ from this study's later 2SLS results, using both OLS and 2SLS to test models here provides one way of examining whether differences discovered with older studies are substantive, or perhaps just due to choice of estimation technique.

Results for the deficit, consumer borrowing and business cycle control variables are printed in boldface in each model below to emphasize the test's key findings.

Model 5.1 OLS Estimates of the effects of the government deficit ($T_T - G_{T\&I}$) and consumer borrowing (C_B) on consumer spending (C_T).

(Current year GDP used as business cycle control)

$$\underset{(t=)}{\Delta C_T} = \underset{(3.3)}{0.21\Delta(Y - T_T)} + \underset{(3.4)}{0.25\boldsymbol{\Delta}(\mathbf{T_T} - \mathbf{G_{T\&I}})}$$

$$- \underset{(-5.9)}{12.36\Delta PR} + \underset{(4.8)}{0.45\,\Delta DJ_{-2}} + \underset{(1.9)}{3.14\,\Delta XR_{AV}} - \underset{(-1.3)}{319.66\Delta POP_{16}}$$

$$+\underset{(2.8)}{0.013\Delta POP} + \underset{(1.1)}{0.31\Delta ICC_{-1}} + \underset{(4.3)}{42.30\Delta M2_{AV}}$$

$$+\underset{(3.4)}{0.11\,\boldsymbol{\Delta}\mathbf{C_{B2}}} + \underset{(4.3)}{0.30\,\boldsymbol{\Delta}\mathbf{GDP_{REAL(0)}}}$$

$$R^2 = 94.8\% \quad D.W. = 1.7\ MSE = 25.49 \qquad (5.1)$$

The results indicate

- a negative relationship between the deficit and consumer spending of 25 cents per dollar of deficit, that is systematic (statistically significant), even after controlling for business cycle effects (all other models below using different, or no, business cycle controls nearly double this estimate of deficit effects. This suggests the high multicollinearity between the current period GDP ($r = 0.70$) and the deficit is resulting in an understatement of the deficits effect)
- that borrowing is a systematic determinant of consumer spending *in addition to* other determinants such as income and wealth, and that
- the finding that both the deficit/spending relationship and the importance of borrowing hold, even controlling for the state of the economy, suggests both findings may hold in recessions as well as good times. Heim (2012a) has found this true for the deficit/spending relationship using dummy variables to separately test this relationship in both recessions and normal times.

In the second model tested, we drop the borrowing variable, that is, drop the hypothesis that borrowing has independent effects on consumption spending. In retesting model 5.1 without it, the estimates for other variables remained very similar to those obtained in model 5.1, indicating the model is robust to at least some model changes, a requirement of good science. Results are shown in Eq. 5.2 below:

Model 5.2 OLS estimates of the effects of crowd out ($T_T - G_{T\&I}$) on consumer spending (C_T), w/o a consumer borrowing (C_{B2}) variable
(Current year GDP ($\text{GDP}_{\text{REAL}(0)}$) used as business cycle control)

$$\underset{(t=)}{\Delta C_T} = \underset{(1.2)}{0.17\Delta(Y - T_T)} + \underset{(3.3)}{0.26\boldsymbol{\Delta}(\mathbf{T_T} - \mathbf{G_{T\&I}})}$$
$$- \underset{(-5.1)}{12.61\Delta \text{PR}} + \underset{(5.0)}{0.41\,\Delta \text{DJ}_{-2}} + \underset{(3.2)}{5.69\,\Delta \text{XR}_{\text{AV}}} - \underset{(-0.8)}{234.57\Delta \text{POP}_{16}}$$
$$+ \underset{(2.4)}{0.011\Delta \text{POP}} + \underset{(0.1)}{0.05\Delta \text{ICC}_{-1}} + \underset{(3.9)}{42.52\Delta \text{M2}_{\text{AV}}} + \underset{(3.0)}{0.36\,\boldsymbol{\Delta}\mathbf{GDP}_{\mathbf{REAL}(0)}}$$
$$R^2 = 93.3\% \quad \text{D.W.} = 1.9 \;\; \text{MSE} = 28.46 \qquad (5.2)$$

As with Model 5.1, most variables initially hypothesized to be related to consumer spending (the "standard model") were found to be statistically significant determinants, as expected. The findings concerning the deficit are virtually identical to model 5.1, despite the change in model specification. This provides some indication multicollinearity may be adequately controlled for, and not be unduly affecting coefficient and *t*-statistic estimates in these models containing many right hand side, potentially multicollinear, variables.

The third model tested is the same as model 5.1 except it uses real GDP-lagged three years as the business cycle control variable:

Model 5.3 OLS estimates of the effects of crowd out and access to borrowing on consumer spending

(GDP-lagged three periods used as business cycle control)

$$\begin{aligned}
\underset{(t=)}{\Delta C_T} &= \underset{(10.0)}{0.46\Delta(Y - T_T)} + \underset{(8.7)}{0.47\boldsymbol{\Delta}(\mathbf{T_T} - \mathbf{G_{T\&I}})} \\
&\quad - \underset{(-5.3)}{12.29\Delta \mathrm{PR}} + \underset{(4.6)}{0.39\,\Delta \mathrm{DJ}_{-2}} + \underset{(2.6)}{3.78\,\Delta \mathrm{XR}_{\mathrm{AV}}} - \underset{(-2.1)}{553.57\Delta \mathrm{POP}_{16}} \\
&\quad + \underset{(4.6)}{0.019\Delta \mathrm{POP}} + \underset{(1.5)}{0.51\Delta \mathrm{ICC}_{-1}} + \underset{(5.3)}{53.25\Delta \mathrm{M2}_{\mathrm{AV}}} \\
&\quad + \underset{(3.0)}{0.13\,\boldsymbol{\Delta}\mathbf{C_{B2}}} + \underset{(1.2)}{0.05\,\boldsymbol{\Delta}\mathbf{GDP_{REAL(-3)}}} \\
&\quad R^2 = 94.1\%\ \ \mathrm{D.W.} = 1.9\ \ \mathrm{MSE} = 27.02
\end{aligned} \tag{5.3}$$

The estimated effect of borrowing on spending remains about the same. The estimated effect of the business cycle variable on consumer spending drops considerably from 0.30 to 0.05. The increase in the estimate of the deficits effect on spending increases by nearly as much (0.47 versus 0.26), suggesting that the strong correlation of current period GDP and the deficit (0.70) is distorting (dampening) the measured effect. Though three years ago's GDP is more strongly correlated with current deficits than is current year GDP, it is not as good an indicator of current economic conditions (which are less well correlated with current period deficits). Model 5.1's deficit effect estimate (0.26) compared to the model 5.3 estimate (0.47) suggests that GDP_{-3}, that while the deficit moves more systematically with GDP_{-3}, current GDP/spending relationships are also negative, and these are not as well controlled for in 5.3, causing it to pick up both sources of variation. However, in all three of these tests we see a statistically significant negative relationship of deficits and private spending, supporting the crowd out hypothesis.

Without borrowing as an explanatory variable, model 5.4 shows the three-year lagged GDP model estimates of the deficits effect are roughly the same as in model 5.3. The slight increase may indicate the loanable funds pool declines in recessions reducing funds available spending for reasons other than deficit induced crowd out.

Model 5.4 OLS estimates of the effects of crowd out W/O access to borrowing variable

(Lagged GDP used as business cycle control)

$$\underset{(t=)}{\Delta C_T} = \underset{(6.1)}{0.48\Delta(Y - T_T)} + \underset{(7.4)}{0.54\boldsymbol{\Delta}(\mathbf{T}_{\mathrm{T}} - \mathbf{G}_{\mathrm{T\&I}})}$$

$$- \underset{(-5.6)}{13.15\Delta \mathrm{PR}} + \underset{(4.8)}{0.36\Delta \mathrm{DJ}_{-2}} + \underset{(3.0)}{6.67\,\Delta \mathrm{XR}_{\mathrm{AV}}} - \underset{(-1.8)}{500.88\Delta \mathrm{POP}_{16}}$$

$$+ \underset{(4.3)}{0.019\Delta \mathrm{POP}} + \underset{(0.4)}{0.21\Delta \mathrm{ICC}_{-1}} + \underset{(5.0)}{58.21\Delta \mathrm{M2}_{\mathrm{AV}}}$$

$$+ \underset{(0.6)}{0.02\,\boldsymbol{\Delta}\mathbf{GDP}_{\mathbf{REAL}(-3)}} \quad R^2 = 92.1\% \quad \mathrm{D.W.} = 2.1$$

$$\mathrm{MSE} = 31.02 \tag{5.4}$$

Here again, deficits appear to be significantly related to consumer spending, even controlling for the phase of the economy. As an alternative business cycle control, current year unemployment was also tested, yielding the Model 5.5 results. As noted earlier, high levels of multicollinearity with government receipts result in a sign opposite the negative sign expected for this variable. Removing the receipts part of the deficit variable or lagging the deficit one year to reduce this problem restores the expected negative sign. The variable also remains statistically significant.

Model 5.5 OLS estimates of the effects of 1 variable crowd out and access to borrowing on consumer demand

(Unemployment business cycle control)

$$\underset{(t=)}{\Delta C_T} = \underset{(12.4)}{0.52\Delta(Y - T_T)} + \underset{(11.1)}{0.54\boldsymbol{\Delta}(\mathbf{T}_{\mathrm{T}} - \mathbf{G}_{\mathrm{T\&I}})}$$

$$- \underset{(-5.6)}{10.80\Delta \mathrm{PR}} + \underset{(5.5)}{0.43\,\Delta \mathrm{DJ}_{-2}} + \underset{(2.5)}{3.24\,\Delta \mathrm{XR}_{\mathrm{AV}}} - \underset{(-2.2)}{555.63\Delta \mathrm{POP}_{16}}$$

$$+ \underset{(4.6)}{0.017\Delta \mathrm{POP}} + \underset{(2.6)}{0.77\Delta \mathrm{ICC}_{-1}} + \underset{(7.4)}{57.61\Delta \mathrm{M2}_{\mathrm{AV}}}$$

$$+ \underset{(3.4)}{0.13\,\boldsymbol{\Delta}\mathbf{C}_{\mathbf{B2}}} + \underset{(3.3)}{20.03\,\boldsymbol{\Delta}\mathbf{UNEM}}$$

$$R^2 = 94.6\% \quad \mathrm{D.W.} = 1.8\ \mathrm{MSE} = 25.96 \tag{5.5}$$

Results for the borrowing variable are about the same as that obtained using either the other business cycle control variables, but estimates of the negative impact of deficits are the strongest yet, though similar to the results obtained using lagged GDP as a business cycle control. That said, the current period unemployment rate, though a significant control, has the wrong sign. As noted in the methodology section, this appears to be a multicollinearity issue, since its intercorrelation with government receipts is the highest of any two explanatory variables (0.76) in the whole first difference data set. Lagging the unemployment rate two years provides a regression coefficient and *t*-statistic of −5.43(−1.9), much more in line with what theory would lead us to expect, but is not strongly related to current year deficits, and therefore, not as useful to us.

In model 5.5.a. below, we use lagged unemployment as the business cycle control, and obtain the expected sign.

Model 5.5.a OLS estimates of the effects of one-variable crowd out on consumer demand with access to borrowing variable

(Unemployment lagged two periods used as business cycle control)

$$\underset{(t=)}{\Delta C_T} = \underset{(10.7)}{0.48\Delta(Y - T_T)} + \underset{(9.2)}{0.47\boldsymbol{\Delta}(\mathbf{T_T} - \mathbf{G_{T\&I}})}$$

$$- \underset{(-6.0)}{12.22\Delta PR} + \underset{(4.0)}{0.39\,\Delta DJ_{-2}} + \underset{(2.3)}{6.68\,\Delta XR_{AV}} - \underset{(-1.9)}{565.82\Delta POP_{16}}$$

$$+ \underset{(5.3)}{0.02\Delta POP} + \underset{(1.6)}{0.47\Delta ICC_{-1}} + \underset{(5.3)}{55.68\Delta M2_{AV}} \; \underset{(3.2)}{13\boldsymbol{\Delta}\mathbf{C_{B2}}}$$

$$- \underset{(-1.9)}{5.44\,\boldsymbol{\Delta}\mathbf{UNEM_{-2}}} \quad R^2 = 94.1\ \% \quad D.W. = 1.7$$

$$MSE = 27.14 \tag{5.5a}$$

We note again that model 5.5.a indicates that using the unemployment rate lagged two years not only has the expected sign, and the model continues to show virtually the same strong statistically significant negative effect of deficits on consumer spending, indicating the problem leading to the wrong sign on the unemployment rate control variable is not also distorting our crowd out results.

The next test (model 5.6) indicates that without controlling for borrowing availability, the estimated effects of crowd out are slightly larger, as was the case with model 5.4, using the GDP_{-3} business cycle control variable. This may reflect a tendency for the loanable funds pool to drop faster than the demand for loanable funds in recessions, an additional channel (besides unemployment) through which recessionary effects may influence consumption, but one which is correlated with deficit size. Or it may be our inability to obtain more precise estimates of deficit effects: clearly this estimate is within the confidence intervals around most of our earlier point estimates: (0.45) – (0.50).

Model 5.6 OLS estimates of the effects of one-variable crowd out on consumer demand W/O access to borrowing variable

(Unemployment business cycle control)

$$\underset{(t=)}{\Delta C_T} = \underset{(7.8)}{0.53\Delta(Y - T_T)} + \underset{(7.3)}{0.60\mathbf{\Delta}(\mathbf{T}_{\mathrm{T}} - \mathbf{G}_{\mathrm{T\&I}})}$$

$$- \underset{(-5.5)}{11.48\Delta \mathrm{PR}} + \underset{(5.0)}{0.38\,\Delta \mathrm{DJ}_{-2}} + \underset{(3.5)}{6.35\,\Delta \mathrm{XR}_{\mathrm{AV}}} - \underset{(-2.0)}{505.42\Delta \mathrm{POP}_{16}}$$

$$+ \underset{(4.3)}{0.017\Delta \mathrm{POP}} + \underset{(1.1)}{0.47\Delta \mathrm{ICC}_{-1}} + \underset{(5.8)}{60.83\Delta \mathrm{M2}_{\mathrm{AV}}}$$

$$+ \underset{(2.5)}{18.01\,\mathbf{\Delta UNEM}} \quad R^2 = 92.6\% \quad \mathrm{D.W.} = 2.1 \ \mathrm{MSE} = 29.98 \qquad (5.6)$$

Most coefficient estimates and significance levels when controlling for economic conditions using unemployment were similar to results using GDP_{-3}, especially for crowd out and borrowing. The results for the crowd out variable when using current GDP as the business cycle control showed coefficients on the deficit variable that were smaller, suggesting a smaller net effect after controlling for business cycle conditions. But as noted earlier, the current GDP, though strongly related to current consumption, is not well related to the current deficit. Hence, any significant finding for the crowd out variable when using current year GDP as the control is unlikely to result from confounding business cycle and crowd out effects. This suggests about half the measured deficit effect on consumption is due to business cycle effects, the rest due to crowd out. (In regressions of the deficit on Y_0, Y_{-3} and UNEM, Y_0 has by far the weakest relationship. It is statistically insignificant, and has the wrong sign). This suggests the current GDP is not much related to the current deficit, and therefore is not a good variable to use when trying to control for business cycle effects on deficits and consumer spending in the same period.

Finally, model 5.7 tests the robustness of our crowd out findings if no business cycle control is used.

Model 5.7 OLS estimates of the effects of one-variable crowd out and access to borrowing on consumer demand
(No explicit business cycle control)

$$\underset{(t=)}{\Delta C_T} = \underset{(10.5)}{0.48\Delta(Y - T_T)} + \underset{(9.8)}{0.48\boldsymbol{\Delta}(\mathbf{T_T} - \mathbf{G_{T\&I}})}$$
$$- \underset{(-6.9)}{13.05\Delta \mathrm{PR}} + \underset{(4.3)}{0.43\ \Delta \mathrm{DJ}_{-2}} + \underset{(2.2)}{3.44\ \Delta \mathrm{XR_{AV}}} - \underset{(-1.9)}{547.55\Delta \mathrm{POP}_{16}}$$
$$+ \underset{(5.0)}{0.020\Delta \mathrm{POP}} + \underset{(1.4)}{0.46\Delta \mathrm{ICC}_{-1}} + \underset{(5.7)}{56.11\Delta \mathrm{M2_{AV}}}\ (2)$$
$$+ \underset{(3.1)}{0.12\ \boldsymbol{\Delta}\mathbf{C_{B2}}} \quad R^2 = 93.9\% \quad \mathrm{D.W.} = 1.7\ \mathrm{MSE} = 27.27 \qquad (5.7)$$

And the same model without a borrowing variable, model 5.8, gives:

Model 5.8 OLS estimates of the effects of one-variable crowd out and access to borrowing on consumer demand
(No explicit business cycle control)

$$\underset{(t=)}{\Delta C_T} = \underset{(6.5)}{0.48\Delta(Y - T_T)} + \underset{(7.5)}{0.54\boldsymbol{\Delta}(\mathbf{T_T} - \mathbf{G_{T\&I}})}$$
$$- \underset{(-6.3)}{13.49\Delta \mathrm{PR}} + \underset{(4.5)}{0.38\ \Delta \mathrm{DJ}_{-2}} + \underset{(3.3)}{6.42\ \Delta \mathrm{XR_{AV}}} - \underset{(-1.7)}{499.77\Delta \mathrm{POP}_{16}}$$
$$+ \underset{(4.7)}{0.020\Delta \mathrm{POP}} + \underset{(0.4)}{0.19\Delta \mathrm{ICC}_{-1}} + \underset{(4.8)}{59.38\Delta \mathrm{M2_{AV}}}\ (2)$$
$$R^2 = 92.0\ \% \quad \mathrm{D.W.} = 2.0\ \mathrm{MSE} = 30.76 \qquad (5.8)$$

Estimates of negative deficit effects on consumer spending are essentially identical to those obtained using our two strongest business cycle control variables: the current unemployment rate and the GDP-lagged three periods.

(Note: ICC_{-1} becomes statistically significant at the1 % level for all four of the above models if the wealth measure used is $\Delta \mathrm{DJ}_{-0,\ \mathrm{or}-3,\ \mathrm{or}\ -4}$, not $\Delta \mathrm{DJ}_{-2}$, and its statistical significance stays high under these conditions even if other the business cycle controls (or no control) used. Even worse results for ICC_{-1} are obtained if DJ_{-1} is used. This suggests a multicollinearity problem. Use of DJ_{-2} does result in a R^2 about 1.2 % higher than obtained using other lags with ICC_{-1}, so we with that wealth variable. However, the dependence of the significance of ICC_{-1} on the particular lag of DJ used leaves the reliability of ICC_{-1} estimates in question. It leaves some question as to whether stock market wealth or consumer confidence is actually causing change in consumption.

5.1.1 OLS Spending Model Conclusions Summarized

Table 5.1 below summarizes the spending model findings.

5.1.2 Do Deficit Effects Differ With the Type of Government Spending Increase, or the Level of Government Cutting Taxes?

Orszag and Gale (2006) found that Federal, but not state and local, government tax cuts to have a net positive stimulus effect on consumption, as did increased government spending on transfer payments, but not any other type of government spending. We attempted to replicate their findings using the models tested in Chap. 5 (Sect 5.1) above, with total government receipts broken into two separate variables: federal taxes and state/local taxes, and also letting total government spending to be divided into two separate variables: transfer spending and all other spending. We were unable to replicate their finding that tax cuts had a positive effect on consumption.

Attempts to duplicate Orszag and Gale's findings for the positive stimulus effects of transfer payments spending were mixed, varying with the business cycle phase control used. Results are shown below in models 5.9a–d, which are identical except for their use of different business cycle control variables. Model 5.9.a uses the unemployment rate lagged two years as the business cycle control variable. Results using the other business cycle control variables in models 5.9.b-d were very similar, and were robust to other time periods tested (1960—92, or 1960–2002, the time period used by Orszag and Gale).

Table 5.1 OLS consumer spending model findings summarized

	$\Delta(T_T - G_{T\&I})$	$\Delta(BORR)$	*Bus. cycle*
Model#	β (*t-stat.*)	β (*t-stat.*)	*Control*
5.1	0.25 (3.4)	0.11 (3.4)	GDP $_{Real(0)}$
5.2	0.26 (3.3)		
5.3	0.47 (8.7)	**0.13 (3.0)**	GDP $_{Real(-3)}$
5.4	0.54 (7.4)		
5.5	0.54 (11.1)	**0.13 (3.4)**	Unem
5.5.a	0.47 (9.2)	0.13 (3.2)	
5.6	0.60 (7.3)		
5.7	0.48 (9.8)	0.12 (3.1)	None
5.8	0.54 (7.5)		
Average	0.46 (7.3)	0.12 (3.2)	

Model 5.9a OLS estimates of the effects of one variable crowd out on consumer demand
(Unemployment lagged 2 periods used as business cycle control)

$$\underset{(t=)}{\Delta C_T} = \underset{(11.7)}{0.50\Delta(Y - T_T)} + \underset{(11.0)}{0.57\boldsymbol{\Delta}(\mathbf{T}_\mathrm{F})} + \underset{(3.8)}{0.54\boldsymbol{\Delta}(\mathbf{T}_\mathrm{S\&L})}$$
$$- \underset{(-1.3)}{0.14\boldsymbol{\Delta}(\mathbf{G}_\mathrm{Trans})} - \underset{(-4.3)}{0.43\boldsymbol{\Delta}(\mathbf{G}_\mathrm{Other})} - \underset{(-5.9)}{12.59\Delta \mathrm{PR}}$$
$$+ \underset{(4.6)}{0.41\,\Delta \mathrm{DJ}_{-2}} + \underset{(2.9)}{4.41\,\Delta \mathrm{XR}_\mathrm{AV}} - \underset{(-1.7)}{396.61\Delta \mathrm{POP}_{16}}$$
$$+ \underset{(1.8)}{0.015\Delta \mathrm{POP}} + \underset{(4.7)}{0.60\Delta \mathrm{ICC}_{-1}} + \underset{(2.5)}{45.70\Delta \mathrm{M2}_\mathrm{AV}}$$
$$+ \underset{(-0.5)}{0.10\boldsymbol{\Delta}\mathbf{C}_\mathrm{B2}} - 1.84\,\boldsymbol{\Delta}\mathbf{UNEM}_{-2}$$
$$R^2 = 95.0\ \%\quad \mathrm{D.W.} = 1.7\ \mathrm{MSE} = 25.88 \tag{5.9a}$$

Model 5.9b OLS estimates of the effects of one-variable crowd out on consumer demand
(GDP-lagged three periods used as business cycle control)

$$\underset{(t=)}{\Delta C_T} = \underset{(11.5)}{0.49\Delta(Y - T_T)} + \underset{(11.6)}{0.56\boldsymbol{\Delta}(\mathbf{T}_\mathrm{F})} + \underset{(4.0)}{0.56\boldsymbol{\Delta}(\mathbf{T}_\mathrm{S\&L})}$$
$$- \underset{(-1.4)}{0.15\boldsymbol{\Delta}(\mathbf{G}_\mathrm{Trans})} - \underset{(-4.5)}{0.41\boldsymbol{\Delta}(\mathbf{G}_\mathrm{Other})} - \underset{(-5.4)}{12.23\Delta \mathrm{PR}}$$
$$+ \underset{(4.8)}{0.40\,\Delta \mathrm{DJ}_{-2}} + \underset{(3.0)}{4.44\,\Delta \mathrm{XR}_\mathrm{AV}} - \underset{(-1.7)}{379.81\Delta \mathrm{POP}_{16}}$$
$$+ \underset{(2.9)}{0.013\Delta \mathrm{POP}} + \underset{(1.8)}{0.60\Delta \mathrm{ICC}_{-1}} + \underset{(4.1)}{43.49\Delta \mathrm{M2}_\mathrm{AV}}$$
$$+ \underset{(2.5)}{0.11\boldsymbol{\Delta}\mathbf{C}_\mathrm{B2}} + \underset{(1.1)}{0.03\,\boldsymbol{\Delta}\mathbf{GDP}_{-3}}$$
$$R^2 = 95.2\ \%\quad \mathrm{D.W.} = 1.8\ \mathrm{MSE} = 25.60 \tag{5.9b}$$

Model 5.9c OLS estimates of the effects of one-variable crowd out on consumer demand
(Unemployment lagged 0 periods used as business cycle control)

$$\underset{(t=)}{\Delta C_T} = \underset{(15.1)}{0.55\Delta(Y - T_T)} + \underset{(12.0)}{0.62\mathbf{\Delta}(\mathbf{T}_{\mathrm{F}})} + \underset{(44.7)}{0.66\mathbf{\Delta}(\mathbf{T}_{\mathrm{S\&L}})}$$
$$- \underset{(-2.2)}{0.26\mathbf{\Delta}(\mathbf{G}_{\mathrm{Trans}})} - \underset{(-4.1)}{0.38\mathbf{\Delta}(\mathbf{G}_{\mathrm{Other}})} - \underset{(-5.5)}{10.10\Delta \mathrm{PR}}$$
$$+ \underset{(5.5)}{0.43\,\Delta \mathrm{DJ}_{-2}} + \underset{(2.4)}{3.47\,\Delta \mathrm{XR}_{\mathrm{AV}}} - \underset{(-1.6)}{336.42\Delta \mathrm{POP}_{16}}$$
$$+ \underset{(2.7)}{0.010\Delta \mathrm{POP}} + \underset{(2.7)}{0.77\Delta \mathrm{ICC}_{-1}} + \underset{(6.0)}{45.10\Delta \mathrm{M2}_{\mathrm{AV}}}$$
$$+ \underset{(2.9)}{0.11\mathbf{\Delta C}_{\mathbf{B2}}} + \underset{(2.8)}{20.36\,\mathbf{\Delta UNEM}_{-0}}$$
$$R^2 = 95.7\ \% \quad \text{D.W.} = 1.9 \ \text{MSE} = 24.20 \qquad (5.9c)$$

Model 5.9d OLS estimates of the effects of one-variable crowd out on consumer demand W/Access to borrowing variable

(No business cycle control used)

$$\underset{(t=)}{\Delta C_T} = \underset{(11.6)}{0.50\Delta(Y - T_T)} + \underset{(8.1)}{0.58\mathbf{\Delta}(\mathbf{T}_{\mathrm{F}})} + \underset{(2.1)}{0.53\mathbf{\Delta}(\mathbf{T}_{\mathrm{S\&L}})}$$
$$- \underset{(-1.3)}{0.14\mathbf{\Delta}(\mathbf{G}_{\mathrm{Trans}})} - \underset{(-4.1)}{0.40\mathbf{\Delta}(\mathbf{G}_{\mathrm{Other}})} - \underset{(-5.6)}{12.84\Delta PR}$$
$$+ \underset{(4.7)}{0.42\,\Delta \mathrm{DJ}_{-2}} + \underset{(2.8)}{4.23\,\Delta \mathrm{XR}_{\mathrm{AV}}} - \underset{(-1.6)}{368.92\Delta \mathrm{POP}_{16}}$$
$$+ \underset{(3.2)}{0.014\Delta \mathrm{POP}} + \underset{(1.8)}{0.57\Delta \mathrm{ICC}_{-1}} + \underset{(4.7)}{45.07\Delta \mathrm{M2}_{\mathrm{AV}}}$$
$$+ \underset{(2.7)}{0.10\mathbf{\Delta C}_{\mathbf{B2}}} \quad R^2 = 95.0\ \% \quad \text{D.W.} = 1.7$$
$$\text{MSE} = 25.58 \qquad (5.9d)$$

All formulations of the crowd out effect show deficits induced by spending increases, including transfer spending increases, to have a negative effect on consumer spending. However, the transfer spending increase's effect on consumer spending, though negative, is only significant at the 20 % level when lagged GDP or the lagged unemployment rate is used as the business cycle control (or no control is used). When the current unemployment rate is used as the control, the results show transfer spending increases as negative and significant at the 3.5 % level. Hence, our point estimates all indicate that even deficits induced by transfer payments have a negative crowd out effect, though not as great as other types of government spending, but the level of statistical significance of this finding is unclear.

Though our transfer spending results vary in statistical significance, the coefficient sign is consistently negative and non-zero. In such situations, Triola (2012) notes our best estimate is our point estimate of mean effect, not zero, as we might consider doing, at least in cases where we lack statistical significance. Because of severe multicollinearity issues, the model would not run with current year GDP as a business cycle control.

Orszag and Gale did not test for crowd out effects on investment. In models 5.9.e–h below, we show regression results for the effects of different types of government spending and levels of taxation on investment, using different business cycle controls. Variables used are defined in the methodology chapter (Chap. 3) and consumption and investment chapters (Chaps. 5 and 6) found later in this paper.

Model 5.9.e OLS estimates of the effects of one-variable crowd out with borrowing

(Two-period lagged unemployment rate business cycle control)

$$\underset{(t=)}{\Delta I_T} = +\underset{(5.3)}{0.34\Delta ACC)} + \underset{(1.9)}{0.21\mathbf{\Delta}(\mathbf{T}_F)} + \underset{(1.5)}{0.60\mathbf{\Delta}(\mathbf{T}_{S\&L})}$$
$$- \underset{(-3.6)}{0.49\mathbf{\Delta}(\mathbf{G}_{Trans})} - \underset{(-3.1)}{0.41\mathbf{\Delta}(\mathbf{G}_{Other})}$$
$$+ \underset{(2.5)}{0.83\Delta DEP} \ \underset{(1.6)}{3.29\Delta CAP_{-1}} - \underset{(-1.5)}{4.66\Delta r_{-2}} + \underset{(0.0)}{0.00\ \Delta DJ_{-0}}$$
$$+ \underset{(2.0)}{0.14\Delta PROF_{-0}} + \underset{(2.4)}{5.49\Delta XR_{AV}} + \underset{(2.0)}{0.008\Delta POP}$$
$$+ \underset{(1.5)}{0.09\ \mathbf{\Delta I}_{\mathbf{B}(-1)}} - \underset{(-0.9)}{5.17\ \mathbf{\Delta GDP}_{\mathbf{REAL}(-3)}}$$
$$R^2 = 93.6\ \%, DW = 2.1, MSE = 33.25 \qquad (5.9.e)$$

Model 5.9.f OLS estimates of the effects of one-variable crowd out with borrowing

(Two-period lagged unemployment rate business cycle control)

$$\underset{(t=)}{\Delta I_T} = \underset{(5.3)}{+0.34\Delta \mathrm{ACC})} \underset{(1.9)}{+0.21\boldsymbol{\Delta}(\mathbf{T}_{\mathrm{F}})} \underset{(1.5)}{+0.60\boldsymbol{\Delta}(\mathbf{T}_{\mathrm{S\&L}})}$$
$$\underset{(-3.6)}{-0.49\boldsymbol{\Delta}(\mathbf{G}_{\mathrm{Trans}})} \underset{(-3.1)}{-0.41\boldsymbol{\Delta}(\mathbf{G}_{\mathrm{Other}})} \underset{(2.5)}{+0.83\Delta \mathrm{DEP}} \underset{(1.6)}{3.29\Delta \mathrm{CAP}_{-1}}$$
$$\underset{(-1.5)}{-4.66\Delta \mathrm{r}_{-2}} \underset{(0.0)}{+0.00\,\Delta \mathrm{DJ}_{-0}} \underset{(2.0)}{+0.14\Delta \mathrm{PROF}_{-0}}$$
$$\underset{(2.4)}{+5.49\Delta \mathrm{XR}_{\mathrm{AV}}} \underset{(2.0)}{+0.008\Delta \mathrm{POP}} \underset{(1.5)}{+.09\,\boldsymbol{\Delta}\mathbf{I}_{\mathbf{B}(-1)}}$$
$$\underset{(-0.9)}{-5.17\,\boldsymbol{\Delta}\mathbf{UNEM}_{(-2)}} \quad R^2 = 93.6\ \%, \mathrm{DW} = 2.1, \mathrm{MSE} = 33.25 \qquad (5.9.\mathrm{f})$$

Model 5.9.g OLS estimates of the effects of one-variable crowd out with borrowing
(Current period unemployment rate business cycle control)

$$\underset{(t=)}{\Delta I_T} = \underset{(4.5)}{+0.32\Delta \mathrm{ACC})} \underset{(1.4)}{+0.16\boldsymbol{\Delta}(\mathbf{T}_{\mathrm{F}})} \underset{(1.3)}{+0.57\boldsymbol{\Delta}(\mathbf{T}_{\mathrm{S\&L}})}$$
$$\underset{(-2.2)}{-0.40\boldsymbol{\Delta}(\mathbf{G}_{\mathrm{Trans}})} \underset{(-3.0)}{-0.42\boldsymbol{\Delta}(\mathbf{G}_{\mathrm{Other}})}$$
$$\underset{(2.6)}{+0.82\Delta \mathrm{DEP}} \underset{(1.2)}{2.69\Delta \mathrm{CAP}_{-1}} \underset{(-1.2)}{-2.80\Delta \mathrm{r}_{-2}} \underset{(0.3)}{+0.09\,\Delta \mathrm{DJ}_{-0}}$$
$$\underset{(1.9)}{+0.12\Delta \mathrm{PROF}_{-0}} \underset{(2.4)}{+5.25\Delta \mathrm{XR}_{\mathrm{AV}}} \underset{(1.9)}{+0.008\Delta \mathrm{POP}}$$
$$\underset{(1.2)}{+0.07\,\boldsymbol{\Delta}\mathbf{I}_{\mathbf{B}(-1)}} \underset{(-1.3)}{-11.98\,\boldsymbol{\Delta}\mathbf{UNEM}_{(-0)}}$$
$$R^2 = 93.8\ \%, \mathrm{DW} = 2.0, \mathrm{MSE} = 32.83 \qquad (5.9.\mathrm{g})$$

Model 5.9.h OLS estimates of the effects of one-variable crowd out with borrowing
(No business cycle control)

$$\underset{(t=)}{\Delta I_T} = \underset{(5.4)}{+0.34\Delta \mathrm{ACC})} \underset{(1.9)}{+0.21\boldsymbol{\Delta}(\mathbf{T}_{\mathrm{F}})} \underset{(1.6)}{+0.61\boldsymbol{\Delta}(\mathbf{T}_{\mathrm{S\&L}})}$$
$$\underset{(-3.5)}{-0.49\boldsymbol{\Delta}(\mathbf{G}_{\mathrm{Trans}})} \underset{(-3.0)}{-0.40\boldsymbol{\Delta}(\mathbf{G}_{\mathrm{Other}})}$$
$$\underset{(2.5)}{+0.89\Delta \mathrm{DEP}} \underset{(1.8)}{3.66\Delta \mathrm{CAP}_{-1}} \underset{(-1.3)}{-3.11\Delta \mathrm{r}_{-2}} \underset{(0.0)}{+0.00\,\Delta \mathrm{DJ}_{-0}}$$
$$\underset{(2.1)}{+0.13\Delta \mathrm{PROF}_{-0}} \underset{(2.4)}{+5.23\Delta \mathrm{XR}_{\mathrm{AV}}} \underset{(1.8)}{+0.008\Delta \mathrm{POP}}$$
$$\underset{(1.4)}{+0.08\,\boldsymbol{\Delta}\mathbf{I}_{\mathbf{B}(-1)}} \quad R^2 = 93.6\ \%, \mathrm{DW} = 2.0,$$
$$\mathrm{MSE} = 32.96 \qquad (5.9.\mathrm{h})$$

All spending deficits had a significant negative effect on investment. For tax cuts, in three of four tests, federal tax cut deficits has at least a marginally negative effect also. In the fourth case they were insignificant. State and local tax cuts were not significantly related to investment in any test.

5.1.3 OLS Estimates of Crowd Out Effects on Consumer Borrowing

Crowd out theory argues that the negative correlation between deficits and consumer spending is caused by government borrowing to finance deficits. Government borrowing reduces the pool of loanable funds available to consumers to finance consumption beyond what incomes alone will allow. In turn, reduced consumer borrowing reduces consumer spending, since spending is driven by both income and access to borrowing, that is, total purchasing power. The borrowing component is constrained by the availability of loanable funds, which have to finance both private and public sector borrowing.

The next set of models tests this theory to see if consumer borrowing is directly affected by government deficits, controlling for other relevant variables. An in-depth analysis of the determinants of consumer borrowing is beyond the scope of this paper. A reasonable initial hypothesis for testing might be that, in general, consumers borrow only to spend. Therefore, some or all of the variables found to be determinants of spending should be determinants of borrowing. In addition, as noted earlier, some borrowing appears to systematically take place simply because consumers have access to borrowed money, that is, consumers may buy bigger houses if they can borrow than they would if they had to pay cash, or consumers may spend more on home furnishings if they have access to credit cards than they would if they had to pay cash.

To estimate the effects of deficits on borrowing, the models used to test spending are used, with three changes:

- The dependent variable is consumer borrowing, not spending.
- The growth of savings components of the real money supply, (M2 − M1), was added to reflect the statistically significant positive relationship between this variable and consumer borrowing. It is interpreted as a measure of the supply of loanable funds. This particular form of the money supply was used because it was more systematically related to borrowing than either M1 or M2 alone. This probably (sensibly) indicates that the supply of loanable funds is more largely determined by fluctuations in savings channeled into financial assets like savings accounts, certificates of deposit and

money market savings rather than by the Federal Reserve's changes in the M1 money supply. In fact, this component of M2 is typically several times as large as the M1 money supply.

- Experimentation indicated the NYSE composite average lagged one period was far more systematically related to *borrowing* than the two period lag. Earlier, the two-lag version had been found most systematically related to spending. A rising stock market provides an alternative source of funding, which may reduce borrowing.
- These models of consumer borrowing are rough estimates, and do not explain nearly as much variance as did the consumer spending models. They explain only about 58–59 % of borrowing's variance, compared to 92–94 % for spending. Generally lower levels of statistical significance for variables tested is also observed. Nonetheless, as was the case with spending, test results, Models 5.9–5.12 below indicate government deficits have a negative relationship with consumer borrowing, usually systematically, even when the state of the economy is controlled for. This provides direct evidence supporting the claim that borrowing is crowded out by government deficits, which is the crowd out hypothesis. Earlier results indicated spending is related to borrowing. Models 5.9–12 are identical except for the business cycle control used.

Model 5.9 OLS estimates of the effects of one-variable crowd out on borrowing
(Current period real GDP business cycle control)

$$\begin{aligned}
\underset{(t=)}{\Delta C_B} = {} & \underset{(0.7)}{0.26\Delta(Y - T_T)} + \underset{(2.3)}{0.54\boldsymbol{\Delta}(\mathbf{T}_{\mathrm{T}} - \mathbf{G}_{\mathrm{T\&I}})} \\
& - \underset{(-3.9)}{20.63\Delta \mathrm{PR}} - \underset{(-3.5)}{1.60\,\Delta \mathrm{DJ}_{-1}} + \underset{(2.9)}{21.79\,\Delta \mathrm{XR}_{\mathrm{AV}}} \\
& + \underset{(0.8)}{424.67\Delta \mathrm{POP}_{16}} - \underset{(-0.1)}{0.001\Delta \mathrm{POP}} + \underset{(0.4)}{0.43\Delta \mathrm{ICC}_{-1}} \\
& - \underset{(-1.0)}{34.31\Delta \mathrm{M2}_{\mathrm{AV}}} - \underset{(-1.8)}{0.20\,\Delta(\mathrm{M2}_{\mathrm{Real}} - \mathrm{M1}_{\mathrm{Real}})} \\
& + \underset{(0.5)}{0.15\boldsymbol{\Delta}\mathbf{GDP}_{\mathbf{REAL}}} \quad R^2 = 58.6\ \% \quad \mathrm{D.W.} = 2.0 \\
& \mathrm{MSE} = 100.86
\end{aligned} \tag{5.9}$$

The effect of the deficit in the comparable spending model (5.2) was .26 (t = 3.3) using the same business cycle control variable. As we will see below, all borrowing models show deficits having a 10 % to over 100 % larger impact on borrowing than on spending. This may be because in addition to the deficit's direct effect in reducing the loanable funds pool available to consumers, some part of the government tax cut or spending stimulus may be used to finance spending that would otherwise still have occurred, but financed out of borrowed funds (e.g., credit card borrowing for the unemployed now receiving larger transfer payments). If so, this provides two ways borrowing declines: first, because financing the deficit crowds out loanable funds available to consumers, second, some or all of the additional disposable income provided by the deficit-financed stimulus program may be used to fund spending that would have taken place anyway, but out of borrowed money.

Crowd out theory would allow for the borrowing decline to be as much or more than the spending decline. Hence, the borrowing results seem consistent with the spending results.

If we lag the real GDP three periods, we get the following results:

Model 5.10 OLS estimates of the effects of crowd out on borrowing (Lagged real GDP business cycle control)

$$\underset{(t=)}{\Delta C_B} = \underset{(1.7)}{0.42\Delta(Y - T_T)} + \underset{(2.6)}{0.64\boldsymbol{\Delta}(\mathbf{T}_{\mathrm{T}} - \mathbf{G}_{\mathrm{T\&I}})}$$
$$- \underset{(-4.2)}{21.90\Delta \mathrm{PR}} - \underset{(-3.3)}{1.59\,\Delta \mathrm{DJ}_{-1}} + \underset{(2.6)}{20.74\,\Delta \mathrm{XR}_{\mathrm{AV}}}$$
$$+ \underset{(0.6)}{290.41\Delta \mathrm{POP}_{16}} + \underset{(0.5)}{0.01\Delta \mathrm{POP}} + \underset{(0.4)}{0.37\Delta \mathrm{ICC}} - \underset{(-0.7)}{23.25\Delta \mathrm{M2}_{\mathrm{AV}}}$$
$$- \underset{(-1.4)}{0.17\,\Delta(\mathrm{M2}_{\mathrm{Real}} - \mathrm{M1}_{\mathrm{Real}})} - \underset{(-0.9)}{0.10\,\boldsymbol{\Delta}\mathbf{GDP}_{\mathbf{REAL}(-3)}}$$
$$R^2 = 59.1\ \% \quad \mathrm{D.W.} = 2.1\ \mathrm{MSE} = 100.16 \qquad (5.10)$$

This business cycle control results in a higher estimated effect of deficits on borrowing (0.64) than with spending (0.46).

Replacing the lagged real GDP with a more contemporaneous measure of business cycle, the unemployment rate, yields the following results

Model 5.11 OLS estimates of the effects of one-variable crowd out on real borrowing

(Unemployment business cycle control)

$$\underset{(t=)}{\Delta C_B} = \underset{(1.4)}{0.35\Delta(Y - T_T)} + \underset{(2.0)}{0.59\boldsymbol{\Delta}(\mathbf{T}_{\mathrm{T}} - \mathbf{G}_{\mathrm{T\&I}})} - \underset{(-4.1)}{23.28\Delta\mathrm{PR}} - \underset{(-3.4)}{1.64\,\Delta\mathrm{DJ}_{-1}}$$
$$+ \underset{(2.9)}{22.08\,\Delta\mathrm{XR}_{\mathrm{AV}}} + \underset{(0.6)}{307.53\Delta\mathrm{POP}_{16}} + \underset{(0.4)}{0.006\Delta\mathrm{POP}} + \underset{(0.2)}{0.23\Delta\mathrm{ICC}_{-1}}$$
$$- \underset{(-0.8)}{30.20\Delta\mathrm{M2}_{\mathrm{AV}}} - \underset{(-1.8)}{0.19\,\Delta(\mathrm{M2}_{\mathrm{Real}} - \mathrm{M1}_{\mathrm{Real}})} - \underset{(-0.7)}{18.87\boldsymbol{\Delta}\mathbf{UNEM}}$$
$$R^2 = 58.8\ \%\quad \mathrm{D.W.} = 2.1, \mathrm{MSE} = 100.61 \qquad (5.11)$$

Here again, we find deficits negatively related to consumer borrowing (consumer spending using the same model, declined 0.54 per dollar of deficit). It was significantly related to spending. The unemployment rate, like the other two business cycle controls, does not seem significantly related to borrowing (it was significantly related to spending), suggesting that much consumer borrowing, undertaken to finance cars, houses and other long-term investments, is inelastic to the short-term ups and downs of the economy, (or perhaps these ups and downs are well captured in the other variables hypothesized as determinants). The crowd out effects of deficits on borrowing were found significant in all the above models.

Finally, model 5.12 presents the borrowing model without a business cycle control variable. It yielded the following results:

Model 5.12 OLS estimates of the effects of crowd out on real borrowing (No business cycle control)

$$\underset{(t=)}{\Delta C_B} = \underset{(1.7)}{0.40\Delta(Y - T_T)} + \underset{(2.7)}{0.66\boldsymbol{\Delta}(\mathbf{T}_{\mathrm{T}} - \mathbf{G}_{\mathrm{T\&I}})}$$
$$- \underset{(-3.9)}{21.25\Delta\mathrm{PR}} - \underset{(-3.5)}{1.63\,\Delta\mathrm{DJ}_{-1}} + \underset{(2.9)}{22.05\,\Delta\mathrm{XR}_{\mathrm{AV}}}$$
$$+ \underset{(0.7)}{309.21\Delta\mathrm{POP}_{16}} + \underset{(0.2)}{0.003\Delta\mathrm{POP}} + \underset{(0.5)}{0.52\Delta\mathrm{ICC}_{-1}}$$
$$- \underset{(-0.9)}{28.01\Delta\mathrm{M2}_{\mathrm{AV}}} - \underset{(-1.8)}{0.20\,\Delta(\mathrm{M2}_{\mathrm{Real}} - \mathrm{M1}_{\mathrm{Real}})}$$
$$R^2 = 58.5\ \%\quad \mathrm{D.W.} = 2.1, \mathrm{MSE} = 99.76 \qquad (5.12)$$

By comparison, consumer spending was estimated to decline 0.48 per dollar of deficit using the no business cycle control model.

All four models above show the same factors drive consumer borrowing:

- The government deficit
- The prime interest rate
- Wealth, lagged a year (negatively related to borrowing)
- The exchange rate, and
- Available savings, M2 – M1 (negatively related to borrowing, but not quite as systematically)

The negative relationship of a dollar change in deficits to consumer borrowing, is summarized in Section 5.1.4.

5.1.4 OLS Borrowing Model Conclusions Summarized

Table 5.2 below summarizes the borrowing model findings.

The borrowing models show a definite statistically significant negative relationship between deficits and borrowing. The evidence suggests deficits are related to a larger contraction in consumer borrowing than in consumer spending. We interpret this to mean that some stimulus money is used to finance spending that can no longer by financed out of (less available) borrowed funds.

The borrowing models explain substantially less variance than the spending models (58–60 % vs. 92–95 %). Lower *t*-statistics are to be expected and were found in these less completely specified borrowing models, but the deficit was still found significant at the 5 % level or better.

Hence, using OLS as the tool of investigation, we conclude the findings provide strong evidence that crowd out is the reason we observe a negative relationship between deficits and both consumer borrowing and spending. The results hold even controlling for the effects on deficits and consumption of variations in the business cycle.

Table 5.2 OLS consumer borrowing model conclusions summarized

Model#	$\Delta(T_T - G_{T\&I})$ β (*t-stat.*)	*Bus. Cycle Control*
5.9	0.54 (2.3)	$GDP_{Real(0)}$
510	0.64 (2.6)	$GDP_{Real(-3)}$
5.11	0.59 (2.0)	Unemployment rate
5.12	0.66 (2.7)	None
Average	0.61 (2.4)	

5.2 2SLS Models

The evidence above for the conclusions regarding crowd out was obtained using OLS regression. If there is endogeneity in the models (e.g., between consumption and income), an instrumental variables technique such as Two Stage Least Squares (2SLS) would be a better tool of investigation, since it avoids the simultaneous equation bias problem. In the presence of endogeneity, OLS is biased and inconsistent and the 2SLS instrumental variable technique provides a consistent estimator. Hence, 2SLS provides a better tool for scientific inquiry when endogeneity is present. In this section, we retest the same models we tested in Chap. 5 (Sect. 5.1) using OLS, but now 2SLS is used as the tool of investigation.

We might suspect such variables as disposable income, the government deficit, the accelerator, the real GDP and the unemployment rate to be endogenous with consumption spending, since consumption is a part of GDP, and GDP is a component or a determinant of all these variables. Prior testing for endogeneity had indicated current year depreciation expense was also endogenous, presumably because depreciation expense can often be taken on new investment plant and equipment in the year it purchased and this might have a positive effect on consumption. Hence, variables "suspected" *a priori* as being simultaneously affected by (error term driven) changes in consumer spending models are given in Table 5.3.

The actual endogeneity of these "suspect" variables was then tested, using the Hausman endogeneity test. The Hausman procedure calls for regressing individual variables suspected of endogeneity on the remainder of the variables in the system, that is, the variables considered exogenous or lagged, in an attempt to strip the non-endogenous parts of the suspect variable from it, leaving only the endogenous portion. The residuals from this regression are then entered as an additional explanatory variable in the consumption function's structural model (the same one tested in the OLS section), and tested using OLS. If the residual variable is statistically

Table 5.3 Determinants of consumption and investment initially assumed endogenous when applying endogeneity tests

- Current year real GDP
- Disposable income
- The government deficit
- The accelerator
- Depreciation allowances
- Unemployment rate

Table 5.4 Determinants of consumption and investment initially assumed exogenous or lagged when applying endogeneity tests (subscripts denote lags)

Capacity utilization rate$_{-1}$
Real prime interest rate$_{-2}$
Dow Jones composite index$_{-2}$
Exchange rate, 4 year Average $_{(0\ \text{through}-3)}$
Profits$_{-2}$
Population size$_{0}$
Population distribution$_{0}$ (20–24 year olds/65+ year olds)
Real M2$_{AV(-2\ \text{through}\ -4)}$
Real (M2 − M1)$_{0}$
Consumer confidence$_{-1}$
Exports$_{0}$
GDP$_{-3}$

significant (5 % significance level), the suspect variable is treated as endogenous and replaced by a 2SLS instrument when the structural model is actually tested. (Griffiths, Hill & Lim 2008)

All other explanatory variables beside those listed in Table 5.4, used in either the consumption and investment models were *initially* assumed to be exogenous or only affect consumption after a lag, including variables (e.g. lagged GDP) which might be endogenous in if their current period values were used. The Hausman test was then used to test each of these current period variables initially presumed exogenous, to also confirm their lack of endogeneity with consumption spending.

The instruments for all Hausman endogenous variables were developed in the standard way. Each instrument was developed by regressing an endogenous variable on the Hausman test-verified exogenous and lagged variables. (In some tests identified below as "Alt2", these components included any "suspect" variables later found exogenous). The fitted values were used as the instrument, that is, each instrument becomes a weighted average of the exogenous and lagged variables, with weights determined by the regression procedure. In addition to the variables initially hypothesized, current year consumer confidence and exports were added, though not used in either the consumption or investment structural equations. They were added to some instruments because they strengthened an instrument's ability to explain variance in the variable it was replacing. The Wald test for weak instruments was used to ensure the instruments were not weak instruments. The Sargan test was used to ensure the instruments themselves were not also endogenously determined with consumption. (Griffiths, Hill & Lim 2008). Conceptually, the Sargan test takes the instrument that has been substituted for the endogenous variable, and regresses it against the residuals from the structural model using instruments, to ensure little or no correlation (endogeneity) exits in the instrument replacing the endogenous variable.

Two slightly different versions of the consumer borrowing variable were available. The first represents yearly averages (C_B), described in Eqs. 5. A.13–5.A.24 below, and the second represents year end totals ($\mathbf{C_{B2}}$), described in Eqs. 5.13.a–5.24.a below.

The first consumer spending model (model 5.13) includes both a borrowing variable and the current year real GDP to control for business cycle effects. As noted in the methodology section, the current real GDP is actually more poorly correlated with the current deficit than the three-lagged real GDP or the current year unemployment rate, and hence, less useful in measuring changes in the business cycle which may be causing simultaneous changes in deficits, confounding which is responsible for changes in spending. Hence, it is presented here largely for reference purposes. Results below identify which variables were found Hausman-endogenous and were instrumented, whether their test results met the Wald t or F test criteria, and the Sargan X^2 test criteria.

Model 5.13 Standard consumer spending model, with borrowing included, current GDP used as a business cycle control.

(Disp. income ($Y - T_T$) was found Endogenous, and Instrumented) (Wald $F = 29.78 > F = 10$ Wald Test Criteria; Sargan Test $nR^2 = 6.63 < X^2_{(95,16)} = 26.30$ Test Criteria)

$$\underset{(t=)}{\Delta C_T} = \underset{(1.8)}{0.37\Delta(Y - T_T)} + \underset{(2.6)}{0.38\mathbf{\Delta}(\mathbf{T_T} - \mathbf{G_{T\&I}})}$$

$$- \underset{(-4.7)}{12.14\Delta PR} + \underset{(4.5)}{0.46\,\Delta DJ_{-2}} + \underset{(2.7)}{3.87\,\Delta XR_{AV}} - \underset{(-1.3)}{417.79\Delta POP_{16}}$$

$$+ \underset{(3.5)}{0.016\Delta POP} + \underset{(0.3)}{0.10\Delta ICC_{-1}} + \underset{(4.7)}{50.16\Delta M2_{AV}}$$

$$+ \underset{(1.9)}{0.11\,\mathbf{\Delta C_B}} + \underset{(0.8)}{0.14\,\mathbf{\Delta GDP_{Real(0)}}} \quad R^2 = 93.6\ \%$$

$$\text{D.W.} = 2.1 \ \text{MSE} = 28.09 \tag{5.13}$$

The results clearly indicate increasing deficits are associated with decreased consumption, controlling for the phase of the business cycle and a wide range of other variables. The results also indicate that access to loanable funds increases consumer spending above what would be based on income alone. In both respects, our 2SLS results are similar to earlier model 5.1 OLS test findings, repeated here for easy comparison:

Model 5.1 (Repeated) Standard OLS consumer spending model, with borrowing included, current GDP used as a business cycle control

$$\begin{aligned}\underset{(t=)}{\Delta C_T} = {} & \underset{(3.3)}{0.21\Delta(Y - T_T)} + \underset{(3.4)}{0.25\boldsymbol{\Delta}(\mathbf{T}_{\mathrm{T}} - \mathbf{G}_{\mathrm{T\&I}})} \\ & - \underset{(-5.9)}{12.36\Delta \mathrm{PR}} + \underset{(4.8)}{0.45\ \Delta \mathrm{DJ}_{-2}} + \underset{(1.9)}{3.14\ \Delta \mathrm{XR}_{\mathrm{AV}}} - \underset{(-1.3)}{319.66\Delta \mathrm{POP}_{16}} \\ & + \underset{(2.8)}{0.013\Delta \mathrm{POP}} + \underset{(1.1)}{0.31\Delta \mathrm{ICC}_{-1}} + \underset{(4.3)}{42.30\Delta \mathrm{M2}_{\mathrm{AV}}} \\ & + \underset{(3.4)}{0.11\ \boldsymbol{\Delta}\mathbf{C}_{\mathbf{B}}} + \underset{(4.3)}{0.30\ \boldsymbol{\Delta}\mathbf{GDP}_{\mathbf{REAL}(0)}} \quad R^2 = 94.8\ \% \\ & \mathrm{D.W.} = 1.7\ \mathrm{MSE} = 25.49 \end{aligned} \tag{5.1}$$

With one exception, the same variables were found statistically significant in both the OLS and 2SLS models, and most regression coefficients were reasonably similar.

Model 5.13.a Standard consumer spending model, with borrowing included as a determinant of consumer spending. B2 version of borrowing used, current GDP used as a business cycle control

(Disp. income ($\Upsilon - T_T$) was found Endogenous, and Instrumented) (Wald $F = 30.52 > F = 10$ Test Criteria; Sargan Test $X^2 = 7.65 < {}^2_{(95,16)} = 26.30$ Test Criteria)

$$\begin{aligned}\underset{(t=)}{\Delta C_T} = {} & \underset{(2.4)}{0.38\Delta(Y - T_T)} + \underset{(2.9)}{0.37\boldsymbol{\Delta}(\mathbf{T}_{\mathrm{T}} - \mathbf{G}_{\mathrm{T\&I}})} \\ & - \underset{(-5.9)}{12.69\Delta \mathrm{PR}} + \underset{(4.8)}{0.43\ \Delta \mathrm{DJ}_{-2}} + \underset{(1.9)}{3.10\ \Delta \mathrm{XR}_{\mathrm{AV}}} - \underset{(-1.5)}{442.71\Delta \mathrm{POP}_{16}} \\ & + \underset{(3.9)}{0.016\Delta \mathrm{POP}} + \underset{(1.3)}{0.38\Delta \mathrm{ICC}_{-1}} + \underset{(4.3)}{47.30\Delta \mathrm{M2}_{\mathrm{AV}}} \\ & + \underset{(3.0)}{0.12\ \boldsymbol{\Delta}\mathbf{C}_{\mathbf{B2}}} + \underset{(1.0)}{0.14\ \boldsymbol{\Delta}\mathbf{GDP}_{\mathbf{Real}(0)}} \quad \mathbf{R}^2 = 94.4\ \% \\ & \mathrm{D.W.} = 1.8\ \mathrm{MSE} = 26.25 \end{aligned} \tag{5.13.a}$$

Generally, results do not differ significantly for most variables in the model, regardless of whether the year average (B) or end of year total form (B2) of the borrowing variable is used. Exceptions are the borrowing variable and consumer confidence variables, whose statistical significance was more noticeably increased using the end of year total version (ΔC_{B2}) of the borrowing data. Model 5.14 below excludes the borrowing variable.

Model 5.14 Standard consumer spending model, w/o borrowing included, current GDP used as a business cycle control

(Endogenous variable was the ratio of young to old in the population, I.E., POP_{16})

(Wald (weak) instrument $F = 0.64$, No $t >= 3.3$; Sargan Test $X^2 = 2.19 < X^2_{(95,12)} = 26.30$ Test Criteria)

$$\underset{(t=)}{\Delta C_T} = \underset{(-0.3)}{-0.09\Delta(Y - T_T)} + \underset{(0.2)}{0.04\mathbf{\Delta}(\mathbf{T}_\mathrm{T} - \mathbf{G}_{\mathrm{T\&I}})}$$
$$- \underset{(-2.8)}{10.89\Delta \mathrm{PR}} + \underset{(3.3)}{0.47\,\Delta \mathrm{DJ}_{-2}} + \underset{(1.1)}{3.49\,\Delta \mathrm{XR}_{\mathrm{AV}}}$$
$$- \underset{(-0.9)}{1435.50\Delta \mathrm{POP}_{16}} + \underset{(0.5)}{0.005\Delta \mathrm{POP}} + \underset{(0.0)}{0.01\Delta \mathrm{ICC}_{-1}}$$
$$+ \underset{(2.0)}{30.82\Delta \mathrm{M2}_{\mathrm{AV}}} + \underset{(1.9)}{0.65\,\mathbf{\Delta}\,\mathbf{GDP}_{\mathbf{Real}(0)}} \quad \mathbf{R}^2 = 86.7\ \%$$
$$\mathrm{D.W.} = 1.4 \ \mathrm{MSE} = 40.13 \qquad (5.14)$$

The results in 5.14 are unusually weak compared to any other findings in this study. The poor quality of the instrument used for the young/old ratio in the population (POP_{16}) variable seems responsible. POP_{16} was only marginally ($t = 2.0$) judged endogenous by the Hausman procedure. If we augment the variables used to calculate the instrument by adding the one-year lagged value of POP_{16}, the instrument becomes a Wald-test not-weak instrument, and results are markedly more in line with the rest of the tests in this study, as shown in 5.14(Alt) below.

Model 5.14.Alt Standard consumer spending model, w/o borrowing included. (Strong instrument alternative to 5.14.) (Endogenous: The ratio of young to old in the population, I.E., POP_{16})

(Wald $F = 2.55$ but $t > 3.3$ for lagged POP_{16}. Sargan Test $nR^2 = 6.12 < X^2_{(95,16)} = 26.30$ Test Criteria)

$$\underset{(t=)}{\Delta C_T} = \underset{(0.8)}{0.12\Delta(Y - T_T)} + \underset{(2.4)}{0.22\mathbf{\Delta}(\mathbf{T}_{\mathrm{T}} - \mathbf{G}_{\mathrm{T\&I}})}$$
$$- \underset{(-4.9)}{12.18\Delta \mathrm{PR}} + \underset{(2.9)}{0.42\,\Delta \mathrm{DJ}_{-2}} + \underset{(3.0)}{5.27\,\Delta \mathrm{XR}_{\mathrm{AV}}}$$
$$+ \underset{(0.3)}{132.38\Delta \mathrm{POP}_{16}} + \underset{(1.8)}{0.01\Delta \mathrm{POP}} + \underset{(0.2)}{0.06\Delta \mathrm{ICC}_{-1}}$$
$$+ \underset{(4.1)}{40.57\Delta \mathrm{M2}_{\mathrm{AV}}} + \underset{(3.1)}{0.41\,\mathbf{\Delta}\,\mathbf{GDP}_{\mathbf{Real}(0)}}$$
$$\mathbf{R}^2 = 92.9\ \%\mathrm{D.W.} = 1.9\ \mathrm{MSE} = 29.46 \qquad (10.1.\mathrm{A}.1414.\mathrm{aAlt.})$$

The stronger instrument results in a statistically significant crowd out variable, consistent with the OLS findings for the same model.

The next test (model 5.15) uses the three-year lagged real GDP as the business cycle control variable, since it was found to be a better indicator of the effects of the business cycle on the deficit than the current year GDP variable used in models 5.13 & 5.14 above:

Model 5.15 Standard consumer spending model, with borrowing included, lagged GDP used as a business cycle control

(Endogenous variables were disposable income and exchange rate average) (Instrument for $(\Upsilon - T_{\mathrm{T}})$:

Wald $F = 30.00$; Instrument For $\mathrm{XR_{AV}}$ Wald $F = 2.7$ Sargan Test $nR^2 = 5.50 < X^2(95.16) = 26.30$ Test Criteria)

$$\underset{(t=)}{\Delta C_T} = \underset{(6.5)}{0.49\Delta(Y - T_T)} + \underset{(8.1)}{0.49\mathbf{\Delta}(\mathbf{T}_{\mathrm{T}} - \mathbf{G}_{\mathrm{T\&I}})} - \underset{(-3.9)}{12.03\Delta \mathrm{PR}} + \underset{(4.4)}{0.41\,\Delta \mathrm{DJ}_{-2}}$$
$$+ \underset{(1.7)}{5.08\,\Delta \mathrm{XR}_{\mathrm{AV}}} - \underset{(-1.9)}{532.75\Delta \mathrm{POP}_{16}} + \underset{(4.2)}{.018\Delta \mathrm{POP}} + \underset{(0.4)}{0.16\Delta \mathrm{ICC}_{-1}}$$
$$+ \underset{(4.8)}{53.82\Delta \mathrm{M2}_{\mathrm{AV}}} + \underset{(1.2)}{0.10\,\mathbf{\Delta}\,\mathbf{C}_{\mathbf{B}}} + \underset{(0.8)}{0.03\,\mathbf{\Delta}\,\mathbf{GDP}_{\mathbf{Real}(-3)}}$$
$$R^2 = 92.9\ \%\ \ \mathrm{D.W.} = 2.2\ \mathrm{MSE} = 29.74 \qquad (5.15)$$

We eliminate the weak instrument for $\mathrm{XR_{AV}}$ in 5.15 by adding a one-lagged $\mathrm{XR_{AV}}$ variable to those used as regressors to make the instrument. Doing so give the following (5.15.Alt) strong instrument results:

Model 5.15.Alt Standard consumer spending model, with borrowing included, lagged GDP used as a business cycle control

(Strong instrument–Endogenous variables were Disp.income, Exchange Rate Average) (Instrument For $(\Upsilon - T_T)$:

Wald $F = 30.00$; Instrument For XR_{AV} Wald $F = 11.1$ Sargan Test $nR^2 = 5.10 < X^2(95.17) = 27.59$ Test Criteria)

$$\underset{(t=)}{\Delta C_T} = \underset{(6.4)}{0.48\Delta(Y - T_T)} + \underset{(8.5)}{0.47\mathbf{\Delta}(\mathbf{T_T} - \mathbf{G_{T\&I}})} - \underset{(-4.2)}{11.86\Delta PR} + \underset{(4.2)}{0.43\ \Delta DJ_{-2}}$$

$$+ \underset{(1.7)}{2.82\ \Delta XR_{AV}} - \underset{(-1.7)}{500.04\Delta POP_{16}} + \underset{(4.2)}{0.019\Delta POP} + \underset{(0.6)}{0.24\Delta ICC_{-1}}$$

$$+ \underset{(4.9)}{53.72\Delta M2_{AV}} + \underset{(1.9)}{0.13\ \mathbf{\Delta\ C_B}} + \underset{(0.7)}{0.02\ \mathbf{\Delta\ GDP_{Real(-3)}}}$$

$$R^2 = 92.9\ \%\quad D.W. = 2.2\ MSE = 29.74 \qquad (5.15.Alt)$$

Model 5.15.a is the same as model 5.15 except it used the B2 version of the borrowing variable:

Model 5.15.a Standard consumer spending model, with borrowing included, lagged GDP used as a business cycle control

(Endogenous variable was Disposable Income) (Instrument for $(Y - T_T)$: Wald $F = 28.09$; Sargan test $nR^2 = 10.20 < X^2_{(95,17)} = 27.59$ Test criteria)

$$\underset{(t=)}{\Delta C_T} = \underset{(9.0)}{0.50\Delta(Y - T_T)} + \underset{(8.3)}{0.47\mathbf{\Delta}(\mathbf{T_T} - \mathbf{G_{T\&I}})} - \underset{(-4.7)}{12.35\Delta PR} + \underset{(4.5)}{0.39\ \Delta DJ_{-2}}$$

$$+ \underset{(2.2)}{3.39\ \Delta XR_{AV}} - \underset{(-2.1)}{550.34\Delta POP_{16}} + \underset{(4.1)}{0.017\Delta POP} + \underset{(1.5)}{0.49\Delta ICC_{-1}}$$

$$+ \underset{(4.9)}{49.69\Delta M2_{AV}} + \underset{(2.5)}{0.13\ \mathbf{\Delta C_{B2}}} + \underset{(1.0)}{0.04\ \mathbf{\Delta\ GDP_{Real(-3)}}}$$

$$R^2 = 94.0\ \%\quad D.W. = 1.9\ MSE = 27.30 \qquad (5.15.a)$$

Here again, most estimates using either of the borrowing estimates are similar, but the statistical significance of the consumer confidence and borrowing variables is noticeably higher.

The same model used in 5.15 and 5.15.s but without a borrowing variable on the right side yields the following results:

Model 5.16 Standard consumer spending model, w/o borrowing included, lagged GDP used as a business cycle control

(No Hausman-endogenous variables found, so OLS Eq. 5.4 results repeated here as Eq. 5.16.

$$\underset{(t=)}{\Delta C_T} = \underset{(6.1)}{0.48\Delta(Y - T_T)} + \underset{(7.4)}{0.54\mathbf{\Delta}(\mathbf{T}_{\mathrm{T}} - \mathbf{G}_{\mathrm{T\&I}})} - \underset{(-5.6)}{13.16\Delta \mathrm{PR}} + \underset{(4.8)}{0.36\,\Delta \mathrm{DJ}_{-2}}$$
$$+ \underset{(3.0)}{6.67\,\Delta \mathrm{XR}_{\mathrm{AV}}} - \underset{(-1.8)}{500.88\Delta \mathrm{POP}_{16}} + \underset{(4.3)}{0.019\Delta \mathrm{POP}} + \underset{(0.4)}{0.21\Delta \mathrm{ICC}_{-1}}$$
$$+ \underset{(5.0)}{58.21\Delta \mathrm{M2}_{\mathrm{AV}}} + \underset{(0.6)}{0.02\,\mathbf{\Delta}\,\mathbf{GDP}_{\mathbf{Real}(-3)}}$$
$$R^2 = 92.1\ \%\quad \mathrm{D.W.} = 2.1\ \mathrm{MSE} = 31.02 \qquad (5.16)$$

Notice crowd out effect estimates are significant and about the same in models with and without a borrowing variable on the right hand side.

The next test (5.17) uses the unemployment rate as the business cycle control variable

Model 5.17 Standard consumer spending model, with borrowing included, unemployment rate used as a business cycle control

(Unemployment rate (UNEM) found endogenous and instrumented) (Wald $F = 10.90$; Sargan $nR^2 = 17.65 < X^2_{(95,18)} = 28.87$)

$$\underset{(t=)}{\Delta C_T} = \underset{(3.8)}{0.45\Delta(Y - T_T)} + \underset{(4.5)}{0.48\mathbf{\Delta}(\mathbf{T}_{\mathrm{T}} - \mathbf{G}_{\mathrm{T\&I}})} - \underset{(-3.1)}{12.62\Delta \mathrm{PR}} + \underset{(4.2)}{0.46\,\Delta \mathrm{DJ}_{-2}}$$
$$+ \underset{(2.8)}{4.29\,\Delta \mathrm{XR}_{\mathrm{AV}}} - \underset{(-1.7)}{519.98\Delta \mathrm{POP}_{16}} + \underset{(2.8)}{0.021\Delta \mathrm{POP}} + \underset{(0.2)}{0.14\Delta \mathrm{ICC}_{-1}}$$
$$+ \underset{(5.5)}{59.97\Delta \mathrm{M2}_{\mathrm{AV}}} + \underset{(2.1)}{0.12\,\mathbf{\Delta C_B}} - \underset{(-0.0)}{1.42\,\mathbf{\Delta UNEM}}$$
$$\mathbf{R}^2 = 93.8\ \%\quad \mathrm{D.W.} = 2.0\ \mathrm{MSE} = 28.85 \qquad (5.17)$$

Model 5.17.a is identical except for using the B2 form of the borrowing variable.

Model 5.17.a Standard consumer spending model, with borrowing included, unemployment rate used as a business cycle control

(Endogenous: Disp. Inc. and Prime Rate) (Instrumented: Disp. Inc.; Wald $F = 28.29$, PR:

Wald (Weak Instrument) $F = 4.17$, No $t >= 3.3$; Sargan $nR^2 = 8.16 < X^2_{(95,18)} = 28.87$)

$$\underset{(t=)}{\Delta C_T} = 0.57\underset{(10.0)}{\Delta(Y - T_T)} + 0.57\underset{(10.2)}{\mathbf{\Delta}(\mathbf{T}_{\mathrm{T}} - \mathbf{G}_{\mathrm{T\&I}})} - 16.79\underset{(-3.1)}{\Delta \mathrm{PR}} + 0.41\underset{(4.4)}{\Delta \mathrm{DJ}_{-2}}$$

$$+ 2.72\underset{(1.8)}{\Delta \mathrm{XR}_{\mathrm{AV}}} - 583.55\underset{(-2.2)}{\Delta \mathrm{POP}_{16}} + 0.015\underset{(3.9)}{\Delta \mathrm{POP}} + 0.94\underset{(2.5)}{\Delta \mathrm{ICC}_{-1}}$$

$$+ 57.20\underset{(5.1)}{\Delta \mathrm{M2}_{\mathrm{AV}}} + 0.12\underset{(2.4)}{\mathbf{\Delta C}_{\mathbf{B2}}} + 17.52\underset{(2.8)}{\mathbf{\Delta UNEM}}$$

$$R^2 = 93.6\ \%\quad \mathrm{D.W.} = 1.8\ \mathrm{MSE} = 28.11 \qquad (10.1.\mathrm{A}.17.\mathrm{a})$$

To eliminate the weak instrument (PR), the real M1 money supply was added to the variables used to develop the instruments. The alternative, strong instrument, version of 5.17.a results are:

Model 5.17.a.Alt Standard consumer spending model, with borrowing included, unemployment rate used as a business cycle control, strong instrument used

(Endogenous: Disp. Inc. And Prime Rate) (Instrumented: Disp. Inc.; Wald $F = 26.98$,

PR: Wald $F = 5.90$, But One $t > 3.3$, So Strong Inst.; Sargan $nR^2 = 9.69 < X^2_{(95,19)} = 30.14$

$$\underset{(t=)}{\Delta C_T} = 0.57\underset{(11.8)}{\Delta(Y - T_T)} + 0.57\underset{(10.9)}{\mathbf{\Delta}(\mathbf{T}_{\mathrm{T}} - \mathbf{G}_{\mathrm{T\&I}})} - 14.74\underset{(-3.8)}{\Delta \mathrm{PR}} + 0.42\underset{(4.7)}{\Delta \mathrm{DJ}_{-2}}$$

$$+ 2.72\underset{(1.9)}{\Delta \mathrm{XR}_{\mathrm{AV}}} - 574.93\underset{(-2.2)}{\Delta \mathrm{POP}_{16}} + 0.015\underset{(4.0)}{\Delta \mathrm{POP}} + 0.92\underset{(2.6)}{\Delta \mathrm{ICC}_{-1}}$$

$$+ 55.75\underset{(6.2)}{\Delta \mathrm{M2}_{\mathrm{AV}}} + 0.12\underset{(2.5)}{\mathbf{\Delta C}_{\mathbf{B2}}} + 20.09\underset{(3.1)}{\mathbf{\Delta UNEM}}$$

$$R^2 = 93.6\ \%\quad \mathrm{D.W.} = 1.8\ \mathrm{MSE} = 28.11 \qquad (5.17.\mathrm{a.Alt})$$

Strengthening the instrument changed the estimates of marginal effect very little, but increased statistical significance of all variables.

When testing for Hausman endogeneity, we also used a second, more conservatively estimated group of variables as exogenous or lagged. These included only eight variables: CAP_{-1}, PR_{-2}, DJ_{-2}, Prof_{-2}, POP_{16}, POP, $\mathrm{M2}_{\mathrm{AV\text{-}2\text{-}4}}$ and ICC_{-1}, (and Υ_{-3} , but only in models using that variable as the business cycle control). Here, only the PR_0 variable was found Hausman-endogenous, but the parameter estimates and significance levels were very similar to those obtained in 5.17.a.Alt.

For tests described in this paper as "Alt2", Wald weak instrument tests are applied a little differently. In Alt2 tests, variables are tested for Wald instrument strength utilizing not only the eight exogenous/lagged variables as regressors, but all "suspect" variables that tested non-endogenous, plus any additional variables needed to pass Wald weak instrument tests. Strong instruments not bearing the Alt2 label, typically were tested using the originally assumed exogenous/lagged variables and any additional variables that had to be added to meet Wald F and t test requirements, but excluding variables in the model originally considered suspect and tested for endogeneity, but found non-Hausman endogenous, for example, in some cases, disposable income, the deficit, and so on.

That said, changing and strengthening the instrument in this way, resulted in little change in the point estimates for crowd out or other variables, but generally did lower statistical significance levels for all variables, though most remained significant at the 5 % level or better.

Therefore, results, particularly point estimates, appear to be robust to variations in variables classified as exogenous in Hausman tests and Wald techniques used to determine instrument strength, an important way of testing the robustness of model results. Results are shown in 5.17.a.Alt2 below:

Model 5.17.a.Alt2 Standard consumer spending model, with borrowing included, unemployment rate used as a business cycle control, strong instrument used, alternative endogeneity test

(Endogenous: The Prime Interest Rate: $PR_{0)}$ (Instrument; Wald $F = 5.3$, But $t = 3.9$, for $(T - G)$, So Strong Instrument; Sargan $nR^2 = 9.69 < X^2_{(95,14)} = 23.68$)

$$\underset{(t=)}{\Delta C_T} = \underset{(3.7)}{0.53\Delta(Y - T_T)} + \underset{(3.8)}{0.62\boldsymbol{\Delta}(\mathbf{T}_{\mathrm{T}} - \mathbf{G}_{\mathrm{T\&I}})} - \underset{(-2.4)}{18.64\Delta \mathrm{PR}} + \underset{(4.5)}{0.42\,\Delta \mathrm{DJ}_{-2}}$$

$$+ \underset{(2.1)}{3.04\,\Delta \mathrm{XR}_{\mathrm{AV}}} - \underset{(-2.2)}{602.55\Delta \mathrm{POP}_{16}} + \underset{(1.7)}{0.016\Delta \mathrm{POP}} + \underset{(1.3)}{1.16\Delta \mathrm{ICC}_{-1}}$$

$$+ \underset{(6.2)}{65.29\Delta \mathrm{M2}_{\mathrm{AV}}} + \underset{(2.9)}{0.12\,\boldsymbol{\Delta}\mathbf{C}_{\mathbf{B2}}} + \underset{(0.5)}{24.10\,\boldsymbol{\Delta}\mathbf{UNEM}}$$

$$R^2 = 93.0\ \%\quad \mathrm{D.W.} = 1.8\ \mathrm{MSE} = 29.46 \qquad (5.17.\mathrm{a.Alt2})$$

Models 5.18 & 18.a Same as 5.17, but without borrowing variable included, unemployment rate used as a business cycle control

(The Unemployment rate was found endogenous and instrumented) (Wald $F = 15.14$, Sargan $nR^2 = 2.65 < X^2_{(95,13)} = 22.36$)

$$\underset{(t=)}{\Delta C_T} = \underset{(2.5)}{0.44\Delta(Y - T_T)} + \underset{(3.3)}{0.48\boldsymbol{\Delta}(\mathbf{T}_{\mathrm{T}} - \mathbf{G}_{\mathrm{T\&I}})} - \underset{(-2.8)}{15.24\Delta \mathrm{PR}} + \underset{(3.6)}{0.38\ \Delta \mathrm{DJ}_{-2}}$$

$$+ \underset{(2.9)}{6.48\ \Delta \mathrm{XR}_{\mathrm{AV}}} - \underset{(-1.4)}{494.83\Delta \mathrm{POP}_{16}} + \underset{(2.1)}{0.023\Delta \mathrm{POP}} - \underset{(-0.1)}{0.05\Delta \mathrm{ICC}_{-1}}$$

$$+ \underset{(4.4)}{58.11\Delta \mathrm{M2}_{\mathrm{AV}}} - \underset{(-0.3)}{15.72\ \boldsymbol{\Delta}\mathbf{UNEM}}$$

$$\mathbf{R}^2 = 90.6\ \%\quad \mathrm{D.W.} = 1.9\ \mathrm{MSE} = 33.84 \qquad (5.18)$$

Notice that again, dropping the borrowing variable restores the expected negative sign to the unemployment variable, indicating the positive sign observed in equations with borrowing is a distortion caused by multicollinearity between the two variables.

Finally, we note that the business cycle control variables generally proved statistically insignificant in a majority of the 2SLS models tested above, but even where significant, the government deficit variable's coefficient and statistical significance were essentially the same with the control or without it. This suggests adding the control has little effect on consumption crowd out estimates, and indicates the other variables explain almost all variation in consumer behavior. We conclude that in 2SLS models controlling for the business cycle effects, the government deficit remains negatively related to consumer spending and statistically significant. This provides support for the assertion that crowd out is a real problem that reduces or eliminates the beneficial effects of stimulus programs, and isn't simply a mischaracterization of the fact that many deficits occur/grow in recessions, when declines in consumption spending are due to deteriorating economic conditions.

Next, we re-estimate the standard model without a business cycle control variable:

Model 5.19 Standard consumer spending model, with borrowing included, no business cycle control

(No Hausman-endogenous variables: Earlier Eq. 5.7 OLS results repeated here as 5.19)

$$\underset{(t=)}{\Delta C_T} = \underset{(10.5)}{0.48\Delta(Y - T_T)} + \underset{(9.8)}{0.48\mathbf{\Delta}(\mathbf{T}_\mathrm{T} - \mathbf{G}_{\mathrm{T\&I}})} - \underset{(-6.9)}{13.05\Delta \mathrm{PR}} + \underset{(4.3)}{0.43\,\Delta \mathrm{DJ}_{-2}}$$
$$+ \underset{(2.2)}{3.44\,\Delta \mathrm{XR}_{\mathrm{AV}}} - \underset{(-1.9)}{547.55\Delta \mathrm{POP}_{16}} + \underset{(5.0)}{0.020\Delta \mathrm{POP}} + \underset{(1.4)}{0.46\Delta \mathrm{ICC}_{-1}}$$
$$+ \underset{(5.7)}{56.11\Delta \mathrm{M2}_{\mathrm{AV}}}\ (2) + \underset{(3.1)}{0.12\,\mathbf{\Delta C_B}}$$
$$R^2 = 93.9\ \%\quad \mathrm{D.W.} = 1.7\ \mathrm{MSE} = 27.27 \qquad (5.7\mathrm{and}5.19)$$

Model 5.19.a is identical to 5.19, except the B2 version of the borrowing variable is used.

Model 5.19.a Standard consumer spending model, with B2 borrowing included, no business cycle control

(Unemployment rate was Hausman-endogenous)

(Wald $F = 11.93$, Sargan $nR^2 = 4.59 < X^2_{(95,16)} = 26.30$)

$$\underset{(t=)}{\Delta C_T} = \underset{(9.0)}{0.52\Delta(Y - T_T)} + \underset{(8.1)}{0.53\mathbf{\Delta}(\mathbf{T}_\mathrm{T} - \mathbf{G}_{\mathrm{T\&I}})} - \underset{(-3.3)}{20.88\Delta \mathrm{PR}} + \underset{(3.9)}{0.41\,\Delta \mathrm{DJ}_{-2}}$$
$$+ \underset{(1.7)}{2.90\,\Delta \mathrm{XR}_{\mathrm{AV}}} - \underset{(-1.9)}{588.31\Delta \mathrm{POP}_{16}} + \underset{(4.3)}{0.019\Delta \mathrm{POP}} + \underset{(1.8)}{0.75\Delta \mathrm{ICC}_{-1}}$$
$$+ \underset{(4.2)}{58.45\Delta \mathrm{M2}_{\mathrm{AV}}} + \underset{(2.1)}{0.12\mathbf{\Delta C_{B2}}}$$
$$R^2 = 92.3\ \%\quad \mathrm{D.W.} = 1.7\ \mathrm{MSE} = 30.46 \qquad (5.19\mathrm{a})$$

Model 5.20 & 20.a below Is identical to 5.19 and 5.19.a, except the borrowing variable is dropped.

Model 5.20 & 5.20.a Standard consumption model, without borrowing variable, no business cycle control

(No Hausman-endogenus variables: Earlier OLS Eq. 5.8 results repeated)

$$\underset{(t=)}{\Delta C_T} = \underset{(6.5)}{0.48\Delta(Y - T_T)} + \underset{(7.5)}{0.54\mathbf{\Delta}(\mathbf{T}_\mathrm{T} - \mathbf{G}_{\mathrm{T\&I}})} - \underset{(-6.3)}{13.49\Delta \mathrm{PR}}$$
$$+ \underset{(4.5)}{0.38\,\Delta \mathrm{DJ}_{-2}} + \underset{(3.3)}{6.42\Delta \mathrm{XR}_{\mathrm{AV}}} - \underset{(-1.7)}{499.77\Delta \mathrm{POP}_{16}}$$
$$+ \underset{(4.7)}{0.020\Delta \mathrm{POP}} + \underset{(0.4)}{0.19\Delta \mathrm{ICC}_{-1}} + \underset{(4.8)}{59.38\Delta \mathrm{M2}_{\mathrm{AV}}}$$
$$\mathbf{R}^2 = 92.0\ \%\quad \mathrm{D.W.} = 2.0\ \mathrm{MSE} = 30.76 \qquad (5.8\mathrm{and}5.20)$$

Table 5.5 2SLS consumer spending model conclusions summarized, compared to OLS

2SLS spending model conclusions summarized				*OLS results (repeated from above)*		
Model#	$\Delta(T_T - G_{T\&I})$ β (*t-stat.*)	$\Delta(BORR)$ β (*t-stat.*)	*Bus. cycle control*	*Model#*	$\Delta(T_T - G_{T\&I})$	$\Delta(BORR)$
5.13	0.38 (2.6)	0.11(1.9)	GDP $_{Real(0)}$	5.1	0.25(3.4)	0.11(3.4)
5.13.a	0.37 (2.9)	0.12(3.0)				
5.14	0.04 (0.2)			5.2	0.26(3.3)	
5.14 (Alt.)	0.22 (2.4)					
5.15	0.49 (8.1)	0.10(1.2)	GDP $_{Real(-3)}$	5.3	0.47(8.7)	0.13(3.0)
5.15.Alt	0.47 (8.5)	0.13(1.9)				
5.15.a	0.47 (8.3)	0.13(2.5)				
5.16	0.54 (7.4)			5.4	0.54(7.4)	
5.17	0.48 (4.5)	0.12(2.1)	% Unem	5.5	0.54(11.1)	0.13(3.4)
5.17.a	0.57(10.2)	0.12(2.4)		5.5.c	0.47(9.2)	0.13(3.2)
5.17.a.Alt	0.57(10.9)	0.12(2.5)				
5.17.a. Alt2	0.62 (3.8)	0.12(2.9)				
5.18&.18.a	0.48 (3.3)			5.6	0.60(7.3)	
5.19	0.48 (9.8)	0.12(3.1)	None	5.7	0.48(9.8)	0.12(3.1)
5.19.a	0.53 (8.1)	0.12(2.1)				
5.20	0.54 (7.5)			5.8	0.54(7.5)	

Notes: "a" models use C_{b2} form; "Alt" models are strong instrument versions of same model
"Alt2" are strong instruments that include originally suspect variables not endogenous. See text.

5.2.1 *2SLS Spending Model Findings Summarized, Compared to OLS*

Table 5.5 summarizes the 2SLS findings and compares them with the OLS findings.

Clearly, the magnitude and statistical significance of the crowd out and borrowing variables in the 2SLS and the OLS consumer spending models were very similar. Both sets of tests support the hypothesis that

- as Government deficits increase, consumer spending decreases due to crowd out.
- access to borrowing has an impact on spending levels that is independent of that of income, interest rates, wealth, and so on.
- controlling for business cycle effects on spending does reduce the magnitude or statistical significance of the deficit's negative

> relationship by about half, but it remains a statistically significant factor. If the deficit was just a proxy for the state of the economy, we would have expected that by controlling for the state of the economy, we would have found the deficit's effect reduced to non-significance.

Adding a borrowing variable to the consumer spending model positively affects consumer spending, in addition to the effects of other commonly hypothesized variables. This provides an empirical basis for hypothesizing that the marginal propensity to consume is determined out of *total access to purchasing power*, that is, income and *credit*. If tests show that borrowing-financed government deficits are negatively related to consumer borrowing, it provides strong evidence the crowd out problem is the source of the negative relationship also seen between deficits and consumer spending.

5.2.2 2SLS Estimates of Crowd Out Effects On Consumer Borrowing

The hypothesized determinants of consumer borrowing were nearly the same as those for consumer spending. As was the case with earlier OLS estimates, there were three changes:

- Consumer borrowing rather than spending was the dependent variable.
- The growth of non-M1 (savings) components of the money supply, (Real M2−M1), was added to reflect an essential determinant affecting both the supply and demand of loanable funds.
- Experimenting with the data indicated the Dow Jones composite average lagged one period was far more systematically related to borrowing than the two-lag version used in spending models, so the one-lag version was used.

These models of the determinants of consumer borrowing are rough at best, and do not explain nearly as much of the variance in borrowing as they do in total consumer spending. These results in general lower levels of statistical significance for each of the variables tested. Nonetheless, government deficits are found to be negatively and systematically related to borrowing in the three best models of the four tested, providing support for the crowd out argument.

Endogeneity

The same five variables were found endogenously related to borrowing in each of the four borrowing models, each model the same except for having a different business cycle control variable. The variables found endogenously in all four were

- the deficit,
- the current year real GDP,
- the ratio of young to old in the population,
- the exchange rate, and
- the level of exports.

The first four of these endogenous variables were used in the consumption function, and so were instrumented to remove endogeneity.

2SLS tests of the model using current year real GDP as the business cycle control variable produced the following results. Instruments for GDP_0, Deficit, Young/old Ratio and XR_{AV} were used. Wald weak instrument test results were

$$T_T - G_{T\&I} = F = 23.50$$
$$Y_{\text{Real}(0)} = F = 59.45$$
$$XR_{AV} = F = 1.93 \text{ (two } t\text{-stats of 2.6 \& 2.8, but none of 3.3)}$$
$$POP_{16} = F = 0.34 \text{ (no } t \text{ values close to 3.3)}$$

These Wald tests are the same for all four models, since the (non-endogenous) variables used to develop the instruments were the same. The first two are strong instruments by Wald criteria: one component of the instrument with $t >= 3.3$ or $F >= 10$ for the whole instrument model. Strong instruments, discussed further below, were developed for the second two.

Results (labeled "Alt" below) are results after eliminating the weak instrument problem for the XR_{AV} and POP_{16} variables. For POP_{16} this was done by eliminating the variable from the structural model (and therefore the need to find an instrument to replace it). This seemed reasonable since neither theory dictates it be included nor did the empirical results indicate it was making any statistically significant contribution to explanatory power.

For the XR_{AV} variable, elimination of some non-significant regressors used to construct the original instrument was enough to raise at least one regressor's t-statistic above the Wald test t-statistic criteria. The additional variables deleted from the total list of system variables were DEP, CAP_{-1}, ICC_0, and of course, the POP_{16} variable had already been eliminated. This raised the Wald F test results for XR_{AV} to only $F = 2.2$ but left one variable in the instrument with a $t = 3.5$, meeting the alternative Wald criteria. The alternative results, using strong instruments, are presented in Model 5.2.1.Alt below.

As before, "a" versions, indicate the borrowing variable used (as dependent variable) was C_{B2}, not C_B.

The weak instrument version is given in Model 5.21 below.

Model 5.21 2SLS estimates of the effects of crowd out on consumer borrowing, current period real GDP business cycle control used)

Wald test (weak instrument: see above) (Sargan Test $NR^2 = 1.0$; Sargan Criteria $X^2_{(.95,15)} = 25.00$)

$$\underset{(t=)}{\Delta C_B} = \underset{(0.4)}{0.52\Delta(Y - T_T)} + \underset{(0.5)}{0.64\boldsymbol{\Delta}(\mathbf{T_T} - \mathbf{G_{T\&I}})} - \underset{(-1.7)}{21.73\Delta PR} - \underset{(-1.2)}{0.84\,\Delta DJ_{-1}}$$
$$+ \underset{(1.7)}{20.19\,\Delta XR_{AV}} + \underset{(0.6)}{4601.74\Delta POP_{16}} + \underset{(0.0)}{0.000\Delta POP} + \underset{(1.3)}{1.95\Delta ICC_{-1}}$$
$$- \underset{(-0.1)}{3.14\Delta M2_{AV}} - \underset{(-1.3)}{0.39\,\Delta(M2_{Real} - M1_{Real})} - \underset{(-0.0)}{0.01\boldsymbol{\Delta}\mathbf{GDP_{REAL(0)}}}$$
$$R^2 = 28.9\,\% \quad D.W. = 1.0 \; MSE = 112.78 \tag{5.21}$$

And the strong instrument version of 5.21 is given in 5.21.Alt below

Model 5.21.Alt 2SLS estimates of the effects of crowd out on borrowing, current period real GDP business cycle control used

(Sargan Test $NR^2 = 1.02 <$ Sargan Criteria $X^2_{(.95,12)} = 21.03$) (Strong Inst.)

$$\underset{(t=)}{\Delta C_B} = \underset{(1.5)}{1.49\Delta(Y - T_T)} + \underset{(1.5)}{1.55\boldsymbol{\Delta}(\mathbf{T_T} - \mathbf{G_{T\&I}})} - \underset{(-2.6)}{29.18\Delta PR} - \underset{(-2.4)}{1.96\,\Delta DJ_{-1}}$$
$$+ \underset{(2.0)}{18.99\,\Delta XR_{AV}} + \underset{(NA)}{(NA)\Delta POP_{16}} + \underset{(0.8)}{0.030\Delta POP} + \underset{(0.8)}{2.22\Delta ICC_{-1}}$$
$$+ \underset{(0.3)}{12.22\Delta M2_{AV}} - \underset{(-1.5)}{0.23\,\Delta(M2_{Real} - M1_{Real})} - \underset{(-1.0)}{1.13\boldsymbol{\Delta}\mathbf{GDP_{REAL(0)}}}$$
$$R^2 = 49.0\,\% \quad D.W. = 2.2 \; MSE = 110.60 \tag{5.21.Alt}$$

This test, using the current year GDP as the business cycle control, provides a coefficient estimate (+1.55) much greater than that of the other borrowing models, but one that is not statistically significant at more than the 15 % level. In the other strong instrument tests using either GDP_{-3} or unemployment business cycle controls, or no controls, crowd out is found to be a more statistically significant factor.

Next, we repeat the standard borrowing model, except using GDP-lagged three periods as the business cycle control variable. Results are as follows

Model 5.22 2SLS estimates of the effects of crowd out on borrowing, lagged real GDP business cycle control

(Sargan Test nR^2 = 1.78; Sargan Criteria $X^2_{(.95,15)}$ = 25.00) (Weak Instrument Version)

$$\underset{(t=)}{\Delta C_B} = \underset{(2.5)}{0.51\Delta(Y - T_T)} + \underset{(3.2)}{0.62\boldsymbol{\Delta}(\mathbf{T_T} - \mathbf{G_{T\&I}})} - \underset{(-2.6)}{21.72\Delta PR}$$
$$-\underset{(-2.2)}{0.83\,\Delta DJ_{-1}} + \underset{(1.6)}{19.88\,\Delta XR_{AV}} + \underset{(1.2)}{4582.98\Delta POP_{16}}$$
$$+\underset{(0.0)}{0.000\Delta POP} + \underset{(1.3)}{1.93\Delta ICC_{-1}} - \underset{(-0.1)}{3.67\Delta M2_{AV}}$$
$$-\underset{(-2.1)}{0.38\,\Delta(M2_{Real} - M1_{Real})} - \underset{(-0.1)}{0.01\boldsymbol{\Delta}\mathbf{GDP_{REAL(-3)}}}$$
$$R^2 = 29.6\ \%\ \ \text{D.W.} = 1.0\ \text{MSE} = 112.26 \qquad (5.22)$$

Model 5.22.Alt 2SLS estimates of the effects of crowd out on borrowing, lagged real GDP business cycle control

(Sargan Test NR^2 = 3.06 ; Sargan Criteria $X^2_{(.95,12)}$ = 21.02) (Strong Instrument Version)

$$\underset{(t=1)}{\Delta C_B} = \underset{(2.3)}{0.49\Delta(Y - T_T)} + \underset{(2.3)}{0.59\boldsymbol{\Delta}(\mathbf{T_T} - \mathbf{G_{T\&I}})} - \underset{(-2.7)}{29.40\Delta PR} - \underset{(-2.7)}{1.86\,\Delta DJ_{-1}}$$
$$+\underset{(2.1)}{17.30\,\Delta XR_{AV}} + \underset{(NA)}{(NA)\Delta POP_{16}} + \underset{(0.5)}{0.007\Delta POP} + \underset{(0.8)}{2.35\Delta ICC_{-1}}$$
$$-\underset{(-0.7)}{34.03\Delta M2_{AV}} - \underset{(-1.3)}{0.21\,\Delta(M2_{Real} - M1_{Real})} - \underset{(-0.7)}{0.10\boldsymbol{\Delta}\mathbf{GDP_{REAL(-3)}}}$$
$$R^2 = 56.5\ \%\ \ \text{D.W.} = 2.20\ \text{MSE} = 102.08 \qquad (5.22.\text{Alt})$$

Here, a highly significant negative relationship between government deficits and consumer borrowing is observed, and explained variance is almost doubled using the strong instrument. This enhances the credibility of our individual explanatory variable results, since higher R^2 implies less potential for "left out" variables which could be correlated with an included explanatory variable, affecting the regression estimate.

As was the case with consumer spending model 5.17.a. Alt2 above, when testing for Hausman endogeneity, we also used a second, more conservatively estimated group of variables as exogenous or lagged. These included only eight variables: CAP_{-1}, PR_{-2}, DJ_{-2}, $Prof_{-2}$, POP_{16}, POP, $M2_{AV-2-4}$ and ICC_{-1}, (and Y_{-3} but only in models using that variable as the business cycle control). In that earlier Alt 2 model, only the PR_0 variable was found Hausman-endogenous, and results are very similar to those obtained in 5.17.a.Alt. using the broader definition of exogenous variables. For tests described as "Alt2", Wald weak instrument tests are applied a little differently also. In Alt2 tests, variables are tested for instrument strength utilizing not only the eight exogenous/lagged variables as regressors but also all "suspect" variables that have tested non-endogenous, plus any additional variables needed to pass Wald weak instrument tests. Strong instruments not bearing the Alt2 label, typically were tested using the originally assumed exogenous/lagged variables and any additional variables that had to be added to meet Wald *F* and *t* test requirements, but excluding any variables in the model originally tested for endogeneity, but found non-Hausman-endogenous, for example, in some cases, disposable income, the deficit and so on.

That said, changing and strengthening the instrument in this way resulted in little change in the estimates for crowd out or most other variables, showing our results to be reasonably robust to variations in Hausman and Wald techniques used to determine endogeneity and instrument strength. Results are shown in 5.22.Alt2 below:

Model 5.22.Alt2 2SLS estimates of the effects of crowd out on borrowing, lagged real GDP business cycle control used, alternative endogeneity test used

($T-G$) found endogenous) (Wald Test: $F = 4.4$, but $t = 4.6$ on $M2_{AV}$. Sargan Test $NR^2 = 5.25$ <Sargan Criteria $X^2_{(.95,14)} = 23.68$) (Strong Instrument)

$$\underset{(t=)}{\Delta C_B} = 0.70\underset{(2.6)}{\Delta(Y - T_T)} + 0.61\underset{(2.6)}{\mathbf{\Delta(T_T - G_{T\&I})}} - 25.00\underset{(-4.8)}{\Delta PR} - 1.73\underset{(-3.2)}{\Delta DJ_{-1}}$$

$$+ 18.73\underset{(2.6)}{\Delta XR_{AV}} + 351.86\underset{(0.7)}{\Delta POP_{16}} + 0.000\underset{(0.0)}{\Delta POP} + 0.73\underset{(0.8)}{\Delta ICC_{-1}}$$

$$- 47.55\underset{(-1.2)}{\Delta M2_{AV}} - 0.26\underset{(-2.9)}{\Delta(M2_{Real} - M1_{Real})} - 0.12\underset{(-1.0)}{\mathbf{\Delta GDP_{REA(-3)}}}$$

$$R^2 = 57.0\ \%\ \ D.W. = 2.3\ MSE = 104.10 \qquad (5.22.Alt2)$$

Even with revised criteria for endogeneity and Wald tests, crowd out results were nearly identical.

In Models 5.23, 5.23.Alt and 5.23.Alt2 below, we replaced the lagged real GDP with the unemployment rate as the control for the effects of the business cycle, yielding the following results:

Model 5.23 2SLS estimates of the effects of 1 variable crowd out on borrowing, unemployment rate business cycle control used

(Sargan Test NR^2 = 1.40; Sargan Criteria $X^2_{(.95,15)}$ = 25.00) (weak Instrument)

$$\underset{(t=)}{\Delta C_B} = 0.44\underset{(1.7)}{\Delta(Y - T_T)} + 0.51\underset{(1.6)}{\mathbf{\Delta(T_T - G_{T\&I})}} - 24.00\underset{(-2.0)}{\Delta PR} - 0.86\underset{(-2.2)}{\Delta DJ_{-1}}$$

$$+ 20.35\underset{(2.0)}{\Delta XR_{AV}} + 4112.89.04\underset{(1.0)}{\Delta POP_{16}} + 0.003\underset{(0.2)}{\Delta POP} + 1.55\underset{(1.3)}{\Delta ICC_{-1}}$$

$$- 9.80\underset{(-0.3)}{\Delta M2_{AV}} - 0.37\underset{(-2.2)}{\Delta(M2_{Real} - M1_{Real})} - 27.19\underset{(-0.5)}{\mathbf{\Delta UNEM}}$$

$$R^2 = 40.0\ \%\ \ D.W. = 1.1, MSE = 105.40 \qquad (5.23)$$

5.23.a.Alt 2SLS estimates of the effects of 1 variable crowd out on borrowing, unemployment rate business cycle control used

(Sargan Test NR^2 = 3.57; Sargan Criteria $X^2_{(.95,12)}$ = 21.03) (Strong Instrument)

$$\underset{(t=)}{\Delta C_B} = \underset{(2.2)}{0.47\Delta(Y - T_T)} + \underset{(2.1)}{0.61\boldsymbol{\Delta}(\mathbf{T}_{\mathrm{T}} - \mathbf{G}_{\mathrm{T\&I}})} - \underset{(-2.5)}{29.24\Delta \mathrm{PR}} - \underset{(-2.5)}{1.90\,\Delta \mathrm{DJ}_{-1}}$$
$$+ \underset{(2.7)}{20.97\,\Delta \mathrm{XR}_{\mathrm{AV}}} + \underset{(\mathrm{NA})}{(\mathrm{NA})0.04\Delta \mathrm{POP}_{16}} + \underset{(0.4)}{0.004\Delta \mathrm{POP}} + \underset{(0.6)}{2.70\Delta \mathrm{ICC}_{-1}}$$
$$- \underset{(-0.7)}{35.32\Delta \mathrm{M2}_{\mathrm{AV}}} - \underset{(-1.6)}{0.26\,\Delta(\mathrm{M2}_{\mathrm{Real}} - \mathrm{M1}_{\mathrm{Real}})} + \underset{(0.1)}{2.33\boldsymbol{\Delta}\mathbf{UNEM}}$$
$$R^2 = 55.6\ \%\quad \mathrm{D.W.} = 2.1, \mathrm{MSE} = 103.20 \qquad (5.23\mathrm{Alt})$$

The unemployment rate also seems insignificantly related to borrowing, again suggesting that the business cycle effects have a limited effect on borrowing, or that the other control variables, such as disposable income, are picking this effect up. Again, crowd out effects of deficits on borrowing were found significant (11 % significance level in model 23, 4 % Level in 5.23.Alt.), consistent with crowd out theory and the spending model findings presented earlier.

Using the second variant (Alt2) for testing endogeneity and developing strong instruments described in 5.22.Alt2 and 5.17.a.Alt2. above, we have

Model 5.23.a.Alt2 2SLS estimates of the effects of 1 variable crowd out on borrowing, unemployment rate business cycle control), alternative endogeneity test

(Unem. Rate Endogenous: (Wald Test: $F = 14.29$, $t = 5.3$ for $(T - G)$, Sargan Test $\mathrm{NR}^2 = 3.00 <$ Sargan Criteria $X^2_{(.95,14)} = 23.68$) (Strong Instrument)

$$\underset{(t=)}{\Delta C_B} = \underset{(1.9)}{0.63\Delta(Y - \mathrm{T}_{\mathrm{T}})} + \underset{(2.3)}{0.96\boldsymbol{\Delta}(\mathbf{T}_{\mathrm{T}} - \mathbf{G}_{\mathrm{T\&I}})} - \underset{(-1.1)}{11.67\Delta \mathrm{PR}} - \underset{(-3.1)}{1.58\,\Delta \mathrm{DJ}_{-1}}$$
$$+ \underset{(2.7)}{21.99\,\Delta \mathrm{XR}_{\mathrm{AV}}} + \underset{(0.4)}{309.59.04\Delta \mathrm{POP}_{16}} - \underset{(-0.6)}{0.01\Delta \mathrm{POP}} + \underset{(0.9)}{1.87\Delta \mathrm{ICC}_{-1}}$$
$$- \underset{(-0.5)}{17.74\Delta \mathrm{M2}_{\mathrm{AV}}} - \underset{(-1.4)}{0.23\Delta(\mathrm{M2}_{\mathrm{Real}} - \mathrm{M1}_{\mathrm{Real}})} + \underset{(1.0)}{87.153\boldsymbol{\Delta}\mathbf{UNEM}}$$
$$R^2 = 48.8\ \%\quad \mathrm{D.W.} = 1.9, \mathrm{MSE} = 113.61 \qquad (5.23\mathrm{Alt2})$$

Model 5.24 below presents the last form of the standard borrowing model examined; the one that has no control for the business cycle.

Model 5.24 2SLS Estimates of the Effects of Crowd out on Borrowing, No Business Cycle Control Used

(Sargan test $nR^2 = 1.78$; Sargan Criteria $X^2_{(.95,15)} = 25.00$) (Weak Instrument)

$$\underset{(t=)}{\Delta C_B} = \underset{(2.5)}{0.51\Delta(Y - T_T)} + \underset{(3.2)}{0.63\boldsymbol{\Delta}(\mathbf{T}_{\mathrm{T}} - \mathbf{G}_{\mathrm{T\&I}})} - \underset{(-2.6)}{21.65\Delta \mathrm{PR}} - \underset{(-2.2)}{0.83\,\Delta \mathrm{DJ}_{-1}}$$

$$+ \underset{(1.8)}{20.21\,\Delta \mathrm{XR}_{\mathrm{AV}}} + \underset{(1.2)}{4647.79\Delta \mathrm{POP}_{16}} + \underset{(0.0)}{0.000\Delta \mathrm{POP}} + \underset{(1.3)}{1.94\Delta \mathrm{ICC}_{-1}}$$

$$- \underset{(-0.1)}{3.47\Delta \mathrm{M2}_{\mathrm{AV}}} - \underset{(-2.3)}{0.39\,\Delta(\mathrm{M2}_{\mathrm{Real}} - \mathrm{M1}_{\mathrm{Real}})}$$

$$\mathbf{R}^2 = 28.3\ \%\quad \mathrm{D.W.} = 1.4\ \mathrm{MSE} = 111.91 \qquad (5.24)$$

And the strong instrument version of 5.24 is 5.24.Alt.

Model 5.24.Alt 2SLS estimates of the effects of crowd out on borrowing, strong instrument, no business cycle control (Sargan test $nR^2 = 3.57$; Sargan Criteria $X^2_{(.95,12)} = 21.03$)

$$\underset{(t=)}{\Delta C_B} = \underset{(2.0)}{0.46\Delta(Y - T_T)} + \underset{(2.4)}{0.61\boldsymbol{\Delta}(\mathbf{T}_{\mathrm{T}} - \mathbf{G}_{\mathrm{T\&I}})} - \underset{(-2.8)}{29.11\Delta \mathrm{PR}} - \underset{(-2.9)}{1.89\,\Delta \mathrm{DJ}_{-1}}$$

$$+ \underset{(3.4)}{21.15\,\Delta \mathrm{XR}_{\mathrm{AV}}} + \underset{(\mathrm{NA})}{(\mathrm{NA})\Delta \mathrm{POP}_{16}} + \underset{(0.3)}{0.004\Delta \mathrm{POP}} + \underset{(0.9)}{2.56\Delta \mathrm{ICC}_{-1}}$$

$$- \underset{(-0.8)}{35.12\Delta \mathrm{M2}_{\mathrm{AV}}} - \underset{(-1.9)}{0.27\,\Delta(\mathrm{M2}_{\mathrm{Real}} - \mathrm{M1}_{\mathrm{Real}})}$$

$$\mathbf{R}^2 = 55.9\ \%\quad \mathrm{D.W.} = 2.2\ \mathrm{MSE} = 101.58 \qquad (5.24.\mathrm{Alt})$$

In summary, the findings generally indicate a statistically significant negative relationship between deficits and consumer borrowing, providing support for the crowd out theory argument. Substituting in the strong instrument version of the exchange rate variable, almost doubles explained variance.

5.2.3 2SLS Borrowing Model Conclusions Summarized, Compared to OLS

Table 5.6 summarizes test findings for the borrowing models.

The mean 2SLS estimate of borrowing's effect on crowd out is roughly the same as the mean OLS estimate, and the average level of statistical significance for the OLS and 2SLS estimates are very similar. We conclude it is strong evidence that crowd out adversely affects consumer borrowing (and therefore, spending). This finding holds whether the tool of

Table 5.6 Consumer borrowing model findings summarized, compared to OLS

2SLS borrowing models			*OLS borrowing models*		
Model#	$\Delta(T_T - G_{T\&I})$ β *(t-stat.)*	*Bus. cycle control*	*Model#*	$\Delta(T_T - G_{T\&I})$ β *(t-stat.)*	*Bus. cycle control*
5.21	0.64 (0.5)	$GDP_{Real(0)}$	5.9	0.54 (2.3)	$GDP_{Real(0)}$
5.21.a.Alt.	1.55 (1.5)				
5.22	0.62 (3.2)	$GDP_{Real(-3)}$	5.10	0.64 (2.6)	$GDP_{Real(-3)}$
5.22.a.Alt	0.59 (2.3)				
5.22 Alt2	0.61 (2.6)				
5.23	0.51 (1.6)	Unem. rate	5.11	0.59 (2.0)	Unem. rate
5.23.a.Alt.	0.61 (2.1)				
5.23.a.Alt2.	0.96 (2.3)				
5.24	0.63 (3.2)	None	5.12	0.66 (2.8)	None
5.24.Alt.	0.61 (2.4)				
Average (All)	0.74 (2.2)			0.61 (2.4)	
Av.(Strong Inst.)	0.81 (2.2)				

Note: "a", "Alt" designations as noted in Table 5.5. Alt2 is strong instrument developed using original list of exogenous variables, plus "suspect" variables found not endogenous. Alt2 not needed for models 5.21.a and 5.24.a; nothing left endogenous.

investigation is OLS or 2SLS. Though results are similar, the endogeneity issue makes the 2SLS estimates the preferred estimates. Because of the similarity with OLS results, others who may investigate crowd out in the future (or past), even using more traditional regression tools like OLS, are likely to arrive at the same conclusions as were reached here.

The strong instrument borrowing models explain substantially less variance than the spending models (about 55 % vs. 94 %). Due to this, lower t-statistics are to be expected, and generally were found, but most crowd out coefficients were still significant at the 5 % significance level or greater. This, coupled with the consistent failure of controls for business cycle effects to eliminate the deficit's estimated negative effect on consumer borrowing, provides strong evidence supporting the hypothesis that a decline in consumer borrowing is responsible for the decline in consumer spending associated with deficits. The findings provide little support for the hypothesis that it is not crowd out, but just normal business cycle effects that cause the observed negative relationship between consumer spending and deficits, since consumer borrowing crowd out estimates are about the same in models with or without business cycle controls.

5.3 OLS and 2SLS Spending and Borrowing Findings Summarized

Table 5.7 summarizes all 39 consumption spending and borrowing test results.

46 Consumer spending and borrowing models were analyzed, not counting robustness tests. Each used the one variable definition of the deficit. Testing the deficit as one variable, $(T - G)$, means our estimated effect is an average of tax cut induced effects, and government spending

Table 5.7 Summary of all consumption OLS and 2SLS spending and borrowing results

	2SLS spending model findings summarized				*OLS spending findings summarized*	
Model#	$\Delta(T_T - G_{T\&I})$ β *(t-stat.)*	*Δ (Bor) β (t-stat.)*	*Bus. cycle control*	*Model#*	$\Delta(T_T - G_{T\&I})$	*Δ (Bor)*
5.13	0.38 (2.6)	0.11(1.9)	$GDP_{Real(0)}$	5.1	0.25 (3.4)	0.11 (3.4)
5.13.a	0.37 (2.9)	0.12(3.0)				
5.14&14.a	0.04 (0.2)			5.2	0.26 (3.3)	
5.14&14.a. (Alt.)	0.22 (2.4)					
5.15	0.49 (8.1)	0.10(1.2)	$GDP_{Real(-3)}$	5.3	0.47 (8.7)	0.13 (3.0)
5.15.Alt	0.47 (8.5)	0.13(1.9)				
5.15.a	0.47 (8.3)	0.13(2.5)				
5.16&16.a	0.54 (7.4)			5.4	0.54 (7.4)	
5.17	0.48 (4.5)	0.12(2.1)	% Unem.	5.5	0.54 (11.1)	0.13 (3.4)
5.17.a	0.57(10.2)	0.12(2.4)		5.5.c	0.47 (9.2)	0.13 (3.2)
5.17.a.Alt	0.57(10.9)	0.12(2.5)				
5.17.a.Alt2	0.62 (3.8)	0.12(2.9)				
5.18&.18.a	0.48 (3.3)			5.6	0.60 (7.3)	
5.19	0.48 (9.8)	0.12(3.1)	None	5.7	0.48 (9.8)	0.12 (3.1)
5.19.a	0.53 (8.1)	0.12(2.1)				
5.20	0.54 (7.5)			5.8	.54 (7.5)	
Average (All):	0.45 (6.2)	0.12(2.3)		Average	0.46 (7.4)	.12 (3.2)
Av.(Str. Inst.Only)	0.46 (5.5)	0.12(2.4)				

Notes: "a" models use C_{b2} form; "Alt" models are strong instrument versions of same model; "Alt2" are strong instruments that include originally suspect variables not endogenous. See text.; "c" model uses $Unem_{-2}$. S=strong inst. W=weak inst.

induced deficit effects. Later in this paper we will test these effects separately to see if spending and tax cut deficits have different effects.

Mean results of OLS and 2SLS tests were virtually identical for spending models. They were also reasonably close for borrowing, where the 2SLS results show a larger crowd out effect than the OLS results, but the differences were statistically insignificant. Within each group, the results for different models tested generally cluster closely around the group mean. Hence, group averages meaningfully reflect individual test results.

The estimates of the effect of deficits on borrowing are generally about 1/3 larger than estimates of their effect on spending. As noted earlier, if stimulus income doesn't finance new spending, but just replaces spending that without the stimulus would have been done anyway, but out of borrowed money, we should find the borrowing effect to be larger. Private borrowing is reduced not only by the reduction in loanable funds available, because they are diverted to fund the deficit, but also because of the reduced need to borrow due to availability of new income from the stimulus program.

The finding that both borrowing and spending decline as deficits rise supports the crowd out hypothesis as an explanation of why this negative relationship occurs. Finding this relationship even when controlling for business cycle effects on deficits and consumer spending also supports the argument that it is crowd out, as well as rising or falling phases of the business cycle that cause the negative relationship between deficits and private spending to occur.

The findings provide no support for the hypothesis that it is not crowd out, but just normal business cycle effects that cause the observed negative relationship between consumer spending and deficits. Estimated crowd out effects on consumer borrowing or spending are about the same in most models where business cycle effects are controlled for, as in models where they are not.

We also conclude these findings are robust for (i.e., remain essentially the same for) a significant range of

- Variables used to control for changes in the business cycle
- Variables used in instruments substituting for endogenous variables
- Estimation Methods used (OLS or 2SLS)
- Robustness of findings over different time periods sampled (See 5.4 below)

Table 5.8 Robustness of consumption models with respect to time period sampled

Spending Model 5.13		*Borrowing Model 5.21*	
Sample period	*Deficit variable* β (t-*stat.*)	*Sample period*	*Deficit variable* β (t-*stat.*)
A. (Current Period Real GDP Rate Business Cycle Control)			
1960–2010	0.38 (2.6)	1960–2010	0.64 (0.5)
1970–2010	0.26 (1.6)	1970–2010	2.25 (2.3)
1960–2000	0.25 (1.2)	1960–2000	0.89 (1.0)
1970–2000	0.25 (1.5)	1970–2000	1.39 (2.1)
B. (3 Period-Lagged Real GDP Rate Business Cycle Control)			
Spending Model 5.15		Borrowing Model 5.22	
1960–2010	0.49 (8.1)	1960–2010	0.62 (3.2)
1970–2010	0.47 (8.1)	1970–2010	0.62 (2.8)
1960–2000	0.37 (5.4)	1960–2000	0.65 (1.8)
1970–2000	0.36 (5.1)	1970–2000	0.75 (2.3)
C. (Unemployment Rate Business Cycle Control)			
Spending Model 5.17		Borrowing Model 5.23	
1960–2010	0.48 (4.5)	1960–2010	0.51 (1.6)
1970–2010	0.50 (8.1)	1970–2010	0.33 (1.3)
1960–2000	0.41 (4.9)	1960–2000	0.84 (1.6)
1970–2000	0.37 (4.6)	1970–2000	0.46 (1.3)
(No Business Cycle Control)			
Spending Model 5.19		Borrowing Model 5.24	
1960–2010	0.48 (9.8)	1960–2010	0.63 (3.2)
1970–2010	0.47 (9.8)	1970–2010	0.63 (2.8)
1960–2000	0.34 (5.3)	1960–2000	0.85 (2.8)
1970–2000	0.29 (5.5)	1970–2000	0.64 (4.2)

5.4 Robustness of Findings To Time Period Sampled

To test for robustness of crowd out coefficients and *t*-statistics with respect to period sampled, we examined the above 2SLS models for four different sampling periods.

Generally, the results indicate that whatever the period sampled over the past 50 years, similar crowd out test results are found (Table 5.8). The similarity of results for models, regardless of whether they used the unemployment rate, lagged GDP or no business control variable, also suggests robustness of results to model change, and implies crowd out is as real an offset to stimulus effects in recessions as in good economic times. Only using current GDP as the business cycle control did the results vary with the

Table 5.9 Additional tests of robustness of consumption models with respect to time period sampled (tests based on alternative method of calculating Hausman endogeneity

Spending Model 5.13 (2SLS)			*Borrowing Model 5.9 (OLS)*	
Sample period	*Deficit var.* β (t-*stat.*)	*Borrow. var.* β (t-*stat.*)	*Sample period*	*Deficit variable* β (t-*stat.*)
A. (Real GDP Rate Business Cycle Control)				
1960–2010	0.25 (3.5)	0.09 (2.8)	1960–2010	0.54 (2.3)
1970–2010	0.25 (3.4)	0.09 (2.9)	1970–2010	0.44 (1.3)
1960–2000	0.13 (2.1)	0.11 (2.0)	1960–2000	0.51 (2.6)
1970–2000	0.22 (2.6)	0.12 (2.0)	1970–2000	0.52 (2.3)
B. (3-Lagged Real GDP Rate Business Cycle Control)				
Spending Model 5.15 (2SLS)			Borrowing Model 5.10. (OLS)	
1960–2010	0.48 (8.3)	0.13 (3.1)	1960–2010	0.64 (2.6)
1970–2010	0.47 (8.8)	0.12 (2.8)	1970–2010	0.66 (2.5)
1960–2000	0.31 (5.0)	0.23 (2.9)	1960–2000	0.42 (2.5)
1970–2000	0.31 (6.0)	0.13 (1.6)	1970–2000	0.42 (1.8)
C. (Unemployment Rate Business Cycle Control)				
Spending Model 5.17 (2SLS)			Borrowing Model 5.11 (OLS)	
1960–2010	0.55 (10.1)	0.12 (3.2)	1960–2010	0.59 (2.0)
1970–2010	0.55 (10.3)	0.13 (3.5)	1970–2010	0.47 (1.7)
1960–2000	0.39 (6.0)	0.12 (2.2)	1960–2000	0.43 (2.5)
1970–2000	0.31 (6.0)	0.13 (1.6)	1970–2000	0.40 (2.3)
D. (No Business Cycle Control)				
Spending Model 5.19 (2SLS)			Borrowing Model 5.12 (OLS)	
1960–2010	0.48 (9.1)	0.11 (3.0)	1960–2010	0.66 (2.8)
1970–2010	0.47 (9.0)	0.12 (3.1)	1970–2010	0.68 (2.7)
1960–2000	0.35 (6.5)	0.11 (2.1)	1960–2000	0.51 (4.0)
1970–2000	0.31 (6.8)	0.12 (1.9)	1970–2000	0.59 (3.8)

time period chosen, but this was the control we found least correlated with deficits. Controlling for it did not mean we were controlling for deficits, so it was least useful in determining if deficit size was proxying for differences in economic conditions. In addition, Table 5.9 below, which repeats these robustness tests using a better endogeneity control technique, shows significant deficit effects in all time periods for models using current year GDP as the control. The results in Table 5.8 above using the current GDP control were so at variance with the uniformity of results using other business cycle control variables, we concluded the problem was with the control variable used, not the finding of significant crowd out effects over time.

We conclude that our finding that deficit-financed government stimulus programs are related to reduced private consumption is robust with respect to all four robustness criteria originally established:

- Robust to a range of regression methods (OLS and 2SLS estimates were similar);
- Robust to different instruments
- Robust to a (limited) range of model specifications (changes in business cycle controls), and
- Robust to a range of different time periods (1960 to 2000 or 2010, and 1970 to 2000 or 2010)

5.5 Robustness Using Alternative Definition of Hausman Endogeneity

In the models presented above, the first stage of the Hausman endogeneity test procedure was regression of one of the explanatory variables being tested for endogeneity on only the remaining variables thought with some certainty to be exogenous or lagged. Initially excluded from this list of variables assumed exogenous or lagged were six variables considered "suspect" of endogeneity on a priori grounds: either definitionally, or because prior testing had so suggested. The variables excluded were the real GDP (Y_0), real disposable income ($Y - T_T$), the real deficit ($T_T - G_{T\&I}$), real depreciation allowances (DEP) and the unemployment rate (UNEM). We now wish to see if our crowd out variable estimates were robust with regard to our selection of variables to be designated as endogenous and instrumented, *since the choice of variables to use as regressors in the first stage of a Hausman process regression when testing a variable suspected of endogeneity, can lead to different findings as regards endogeneity.*

To do so, another set of tests were undertaken to determine *endogeneity without making any a priori assumptions that some variables were endogenous.* Hence, all explanatory variables in the consumption and investment models were included as regressors in the first stage Hausman regression (except the one being tested for endogeneity, which became the dependent variable in the first stage test).

Overall, consumer spending model results for all periods sampled using the new endogeneity method were strikingly similar to those obtained using the prior endogeneity tests and their instruments presented in Eqs. 5.1.

A.1–5.1.A.24, *despite the fact that variables ruled Hausman-endogenous using the "new" first stage Hausman test were very different.* In the new tests of consumer spending, only depreciation and the borrowing variable were found Hausman-endogenous, despite the fact that variables like Υ_0 and $(\Upsilon - T_T)$, where, since C_T is a component of those variables, seems definitionally to contain some endogeneity, but apparently not enough to cause the observed crowd out relationship to be sufficiently different from our earlier results.

For the consumer borrowing models, the new Hausman endogeneity tests indicated none of the explanatory variables were endogenous with consumer borrowing, and therefore, OLS was the preferred estimation technique. The OLS results for borrowing models were very robust with regard to different time periods sampled, both in terms of coefficients obtained and their high levels of statistical significance. Recall that using the original method for determining endogeneity in structural models 5.21–5.24, (where suspect variables were not used as regressors in the first stage Hausman test), the deficit, Υ_0, XR_{AV} and POP_{16} were found endogenous and 2SLS was used to estimate them.

CHAPTER 6

Test Results: Investment Spending and Borrowing Models (One-Variable Deficit)

In this chapter, total investment spending (I_T) and business borrowing (I_B) models will be tested and findings regarding the effect of government deficits on them examined. The deficit variable tested is the one-variable formulation ($T_T - G_{T\&I}$) equal to government revenues minus government spending. The two-variable case, which tests for differences in crowd out effects when deficits are caused by tax cuts rather than spending increases, is tested in Chap. 8 below.

Section 6.1 tests 24 OLS models. The first 12 OLS models are spending models, summarized in Section 6.1.2. All 12 find crowd out has a significant negative effect on investment spending. Section 6.1.3 tests 12 OLS single-variable crowd out models of consumer borrowing, and finds crowd out significantly affects consumer borrowing negatively in all of them.

Section 6.2 tests 24 2SLS one-variable models of investment. Section 6.2.2 summarizes 23 tests of consumer spending, and finds crowd out has statistically significant negative effects on spending in all of them. Section 6.2.3 tests one 2SLS consumer borrowing model and finds crowd out has a significant negative effect. (None of the other 11 borrowing models tested had endogeneity problems requiring their earlier OLS tests be replaced by 2SLS.)

Sections 4.4 tests four spending models in four different but overlapping periods of time (16 tests), and four borrowing models in the same four time periods (16 tests). Crowd out is found to have a significant negative effect of investment spending in all 16 tests, and a significant negative effect on borrowing in 10 of 16 tests.

J.J. Heim, *Crowding Out Fiscal Stimulus*,
DOI 10.1007/978-3-319-45967-7_6

Detailed analysis of each of these tests is provided in the remainder of the chapter.

In consumption models tested, the following variables are hypothesized to be determinants of consumer spending and are tested using a variety of regression techniques. Results of the tests are then compared for consistency.

ACC = current year change in GDP accelerator variable ($Y_T - Y_{T-1}$)
($T_T - G_{T\&I}$) = real government deficit: total receipts minus total expenditures on government consumption, Investment, transfers, interest and subsidies
r_{-2} = real prime interest rate defined as the nominal rate minus the average of the past two completed years inflation. The rate used is the two-year lagged real rate.
DEP = current year depreciation allowances
CAP_{-1} = capacity utilization, lagged one year (percentage given in decimal form)
DJ_{-2} = a measure of wealth (NYSE Composite Index), lagged two years
XR_{AV} = the real broad US exchange rate average for current and past three years (foreign currency per dollar)
POP = population size
$I_{B(-1)}$ = total net business borrowing (defined as annual change in consumer debt in current period). The rate used is lagged one year, reflecting its more systematic relationship to investment in the data.

These variables are all variables that have been found significant determinants of investment in past studies, and will constitute our "standard" investment model. In most of the tests below, these variables will be accompanied by one of the following three variables designed to control for business cycle effects on estimates of the impact of the variables above, particularly the government deficit (crowd out) variable:

GDP = current period GDP variable used to control for the business cycle
GDP_{-3} = lagged GDP variable used to control for the business cycle
$UNEM_0$ = unemployment rate variable used to control for the business cycle

Current period values are typically, though not always, denoted without subscript; when subscripts are used, the current period is denoted "0"; other subscripts indicate periods lagged. These variables were found related to consumer spending in previous studies of investment. Lags were determined by assessing which lag was most significantly related to consumption. Our approach to determining the right level of lag to use was that if theory said a variable was a determinant of consumption, then the lag that most strongly demonstrated this relationship should be the lag used.

Some of the models tested, including the first model below (Model 6.1), contain a measure of business borrowing as one of the explanatory variables. Business borrowing is defined as the net annual change in business debt (US Federal Reserve Flow of Funds Accounts). This variable is used to test the hypothesis that investment demand (spending) is a function of availability of borrowed funds as well as income, that is, that investment spending is a function of *purchasing power, not just income related variables. A*ccess to credit may affect investment spending *independently* of its role as a way investment demand driven by other variables, like corporate profits, wealth, and so on, manifests itself. If so, the business borrowing variable will be found to have a positive, statistically significant regression coefficient, even in models in which the other determinants are well described.

Also included in most investment models is a variable controlling for the state of the economy each year in the 1960–2010 sample period. This is included to control for any possible business cycle effects which might cause a negative deficit/consumer spending relationships to occur for reasons having nothing to do with crowd out. By including a business cycle variable, we can control for business cycle effects on the deficit/consumer spending relationship when evaluating crowd out effects. Each model is tested using three different controls: the current GDP, GDP lagged three periods, and the current period unemployment rate. In addition, the model is estimated a fourth way, using no control at all.

6.1 OLS Models

To support crowd out theory, a negative relationship must be found between government deficits and both business borrowing and investment spending. That would be consistent with the theory that funding deficits take funds from the loanable funds pool that otherwise would be available to businesses to borrow and spend on business investment, reducing investment spending.

The first model (Model 6.1) tests whether business borrowing is a determinant of investment spending, using current period GDP as a control for business cycle effects. Preliminary testing indicated one-year lagged borrowing was systematically related to investment (recall it was current period borrowing affected consumer spending). This is not surprising for investment spending, since financing occurs well ahead of most spending: Design and bidding must occur prior to heavy spending on construction of factories, offices and stores, or even for purchases of large capital equipment, which is often built to order.

Model 6.1 OLS estimates of the effects of one-variable crowd out, with borrowing

(Current period real GDP used as business cycle control)

$$\underset{(t=)}{\Delta I_T} = +\underset{(2.5)}{0.12\Delta ACC} + \underset{(4.5)}{0.27\boldsymbol{\Delta}(\mathbf{T_T} - \mathbf{G_{T\&I}})} + \underset{(0.6)}{0.18\Delta DEP}$$
$$- \underset{(-0.6)}{0.94\Delta CAP_{-1}} - \underset{(-0.8)}{2.10\Delta r_{-2}} - \underset{(-3.9)}{0.38\,\Delta DJ_{-2}} - \underset{(-1.2)}{0.10\Delta PROF_{-2}}$$
$$+ \underset{(1.6)}{2.91\Delta XR_{AV}} - \underset{(-1.3)}{0.005\Delta POP} + \underset{(2.5)}{0.11\,\boldsymbol{\Delta}\mathbf{I_{B(-1)}}} + \underset{(4.2)}{0.25\,\boldsymbol{\Delta}\mathbf{GDP_{REAL(0)}}}$$
$$R^2 = 95.5\ \%, DW = 1.9, MSE = 26.46 \qquad (6.1)$$

Clearly the level of business borrowing is a factor influencing the level of investment, independent of the demand generated by investment's other determinants. Crowd out also appears to be a problem, even when controlling for business cycle effects (using the level of the GDP_0. Lagging real GDP one year to avoid simultaneity issues leaves coefficients and *t*-statistics on the deficit and business borrowing variables virtually identical at $\Delta(T_T - G_{T\&I})=.27(t=4.5)$ and $\Delta(I_B = .11(t=2.5)))$

Model 2 repeats the test without the borrowing variable and gives nearly the same estimate of deficit effects. This of course raises questions as to whether, in testing crowd out, a separate business cycle control is even needed. Other business cycle—sensitive variables, like the accelerator or business borrowing may already be adequately controlling for this factor. Model 2, in fact, suggests this: take the borrowing variable out of the model, and the current year GDP becomes a significant control.

Model 6.2 OLS estimates of the effects of one-variable crowd out, without borrowing

(Current period real GDP business cycle control)

$$
\begin{aligned}
\underset{(t=)}{\Delta I_T} = &+\underset{(3.1)}{0.15\Delta ACC}+\underset{(7.0)}{0.33\boldsymbol{\Delta}(\mathbf{T_T}-\mathbf{G_{T\&I}})}+\underset{(1.4)}{0.42\Delta DEP} \\
&-\underset{(-0.1)}{0.01\Delta CAP_{-1}}-\underset{(-1.5)}{3.80\Delta r_{-2}}-\underset{(-4.4)}{0.47\,\Delta DJ_{-2}}-\underset{(-0.1)}{0.01\Delta PROF_{-2}} \\
&+\underset{(3.3)}{4.57\Delta XR_{AV}}-\underset{(-1.6)}{0.006\Delta POP}+\underset{(4.3)}{0.24\,\boldsymbol{\Delta}\mathbf{GDP_{REAL(0)}}}
\end{aligned}
$$

$$R^2 = 95.0\ \%,\quad DW = 2.2, MSE = 27.63 \tag{6.2}$$

Model 3 uses a three-year lagged value of the real GDP, which is the GDP period most strongly correlated with the current year deficit, as the business cycle control. Nonetheless, we again obtain very similar estimates of the deficit's effect on business investment, and borrowing's effect:

Model 6.3 OLS estimates of the effects of one-variable crowd out, with borrowing

(Three-period lagged real GDP business cycle control)

$$
\begin{aligned}
\underset{(t=)}{\Delta I_T} = &+\underset{(8.1)}{0.30\Delta ACC}+\underset{(5.2)}{0.35\boldsymbol{\Delta}(\mathbf{T_T}-\mathbf{G_{T\&I}})}+\underset{(2.9)}{1.05\Delta DEP} \\
&+\underset{(1.6)}{3.52\Delta CAP_{-1}}-\underset{(-2.2)}{4.50\Delta r_{-2}}-\underset{(-3.3)}{0.38\,\Delta DJ_{-2}}-\underset{(-0.5)}{0.05\Delta PROF_{-2}} \\
&+\underset{(4.1)}{5.90\Delta XR_{AV}}+\underset{(0.5)}{0.002\Delta POP}+\underset{(1.8)}{0.10\,\boldsymbol{\Delta}\mathbf{I_{B(-1)}}}+\underset{(1.1)}{0.06\,\boldsymbol{\Delta}\mathbf{GDP_{REAL(-3)}}}
\end{aligned}
$$

$$R^2 = 94.2\ \%, DW = 1.8, MSE = 30.06 \tag{6.3}$$

Clearly the level of business borrowing is a factor related to the level of investment (7 % significance level), independent of its other determinants. Also, even controlling for the business cycle, the government deficit appears to have a negative effect on investment.

Repeating the test without the borrowing variable (Model 4) again leaves the estimate of deficit effects largely unchanged:

Model 6.4 OLS estimates of the effects of one-variable crowd out, without borrowing

(Three-period lagged real GDP business cycle control)

$$\underset{(t=)}{\Delta I_T} = +\underset{(8.8)}{0.33\Delta \mathrm{ACC}} + \underset{(6.9)}{0.40\mathbf{\Delta}(\mathbf{T_T} - \mathbf{G_{T\&I}})} + \underset{(3.4)}{1.23\Delta \mathrm{DEP}}$$
$$+ \underset{(1.9)}{4.17\Delta \mathrm{CAP}_{-1}} - \underset{(-2.6)}{5.91\Delta \mathrm{r}_{-2}} - \underset{(-4.6)}{0.46\,\Delta \mathrm{DJ}_{-2}} + \underset{(0.4)}{0.03\Delta \mathrm{PROF}_{-2}}$$
$$+ \underset{(5.2)}{7.26\Delta \mathrm{XR_{AV}}} + \underset{(0.2)}{0.001\Delta \mathrm{POP}} + \underset{(1.1)}{0.06\,\mathbf{\Delta GDP_{REAL}}(-3)}$$
$$R^2 = 93.8\ \%, \mathrm{DW} = 2.1,\ \ \mathrm{MSE} = 30.74 \qquad (6.4)$$

Model 6.5 is identical to models 6.3 and 6.1, except it uses the unemployment rate as the business cycle control variable. Using this business cycle control does diminish the estimate of crowd out's effect slightly, but still leaves it a highly statistically significant influence.

Model 6.5 OLS estimates of the effects of one-variable crowd out, with borrowing

(Unemployment rate used as business cycle control)

$$\underset{(t=)}{\Delta I_T} = +\underset{(7.2)}{0.27\Delta \mathrm{ACC}} + \underset{(4.0)}{0.29\mathbf{\Delta}(\mathbf{T_T} - \mathbf{G_{T\&I}})} + \underset{(4.5)}{1.34\Delta \mathrm{DEP}}$$
$$+ \underset{(4.5)}{1.34\Delta \mathrm{CAP}_{-1}} - \underset{(-1.8)}{3.91\Delta \mathrm{r}_{-2}} - \underset{(-3.2)}{0.41\,\Delta \mathrm{DJ}_{-2}} - \underset{(-0.8)}{0.07\Delta \mathrm{PROF}_{-2}}$$
$$+ \underset{(2.7)}{4.66\Delta \mathrm{XR_{AV}}} + \underset{(1.2)}{0.004\Delta \mathrm{POP}} + \underset{(1.5)}{0.08\Delta \mathrm{I_{B(-1)}}} - \underset{(-2.1)}{14.70\,\mathbf{\Delta UNEM}}$$
$$R^2 = 94.4\ \%, \mathrm{DW} = 1.7, \mathrm{MSE} = 29.50 \qquad (6.5)$$

Repeating the test without the borrowing variable (again) gives about the same result:

Model 6.6 OLS estimates of the effects of one-variable crowd out, without borrowing

(Unemployment rate used as business cycle control)

$$\underset{(t=)}{\Delta I_T} = +\underset{(7.3)}{0.29\Delta \mathrm{ACC}} + \underset{(5.6)}{0.32\mathbf{\Delta}(\mathbf{T_T} - \mathbf{G_{T\&I}})} + \underset{(5.2)}{1.48\Delta \mathrm{DEP}}$$
$$+ \underset{(0.6)}{1.29\Delta \mathrm{CAP}_{-1}} - \underset{(-2.3)}{5.02\Delta \mathrm{r}_{-2}} - \underset{(-4.1)}{0.48\,\Delta \mathrm{DJ}_{-2}} - \underset{(-0.2)}{0.01\Delta \mathrm{PROF}_{-2}}$$
$$+ \underset{(3.7)}{5.74\Delta \mathrm{XR_{AV}}} + \underset{(0.9)}{0.003\Delta \mathrm{POP}} - \underset{(-2.4)}{16.37\,\mathbf{\Delta UNEM}}$$
$$R^2 = 94.2\ \%, \mathrm{DW} = 1.9, \mathrm{MSE} = 29.84 \qquad (6.6)$$

And results for the model using no business cycle control:

Model 6.7 OLS estimates of the effects of one-variable crowd out, with borrowing
(Using no business cycle control variable)

$$\begin{aligned}\underset{(t=)}{\Delta I_T} &= \underset{(8.1)}{+0.30\Delta ACC} + \underset{(5.0)}{0.33\boldsymbol{\Delta}(\mathbf{T_T} - \mathbf{G_{T\&I}})} + \underset{(4.2)}{1.33\Delta DEP} \\ &\quad \underset{(1.4)}{+2.46\Delta CAP_{-1}} \underset{(-1.9)}{-4.25\Delta r_{-2}} \underset{(-3.1)}{-0.36\,\Delta DJ_{-2}} \underset{(-0.9)}{-0.07\Delta PROF_{-2}} \\ &\quad \underset{(3.0)}{+4.96\Delta XR_{AV}} \underset{(1.8)}{+0.09\Delta I_{B(-1)}} + \underset{(1.1)}{0.004\Delta POP} \\ R^2 &= 94.0\ \%, DW = 1.8,\ \ MSE = 30.35 \end{aligned} \tag{6.7}$$

Here again, the results indicate a significant crowd out effect, and that access to borrowing increases business purchases of investment goods.

And repeating Model 6.7, except without a borrowing variable, gives the results shown in Model 6.8:

Model 6.8 OLS estimates of the effects of one-variable crowd out, without borrowing
(Using no business cycle control variable)

$$\begin{aligned}\underset{(t=)}{\Delta I_T} &= \underset{(9.1)}{+0.33\Delta ACC} + \underset{(6.7)}{0.39\boldsymbol{\Delta}(\mathbf{T_T} - \mathbf{G_{T\&I}})} + \underset{(5.1)}{1.50\Delta DEP} \\ &\quad \underset{(1.7)}{+3.13\Delta CAP_{-1}} \underset{(-2.5)}{-5.65\Delta r_{-2}} \underset{(-4.3)}{-0.44\,\Delta DJ_{-2}} \underset{(0.1)}{+0.00\Delta PROF_{-2}} \\ &\quad \underset{(4.3)}{+6.32\Delta XR_{AV}} \underset{(0.7)}{+0.003\Delta POP} \\ R^2 &= 93.6\ \%, DW = 2.1,\ \ MSE = 30.96 \end{aligned} \tag{6.8}$$

Clearly, all four models show crowd out to have a significant negative effect on business spending and that business borrowing, lagged a year, is positively associated with business spending independent of the effect of other variables.

That said, when our best business cycle control variable (UNEM) was included, crowd out effects were a little smaller ($0.29–0.32 per dollar of deficit) than when there was no business cycle control ($0.33–0.39 per dollar of deficit). Hence, for investment it would seem the underlying business cycle effect explains a small part (~15 %) of the observed negative relationship between deficits and business spending. Crowd out appears to explain the rest.

6.1.1 *Tobin's* q *and Profits Lag Specification Problem*

Though statistically significant in the above tests, estimates of the lagged Tobin's q proxy (DJ_{-2}) have a sign opposite what theory predicts. In addition, unexpectedly, the effects of profits on investment were not significantly different from zero. Both results were sufficiently counterintuitive to suggest the relationship should be investigated further. Examination indicated the correlation level between DJ_{-2} and profits variables ($r = 0.42$) to be among the highest of all explanatory variables in the investment data set, suggesting the relationship should be investigated further for multicollinearity effects. Changing the lag on the profits variable to zero reduced the multicollinearity, but did not change the sign or significance of either variable. However, *changing the lag level of both variables to zero, though not changing the correlation between them, markedly changed their significance level in the regression: current profits became highly significant, the Tobin's q proxy (NYSE Composite index) became insignificantly different from zero.* This held for all four business cycle control variables used. Repeating the same tests changing only the lag level on the Tobin's q proxy (the NYSE composite index) to two years in the future showed the NYSE composite two years in the future strongly positively related to current investment, controlling for the effects of other variables. This finding held regardless of which business cycle control variable was used. This suggests that while the independent effects of the stock market on current investment may be minimal, the reverse is not true: the effect of investment on the stock market in the future appears to be substantial.

Which alternative provides the best estimates of the real relationship between investment and b profits and Tobin's *q*? Our conclusion is that the models using current period versions of both Tobin's *q* and profits are the best. This is because the results are most consistent with theory. The NYSE composite index *t* allows for testing the commonly discussed *q* theory, without having the order of causation backward (DJ_{+2}), or having the sign of the effect perverse (DJ_{-2}).

Additional testing showed today's profits better explain future stock market values than do today's stock market prices explain future profits. In essence, our conclusion is that the data do not support the Tobin's *q* hypothesis, at least not using our proxy for Tobin's *q*, but does support

Table 6.1 Deficit variable coefficient and *t*-statistics using different lags for DJ and PROF variables

Business cycle Control variable	DJ_{-2}, $PROF_{-2}$	DJ_{+0}, $PROF_{-0}$	DJ_{+2}, $PROF_{-0}$
Y_0	0.27 ($t = 4.5$)	0.27 (4.4)	0.31 (6.1)
Y_{-3}	0.35 (5.2)	0.34 (4.1)	0.36 (6.5)
UNEM	0.29 (4.0)	0.28 (2.9)	0.32 (5.5)
None Used	0.33 (5.0)	0.32 (4.1)	0.35 (6.6)

the hypothesis that investment is positively, and significantly, related to current profit levels.

Whatever lag levels are used for Tobin's q and profits leaves the deficit's estimated marginal effect on investment essentially the same. Hence, the lag issue, though interesting, is of somewhat limited relevance to this paper, whose focus is on deficit effects, as shown in Table 6.1 below.

Complete test results for the DJ_0, $PROF_0$ models are presented in Models 6.1.a, 6.3.a, 6.5.a and 6.7.a below. All these models are identical "standard" models, except for differences in the business cycle control variable used.

Model 6.1.a OLS estimates of the effects of one-variable crowd out, with borrowing

(Current period real GDP business cycle control)

$$\underset{(t=)}{\Delta I_T} = \underset{(2.5)}{+0.16\Delta ACC} + \underset{(3.4)}{0.27\boldsymbol{\Delta}(\mathbf{T_T} - \mathbf{G_{T\&I}})} - \underset{(-0.4)}{0.18\Delta DEP}$$
$$- \underset{(-0.4)}{0.73\Delta CAP_{-1}} - \underset{(-0.9)}{1.92\Delta r_{-2}} - \underset{(-0.0)}{0.01\,\Delta DJ_{-0}} + \underset{(2.1)}{11\Delta PROF_{-0}}$$
$$+ \underset{(1.8)}{3.84\Delta XR_{AV}} - \underset{(-0.7)}{0.002\Delta POP} + \underset{(2.4)}{0.13\,\boldsymbol{\Delta}\mathbf{I_{B(-1)}}} + \underset{(3.3)}{0.22\,\boldsymbol{\Delta}\mathbf{GDP_{REAL(0)}}}$$
$$R^2 = 94.2\ \%, DW = 2.0, \quad MSE = 30.07 \qquad (6.1.a)$$

Model 6.3.a OLS estimates of the effects of one-variable crowd out, with borrowing

(Three-period lagged real GDP business cycle control)

$$\underset{(t=)}{\Delta I_T} = +\underset{(6.3)}{0.31\Delta ACC} + \underset{(4.1)}{0.34\mathbf{\Delta}(\mathbf{T_T} - \mathbf{G_{T\&I}})} + \underset{(2.0)}{0.54\Delta DEP}$$
$$+\underset{(1.8)}{3.63\Delta CAP_{-1}} - \underset{(-1.3)}{2.81\Delta r_{-2}} - \underset{(-0.2)}{0.05\,\Delta DJ_{-0}} + \underset{(2.1)}{0.14\Delta PROF_{-0}}$$
$$+\underset{(2.9)}{6.33\Delta XR_{AV}} + \underset{(0.8)}{0.003\Delta POP} + \underset{(2.3)}{0.14\,\mathbf{\Delta I_{B(-1)}}}$$
$$+\underset{(1.4)}{0.07\,\mathbf{\Delta GDP_{REAL(-3)}}}\quad R^2 = 93.3\ \%, DW = 1.9,$$
$$MSE = 32.18 \qquad (6.3.a)$$

Model 6.5.a OLS estimates of the effects of one-variable crowd out, with borrowing

(Unemployment rate used as business cycle control)

$$\underset{(t=)}{\Delta I_T} = +\underset{(5.1)}{0.29\Delta ACC} + \underset{(2.8)}{0.28\mathbf{\Delta}(\mathbf{T_T} - \mathbf{G_{T\&I}})} + \underset{(2.6)}{0.79\Delta DEP}$$
$$+\underset{(0.6)}{1.14\Delta CAP_{-1}} - \underset{(-1.4)}{3.38\Delta r_{-2}} + \underset{(0.2)}{0.04\,\Delta DJ_{-0}} + \underset{(1.8)}{0.12\Delta PROF_{-0}}$$
$$+\underset{(2.2)}{5.29\Delta XR_{AV}} + \underset{(1.6)}{0.005\Delta POP} + \underset{(1.7)}{0.11\Delta I_{B(-1)}} - \underset{(-1.5)}{11.07\,\mathbf{\Delta UNEM}}$$
$$R^2 = 93.3\ \%, DW = 1.9,\quad MSE = 32.44 \qquad (6.5.a)$$

Model 6.7.a OLS estimates of the effects of one-variable crowd out, with borrowing

(Using no business cycle control variable)

$$\underset{(t=)}{\Delta I_T} = +\underset{(6.2)}{0.32\Delta ACC} + \underset{(4.1)}{0.32\mathbf{\Delta}(\mathbf{T_T} - \mathbf{G_{T\&I}})}$$
$$+\underset{(2.7)}{0.85\Delta DEP} + \underset{(1.4)}{2.29\Delta CAP_{-1}} - \underset{(-1.4)}{3.15\Delta r_{-2}} - \underset{(-0.2)}{0.03\,\Delta DJ_{-0}}$$
$$+\underset{(2.0)}{0.13\Delta PROF_{-0}} + \underset{.(2.4)}{5.53\Delta XR_{AV}} + \underset{(2.1)}{0.13\Delta I_{B(-1)}} + \underset{(1.5)}{0.005\Delta POP}$$
$$R^2 = 93.0\ \%,\quad DW = 1.9,\ MSE = 32.60 \qquad (6.7.a)$$

6.1.2 OLS Investment Spending Model Findings Summarized

Table 6.2 summarizes the findings for investment spending models tested above.

Table 6.2 OLS investment spending model conclusions summarized

Model#	*Deficit var. β* (*t-stat.)*	*Borrow. var* β (*t-stat.)*	*Bus. cycle control var*
6.1	0.27 (4.5)	0.11 (2.5)	$GDP_{Real(0)}$
6.1.a	0.27 (3.4)	0.13 (2.4)	$GDP_{Real(0)}$
6.2	0.33 (7.0)		
6.3	0.35 (5.2)	0.10 (1.8)	$GDP_{Real(-3)}$
6.3.a	0.34 (4.1)	0.14 (2.3)	$GDP_{Real(-3)}$
6.4	0.40 (6.9)		
6.5	0.29 (4.0)	0.08 (1.5)	Unem. Rate
6.5.a	0.28 (2.8)	0.11 (1.7)	Unem. Rate
6.6	0.32 (5.6)		
6.7	0.33 (5.0)	0.09 (1.8)	None
6.7.a	0.32 (4.1)	0.13 (2.1)	None
6.8	0.39 (6.7)		
Average	0.34 (5.6)	0.10 (1.9)	(w/o "a" versions)
Average	0.33 (4.9)	0.11 (2.0)	(w/ "a" versions)

All the tests show a very strong negative relationship between the government deficit and investment spending. The evidence that borrowing ability is a separate factor affecting levels of investment (as was the case with consumption), in addition to all other known factors, is less strong, but still substantial enough to warrant attention, with all *t*-statistics for the borrowing variable significant at the 10 % level ($t = 1.7$) or better, except one which was significant only at the 15 % ($t = 1.5$) level.

6.1.3 OLS Estimates of Crowd Out Effects on Business Borrowing

In the models below, it is hypothesized that business borrowing is driven by some or all of the same variables that drive investment spending. The models include a control for the effect of the business cycle on borrowing. The models are the same as those tested for spending, except that the dependent variable is now current year business borrowing, not investment spending. This is the same borrowing variable used on the right side of the equation in spending models (with a one year lag). As was the case with consumer borrowing, using the one period lag on the Dow Jones Composite Index (Tobin's *q* proxy) explained considerably more variance in the borrowing models than the two period lag versions used in the spending models. Also added to the spending models was a variable representing the savings components of M2. This was found systematically related to consumer borrowing, as is tested here for that reason. In theory, one would expect growth in saving to reduce the need for borrowing.

The "a" versions of all tests below rerun the same model previously tested, but using current period specifications for profits while retaining the one period lag for the Tobin's q proxy, (DJ_{-1} and $PROF_0$). This is done to test the theory that it is current values of profits, not two-year lagged values that systematically affect investment borrowing.

The first borrowing model we will test (Model 6.9) uses the current period real GDP as the business cycle control.

Model 6.9 OLS estimates of the effects of one-variable crowd out on real borrowing

(Current period real GDP business cycle control)

$$\begin{aligned} \underset{(t=)}{\Delta I_B} = &+\underset{(0.3)}{0.09\Delta ACC}+\underset{(3.6)}{0.98\boldsymbol{\Delta}(\mathbf{T_T}-\mathbf{G_{T\&I}})}-\underset{(-0.2)}{0.35\Delta DEP} \\ &-\underset{(-1.9)}{17.10\Delta CAP_{-1}}-\underset{(-2.0)}{13.74\Delta r_{-2}}-\underset{(-2.6)}{2.09\,\Delta DJ_{-1}}+\underset{(3.6)}{1.30\Delta PROF_{-2}} \\ &+\underset{(3.3)}{24.26\Delta XR_{AV}}+\underset{(3.0)}{0.04\Delta POP}-\underset{(-0.8)}{0.12\Delta(RealM2-M1)} \\ &-\underset{(-1.1)}{0.27\boldsymbol{\Delta}\mathbf{GDP_{REAL(0)}}} \quad R^2 = 59.5\ \%, DW = 2.0, MSE = 118.45 \end{aligned} \tag{6.9}$$

The negative sign on the DJ index we take to mean the higher the amount that can be raised issuing equity, the less the demand for borrowed funds.

Model 6.9.a OLS estimates of the effects of one-variable crowd out on real borrowing

(Current period real GDP business cycle control)

$$\begin{aligned} \underset{(t=)}{\Delta I_B} = &+\underset{(0.3)}{0.10\Delta ACC}+\underset{(3.1)}{0.73\boldsymbol{\Delta}(\mathbf{T_T}-\mathbf{G_{T\&I}})}-\underset{(-0.4)}{0.94\Delta DEP} \\ &-\underset{(-0.5)}{4.47\Delta CAP_{-1}}+\underset{(0.7)}{6.95\Delta r_{-2}}-\underset{(-0.3)}{0.13\,\Delta DJ_{-1}}+\underset{(4.2)}{1.04\Delta PROF_{-0}} \\ &+\underset{(3.5)}{20.59XR_{AV}}+\underset{(2.7)}{0.05\Delta POP}-\underset{(-0.1)}{0.02\Delta(RealM2-M1)} \\ &-\underset{(-1.8)}{0.45\boldsymbol{\Delta}\mathbf{GDP_{REAL(0)}}} \\ R^2 &= 56.6\ \%, DW = 2.0, MSE = 122.65 \end{aligned} \tag{6.9.a}$$

In both models, government deficits are systematically, and negatively, related to investment borrowing.

Retesting the same models, except using three-period lagged real GDP as the business cycle control variable yields essentially the same results as regards the deficit's negative effect on borrowing. Results are presented in Models 6.10 and 6.10.a below.

Model 6.10 OLS estimates of the effects of one-variable crowd out on real borrowing

(Real GDP lagged three periods used as business cycle control)

$$\underset{(t=)}{\Delta I_B} = -\underset{(-0.4)}{0.11\Delta ACC} + \underset{(3.1)}{0.87\boldsymbol{\Delta}(\mathbf{T_T} - \mathbf{G_{T\&I}})}$$

$$- \underset{(-0.4)}{0.68\Delta DEP} - \underset{(-2.7)}{23.53\Delta CAP_{-1}} - \underset{(-2.0)}{10.99\Delta r_{-2}} - \underset{(-2.6)}{2.10\,\Delta DJ_{-1}}$$

$$+ \underset{(3.3)}{1.23\Delta PROF_{-2}} + \underset{(2.5)}{20.09\Delta XR_{AV}} + \underset{(2.7)}{0.04\Delta POP}$$

$$- \underset{(-1.0)}{0.15\Delta(\mathrm{RealM2} - \mathrm{M1})} - \underset{(-1.0)}{0.17\boldsymbol{\Delta}\mathbf{GDP_{REA(-3)}}}$$

$$R^2 = 59.6;\ DW = 1.9;\ MSE = 118.31 \qquad (6.10)$$

Model 6.10.a OLS estimates of the effects of one-variable crowd out on real borrowing

(Real GDP lagged three periods used as business cycle control)

$$\underset{(t=)}{\Delta I_B} = \underset{(-0.8)}{-0.21\Delta ACC} + \underset{(2.6)}{0.56\boldsymbol{\Delta}(\mathbf{T_T} - \mathbf{G_{T\&I}})} - \underset{(-0.7)}{1.34\Delta DEP}$$

$$- \underset{(-2.2)}{16.56\Delta CAP_{-1}} + \underset{(1.3)}{9.48\Delta r_{-2}} - \underset{(0.6)}{0.34\,\Delta DJ_{-1}}$$

$$+ \underset{(4.1)}{0.95\Delta PROF_0} + \underset{(2.0)}{13.88\Delta XR_{AV}} + \underset{(2.2)}{0.04\Delta POP}$$

$$- \underset{(-0.3)}{0.06\Delta(\mathrm{RealM2} - \mathrm{M1})} - \underset{(-2.2)}{0.29\boldsymbol{\Delta}\mathbf{GDP_{REA(-3)}}}$$

$$R^2 = 58.9;\ DW = 2.0;\ MSE = 119.40 \qquad (6.10.a)$$

Models 6.11 and 6.11.a retest the models above using the unemployment rate as the business cycle control variable:

Model 6.11 OLS estimates of the effects of one-variable crowd out on real borrowing

(Unemployment rate business cycle control; Tobin's *q* proxy (DJ), PROF not lagged)

$$\begin{aligned}
\underset{(t=)}{\Delta I_B} = {} & -\underset{(-0.1)}{0.02\Delta \mathrm{ACC}} + \underset{(3.2)}{1.07\boldsymbol{\Delta}(\mathbf{T_T} - \mathbf{G_{T\&I}})} - \underset{(-1.0)}{1.58\Delta \mathrm{DEP}} \\
& - \underset{(-2.2)}{16.24\Delta \mathrm{CAP}_{-1}} - \underset{(-2.0)}{13.43\Delta \mathrm{r}_{-2}} - \underset{(-2.7)}{2.03\,\Delta \mathrm{DJ}_{-1}} + \underset{(3.5)}{1.32\Delta \mathrm{PROF}_{-2}} \\
& + \underset{(3.1)}{23.44\Delta \mathrm{XR_{AV}}} + \underset{(2.2)}{0.03\Delta \mathrm{POP}} - \underset{(-0.7)}{0.10\Delta(\mathrm{RealM2} - \mathrm{M1})} \\
& + \underset{(1.6)}{39.27\boldsymbol{\Delta}\mathbf{UNEM}} \quad R^2 = 60.2\ \%, \mathrm{DW} = 1.9,\ \ \mathrm{MSE} = 117.44
\end{aligned}$$

(6.11)

Model 6.11.a OLS estimates of the effects of one-variable crowd out on real borrowing

(Unemployment rate business cycle control; Tobin's *q* proxy (DJ), PROF not lagged)

$$\begin{aligned}
\underset{(t=)}{\Delta I_B} = {} & \underset{(-05)}{-0.13\Delta \mathrm{ACC}} + \underset{(3.1)}{0.77\boldsymbol{\Delta}(\mathbf{T_T} - \mathbf{G_{T\&I}})} - \underset{(-1.3)}{2.73\Delta \mathrm{DEP}} \\
& - \underset{(-0.8)}{6.19\Delta \mathrm{CAP}_{-1}} + \underset{(0.9)}{8.42\Delta \mathrm{r}_{-2}} \quad \underset{(-0.3)}{0.14\,\Delta \mathrm{DJ}_{-1}} + \underset{(4.0)}{0.98\Delta \mathrm{PROF}_0} \\
& + \underset{(2.8)}{18.35\Delta \mathrm{XR_{AV}}} + \underset{(1.8)}{0.03\Delta \mathrm{POP}} - \underset{(-0.2)}{0.04\Delta(\mathrm{RealM2} - \mathrm{M1})} \\
& + \underset{(1.6)}{37.17\boldsymbol{\Delta}\mathbf{UNEM}} \quad R^2 = 55.9\ \%, \mathrm{DW} = 1.9,\ \ \mathrm{MSE} = 123.66
\end{aligned}$$

(6.11.a)

Finally, since the business cycle control variable was consistently found statistically insignificant in most of the above tests, Model 6.12 retests without using any business cycle control variable.

Model 6.12 OLS estimates of the effects of one-variable crowd out on real borrowing

(No business cycle control; Tobin's *q* proxy (DJ) lagged one period)

$$\begin{aligned}
\underset{(t=)}{\Delta I_B} = {} & -\underset{(-0.4)}{0.10\Delta \mathrm{ACC}} + \underset{(3.4)}{0.92\boldsymbol{\Delta}(\mathbf{T_T} - \mathbf{G_{T\&I}})} - \underset{(-0.9)}{1.38\Delta \mathrm{DEP}} \\
& - \underset{(-2.8)}{20.54\Delta \mathrm{CAP}_{-1}} - \underset{(-1.9)}{11.57\Delta \mathrm{r}_{-2}} - \underset{(-2.7)}{2.10\,\Delta \mathrm{DJ}_{-1}} + \underset{(3.7)}{1.30\Delta \mathrm{PROF}_{-2}} \\
& + \underset{(3.1)}{22.80\Delta \mathrm{XR_{AV}}} + \underset{(2.4)}{0.03\Delta \mathrm{POP}} - \underset{(-1.2)}{0.17\Delta(\mathrm{RealM2} - \mathrm{M1})}
\end{aligned}$$

$$R^2 = 58.8\ \%,\quad \mathrm{DW} = 2.0, \mathrm{MSE} = 118.05 \qquad (6.12)$$

Model 6.12.a OLS estimates of the effects of one-variable crowd out on real borrowing

(No business cycle control; Tobin's *q* proxy (DJ) and PROF not lagged)

$$\underset{(t=)}{\Delta I_B} = -\underset{(-0.7)}{0.20\Delta ACC} + \underset{(3.1)}{0.63\boldsymbol{\Delta}(\mathbf{T_T} - \mathbf{G_{T\&I}})} - \underset{(-1.3)}{2.52\Delta DEP}$$
$$-\underset{(-1.6)}{10.43\Delta CAP_{-1}} + \underset{(1.1)}{9.79\Delta r_{-2}} - \underset{(-0.5)}{0.25\Delta DJ_{-1}} + \underset{(3.9)}{0.96\Delta PROF_0}$$
$$+\underset{(2.6)}{17.82\Delta XR_{AV}} + \underset{(1.9)}{0.03\Delta POP} - \underset{(-0.6)}{0.10\Delta(RealM2 - M1)}$$
$$R^2 = 54.6\ \%, DW = 2.0, MSE = 123.90 \qquad (6.12.a)$$

Clearly, in all the borrowing models using two period lagged profits with the one period lagged Tobin's *q* and, rising deficits are related to a decline in business borrowing on close to a one-to-one basis. The same was true using the current period Tobin's *q* proxy, but in those models, the deficit coefficient only indicated crowd out's effect averages only \$0.65 per dollar of deficit, compared to \$0.95 when using the two lagged version of profits. The crowd out effect in models using business cycle controls was nearly identical to that in the no-control model.

6.1.4 *OLS Investment Spending and Business Borrowing Model Findings Summarized*

Table 6.3 summarizes the test results from the business borrowing models.

The deficit has a strong negative effect on business borrowing, estimated at between 2/3 to nearly a full dollar per dollar of deficit incurred. The finding is consistent with the crowd out. This was also the case with consumer borrowing. The decline in spending is \$0.30–\$0.34, about 1/3–½ as large. Here again, we also see reductions in borrowing greater than reductions in spending, suggesting two possible causes:

- That businesses draw down savings or sell off other financial assets to offset part of the reduced ability to borrow, or
- Businesses use stimulus money, for example, tax cuts, to finance spending they otherwise had planned to do using borrowed money.

Table 6.3 OLS investment spending and business borrowing model findings summarized

Spending Models				*Borrowing Models:*	
Model#	*Deficit Var. β (t-stat.)*	*Borrow. Var. β (t-stat.)*	*Bus. Cycle Control Var.*	*Model#*	*Deficit Var. β (t-stat.)*
6.1	0.27 (4.5)	0.11 (2.5)	$GDP_{Real(0)}$	6.9.	0.98 (3.6)
6.1.a	0.27 (3.4)	0.13 (2.4)			
6.2	0.33 (7.0)			6.9.a	0.73 (3.1)
6.3	0.34 (5.2)	0.10 (1.8)	$GDP_{Real(-3)}$	6.10	0.87 (3.1)
6.3.a	0.34 (4.1)	0.14 (2.3)			
6.4	0.38 (6.3)			6.10.a	0.56 (2.6)
6.5	0.29 (4.0)	0.08 (1.5)	Unemployment	6.11	1.07 (3.2)
6.5.a	0.28 (2.8)	0.11 (1.7)			
6.6	0.32 (5.6)			6.11.a	0.77 (3.1)
6.7	0.33 (5.0)	0.09 (1.8)	None	6.12	0.92 (3.6)
6.7.a	0.32 (4.1)	0.13 (2.1)			
6.8	0.39 (6.7)			6.12.a	0.63 (3.1)
Aver.(w/o "a"):	0.34 (5.6)	0.10 (1.9)			0.96 (3.4)
Aver. ("a" only)	0.30 (3.6)	0.13 (2.1)			0.65 (2.9)

6.2 2SLS Models

When endogeneity is found in the investment models to be tested, 2SLS is the preferred tool of analysis, providing consistent estimates of model parameters. The process used for determining endogeneity was the same

Table 6.4 Determinants of consumption and investment initially assumed endogenous when applying endogeneity tests

Disposable income	*Depreciation*
The deficit	Unemployment rate
The accelerator	Real GDP
Exchange rate av.	Dow Jones composite av.

as described earlier for consumption models. Of all the variables used on the right hand side of either the consumption or investment functions (plus the exports and current period consumer confidence variables), the variables shown in Table 6.4 were initially assumed to possibly be endogenous, that is, were considered "suspect" and tested for endogeneity:

The remaining variables were initially assumed exogenous, or were lagged, and were used as first-stage Hausman test regressors when testing the endogeneity of any of the variables above. Residuals from that regression were then added to the investment structural equation as an additional variable. If statistically significant, the variable being tested was judged Hausman-endogenous and replaced by an instrument in the actual tests of the structural model reported here.

The standard practice used to develop the first instrument used was to regress the endogenous variable on all the variables determined non-endogenous. The fitted values from this regression were used as the initial or "standard" instrument when estimating the structural equation. If it proved to be a weak instrument, further changes were made to strengthen it. So that the same instrument could be used for all endogenous variables in a model, sometimes additional variables needed to be added to a strong instrument to make it also a strong instrument for a second or third endogenous variable.

If the standard instrument was determined to be weak instrument using the Wald test (F-statistic less than 10 or no individual t-statistic in the instrument equal to 3.3 or more), more variables were added to or subtracted from the instrument until it met either the Wald F or t-test standard. The specific changes made to the standard instrument are noted as they occur with the various models.

Some variables contemporaneous with the dependent variable were initially assumed not endogenous and used as right hand side regressors in the first stage of the Hausman test. However, they were also individually tested

Table 6.5 Determinants of consumption and investment initially assumed exogenous when applying endogeneity tests

Index of consumer confidence$_{-1}$	*M2 average*$_{-2\ to\ -4}$
Dow Jones Composite Index$_{-1\&2}$	Exports
Profits$_{-2}$	$GDP_{Real(-3)}$
Prime Rate$_0$	Business Borrowing (Net)
Population (Young/old Ratio)	Consumer Confidence Index$_0$
Capacity utilization$_{-1}$	Real Prime Int. Rate$_{-2}$

for endogeneity against the remaining variables originally assumed exogenous. The variables assumed exogenous, or which were lagged, are shown in Table 6.5, included the following (lack of a subscript denotes current period values).

The variables identified as endogenous using the Hausman procedure varied depending on which business cycle control variable (Y_0, Y_{-3}, UNEM or none) was being used, and whether the business borrowing variable was an explanatory variable in the model. Separate instruments were developed for each model having different Hausman-endogenous variables.

Instrument components were weighted using the first-stage regression in the 2SLS procedure described in the consumption and methodology sections of this paper. Sargan tests were undertaken to ensure the correlation of error term with endogenous variables had successfully been removed by the instrument. If the (nR^2) Sargan test result was less than the $X^2_{(.95,\ df)}$ test criteria, the endogeneity was deemed removed.

In this section, models labeled "Alt. a" use the alternative current period formulation of Tobin's q (DJ_0) and profits ($PROF_0$) variables instead of their two-year lagged values.

The first model tested (6.13) uses the current year GDP business cycle control variable.

Model 6.13 2SLS estimates of crowd out and business borrowing on investment spending, borrowing included, current GDP used as business cycle control variable

(Real GDP and population found endogenous and instrumented) (Weak instrument) (Real GDP Wald test $F = 32.84$), as was population (Wald test $F = 1.95$, no $t \geq 3.3$)). Sargan test $NR^2 = 12.74$)

$$\underset{(t=)}{\Delta I_T} = +0.23\underset{(3.3)}{\Delta ACC} + 0.30\underset{(4.6)}{\boldsymbol{\Delta}(\mathbf{T_T} - \mathbf{G_{T\&I}})} + 1.01\underset{(2.3)}{\Delta DEP}$$
$$+ 1.19\underset{(0.6)}{\Delta CAP_{-1}} - 3.60\underset{(-1.6)}{\Delta r_{-2}} - 0.38\underset{(-3.8)}{\Delta DJ_{-2}} - 0.08\underset{(-1.0)}{\Delta PROF_{-2}}$$
$$+ 4.06\underset{(2.1)}{\Delta XR_{AV}} - 0.002\underset{(-0.4)}{\Delta POP} + 0.09\underset{(1.9)}{\boldsymbol{\Delta}\mathbf{I_B}} + 0.11\underset{(1.4)}{\boldsymbol{\Delta}\mathbf{GDP_{REAL(0)}}}$$
$$R^2 = 95.1\ \%, DW = 1.9,\ \ MSE = 28.07 \qquad (6.13)$$

Though the initial instrument for the GDP was strong, it was weak for the population variable. To eliminate the weak instrument problem, we removed the variables in the instrument not used in the investment model that were least correlated with POP in the original instrument, and re-applied the Wald test. This did not strengthen the instrument enough to eliminate the weak instrument problem. However, adding two additional variables ($Y_{Real(\geq 2)}$ and r_{-3}) did increase the F to $F = 2.4$ and resulted in $t = 3.6$ on one variable ($M2_{AV}$) used to construct the instrument. The eliminated variables were PR_0, ICC_0, ICC_{-1} and POP_{16}. The new instrument used also improved the F and t-statistics for the real GDP variable. The significant t-statistics were not on the same variables as were significant in the POP instrument. Re-estimating the regression using the new instruments, a strong instrument version of the current real GDP business cycle control model emerged (Eq. 6.13.Alt) and is shown below.

Model 6.13.Alt 2SLS estimates of crowd out and business borrowing on investment spending, borrowing included, current GDP used as business cycle control variable (strong instrument)

(Endogenous: Real GDP (Wald test $F = 28.76$) and Population (Wald test $F = 3.18$, but $t > 3.3$ Wald criteria for $M2_{AV}$ variable in the instrument. Sargan test $NR^2 = 11.02$)

$$\underset{(t=)}{\Delta I_T} = +0.25\underset{(2.7)}{\Delta ACC} + 0.31\underset{(4.5)}{\boldsymbol{\Delta}(\mathbf{T_T} - \mathbf{G_{T\&I}})}$$
$$+ 1.10\underset{(1.8)}{\Delta DEP} \quad + 1.52\underset{(0.6)}{\Delta CAP_{-1}} \quad - 3.79\underset{(-1.7)}{\Delta r_{-2}}$$
$$- 0.37\underset{(-3.7)}{\Delta DJ_{-2}}$$
$$- 0.08\underset{(-1.0)}{\Delta PROF_{-2}} \quad + 4.28\underset{(2.0)}{\Delta XR_{AV}}$$
$$- 0.001\underset{(-0.1)}{\Delta POP} \quad + \quad 0.09\underset{(1.9)}{\boldsymbol{\Delta}\mathbf{I_{B(-1)}}}$$
$$+ 0.08\underset{(0.8)}{\boldsymbol{\Delta}\mathbf{GDP_{REAL(0)}}}$$

$$R^2 = 94.8\ \%, \quad \text{DW} = 1.9, \quad \text{MSE} = 28.60 \quad \text{(Eq.11.1.A.13.Alt)}$$

The use of stronger instruments did not significantly change our regression results, indicating the model is somewhat robust to variation in the choice of instruments.

As was done for consumption (see Eq. 5.17.a.Alt2, 5.22.Alt2, and 5.23. Alt2), when testing for Hausman endogeneity, we also used a second, more conservatively estimated group of variables as exogenous or lagged. These included only eight variables: CAP_{-1}, PR_{-2}, DJ_{-2}, $Prof_{-2}$, POP_{16}, POP, $M2_{AV-2-4}$ and ICC_{-1} (and Υ_{-3} in models using that variable as the business cycle control). Here, only the PR_0 variable was found Hausman-endogenous. For these "Alt2" tests, Wald weak instrument tests are applied a little differently also. In Alt2 tests, variables are tested for weakness utilizing not only the eight exogenous/lagged variables noted earlier in this paragraph as regressors but also any "suspect" variables that have tested non-endogenous. Added to this group are any additional variables added earlier so the instrument could pass Wald weak instrument tests for other endogenous variables in the same structural investment model. By comparison, strong instruments not bearing the Alt2 label, typically were tested using the larger group of originally assumed exogenous/lagged variables and any additional variables that had to be added to meet Wald *F* and *t*-test requirements for other endogenous variables, but excluding variables in the model originally designated as suspect, but found non-Hausman-endogenous, for example, disposable income, the deficit and so on, in some cases.

That said, changing and strengthening the instrument in this way resulted in little change in deficit or other variable estimates, showing our results to be reasonably robust to variations in Hausman and Wald techniques used to determine endogeneity and instrument strength. Results are shown in Model 6.13.Alt2 below.

Model 6.13.Alt.2 2SLS estimates of crowd out and business borrowing on investment, borrowing included, current GDP used as business cycle control variable spending, alternate endogeneity method

(Endogenous: Only depreciation) (Instrumented: Wald test $F = 18.0$) $t > 4.0$ for I_B; $t = 8.4$ for DEP_{-1} Sargan test $NR^2 = 15.5 < X^2_{(.95,15)} = 25.0$ (Strong Instrument)

$$\Delta I_T = +0.20\Delta ACC + 0.31\mathbf{\Delta(T_T - G_{T\&I})} - 0.20\Delta DEP + 0.55\Delta CAP_{-1} - 1.84\Delta r_{-2} + 0.01\,\Delta DJ_{-2} + 0.13\Delta PROF_{-2} + 4.79\Delta XR_{AV} + 0.006\Delta POP + 0.14\mathbf{\Delta I_{B(-1)}} + 0.12\,\mathbf{\Delta GDP_{REAL(0)}}$$

$$\underset{(t=)}{\Delta I_T} = +\underset{(2.6)}{0.20\Delta ACC} + \underset{(3.9)}{0.31\mathbf{\Delta(T_T - G_{T\&I})}} - \underset{(-0.3)}{0.20\Delta DEP} + \underset{(0.3)}{0.55\Delta CAP_{-1}} - \underset{(-0.8)}{1.84\Delta r_{-2}} + \underset{(03)}{0.01\,\Delta DJ_{-2}} + \underset{(1.9)}{0.13\Delta PROF_{-2}} + \underset{(2.0)}{4.79\Delta XR_{AV}} + \underset{(1.4)}{0.006\Delta POP} + \underset{(2.2)}{0.14\mathbf{\Delta I_{B(-1)}}} + \underset{(1.9)}{0.12\,\mathbf{\Delta GDP_{REAL(0)}}}$$

$$R^2 = 93.8\ \%, \quad DW = 2.0, \quad MSE = 31.65 \qquad (11.1.A.13.Alt.2)$$

There is virtually no difference in the deficit variable estimates for the Alt and Alt 2 strong instrument models, even though slightly different methods of assessing Hausman endogeneity and Wald instrument strength were used.

The results from models 6.13 and 6.13.Alt and 6.13.Alt.2 clearly indicate that deficits adversely affect private investment spending by about \$0.31 per dollar of deficit, even when controlling for the phase of the business cycle in which the deficit occurs, using current real GDP as the control for business cycle effects. (As you will recall, the same year's deficit also adversely affects consumer spending by an average of \$0.46 cents per dollar of deficit.)

6.2.1 *Borrowing and Deficit Multicollinearity With Deficit*

The results also indicate that business borrowing may be a factor affecting investment spending, even controlling for other factors, that is, it is not just a proxy through which these other explanatory variables make their effects on investment felt. However, the results are marginal: the $t = 1.9$ statistic (6 % significance level) suggests this is a less statistically significant factor than we might have expected.

This is may be due to the extreme level of multicollinearity between the deficit and business borrowing. The simple correlation (r) between the two is $r = +0.80$, indicating changes in the deficit explain 64 % of the variance in business borrowing. No other correlation among any two right hand side variables is nearly as high. High multicollinearity is often characterized by reduced statistical significance of one of the variables. Removing the deficit from the model markedly improves the statistical significance of the borrowing variable; its t-statistic rises to $t = 6.8$.

The same model without borrowing as an explanatory variable yields the following results:

Model 6.14 2SLS estimates of crowd out on investment spending, borrowing not included, current GDP used as business cycle control variable

(Endogenous: population) (Instrumented: Wald test $F = 2.12$) Sargan test ($NR^2 = 28.92 > X^2_{(.95,17)} = 27.59$) (Weak Instrument)

$$\begin{aligned} \underset{(t=)}{\Delta I_T} = \; & +\underset{(3.1)}{0.15\Delta ACC} + \underset{(7.2)}{0.33\boldsymbol{\Delta}(\mathbf{T_T} - \mathbf{G_{T\&I}})} + \underset{(1.4)}{0.43\Delta DEP} \\ & - \underset{(-0.0)}{0.08\Delta CAP_{-1}} - \underset{(-1.5)}{3.78\Delta r_{-2}} - \underset{(-4.8)}{0.47\,\Delta DJ_{-2}} - \underset{(-0.1)}{0.00\Delta PROF_{-2}} \\ & + \underset{(3.1)}{4.48\Delta XR_{AV}} - \underset{(-1.9)}{0.006\Delta POP} + \underset{(4.7)}{0.25\boldsymbol{\Delta}\mathbf{GDP_{REAL(0)}}} \\ & R^2 = 95.0\ \%, DW = 2.2, MSE = 27.64 \end{aligned} \tag{6.14}$$

The same variables remain significant when the model is re-specified without the borrowing variable, and the coefficients remain similar on these variables. On variables that were insignificant, coefficients tend to fluctuate, but without much meaning relative to findings.

The same stronger instruments used in 6.13.Alt above, minus the borrowing variable for consistency with the structural model being tested, also produced a Wald test t-statistic greater than 3.3 (the $M2_{AV}$), thus allowing us to retest the model with strong instruments. Results are shown in 6.14. Alt below.

Model 6.14.Alt 2SLS estimates of crowd out and business borrowing on investment spending, borrowing included, current GDP used as business cycle control variable

(Endogenous and instrumented variables include current period GDP and population) (Strong Instrument) (Current period real GDP (Wald test $F = 31.36$) and population (Wald test $F = 2.62$, but $M2_{AV}$ had $T = -3.7$). Sargan test ($NR^2 = 11.22 < X^2_{(.95,14)} = 23.69$)

$$\underset{(t=)}{\Delta I_T} = +0.29\underset{(3.0)}{\Delta ACC} + 0.36\underset{(6.8)}{\boldsymbol{\Delta}(\mathbf{T_T} - \mathbf{G_{T\&I}})} + 1.35\underset{(2.4)}{\Delta DEP} + 2.39\underset{(1.0)}{\Delta CAP_{-1}} - 5.30\underset{(-2.4)}{\Delta r_{-2}} - 0.45\underset{(-4.8)}{\Delta DJ_{-2}} - 0.00\underset{(-0.1)}{\Delta PROF_{-2}} + 5.74\underset{(3.2)}{\Delta XR_{AV}} - 0.002\underset{(-0.3)}{\Delta POP} + 0.07\underset{(0.6)}{\boldsymbol{\Delta}\mathbf{GDP_{REAL(0)}}}$$

$$R^2 = 94.2\ \%, DW = 2.1, MSE = 29.76 \qquad (11.1.A.14.Alt)$$

Retesting the same model with a borrowing variable, except using three-period lagged real GDP as the business cycle control we get

Model 6.15 2SLS estimates of crowd out and business borrowing on investment spending, borrowing included, lagged GDP used as business cycle control variable

(Endogenous: DEP (Instrumented: Wald test $F = 6.85$) and population (Instrumented: Wald test $F = 2.12$. Sargan test ($NR^2 = 6.93$) (Weak instrument)

$$\underset{(t=)}{\Delta I_T} = +0.30\underset{(7.6)}{\Delta ACC} + 0.37\underset{(5.3)}{\boldsymbol{\Delta}(\mathbf{T_T} - \mathbf{G_{T\&I}})} + 0.43\underset{(0.8)}{\Delta DEP} + 4.24\underset{(1.8)}{\Delta CAP_{-1}} - 4.27\underset{(-1.9)}{\Delta r_{-2}} - 0.33\underset{(-2.4)}{\Delta DJ_{-2}} - 0.01\underset{(-0.1)}{\Delta PROF_{-2}} + 6.64\underset{(4.1)}{\Delta XR_{AV}} + 0.003\underset{(0.6)}{\Delta POP} + 0.12\underset{(2.2)}{\boldsymbol{\Delta}\mathbf{I_{B(-1)}}} + 0.12\underset{(2.3)}{\boldsymbol{\Delta}\mathbf{GDP_{REAL(-3)}}}$$

$$R^2 = 93.8\ \%, DW = 1.8, MSE = 31.10 \qquad (6.15)$$

Here, we needed strong instruments for the depreciation variable and population variables. Adding depreciation lagged one period, and we were able to meet Wald criteria for non-weak instruments. Results are presented in Eq. 6.15.Alt below.

Model 6.15.Alt 2SLS estimates of crowd out and business borrowing on investment spending, borrowing included, lagged GDP used as business cycle control variable

(Endogenous: Disposable Income, Real GDP (Instrumented: Wald test $F = 27.31$), DEP (Instrumented: Wald test $F = 21.10$) and population (Instrumented: Wald test $F = 3.07$, But $M2_{AV}$ component of instrument had $T > 3.3$, meet Wald Strong Instrument Criteria). Sargan test ($NR^2 = 11.22$) (Strong Instrument)

$$\underset{(t=)}{\Delta I_T} = +0.30\underset{(7.9)}{\Delta \text{ACC}} + 0.37\underset{(5.1)}{\mathbf{\Delta(T_T - G_{T\&I})}} + 0.59\underset{(1.3)}{\Delta \text{DEP}}$$
$$+ 5.01\underset{(2.4)}{\Delta \text{CAP}_{-1}} - 4.23\underset{(-2.1)}{\Delta \text{r}_{-2}} - 0.35\underset{(-2.6)}{\Delta \text{DJ}_{-2}} - 0.03\underset{(-0.4)}{\Delta \text{PROF}_{-2}}$$
$$+ 6.62\underset{(4.6)}{\Delta \text{XR}_{\text{AV}}} + 0.004\underset{(0.9)}{\Delta \text{POP}} + 0.10\underset{(2.1)}{\mathbf{\Delta I_{B(-1)}}}$$
$$+ 0.10\underset{(1.8)}{\mathbf{\Delta GDP_{REAL(-3)}}}$$
$$R^2 = 94.4\ \%,\ \text{DW} = 1.9, \text{MSE} = 30.01 \qquad (6.15.\text{Alt})$$

The strong instrument model results are very similar to those in 6.15, which used a weak instrument for the population variable, again suggesting the models are reasonably robust with regard to the choice of instruments.

Using the alternative current period specification of how the Tobin's *q* proxy (DJ_0) and profits ($PROF_0$) affect investment we have: formulations, we have

Model 6.15.Alt.a 2SLS estimates of crowd out and business borrowing on investment spending, borrowing included, lagged GDP used as business cycle control variable

(Endogenous & instrumented: ACC (Wald $F = 7.7$, but CAP_{-1} $t = -4.2$); DEP (Wald test $F = 14.3$); POP: (Wald test $F = 11.7$); DJ_0 (Wald test $F = 8.6$, but $(T - G)$ $t = 4.6$), And $Prof_0$ (Wald test $F = 7.8$, but $M2_{AV}$ $t = 3.6$). Sargan Test ($NR^2 = 8.5 < X^2_{(.95,17)} = 27.6$)

$$\underset{(t=)}{\Delta I_T} = +0.31\underset{(3.7)}{\Delta \text{ACC}} + 0.33\underset{(4.0)}{\mathbf{\Delta(T_T - G_{T\&I})}} - 0.26\underset{(-0.4)}{\Delta \text{DEP}}$$
$$+ 6.38\underset{(2.0)}{\Delta \text{CAP}_{-1}} - 2.02\underset{(-0.9)}{\Delta \text{r}_{-2}} + 0.11\underset{(0.5)}{\Delta \text{DJ}_0} + 0.14\underset{(1.2)}{\Delta \text{PROF}_0}$$
$$+ 7.47\underset{(3.3)}{\Delta \text{XR}_{\text{AV}}} + 0.007\underset{(1.2)}{\Delta \text{POP}} + 0.14\underset{(1.9)}{\mathbf{\Delta I_{B(-1)}}}$$
$$+ 0.13\underset{(2.0)}{\mathbf{\Delta GDP_{REAL(-3)}}}$$
$$R^2 = 92.9\ \%, \text{DW} = 2.0, \text{MSE} = 33.75 \qquad (6.15.\text{Alt.a})$$

Test results for the Alt.a2 form of this model (current period DJ and profits variables, more conservative endogeneity method) are as follows:

Model 6.15.Alt.a2 2SLS estimates of crowd out and business borrowing on investment spending, borrowing included, lagged GDP used as business cycle control variable

(Endogenous and instrumented: depreciation: (Wald test $F = 19.5$), DJ_0 (Wald test $F = 8.10$, but $t = 3.4$ for $(T - G)$, and $Prof_0$ (Wald test $F = 5.6$, But $t = 5.6$ for $(T - G)$. Sargan test ($NR^2 = 10.0 < X^2_{(.95,14)} = 23.7$) (Strong Instrument)

$$\underset{(t=)}{\Delta I_T} = +\underset{(5.2)}{0.24\Delta ACC} + \underset{(3.1)}{0.37\boldsymbol{\Delta}(\mathbf{T_T} - \mathbf{G_{T\&I}})} - \underset{(1.0)}{1.30\Delta DEP}$$
$$+ \underset{(1.4)}{7.51\Delta CAP_{-1}} - \underset{(-0.3)}{2.08\Delta r_{-2}} + \underset{(0.3)}{0.24\,\Delta DJ_{-0}} + \underset{(0.6)}{0.17\Delta PROF_{-0}}$$
$$+ \underset{(2.8)}{9.25\Delta XR_{AV}} + \underset{(1.1)}{0.007\Delta POP} + \underset{(1.5)}{0.16\boldsymbol{\Delta}\mathbf{I}_{\mathbf{B}(-1)}}$$
$$+ \underset{(1.4)}{0.26\,\boldsymbol{\Delta}\mathbf{GDP}_{\mathbf{REAL}(-3)}}$$
$$R^2 = 89.5\ \%, DW = 2.0, MSE = 41.01 \qquad (6.15.Alta2)$$

Again, both strong instrument models provide about the same estimates of the crowd out effect.

And the lagged GDP, DJ_{-2}, $PROF_{-2}$ model without the borrowing variable is

Model 6.16 2SLS estimates of crowd out on investment spending, borrowing not included, lagged GDP used as business cycle control variable

(Endogenous and Instrumented: DEP (Wald test $F = 6.85$) and Population (Wald test $F = 2.12$)). Sargan Test ($NR^2 = 6.93 < X^2_{(.95,14)} = 23.69$) (Weak Instrument)

$$\underset{(t=)}{\Delta I_T} = +\underset{(9.0)}{0.34\Delta ACC} + \underset{(6.9)}{0.39\boldsymbol{\Delta}(\mathbf{T_T} - \mathbf{G_{T\&I}})} + \underset{(4.1)}{1.37\Delta DEP}$$
$$+ \underset{(2.0)}{4.57\Delta CAP_{-1}} - \underset{(-2.6)}{6.19\Delta r_{-2}} - \underset{(-5.0)}{0.46\,\Delta DJ_{-2}} + \underset{(0.3)}{0.03\Delta PROF_{-2}}$$
$$+ \underset{(5.1)}{7.31\Delta XR_{AV}} - \underset{(-0.5)}{0.002\Delta POP} + \underset{(1.3)}{0.07\,\boldsymbol{\Delta}\mathbf{GDP}_{\mathbf{REAL}(-3)}}$$
$$R^2 = 93.7\ \%, DW = 2.0, MSE = 30.97 \qquad (6.16)$$

To strengthen the instruments used to replace the endogenous variables POP and DEP, the variable DEP_{-1} was added and ICC_{-1} subtracted. Results are shown in 6.16.Alt below

Model 6.16.Alt 2SLS estimates of crowd out on investment spending, borrowing not included, lagged gdp used as business cycle control variable

(Endogenous and instrumented: DEP (Wald Test $F = 20.60$) and population (Wald Test $F = 3.38$, but $T > 3.3$) for $M2_{AV}$ variable, Sargan test ($NR^2 = 12.24 < X^2_{(.95,14)} = 23.69$)

(Strong Instrument)

$$\underset{(t=)}{\Delta I_T} = +0.33\underset{(8.3)}{\Delta ACC} + 0.43\underset{(6.8)}{\boldsymbol{\Delta}(\mathbf{T_T} - \mathbf{G_{T\&I}})} + 0.72\underset{(1.8)}{\Delta DEP}$$
$$+ 5.85\underset{(2.8)}{\Delta CAP_{-1}} - 5.69\underset{(2.6)}{\Delta r_{-2}} - 0.44\underset{(-3.5)}{\Delta DJ_{-2}} + 0.05\underset{(0.6)}{\Delta PROF_{-2}}$$
$$+ 8.14\underset{(6.1)}{\Delta XR_{AV}} + 0.003\underset{(0.8)}{\Delta POP} + 0.10\underset{(1.8)}{\boldsymbol{\Delta}\mathbf{GDP_{REAL(-3)}}}$$
$$R^2 = 94.0\ \%, DW = 2.2, MSE = 30.63 \qquad (6.16.Alt)$$

Here again, generally, the coefficient estimates are robust to the change in model specification, dropping the borrowing variable. The deficit variable continues to show a strong negative relationship to investment spending.

Retesting the 2SLS same model except the unemployment rate is used as a business cycle control.

Model 6.17 2SLS estimates of crowd out and business borrowing on investment spending, unemployment used as business cycle control

(Endogenous and Instrumented: Population: Wald Test $F = 1.96$)). Sargan Test ($NR^2 = 8.67$) (Weak Instrument)

$$\underset{(t=)}{\Delta I_T} = +0.28\underset{(7.4)}{\Delta ACC} + 0.28\underset{(3.9)}{\boldsymbol{\Delta}(\mathbf{T_T} - \mathbf{G_{T\&I}})} + 1.53\underset{(5.1)}{\Delta DEP}$$
$$+ 1.13\underset{(0.6)}{\Delta CAP_{-1}} - 4.22\underset{(-1.9)}{\Delta r_{-2}} - 0.42\underset{(-3.4)}{\Delta DJ_{-2}} - 0.08\underset{(-0.9)}{\Delta PROF_{-2}}$$
$$+ 4.64\underset{(2.7)}{\Delta XR_{AV}} + 0.002\underset{(0.4)}{\Delta POP} + 0.07\underset{(1.3)}{\boldsymbol{\Delta}\mathbf{I_{B(-1)}}} - 14.58\underset{(-2.1)}{\boldsymbol{\Delta}\mathbf{UNEM}}$$
$$R^2 = 94.4\ \%, DW = 1.7, MSE = 29.67 \qquad (6.17)$$

Again the deficit variable is significant. The borrowing variable is not, but remove the deficit from the model and the *t*-statistic on borrowing jumps to 3.4, again pointing to the multicollinearity problem as the fundamental cause for statistical insignificance of investment borrowing, not theoretical deficiency of the notion that access to borrowing affects investment spending.

Using the stronger instruments for POP and current period real GDP used in 6.13, results were similar. (The instruments used were all variables in the system, including X and ICC, subtracting UNEM and PR_0 and adding PR_{-2} and Υ_{-2}.). Results are shown in Eq. 6.17.Alt.

Model 6.17.Alt 2SLS estimates of crowd out and business borrowing on investment spending, unemployment used as business cycle control

(Endogenous and Instrumented: Population; Wald Test $F = 2.5$, But $T > 3.3$ For M2AV Variable; Sargan Test ($NR^2 = 10.50$) (Strong Instrument)

$$\underset{(t=)}{\Delta I_T} = +\underset{(6.6)}{0.30\Delta ACC} + \underset{(3.9)}{0.30\boldsymbol{\Delta}(\mathbf{T_T} - \mathbf{G_{T\&I}})} + \underset{(4.9)}{1.49\Delta DEP}$$
$$+ \underset{(0.8)}{1.79\Delta CAP_{-1}} - \underset{(-2.0)}{4.32\Delta r_{-2}} - \underset{(-3.6)}{0.40\ \Delta DJ_{-2}} - \underset{(-0.9)}{0.07\Delta PROF_{-2}}$$
$$+ \underset{(2.7)}{4.78\Delta XR_{AV}} + \underset{(0.5)}{0.002\Delta POP} + \underset{(1.5)}{0.08\boldsymbol{\Delta}\mathbf{I_{B(-1)}}} - \underset{(-0.6)}{8.01\ \boldsymbol{\Delta}\mathbf{UNEM}}$$
$$R^2 = 93.9\ \%, DW = 1.8, MSE = 30.89 \qquad (6.17.Alt)$$

Here, the negative relationship of the deficit to investment spending is again seen, but whether there is an independent effect of borrowing on spending when the deficit is controlled for is not clear: results show only marginal statistical significance (15 % level) for the borrowing variable.

Model 6.17.Alt.a 2SLS estimates of crowd out and business borrowing on investment spending, using current period DJ and profits, unemployment used as business cycle control

(Endogenous & Instrumented: ACC (Wald $F = 8.8$, but CAP_{-1} $t = -4.2$), DEP: (Wald Test $F = 18.5$), POP: (Wald Test $F = 11.6$), DJ_0 (Wald Test $F = 8.6$, but $(T - G)$ $t = 4.6$), $Prof_0$ (Wald Test $F = 7.6$, but $M2_{AV}$ $t = 3.6$ and POP_{-1} $t = 3.5$). XR_{AV} (Wald $F = 11.6$); Sargan Test ($NR^2 = 8.5 < X^2_{(.95,17)} = 27.6$)
(Strong Instrument)

$$\underset{(t=)}{\Delta I_T} = +\underset{(3.1)}{0.40\Delta ACC} + \underset{(3.1)}{0.30\boldsymbol{\Delta}(\mathbf{T_T} - \mathbf{G_{T\&I}})} + \underset{(1.1)}{0.72\Delta DEP}$$
$$+ \underset{(1.6)}{6.20\Delta CAP_{-1}} - \underset{(-0.3)}{0.93\Delta r_{-2}} - \underset{(-0.1)}{0.03\ \Delta DJ_0} + \underset{(1.7)}{0.13\Delta PROF_0}$$
$$+ \underset{(2.1)}{6.60\Delta XR_{AV}} + \underset{(1.1)}{0.007\Delta POP} + \underset{(1.3)}{.09\boldsymbol{\Delta}\mathbf{I_{B(-1)}}} - \underset{(-0.2)}{2.17\ \boldsymbol{\Delta}\mathbf{UNEM}}$$
$$R^2 = 92.6\ \%, DW = 2.1, MSE = 34.41 \qquad (6.17.Alt.a)$$

And the Alt.a2 strong instrument form is

Model 6.17.Alt.a2 2SLS estimates of crowd out and business borrowing on investment spending, using current period DJ and profits, alternative endogeneity method, unemployment used as business cycle control

(Endogenous: and Instrumented: Depreciation: Wald Test $F = 21.5$), DJ_0 (Instrumented: Wald Test $F = 8.9$, but $t = 3.4$ for $(T - G)$, and $Prof_0$

(Instrumented: Wald Test $F = 6.0$, But $t = 5.3$ for $(T - G)$; Meet Wald Strong Instrument Criteria). Sargan Test ($NR^2 = 4.0 < X^2_{(.95,15)} = 25.0$) (Strong Instrument)

$$\underset{(t=)}{\Delta I_T} = +\underset{(3.2)}{0.25\Delta ACC} + \underset{(4.3)}{0.34\boldsymbol{\Delta}(\mathbf{T_T} - \mathbf{G_{T\&I}})} + \underset{(0.6)}{0.36\Delta DEP}$$
$$+ \underset{(0.8)}{2.34\Delta CAP_{-1}} + \underset{(0.5)}{2.81\Delta r_{-2}} - \underset{(-0.7)}{0.33\,\Delta DJ_0} + \underset{(2.2)}{0.43\Delta PROF_0}$$
$$+ \underset{(2.2)}{6.93\Delta XR_{AV}} + \underset{(1.8)}{0.01\Delta POP} + \underset{(1.5)}{0.22\boldsymbol{\Delta}\mathbf{I_{B(-1)}}} + \underset{(0.1)}{1.52\boldsymbol{\Delta}\mathbf{UNEM}}$$
$$R^2 = 90.3\ \%, DW = 1.8, MSE = 39.34 \qquad \text{(Eq.6.17.Alt.a2)}$$

Retesting the main 6.17 model but without the borrowing variable included, we get

Model 6.18 2SLS estimates of crowd out on investment spending W/O business borrowing variable in model, unemployment used as business cycle control

(Endogenous: Population (Instrumented: Wald Test $F = 2.13$, But $t > 3.3$ For One Variable)). Sargan Test ($NR^2 = 9.18$) (Strong Instrument)

$$\underset{(t=)}{\Delta I_T} = +\underset{(7.6)}{0.30\Delta ACC} + \underset{(5.5)}{0.31\boldsymbol{\Delta}(\mathbf{T_T} - \mathbf{G_{T\&I}})} + \underset{(5.9)}{1.70\Delta DEP}$$
$$+ \underset{(0.8)}{1.48\Delta CAP_{-1}} - \underset{(-2.3)}{5.23\Delta r_{-2}} - \underset{(-4.3)}{0.48\,\Delta DJ_{-2}} - \underset{(-0.2)}{0.02\Delta PROF_{-2}}$$
$$+ \underset{(3.6)}{5.61\Delta XR_{AV}} + \underset{(0.1)}{0.001\Delta POP} \quad \underset{(-2.3)}{16.07\,\boldsymbol{\Delta}\mathbf{UNEM}}$$
$$R^2 = 94.1\ \%, DW = 1.9, MSE = 30.02 \qquad \text{(Eq.6.18)}$$

And with a slightly stronger instrument:

Model 6.18.Alt 2SLS estimates of crowd out W/O business borrowing on investment spending, unemployment used as business cycle control

(Endogenous: Population (Instrumented: Wald Test $F = 2.78$, But One Variable $M2_{AV}$ Meets Wald $t > 3.3$ Criteria). Sargan Test ($NR^2 = 11.22$) (Strong Instrument)

$$\underset{(t=)}{\Delta I_T} = +\underset{(6.0)}{0.32\Delta ACC} + \underset{(5.1)}{0.34\boldsymbol{\Delta}(\mathbf{T_T} - \mathbf{G_{T\&I}})} + \underset{(5.7)}{1.64\Delta DEP}$$
$$+ \underset{(0.9)}{2.27\Delta CAP_{-1}} - \underset{(-2.5)}{5.47\Delta r_{-2}} - \underset{(-4.7)}{0.46\,\Delta DJ_{-2}} - \underset{(-0.1)}{0.01\Delta PROF_{-2}}$$
$$+ \underset{(3.4)}{5.89\Delta XR_{AV}} + \underset{(0.2)}{0.001\Delta POP} - \underset{(-0.6)}{8.83\,\boldsymbol{\Delta}\mathbf{UNEM}}$$
$$R^2 = 94.0\ \%, DW = 2.0, MSE = 30.28 \qquad \text{(Eq.6.18.Alt)}$$

Finally, we test the investment spending model without any business cycle phase control variable

Model 6.19 2SLS estimates of crowd out with business borrowing on investment spending

(Endogenous: Population (Instrumented: Wald Test $F = 1.95$)). Sargan Test ($NR^2 = 11.90$) (Weak Instrument)

$$\begin{aligned} \Delta I_T = {} & \underset{(t=)}{} +\underset{(8.1)}{0.31\Delta ACC} + \underset{(4.9)}{0.33\boldsymbol{\Delta}(\mathbf{T_T} - \mathbf{G_{T\&I}})} + \underset{(4.8)}{1.53\Delta DEP} \\ & + \underset{(1.5)}{2.67\Delta CAP_{-1}} - \underset{(-2.1)}{4.56\Delta r_{-2}} - \underset{(-3.3)}{0.37\Delta DJ_{-2}} - \underset{(-0.9)}{0.07\Delta PROF_{-2}} \\ & + \underset{(3.0)}{4.93\Delta XR_{AV}} + \underset{(0.3)}{0.001\Delta POP} + \underset{(1.6)}{0.09\boldsymbol{\Delta}\mathbf{I_B}} \\ R^2 = {} & 93.9\ \%, DW = 1.8, MSE = 30.51 \end{aligned} \qquad \text{(Eq.6.19)}$$

Using the stronger instruments previously used in 6.13.Alt, 14.Alt, 17. Alt and 18.Alt, we get

Model 6.19.Alt 2SLS estimates of crowd out with business borrowing on investment spending

(Endogenous: Population (Instrumented: Wald Test $F = 2.45$, But One-Variable $M2_{AV}$ Has $t > 3.3$, Meeting Wald Criteria)). Sargan Test ($NR^2 = 10.35$) (Strong Instrument)

$$\begin{aligned} \Delta I_T = {} & \underset{(t=)}{} +\underset{(8.1)}{0.31\Delta ACC} + \underset{(4.9)}{0.33\boldsymbol{\Delta}(\mathbf{T_T} - \mathbf{G_{T\&I}})} + \underset{(4.7)}{1.49\Delta DEP} \\ & + \underset{(1.2)}{2.63\Delta CAP_{-1}} - \underset{(-2.1)}{4.50\Delta r_{-2}} - \underset{(-3.3)}{0.37\Delta DJ_{-2}} - \underset{(-0.9)}{0.07\Delta PROF_{-2}} \\ & + \underset{(3.0)}{4.94\Delta XR_{AV}} + \underset{(0.5)}{0.002\Delta POP} + \underset{(1.7)}{0.09\boldsymbol{\Delta}\mathbf{I_B}} \\ R^2 = {} & 93.9\ \%, DW = 1.8, MSE = 30.51 \end{aligned} \qquad \text{(6.19.Alt)}$$

Results using stronger instruments are virtually identical. Testing the current period Tobin's q and Profits model, we get

Model 6.19.Alt.a 2SLS estimates of crowd out and business borrowing on investment spending

(Endogenous & instrumented: ACC (Wald $F = 11.7$), POP: (Wald Test $F = 14.1$), DJ_0 (Wald Test $F = 9.4$, but $(T-G)$ $t = 4.1$), $PROF_0$ (Wald Test $F = 6.4$, but $M2_{AV}$ $t = 3.4$ and DJ_{-2} $t = -4.0$). Sargan Test ($NR^2 = 4.0 < X^2_{(.95,13)} = 22.4$) (Strong Instrument)

$$\underset{(t=)}{\Delta I_T} = +0.24\underset{(1.9)}{\Delta \text{ACC}} + 0.26\underset{(3.1)}{\boldsymbol{\Delta}(\mathbf{T_T} - \mathbf{G_{T\&I}})} + 0.47\underset{(0.6)}{\Delta \text{DEP}}$$
$$+ 1.74\underset{(0.5)}{\Delta \text{CAP}_{-1}} - 3.15\underset{(-1.0)}{\Delta \text{r}_{-2}} + 0.26\underset{(0.6)}{\Delta \text{DJ}_0} + 0.26\underset{(2.4)}{\Delta \text{PROF}_0}$$
$$+ 6.44\underset{(2.4)}{\Delta \text{XR}_{\text{AV}}} + 0.006\underset{(1.1)}{\Delta \text{POP}} + .13\underset{(1.8)}{\boldsymbol{\Delta}\mathbf{I}_{\mathbf{B}(-1)}}$$
$$R^2 = 91.4\%, \text{DW} = 2.2, \text{MSE} = 36.61 \qquad (6.19.\text{Alt.a})$$

And using the Alta2 strong instrument form we get

Model 6.19.Alt.a2 2SLS estimates of crowd out and business borrowing on investment spending

(Endogenous & instrumented: DJ_0 (Wald Test $F = 8.9$, but $(T-G)$ $t = 3.4$), $PROF_0$ (Wald Test $F = 6.0$, but DJ_{-2} $t = -5.3$). Sargan Test ($NR^2 = 5.0 < X^2_{(.95,13)} = 22.4$)

$$\underset{(t=)}{\Delta I_T} = +0.24\underset{(4.2)}{\Delta \text{ACC}} + 0.33\underset{(4.3)}{\boldsymbol{\Delta}(\mathbf{T_T} - \mathbf{G_{T\&I}})} + 0.35\underset{(0.6)}{\Delta \text{DEP}}$$
$$+ 2.16\underset{(1.1)}{\Delta \text{CAP}_{-1}} + 2.80\underset{(0.5)}{\Delta \text{r}_{-2}} - 0.33\underset{(-0.7)}{\Delta \text{DJ}_0} + 0.43\underset{(2.3)}{\Delta \text{PROF}_0}$$
$$+ 6.89\underset{(2.5)}{\Delta \text{XR}_{\text{AV}}} + 0.01\underset{(1.9)}{\Delta \text{POP}} + 0.22\underset{(1.6)}{\boldsymbol{\Delta}\mathbf{I}_{\mathbf{B}(-1)}}$$
$$R^2 = 90.4\ \%, \text{DW} = 1.8, \text{MSE} = 38.71 \qquad (6.19.\text{Alt.a2})$$

Without a borrowing variable included among the explanatory variables, the same model yields the following test results:

Model 6.20 2SLS estimates of crowd out W/O business borrowing on investment spending

(Endogenous: Population (Instrumented: Wald Test $F = 2.12$); Sargan Test ($NR^2 = 11.60$) (Weak Instrument)

$$\underset{(t=)}{\Delta I_T} = +0.34\underset{(9.4)}{\Delta \text{ACC}} + 0.37\underset{(6.6)}{\boldsymbol{\Delta}(\mathbf{T_T} - \mathbf{G_{T\&I}})} + 1.68\underset{(5.9)}{\Delta \text{DEP}}$$
$$+ 3.29\underset{(1.9)}{\Delta \text{CAP}_{-1}} - 5.85\underset{(-2.5)}{\Delta \text{r}_{-2}} - 0.44\underset{(-4.5)}{\Delta \text{DJ}_{-2}} - 0.00\underset{(-0.0)}{\Delta \text{PROF}_{-2}}$$
$$+ 6.18\underset{(4.2)}{\Delta \text{XR}_{\text{AV}}} + 0.000\underset{(0.0)}{\Delta \text{POP}}$$
$$R^2 = 93.5\%, \text{DW} = 2.0, \text{MSE} = 31.12 \qquad (6.20)$$

Using the stronger instruments, the results become:

Model 6.20.Alt 2SLS estimates of crowd out w/o business borrowing on investment spending

(Endogenous: Population (Instrumented: Wald Test $F = 2.69$, But $t > 3.3$ On $M2_{AV}$); Sargan Test ($NR^2 = 11.00$) (Strong Instrument)

$$\underset{(t=)}{\Delta I_T} = +\underset{(9.3)}{0.34\Delta ACC} + \underset{(6.6)}{0.38\boldsymbol{\Delta}(\mathbf{T_T} - \mathbf{G_{T\&I}})} + \underset{(5.7)}{1.65\Delta DEP}$$
$$+ \underset{(1.8)}{3.26\Delta CAP_{-1}} - \underset{(-2.5)}{5.82\Delta r_{-2}} - \underset{(-4.5)}{0.44\,\Delta DJ_{-2}} - \underset{(-0.0)}{0.00\Delta PROF_{-2}}$$
$$+ \underset{(4.2)}{6.20\Delta XR_{AV}} + \underset{(0.1)}{0.001\Delta POP}$$
$$R^2 = 93.5\ \%, DW = 2.0, MSE = 31.12 \qquad (6.20.\text{Alt})$$

6.2.2 *2SLS Investment Spending Conclusions Summarized, Compared to OLS*

Below in Table 6.6 we present a summary of 2SLS test results on the relationship of government deficits to investment spending (Eqs. 6.13–6.20, including both weak and strong instrument variants).

OLS results for the same structural models are repeated from above for comparison

Note on Table 6.6: 2SLS Instruments were used for all Hausman-endogenous variables. They also passed Sargan test, indicating they were not endogenously related to the dependent variable. Those marked "Alt" also passed the Wald test, indicating they were not weak instruments for the variable they replaced. The population variable was the one that initially had a weak instrument, except in one case, where depreciation also had a weak instrument (See 6.17). Alt.a and Alt.a2 refer to models using the zero lag versions of DJ sand PROF. Alt2 refers to the alternate form of endogeneity testing and strong instrument development done.

All the tests show a very strong negative, statistically significant inverse relationship between the government deficit and investment spending, even controlling for the level of the economy. The results indicated investment spending declined \$0.33 per dollar of deficit incurred (Strong Instrument 2SLS).

The same tests also showed some evidence that borrowing is a separate factor affecting investment spending, and not just a financial manifestation of the desire to invest due to other investment determinants. However, the statistical significance of this finding was marginal in about half the cases, and hence, the strength of this independent effect finding was not as strong as with consumption spending examined earlier. Evidence suggests that perhaps the only reason it does not show an even stronger relationship with spending controlling for all these factors, is that borrowing is highly negatively collinear with collinear with government deficits (r = -.78), and that our model is somewhat flawed as a method of determining the independent effects of borrowing, since holding deficits constant while estimating borrowing's effect amounts to holding a major source of borrowing fluctuation itself constant. One cannot find a statistical relationship where there is no movement. Then again, it may mean that investment plans, to some degree, can be financed from other sources (perhaps profits) when borrowing is unavailable.

The similarity of findings for different instruments suggests the model results are robust to moderate changes in the components of the instruments used. The instruments, of course, are weighted averages, obtained by OLS regression of their component variables on the endogenous variable for which the instrument is being developed.

Note also that these results, whichever set of 2SLS models are used, are nearly identical to each other and to the OLS results

6.2.3 2SLS Estimates of Crowd Out Effects on Investment Borrowing

In this section, the direct effects of government deficits on borrowing are tested using the same four business cycle effects models used to test spending. Testing the sensitivity of business borrowing to changes in the deficit, controlling for other determinants of borrowing, provides a way of directly testing whether the mechanism through which deficits affect spending is "crowd out", that is, reductions in loanable funds available to the private sector. The four borrowing models differ only in the choice of a variable used to control for the effects of the business cycle on deficits and borrowing. The business cycle controls used are current real GDP, real GDP lagged three periods, the unemployment rate and no control at all. The unemployment rate and three- lag income variables are the measures of the business cycle found most systematically related to the deficit. Current year GDP was not found to have any systematic relationship with the current year deficit, and is presented here simply for reference, though certainly it is a good measure of the business cycle.

Because borrowing is now the dependent variable, no borrowing variable is included as an explanatory variable. The hypothesized determinants of business borrowing are the same as used in the investment spending models. We assume that the demand for borrowed money (loanable funds) by businesses reflects a desire to spend on investment goods. To this initial

Table 6.6 2SLS investment spending findings summarized, compared to OLS

2SLS Spending Model#	*Deficit Var.* $\Delta(T_T - G_{T\&I})$ *β (t-stat.)*	*Bor. Var.* $\Delta(I_B)$ *β (t-stat.)*	*Bus. Cycle control*	*OLS Spending Model#*	*Deficit Var.* $\Delta(T_T - G_{T\&I})$ *β (t-stat.)*	*Bor. Var.* $\Delta(I_B)$ *β (t-stat.)*
6.13	0.30 (4.6)	0.09 (1.9)	GDP $_{Real(0)}$	6.1	.27 (4.5)	0.11 (2.5)
6.13.Alt	0.31 (4.5)	0.09 (1.9)		6.1.a	.27 (3.4)	0.13 (2.4)
6.13.Alt. a2	0.31 (3.9)	0.14 (2.2)				
6.14	0.33 (7.1)			6.2	.33 (7.0)	
6.14. Alt	0.36 (6.8)					
6.15	0.37 (5.3)	0.12 (2.2)	GDP$_{Real(-3)}$	6.3	.34 (5.2)	0.10 (1.8)
6.15. Alt	0.37 (5.1)	0.10 (2.1)		6.4	.38 (6.3)	
6.15.Alt. a	0.33 (4.0)	0.14 (1.9)		6.3.a	.34 (4.1)	0.14 (2.3)
6.15.Alt. a2	0.37 (3.1)	0.16 (1.5)				
6.16	0.39 (6.9)					
6.16. Alt	0.42 (6.8)					
6.17	0.28 (3.9)	0.07 (1.3)	Unem. Rate	6.5	.29 (4.0)	0.08 (1.5)
6.17. Alt	0.30 (3.9)	0.08 (1.5)		6.6	.32 (5.6)	
6.17.Alt. a	0.30 (3.1)	0.09 (1.3)		6.5.a	.28 (2.8)	0.11 (1.7)
6.17.Alt. a2	0.34 (4.2)	0.22 (1.5)				
6.18	0.31 (5.5)					
6.18. Alt	0.34 (5.1)					
6.19	0.33 (4.9)	0.09 (1.6)	None	6.7	.33 (5.0)	0.09 (1.8)
6.19. Alt.	0.33 (4.9)	0.09 (1.7)		6.8	.39 (6.7)	
6.19.Alt. a	0.26 (3.1)	0.13 (1.8)		6.7.a	.32 (4.1)	0.13 (2.1)
6.19.Alt. a2	0.33 (4.3)	0.22 (1.6)				
6.20	0.37 (6.6)					
6.20. Alt	0.38 (6.6)					
Average	0.34 (5.6)	0.09 (1.8) 2SLS weak instr.	Average	0.33 (5.5)	0.10 (1.9)—OLS (w/o "a")	
Average	0.35 (5.5)	0.09 (1.8) 2SLS str. instr.(Alt)				

(*continued*)

Table 6.6 (continued)

2SLS Spending Model#	*Deficit Var.* $\Delta(T_T - G_{T\&I})$ *β (t-stat.)*	*Bor. Var.* $\Delta(I_B)$ *β (t-stat.)*	*Bus. Cycle control*	*OLS Spending Model#*	*Deficit Var.* $\Delta(T_T - G_{T\&I})$ *β (t-stat.)*	*Bor. Var.* $\Delta(I_B)$ *β (t-stat.)*
Average	0.30 (3.4)	0.12 (1.7) 2SLS str. Instr (Alt.a)	Average	0.30 (3.6)	0.13 (2.1) ("a" only)	
Average	0.34 (3.9)	0.19 (1.7) 2SLS str. Instr (Alt.a2)				

hypothesis as to what drives the demand for borrowing, a variable is added to represent the effect of the money supply on the pool of loanable funds. The monetary variable most systematically related to business borrowing was the current year growth of the savings (non-M1) components of M2: that is, savings accounts, CDs, money market deposit accounts and individually held money market mutual funds. The variable is denoted as Real (M2−M1). This suggests that banks' principal role in providing loanable funds to borrowers is to transfer recent savings (converted to financial assets) accumulated by the population as a whole. The central bank's role of increasing bank lendable reserves (via open market purchases of bank-owned bonds using M1) seems less important than this general population savings-to-borrowers process of meeting borrower demand. If increases in bank reserves due to open market operations had been the major factor, we would expect to see Ml changes more closely related to changes in borrowing. None of our models showed Ml to be statistically significant when it was added as a separate variable to the model. But M2 entered most significantly when only its non-M1 savings components were used.

The borrowing variable used as the dependent variable is annual business borrowing (current period average). The investment spending models previously examined used the same variable, lagged one period, as a determinant of investment spending.

Methodologically, we again undertake Hausman first-stage regression tests using all variables in the investment and consumption structural models not suspected of endogeneity as the first-stage regressors used to test suspect variables for endogeneity. The additional variable Real (M2-M1) was also used so that we had a complete set of variables used in our structural models. In addition, exports and the current year index of consumer confidence were also used as they tended to increase instrument strength. These variables were regressed against each of the initially hypothesized "suspect" endogenous variables (Y_0, $Y\text{-}T_T$, $T_{T\text{-}GT\&I}$, DEP and UNEM) to determine which in fact were endogenous at a statistically significant level. Then, one by one, each of the originally hypothesized exogenous variables was also regressed against the remaining hypothesized exogenous/lagged variables to determine empirically whether their original assumption of non-endogeneity was warranted.

In the second stage of the Hausman procedure, a variable representing residuals from each first-stage regression of the Hausman procedure was added to the structural investment borrowing model being tested. If found statistically significant, it is treated as endogenous in that model, and an instrument is developed to replace it. The instrument is the systematic portion of the regression of all variables found non-Hausman-endogenous on the endogenous variable.

That said, results for all four borrowing models (using $DJ_{-1}$and $Profits_{-2}$) indicated no variable was Hausman-endogenous with borrowing. Hence, OLS is the appropriate technique here. These OLS tests were already done in Eq. 6.9–6.12 and are not repeated here.

For the revised borrowing model, which used current period profits ($PROF_0$) instead of $PROF_{-2}$ above, a variable was found endogenous with investment borrowing only in the business cycle model using unemployment as a control. In the other business cycle models tested (GDP_{-3} and no control), no variables were found to be Hausman-endogenous with borrowing. (GDP_0 was not tested because it was not found to be related to current period deficits, hence would serve poorly as a control for business cycle effects on the deficit.) A strong instrument 2SLS version of this unemployment business cycle control model is shown below.

Model **6.21.a** 2SLS Estimates of Crowd Out on Business Borrowing, DJ_{-1} and $PROF_0$ Used

(Endogenous and Instrumented: Unemployment Rate: Wald Test $F = 14.65$), Sargan Test ($NR^2 = 25.5 < X^2(.95, 19) = 30.1$)

$$\underset{(t=)}{\Delta I_B} = \underset{(0.1)}{0.02\Delta ACC} + \underset{(3.3)}{1.11\boldsymbol{\Delta}(\mathbf{T_T} - \mathbf{G_{T\&I}})} - \underset{(-1.6)}{3.65\Delta DEP}$$
$$+ \underset{(0.5)}{5.52\Delta CAP_{-1}} + \underset{(0.6)}{5.53\Delta r_{-2}} + \underset{(0.2)}{0.09\,\Delta DJ_{-1}} + \underset{(3.8)}{1.01\Delta PROF_{-0}}$$
$$+ \underset{(3.0)}{19.70\Delta XR_{AV}} + \underset{(1.8)}{0.035\Delta POP} + \underset{(0.6)}{0.13\,\Delta RealM2 - M1}$$
$$+ \underset{(3.4)}{119.82\,\Delta UNEM} \quad R^2 = 50.9\ \%, DW = 1.8, MSE = 132.00 \tag{6.23.a}$$

We presume the sign on the unemployment rate variable indicates poor levels of sales and profits are periods in which businesses need to borrow more to cover costs.

6.2.4 *2SLS Business Borrowing Conclusions Summarized, Compared to OLS*

Table 6.7 summarizes the findings of models testing the effect of crowd out on business borrowing.

As was the case with spending models, *the borrowing models evidence is overwhelming in support of the conclusion that there is a systematic, highly significant, negative relationship between government deficits and business borrowing, and that this relationship is nearly a one-to-one relationship, where business borrowing declines close to $1.00 for every $1.00 increase in the deficit.*

6.3 OLS and 2SLS Spending and Borrowing Findings Summarized

Table 6.8 and 6.9 below presents a summary of all 40 spending and borrowing model test findings

All one-variable deficit/investment spending tests show a very strong negative, statistically significant negative relationship between the government deficit and investment spending, even controlling for the level of the economy. The same tests also showed some evidence that borrowing is a separate factor affecting investment spending, and not just a financial manifestation of the desire to invest due to other investment determinants. However, the statistical significance of this finding was marginal, and hence, the strength of this independent effect finding was not as strong as with consumption data examined earlier. Evidence suggests that perhaps the only reason it does not show an even stronger relationship with spending controlling for all these factors is that borrowing is highly negatively collinear with collinear with government deficits ($r = -0.78$), and that our model is somewhat flawed as a method of determining the independent effects of borrowing, since holding deficits constant while estimating borrowing's effect, in large part, amounts to holding borrowing itself constant. One cannot find a statistical relationship where there is no movement to measure.

The similarity of findings for different 2SLS instruments used suggests the model results are robust to moderate changes in the components of the instruments used to deal with the endogeneity problem. The instruments are weighted averages of their component variables, obtained by OLS regression on the endogenous variable; this process constitutes the first stage of the 2SLS process.

Note also that these results, whichever set of 2SLS models are used, are nearly identical to each other and to the OLS results

As was the case with spending models, *in all five borrowing models, evidence is overwhelming in support of the conclusion that there is a systematic, highly statistically significant, negative relationship between government deficits and business borrowing, and that this relationship is nearly a one-to-one relationship, where business borrowing declines approximately $1.00 for every $1.00 increase in the deficit.*

Table 6.7 Business borrowing model conclusions summarized, compared to OLS

2SLS Model#	$\Delta(T_T - G_{T\&I})$ β (t-*stat.*)	*Bus. cycle control*	*2SLS Method*	*OLS Model#*	$\Delta(T_T - G_{T\&I})$ β (t-*stat.*)
NA		GDP $_{Real(0)}$		6.9	0.98 (3.6)
NA		GDP $_{Real(-3)}$		6.10	0.87 (3.1)
NA		Unem. Rate		6.11	1.07 (3.2)
6.21.a	1.11 (3.3)		Strong Instr.	6.12	0.92 (3.6)
NA		None			
Average	1.11 (3.3)			Average	0.96 (3.4)

Table 6.8 Summary of all investment OLS and 2SLS spending and borrowing findings

2SLS spending models#	*Deficit Var.* $\Delta(T_T - G_{T\&I})$ β (t-stat.)	*Bor. Var.* $\Delta(I_B)$ β (t-stat.)	*Bus. cycle control*	*OLS spending Model#*	*Deficit Var.* $\Delta(T_T - G_{T\&I})$ β (t-stat.)	*Bor. Var.* $\Delta(I_B)$ β (t-stat.)
Spending models						
6.13	0.30 (4.6)	0.09 (1.9)	GDP $_{Real(0)}$	6.1	0.27 (4.5)	0.11 (2.5)
6.13.Alt	0.31 (4.5)	0.09 (1.9)		6.1.a	0.27 (3.4)	0.13 (2.4)
6.13.Alt. a2	0.31 (3.9)	0.14 (2.2)				
6.14	0.33 (7.1)			6.2	0.33 (7.0)	
6.14. Alt	0.36 (6.8)					
6.15	0.37 (5.3)	0.12 (2.2)	GDP $_{Real(-3)}$	6.3	0.34 (5.2)	0.10 (1.8)
6.15. Alt	0.37 (5.1)	0.10 (2.1)		6.4	0.38 (6.3)	
6.15.Alt.a	0.33 (4.0)	0.14 (1.9)		6.3.a	0.34 (4.1)	0.14 (2.3)
6.15.Alt. a2	0.37 (3.1)	0.16 (1.5)				
6.16	0.39 (6.9)					
6.16. Alt	0.42 (6.8)					
6.17	0.28 (3.9)	0.07 (1.3)	Unem. Rate	6.5	0.29 (4.0)	0.08 (1.5)
6.17. Alt	0.30 (3.9)	0.08 (1.5)		6.6	0.32 (5.6)	
6.17.Alt.a	0.30 (3.1)	0.09 (1.3)		6.5.a	0.28 (2.8)	0.11 (1.7)
6.17.Alt. a2	0.34 (4.2)	0.22 (1.5)				
6.18	0.31 (5.5)					

(*continued*)

Table 6.8 (continued)

2SLS spending models#	*Deficit Var.* $\Delta(T_T - G_{T\&I})$ *β (t-stat.)*	*Bor. Var.* $\Delta(I_B)$ *β (t-stat.)*	*Bus. cycle control*	*OLS spending Model#*	*Deficit Var.* $\Delta(T_T - G_{T\&I})$ *β (t-stat.)*	*Bor. Var.* $\Delta(I_B)$ *β (t-stat.)*
Spending models						
6.18. Alt	0.34 (5.1)					
6.19	0.33 (4.9)	0.09 (1.6)	None	6.7	0.33 (5.0)	0.09 (1.8)
6.19. Alt.	0.33 (4.9)	0.09 (1.7)		6.8	0.39 (6.7)	
6.19.Alt.a	0.26 (3.1)	0.13 (1.8)		6.7.a	0.32 (4.1)	0.13 (2.1)
6.19.Alt. a2	0.33 (4.3)	0.22 (1.6)				
6.20	0.37 (6.6)					
6.20. Alt	0.38 (6.6)					
Average	.34 (5.6)	.09 (1.8) 2SLS weak instr.	Average	0.33 (5.5)	0.10 (1.9) - OLS (w/o "a")	
Average	.35 (5.5)	.09 (1.8) 2SLS str. instr.(Alt)				
Average	.30 (3.4)	.12 (1.7) 2SLS str.Instr (Alt.a)	Average	0.30 (3.6)	0.13 (2.1) ("a" only)	
Average	.34 (3.9)	.19 (1.7) 2SLS str.Instr (Alt. a2)				

Results for investment spending and borrowing show little support for the hypothesis that it is just normal business cycle effects, not crowd out, that cause the observed negative relationship between deficits and investment spending or borrowing.

Table 6.9 Summary of findings for 5 borrowing models

2SLS Model#	$\Delta(T_T\text{-}G_{T\&I})$ β (t-*stat.)*	*Bus. cycle control*	*2SLS method*	*OLS Model#*	$\Delta(T_T\text{-}G_{T\&I})$ β (t-*stat.)*
Borrowing Models:					
NA		GDP $_{Real(0)}$	Strong Instr.	6.9	0.98 (3.6)
NA		GDP $_{Real(-3)}$		6.10	0.87 (3.1)
NA		Unem. Rate		6.11	1.07 (3.2)
6.21.a	1.11 (3.3)	Unem. Rate			
NA		None		6.12	0.92 (3.6)
Average	1.11 (3.3)			Average	0.96 (3.4)

6.4 Robustness of Findings To Period Sampled

In Table 6.10 below, we examine the robustness of our findings by testing the same spending and borrowing models over different four sample periods.

Investment spending and borrowing results are robust for differences in time period examined, and over time the average results indicate a dollar of deficit is related to a $0.82 reduction in business borrowing, and an average decline of $0.32 in investment spending. Businesses borrow for other reasons beside investment (e.g., cash flow issues), and this may explain the larger borrowing effect, but it may also indicate businesses have some flexibility in investment funding, for example, deciding the level of retained earnings to use in lieu of borrowing. A third possible reason is that government deficits that provide additional money to businesses used to finance previously planned spending that absent the stimulus would have been financed by borrowing. This would mean that in addition to reduction in business borrowing resulting directly from the deficit's crowd out effect, additional reductions would take place to the extent the deficit provided funds to businesses they otherwise would have borrowed. This study concludes business borrowing and investment spending findings are robust for (i.e., are consistent for)

- regression technique used (though 2SLS not required but once)
- the specific business cycle control variables included in the model tested
- the time period sampled.

Table 6.10 Robustness of investment models with respect to period sampled

Investment			*Investment*		
2SLS Spending Model 6.15Alt., 17Alt. (Current Year GDP Or No Control Used as Business Cycle Control)			*OLS Borrowing Model 6.11, 6.10. (Current Year Unemployment or GDP_{-3} Used as Business Cycle Control)*		
Sample period	*Using Unem. Deficit Var.* β (*t-stat.*)	*Using GDP_{-3} Deficit Var.* β (*t-stat.*)	*Sample period*	*Using Unem. Deficit Var.* β (*t-stat.*)	*Using GDP_{-3} Deficit Var.* β (*t-stat.*)
1960–2010	0.30 (3.9)	0.37 (5.1)	1960–2010	1.07 (3.2)	0.87 (3.1)
1970–2010	0.31 (3.7)	0.40 (5.6)	1970–2010	1.22 (3.2)	0.95 (3.1)
1960–2000	0.32 (3.9)	0.38 (5.0)	1960–2000	.70 (1.7)	0.50 (1.8)
1970–2000	0.37 (3.8)	0.45 (6.6)	1970–2000	1.04 (2.0)	0.60 (1.9)

Investment			*Investment*		
2SLS Spending Model 6.13Alt, 19Alt. (Current Year GDP Or No Control Used as Business Cycle Control)			*OLS Borrowing Model 6. 9, 6.12. (Current Year GDP Or No Control Used as Business Cycle Control)*		
Sample period	*Using GDP_0. Deficit Var.* β (*t-stat.*)	*No Control Deficit Var.* β (*t-stat.*)	*Sample period*	*Using GDP_0. Deficit Var.* β (*t-stat.*)	*No Control Deficit Var.* β (*t-stat.*)
1960–2010	0.30 (4.4)	0.33 (4.9)	1960–2010	0.98 (3.6)	0.92 (3.6)
1970–2010	0.33 (4.5)	0.36 (5.1)	1970–2010	0.55 (1.4)	1.01 (3.5)
1960–2000	0.31 (4.8)	0.36 (5.1)	1960–2000	0.66 (2.2)	0.50 (1.8)
1970–2000	0.37 (5.4)	0.43 (6.5)	1970–2000	0.91 (2.7)	0.61 (1.8)

6.5 Expected Robustness With Future Studies

Models that indicate the economy can be stimulated by government spending or tax cut deficits are usually derived from demand-driven models of how the economy behaves. Keynesian models are the most popular demand-driven models. This paper tests crowd out by inserting it into such models' consumption and investment functions. Results indicate the crowd out effect, though generally ignored in earlier studies, is real and offsets the stimulus effects of deficit-driven fiscal policy that Keynesian models are noted for. That is not to say there is anything fundamentally incorrect about Keynesian theory *as it is usually presented*, only that such presentations *are incomplete* without incorporating a deficit variable in the model to account for potential crowd out effects. Models tested here are such Keynesian models, and explain as much as 95 % of the variance in key macroeconomic variables over 50 years. Failure to include a variable in the model for crowd out effects of deficits has led to erroneous policy conclusions in the past regarding the positive stimulus effects deficits.

It was a relatively simple application of econometric science to macroeconomics that led to this finding, and it is reasonable to ask why it has taken so long for the answer to the question of whether crowd out offsets stimulus effects of deficits. Certainly the issue has been argued endlessly in the popular press for decades. Economists such as Solow and Mankiw have suggested that in retrospect, the change in economics in recent decades from a more scientific (or "engineering") approach of econometric modeling and testing to a more mathematically deductive, philosophical approach may not have been as successful as desired in helping us obtain answers to everyday economic problems. (Mankiw 2006, Solow 2010).

The exhaustiveness of the testing in this study, and the uniformity of findings resulting from it, suggest that in the future, other researchers, testing other reasonably well-specified structural models of consumption or investment or other time periods will almost certainly come up with similar conclusions.

CHAPTER 7

Test Results: Consumer Spending and Borrowing Models (Two-Variable Deficit)

Consumption test results of Chap. 5 indicated deficits were strongly related to the crowd out problem, but did not indicate whether the effects of government spending and tax deficits were the same or different. In this section, some of the same consumption spending and borrowing models used in consumption Chap. 5 are retested, except that the deficit components T_T and $G_{T\&I}$ are tested separately to determine if their effects are the same or different. Though these two variables appear to measure total government revenues and spending, not deficits, recall that in any one regression, our regression coefficients on these two variables indicate how any one of them affects consumer spending holding the other constant, that is, by changing the deficit.

Tests are run using either GDP lagged three periods, the unemployment rate as business cycle control variables or no business cycle control variable at all. Earlier tests showed no relationship between current period GDP and deficit size, so that model is not tested here. Borrowing models are tested further below. OLS and 2SLS results for each specific model are presented together here. In Chaps. 5 and 6, they were separated into different sections of the chapter.

Section 7.1 tests 6 OLS and 2SLS models of consumer spending, each using the two-variable definition of crowd out. Section 7.1.1 summarizes the six test results and finds that in all of them, both tax cut and spending crowd out variables had statistically significant negative effects on spending. Tax cut deficits had twice as large a negative effect on consumption as did spending deficits.

J.J. Heim, *Crowding Out Fiscal Stimulus*,
DOI 10.1007/978-3-319-45967-7_7

Section 7.2 tests 11 OLS and 2SLS models of consumer borrowing, each using the two-variable definition of crowd out. In 10 of the 11 tests, tax cut-caused deficits had significant negative effects on consumer borrowing, as did two of the 11 spending deficit tests. Tax cut deficits had a slightly larger adverse effect on borrowing than did spending deficits.

Detailed analysis of each of these tests is provided in the remainder of the chapter.

7.1 OLS and 2SLS Spending Models

Model 7.1 OLS standard consumer spending model, with borrowing included, GDP lagged three years used as business cycle control

(Hausman tests indicated no explanatory variables endogenous, So No 2SLS tests undertaken)

$$\begin{aligned}\underset{(t=)}{\Delta C_T} &= \underset{(11.4)}{0.50\Delta(Y - T_T)} + \underset{(11.4)}{0.54\boldsymbol{\Delta}(\mathbf{T}_\mathrm{T})} - \underset{(-3.7)}{0.26\boldsymbol{\Delta}(\mathbf{G}_{\mathrm{T\&I}})} \\ &- \underset{(-5.1)}{11.81\Delta \mathrm{PR}} + \underset{(5.3)}{0.42\,\Delta \mathrm{DJ}_{-2}} + \underset{(2.3)}{3.42\,\Delta \mathrm{XR}_{\mathrm{AV}}} - \underset{(-1.3)}{336.65\Delta \mathrm{POP}_{16}} \\ &+ \underset{(2.6)}{0.012\Delta \mathrm{POP}} + \underset{(1.3)}{0.36\Delta \mathrm{ICC}_{-1}} + \underset{(3.8)}{40.86\Delta \mathrm{M2}_{\mathrm{AV}}} \\ &+ \underset{(3.1)}{0.12\,\boldsymbol{\Delta}\mathbf{C}_{\mathbf{B2}}} + \underset{(1.1)}{0.04\,\boldsymbol{\Delta}\mathbf{GDP}_{\mathbf{Real}(-3)}} \quad \mathbf{R}^2 = 94.9\ \% \\ &\mathrm{D.W.} = 1.8\ \mathrm{MSE} = 25.45 \end{aligned} \quad (7.1)$$

Model 7.2 OLS standard consumer spending model, with borrowing included, unemployment rate used as business cycle control

(Hausman tests indicate XR_{av} and Pop_{16} variables endogenous. 2SLS tests provided in Eq. 7.2.a below.)

$$\begin{aligned}\underset{(t=)}{\Delta C_T} &= \underset{(15.4)}{0.57\Delta(Y - T_T)} + \underset{(12.2)}{0.63\boldsymbol{\Delta}(\mathbf{T}_\mathrm{T})} - \underset{(-4.5)}{0.31\boldsymbol{\Delta}(\mathbf{G}_{\mathrm{T\&I}})} \\ &- \underset{(-6.0)}{9.87\Delta \mathrm{PR}} + \underset{(5.8)}{0.45\,\Delta \mathrm{DJ}_{-2}} + \underset{(2.2)}{2.91\,\Delta \mathrm{XR}_{\mathrm{AV}}} - \underset{(-1.6)}{313.06\Delta \mathrm{POP}_{16}} \\ &+ \underset{(2.3)}{0.009\Delta \mathrm{POP}} + \underset{(2.6)}{0.64\Delta \mathrm{ICC}_{-1}} + \underset{(5.8)}{42.98\Delta \mathrm{M2}_{\mathrm{AV}}} \\ &+ \underset{(3.6)}{0.12\,\boldsymbol{\Delta}\mathbf{C}_{\mathbf{B2}}} + \underset{(3.4)}{21.72\,\boldsymbol{\Delta}\mathbf{UNEM}} \quad \mathbf{R}^2 = 95.6\ \% \\ &\mathrm{D.W.} = 1.9\ \mathrm{MSE} = 23.67 \end{aligned} \quad (7.2)$$

Model 7.2.a 2SLS standard consumer spending model, with borrowing included, unemployment rate used as business cycle control

(Hausman tests indicate XR_{AV} and POP_{16} variables endogenous (Instrumented: XR_{AV} Wald $F = 2.23$; POP_{16}: Wald $F = 5.90$, neither with a $t \geq 3.3$, so these are weak instruments; Sargan test $NR^2 = (51)(0.43) = 21.93$, $< X^2_{(95,18)} = 28.87$)

$$
\begin{aligned}
\underset{(t=)}{\Delta C_T} = {} & \underset{(13.0)}{0.58\Delta(Y - T_T)} + \underset{(14.4)}{0.63\mathbf{\Delta}(\mathbf{T}_\mathrm{T})} - \underset{(-3.7)}{0.28\mathbf{\Delta}(\mathbf{G}_{\mathrm{T\&I}})} \\
& - \underset{(-5.8)}{9.79\Delta \mathrm{PR}} + \underset{(5.4)}{0.46\,\Delta \mathrm{DJ}_{-2}} + \underset{(0.4)}{1.48\,\Delta \mathrm{XR}_{\mathrm{AV}}} - \underset{(-0.4)}{211.09\Delta \mathrm{POP}_{16}} \\
& + \underset{(1.8)}{0.008\Delta \mathrm{POP}} + \underset{(2.0)}{0.70\Delta \mathrm{ICC}_{-1}} + \underset{(4.8)}{40.96\Delta \mathrm{M2}_{\mathrm{AV}}} \\
& + \underset{(2.6)}{0.13\,\mathbf{\Delta C}_{\mathbf{B2}}} + \underset{(3.3)}{22.17\,\mathbf{\Delta UNEM}} \quad \mathbf{R}^2 = 95.5\,\% \\
& \mathrm{D.W.} = 1.9 \ \mathrm{MSE} = 23.98 \qquad (7.2.\mathrm{a})
\end{aligned}
$$

The initial instruments were developed regressing all non-endogenous right hand side variables in the C_T and I_T models, plus the current period exports and index of consumer confidence variables, on each of the two endogenous variables, following the same process used in Chaps. 5 and 6.

Since the instruments were weak, explaining relatively little variance in the endogenous variables, they were not good substitutes for the endogenous variables. Stronger Wald test instruments were developed. The same variables used to formulate the original (weak) instruments were used, but two additional variables were added: the lagged values of the two endogenous variables, that is, XR_{AV-1} and $POP16_{-1}$. Results are shown in model 7.2.Alt. below:

Model 7.2.a.Alt 2SLS standard consumer spending model, with borrowing included as a determinant of consumer spending, unemployment rate used as the business cycle control

(XR_{AV} And POP_{16} endogenous and (instrumented: XR_{AV}: Wald $F = 10.29$, POP_{16}: Wald $F = 1.90$, but with $t = 4.37$ for one component of the instrument so this is not a weak instrument; Sargan test $nR^2 = (51)(0.43) = 21.93$, $< X^2_{(95,20)} = 31.40$)

(Strong Instrument)

$$\underset{(t=)}{\Delta C_T} = \underset{(13.3)}{0.57\Delta(Y - T_T)} + \underset{(12.0)}{0.64\boldsymbol{\Delta}(\mathbf{T}_{\mathrm{T}})} - \underset{(-3.9)}{0.28\boldsymbol{\Delta}(\mathbf{G}_{\mathrm{T\&I}})}$$
$$- \underset{(-5.7)}{9.46\Delta \mathrm{PR}} + \underset{(5.8)}{0.45\,\Delta \mathrm{DJ}_{-2}} + \underset{(2.0)}{2.57\,\Delta \mathrm{XR}_{\mathrm{AV}}} - \underset{(-0.1)}{30.03\Delta \mathrm{POP}_{16}}$$
$$+ \underset{(1.8)}{0.009\Delta \mathrm{POP}} + \underset{(2.4)}{0.67\Delta \mathrm{ICC}_{-1}} + \underset{(6.3)}{41.97\Delta \mathrm{M2}_{\mathrm{AV}}}$$
$$+ \underset{(3.9)}{0.11\,\boldsymbol{\Delta}\mathbf{C}_{\mathrm{B2}}} + \underset{(3.0)}{22.12\,\boldsymbol{\Delta}\mathbf{UNEM}} \quad \mathbf{R}^2 = 95.4\%$$
$$\mathrm{D.W.} = 1.9\ \mathrm{MSE} = 24.34 \qquad (7.2.\mathrm{Alt})$$

(Lagging Unemployment one period gives it the theoretically appropriate negative sign (but statistically insignificant) and leaves the coefficients and statistical significance of the deficit variables only marginally changed: 0.57 (12.7) ΔT and −0.21 (−2.6) ΔG. A collinearity problem is affecting the sign of current period UNEM variable: the simple correlation between taxes and the unemployment rate is −0.76, the highest in the model. Remove the taxes variable from the model and the sign, coefficient and significance of the UNEM variable become −21.33 (−1.8). By comparison, the correlation between unemployment lagged one period and taxes is only −0.19.)

Both the 2SLS weak and strong instrument models using the unemployment rate provide virtually identical estimates of the effects of crowd out: weak (Tax = 0.63, Spending = −0.28, and strong (0.64, −0.28), and that these are very close to the OLS results (0.63,−0.31), which themselves are very similar to the OLS results (0.54,−0.26) using lagged GDP as the business cycle control. In short, despite the differences in test method employed, the results consistently indicate government deficits are strongly related to consumer spending.

Tax cut deficits were found to have about twice the adverse effect on consumer spending as government spending deficits. One explanation is that borrowing a dollar from banks to finance a dollar of tax cuts reduces consumer spending out of borrowed funds by a dollar. This is partially offset by the \$0.42–\$0.43 that is saved out of each dollar of tax cut the pool of loanable funds is augmented by the marginal propensity to save out of the tax cut, (1-MPC). Hence, from the consumption function data, we would predict only a \$0.57–\$58 increase in spending from the tax cut. This is close to the \$0.63–\$0.64 we actually obtained. Hence, the reduced borrowing of \$0.57–\$0.58, which represented reduced consumer spending, just offset the \$0.57–\$58 increase in spending that occurs because of the tax cut's effect of increasing disposable income. The spending deficit crowd out effect of $0.28 for the 2SLS tests may suggest the MPS for spending recipients is lower than the $0.41–$42 average implied by the disposable income coefficient (which averages business and consumer saving). Since much government spending is aimed toward lower income groups, the lower MPS implied may be reasonable.

Equation 7.2.a.Alt. Graphed: Actual Consumption Versus consumption Explained By Model 7.2.a Alt. 1960–2010

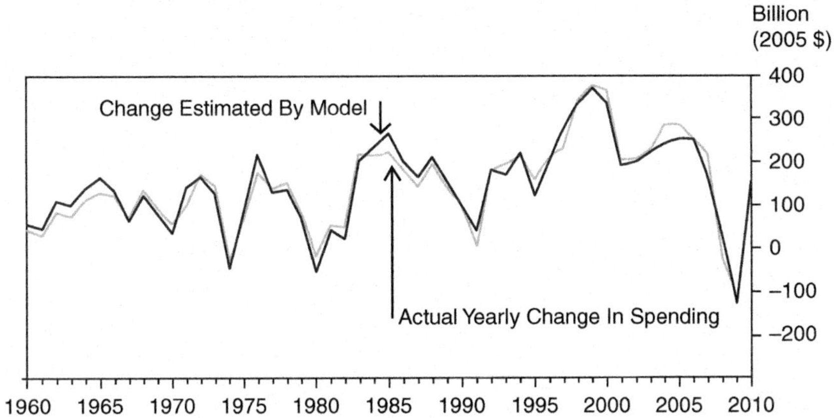

Equation 7.2.a.Alt.2 below is exactly the same as 7.2.a.Alt except the borrowing variable (C_{B2}) is not included in either the structural equation or the instrument. Otherwise, the same variables were assumed endogenous, exogenous or lagged). The same variables are found significant, except the lagged consumer confidence index (ICC_{-1}).

Model 7.2.a.Alt.2 2SLS standard consumer spending model, with borrowing not included as a determinant of consumer spending, unemployment rate used as the business cycle control

(Same variables assumed endogenous, exogenous or lagged as in 7.2.a. Alt above, except C_{B2})

$$\underset{(t=)}{\Delta C_T} = \underset{(9.8)}{0.58\Delta(Y - T_T)} + \underset{(7.9)}{0.71\mathbf{\Delta}(\mathrm{T_T})} - \underset{(-3.1)}{0.28\mathbf{\Delta}(\mathbf{G}_{\mathrm{T\&I}})}$$
$$- \underset{(-4.9)}{9.84\Delta \mathrm{PR}} + \underset{(4.8)}{0.42\,\Delta \mathrm{DJ}_{-2}} + \underset{(3.2)}{5.40\,\Delta \mathrm{XR_{AV}}} + \underset{(0.31)}{97.50\Delta \mathrm{POP}_{16}}$$
$$+ \underset{(1.3)}{0.007\Delta \mathrm{POP}} + \underset{(1.0)}{0.37\Delta \mathrm{ICC}_{-1}} + \underset{(5.3)}{41.99\Delta \mathrm{M2_{AV}}}$$
$$+ \underset{(3.0)}{20.59\,\mathbf{\Delta UNEM}} \quad \mathbf{R}^2 = 93.7\ \%$$
$$\mathrm{D.W.} = 2.0\ \mathrm{MSE} = 28.04 \qquad (7.2.\mathrm{a.Alt2})$$

Model 7.3 OLS standard consumer spending model, with borrowing included, no business cycle control used

(No variable found endogenous, so no 2SLS Models)

$$\underset{(t=)}{\Delta C_T} = \underset{(12.1)}{0.51\Delta(Y - T_T)} + \underset{(12.5)}{0.55\mathbf{\Delta}(\mathrm{T_T})} - \underset{(-3.4)}{0.25\mathbf{\Delta}(\mathbf{G}_{\mathrm{T\&I}})}$$
$$- \underset{(-5.9)}{12.35\Delta \mathrm{PR}} + \underset{(4.8)}{0.45\,\Delta \mathrm{DJ}_{-2}} + \underset{(1.9)}{3.14\,\Delta \mathrm{XR_{AV}}} - \underset{(-1.3)}{319.66\Delta \mathrm{POP}_{16}}$$
$$+ \underset{(2.8)}{0.013\Delta \mathrm{POP}} + \underset{(1.1)}{0.31\Delta \mathrm{ICC}_{-1}} + \underset{(4.3)}{42.30\Delta \mathrm{M2_{AV}}} + \underset{(3.4)}{0.11\,\mathbf{\Delta C_{B2}}}$$
$$\mathbf{R}^2 = 94.8\% \quad \mathrm{D.W.} = 1.7\ \mathrm{MSE} = 25.49 \qquad (7.3)$$

Note that estimates of crowd out effects are slightly smaller when no business cycle control variable is used, but not significantly so. Nonetheless, these point estimates of the effects of deficits on consumption are just the opposite of what we would expect if the negative relationship between deficits and consumer spending was (in part) really just a proxy for the effect of changes in the economy (business cycle). Were that hypothesis true, we would expect that, controlling for the state of the economy (i.e., the business cycle), we would see smaller estimates of the deficit's effect on spending, since we would only be measuring the crowd out effect. Instead, we see estimates of deficit effects which are essentially the same, regardless of whether or not we control for business cycle effects or not.

Otherwise, in the no-control model, the same variables appear significant as in models with controls, except for the Index of consumer confidence. The correlation between ICC_{-1} and the condition of the economy is high. For ICC_{-1} and unemployment, it is −0.65, which may explain this problem.

Table 7.1 2SLS consumer spending findings summarized, compared to OLS (two-variable deficit effects)

Model#	*Δ* (T_T) β (t-*stat.*)	*Δ* ($G_{T\&I}$) β (t-*stat.*)	*Δ* (*BOR*) β (t-*stat.*)	*Bus. cycle control*	*Method*
7.1	0.55 (11.4)	−0.26 (−3.7)	0.12 (3.1)	GDP $_{Real(-3)}$	OLS only (No Endog.)
7.2	0.63 (12.2)	−0.31 (−4.5)	0.12 (3.6)	Unem. rate	OLS only
7.2.a	0.63 (14.4)	−0.28 (−3.7)	0.13 (2.6)		2SLS (Weak Inst.)
7.2.a.(Alt.)	0.64 (12.0)	−0.28 (−3.9)	0.11 (3.9)		2SLS (Strong Inst.)
7.2.a.(Alt2)*	0.71 (7.9)	−0.28 (−3.1)	NA		2SLS
7.3	0.55 (12.5)	−0.25 (−3.4)	0.11 (3.4)	(None)	OLS Only (No Endog.)
Average	0.60 (12.5)	−0.28 (−3.8)	0.12 (3.3)		
Av. (All except weak inst.)	0.59 (12.0)	−0.28 (−3.8)	0.12 (3.5)		

*7.2.a.Alt3 model is the same as Alt model, except without the borrowing variable included.

7.1.1 2SLS Consumer Spending Conclusions Summarized, Compared to OLS (Two-Variable Deficit Models)

Table 7.1 below summarizes 2SLS spending model findings regarding crowd out, and compares them to OLS findings obtained testing the same structural models.

Overall, both the OLS and 2SLS estimates indicate a highly statistically significant crowd out effect for both tax cut and spending increase government deficits, with tax cut deficits having about twice the negative effect on consumer spending as spending deficits. The results also indicate that every dollar of additional consumer borrowing results in about $0.13 in *additional* spending not attributable to changes in other determinants of consumption. To the extent deficits also reduce this general access to borrowing, this effect, which is shown below to be significant, should be added to the deficit variables' effect, for example, if deficits reduced consumer borrowing by $1.00, then, the tax cut deficits' total crowd out effect is now estimated to be $0.70 per dollar of deficit ($.58 + 0.12), the spending deficit's effect is now $0.40 ($0.28 + 0.12).

7.2 OLS and 2SLS Borrowing Models

To test the direct effects of deficits on consumer borrowing (ΔC_{B2}), we test the same models as tested for consumption spending, with the usual three changes. The three differences in the right hand side of the borrowing model compared to the spending model are:

- There is no borrowing variable on the right hand side. It is now the dependent variable.
- The NYSE average is lagged only one period, instead of two. By strengthening the wealth variable this way, the explanatory power of the consumer borrowing model is nearly doubled (though for spending models, the two period lagged version remains a better explainer of variance).
- A monetary variable Real (M2−M1) is added to the right side to reflect the fact that the money supply has an influence on the supply of loanable funds. As noted in Sections 5 and 6, this form explained the most variance.

Model 7.4 OLS estimates of borrowing, using real GDP_{-3} as the business cycle control variable

$$\begin{aligned}
\underset{(t=)}{\Delta C_{B2}} = {} & \underset{(1.8)}{0.44\Delta(Y - T_T)} + \underset{(2.4)}{0.68\mathbf{\Delta}(\mathbf{T}_T)} - \underset{(-2.3)}{0.48\mathbf{\Delta}(\mathbf{G}_{T\&I})} \\
& - \underset{(-4.2)}{21.15\Delta PR} - \underset{(3.3)}{1.55\,\Delta DJ_{-1}} + \underset{(2.5)}{20.34\,\Delta XR_{AV}} + \underset{(0.8)}{436.90\Delta POP_{16}} \\
& + \underset{(0.2)}{0.003\Delta POP} + \underset{(0.2)}{0.25\Delta ICC_{-1}} - \underset{(-1.0)}{31.04\Delta M2_{AV}} \\
& - \underset{(-1.3)}{0.17\,\Delta(M2 - M1)_{Real}} - \underset{(-0.9)}{0.10\,\mathbf{\Delta GDP_{Real(-3)}}} \\
& R^2 = 59.3\% \quad D.W. = 2.0 \quad MSE = 101.21
\end{aligned} \tag{7.4}$$

Model 7.4.a 2SLS estimates of borrowing, using real GDP_{-3} as the business cycle control variable

(Hausman tests indicate T_T, (Wald $F = 20.02$), XR_{AV} (Wald $F = 0.68$, no $t \geq 3.3$) and POP_{16} (Wald $F = 2.30$, no $t \geq 3.3$) Endogenous. Sargan Test $nR^2 = (50)(0.29) = 14.5$, $< X^2_{(95,17)} = 27.59$) (Strong instrument Tests Provided Further Below in Eq. 7.4.a.Alt).

$$\underset{(t=)}{\Delta C_{B2}} = 0.40\underset{(1.4)}{\Delta(Y - T_T)} + 0.83\underset{(3.1)}{\boldsymbol{\Delta}(\mathbf{T_T})} + 0.11\underset{(0.1)}{\boldsymbol{\Delta}(\mathbf{G_{T\&I}})}$$
$$- 13.82\underset{(-1.1)}{\Delta PR} - 1.03\,\underset{(1.8)}{\Delta DJ_{-1}} + 35.37\,\underset{(3.1)}{\Delta XR_{AV}} + 5557.01\underset{(1.2)}{\Delta POP_{16}}$$
$$- 0.010\underset{(-0.5)}{\Delta POP} - 0.27\underset{(-0.1)}{\Delta ICC_{-1}} - 25.37\underset{(0.4)}{\Delta M2_{AV}}$$
$$- 0.44\,\underset{(-2.3)}{\Delta(M2 - M1)_{Real}} + 0.007\,\underset{(0.4)}{\boldsymbol{\Delta}\mathbf{GDP_{Real(-3)}}}$$
$$R^2 = 16.6\% \quad D.W. = 1.1 \; MSE = 145.01 \qquad (7.4.a)$$

Since the instruments developed for XR and POP_{16} were Wald-weak, stronger instruments were developed adding XR_{AV-1} and $POP16_{-1}$ to the standard variable group used to initially develop all instruments. Results are presented in the Alternate version of 7.4.a shown below.

Model 7.4.a.Alt 2SLS estimates of borrowing, using real GDP_{-3} as the business cycle control variable

(Hausman tests indicate endogeneity for: T_T, (Wald $F = 23.46$) XR_{AV} (Wald $F = 10.94$, with $t = 8.5$ for $XR_{AV(-1)}$) and POP_{16} (Wald $F = 2.20$, But $T = 4.5$ for $Pop_{16(-1)}$). Sargan test $nR^2 = (50)(0.54) = 0.27$, $< X^2_{(95,19)} = 30.14$) (Strong instrument model).

$$\underset{(t=)}{\Delta C_{B2}} = 0.41\underset{(1.6)}{\Delta(Y - T_T)} + 0.61\underset{(2.2)}{\boldsymbol{\Delta}(\mathbf{T_T})} - 0.57\underset{(1.9)}{\boldsymbol{\Delta}(\mathbf{G_{T\&I}})}$$
$$- 20.39\underset{(-4.1)}{\Delta PR} - 1.55\,\underset{(3.2)}{\Delta DJ_{-1}} + 22.11\underset{(2.4)}{\Delta XR_{AV}} + 78.30\underset{(0.1)}{\Delta POP_{16}}$$
$$+ 0.007\underset{(0.4)}{\Delta POP} + 0.39\underset{(0.4)}{\Delta ICC_{-1}} - 25.04\underset{(-0.8)}{\Delta M2_{AV}}$$
$$- 0.18\,\underset{(-1.2)}{\Delta(M2 - M1)_{Real}} - 0.10\,\underset{(-0.8)}{\boldsymbol{\Delta}\mathbf{GDP_{Real(-3)}}}$$
$$\mathbf{R^2} = 59.0\% \quad D.W. = 2.0 \; MSE = 102.92 \qquad (7.4.a.Alt)$$

Using the Alt2 form of strong instruments (see 5.17.a.Alt2 for explanation) we have

Model 7.4.a.Alt2 2SLS estimates of borrowing, using real GDP_{-3} as the business cycle control variable

(Hausman tests indicate ($Y - T_T$) endogenous: Wald $F = 4.1$, but $t = 4.5$ for $M2_{AV}$. $G_{T\&I}$ also ndogenous (Wald $F = 3.2$, but $t > 3.3$ for $M2_{AV}$ and Dep_{-1}. Sargan test: $NR^2 = 5.4$, $< X^2(.95,16) = 26.30$)

$$\underset{(t=)}{\Delta C_{B2}} = \underset{(1.1)}{0.36\Delta(Y - T_T)} + \underset{(2.2)}{0.64\boldsymbol{\Delta}(\mathbf{T}_T)} - \underset{(-1.7)}{1.04\boldsymbol{\Delta}(\mathbf{G}_{T\&I})}$$
$$- \underset{(-3.9)}{25.27\Delta PR} - \underset{(-4.3)}{1.72\,\Delta DJ_{-1}} + \underset{(2.7)}{21.94\Delta XR_{AV}} - \underset{(-0.1)}{42.00\Delta POP_{16}}$$
$$+ \underset{(0.6)}{0.017\Delta POP} + \underset{(0.5)}{0.57\Delta ICC_{-1}} - \underset{(-0.1)}{4.83\Delta M2_{AV}}$$
$$- \underset{(-1.2)}{0.16\,\Delta(M2 - M1)_{Real}} - \underset{(-0.6)}{0.08\,\boldsymbol{\Delta}\mathbf{GDP}_{\mathbf{Real}(-3)}}$$
$$\mathbf{R}^2 = 57.6\% \quad D.W. = 2.1 \; MSE = 106.12 \qquad (7.4.a.Alt2)$$

Using lagged GDP as the business cycle control, the best 2SLS findings (Eq. 7.4.a, 7.4.aAlt) indicate tax cut deficits and spending deficits generally have about the same direct impact on consumer borrowing, or spending somewhat more. OLS results were reasonably close. The low, non-significant effect for government spending deficits obtained using weak instruments, we discount as an instrument problem.

Next, we wish to test deficit effects using the unemployment rate as the business cycle control variable.

Model 7.5 OLS estimates of borrowing, using the unemployment rate as the business cycle control variable

$$\underset{(t=)}{\Delta C_{B2}} = \underset{(1.5)}{0.37\Delta(2 - T_T)} + \underset{(1.8)}{0.62\boldsymbol{\Delta}(\mathbf{T}_T)} - \underset{(-2.0)}{0.49\boldsymbol{\Delta}(\mathbf{G}_{T\&I})}$$
$$- \underset{(-3.8)}{22.66\Delta PR} - \underset{(3.5)}{1.61\,\Delta DJ_{-1}} + \underset{(2.8)}{21.86\,\Delta XR_{AV}} + \underset{(0.7)}{406.63\Delta POP_{16}}$$
$$+ \underset{(0.2)}{0.002\Delta POP} + \underset{(0.2)}{0.16\Delta ICC_{-1}} - \underset{(1.0)}{35.51\Delta M2_{AV}}$$
$$- \underset{(-1.8)}{0.19\,\boldsymbol{\Delta}(\mathbf{M2} - \mathbf{M1})_{\mathbf{Real}}} - \underset{(-0.6)}{18.00\,\boldsymbol{\Delta}\mathbf{UNEM}}$$
$$\mathbf{R}^2 = 58.9\% \quad D.W. = 2.1 \; MSE = 101.79 \qquad (7.5)$$

Model 7.5.a 2SLS estimates of borrowing, using unemployment rate as the business cycle control variable .

(Hausman tests indicate XR_{AV} (Wald $F = 2.23$, no $t >= 3.3$) and POP_{16} (Wald $F = 1.00$, no $t >= 3.3$) Variables endogenous (Sargan test $NR^2 = 6 < X^2_{(95,\, 17)} = 27.59$) (Weak Instrument)

$$\underset{(t=)}{\Delta C_{B2}} = 0.36\underset{(1.1)}{\Delta(Y - T_T)} + 0.79\underset{(2.3)}{\boldsymbol{\Delta}(\mathbf{T_T})} + 0.12\underset{(0.2)}{\boldsymbol{\Delta}(\mathbf{G_{T\&I}})}$$
$$- 15.68\underset{(-1.0)}{\Delta PR} - 1.04\underset{(1.7)}{\Delta DJ_{-1}} + 35.70\underset{(3.6)}{\Delta XR_{AV}} + 5403.49\underset{(1.1)}{\Delta POP_{16}}$$
$$- 0.007\underset{(-0.3)}{\Delta POP} - 0.50\underset{(-0.3)}{\Delta ICC_{-1}} - 25.31\underset{(-0.5)}{\Delta M2_{AV}}$$
$$- 0.43\underset{(-2.6)}{\Delta(M2 - M1)_{Real}} - 13.18\underset{(-0.2)}{\boldsymbol{\Delta}\mathbf{UNEM}}$$
$$R^2 = 18.3\% \quad D.W. = 1.1 \; MSE = 143.49 \qquad (7.5.a)$$

Since the instruments developed for XR and POP_{16} were Wald-weak, substantially stronger instruments were developed adding XR_{AV-1} and $POP_{16(-1)}$ to the standard variable group used to initially develop all instruments. Results are presented in the Alternate version of 7.5.a shown below.

Model 7.5.a.Alt 2SLS estimates of borrowing, using unemployment rate as the business cycle control

(Hausman tests indicate variables endogenous with consumption include XR_{AV} (Wald $F = 10.33$, with $t = 8.3$ for $XR_{AV}(-1)$) and POP_{16} (Wald $F = 1.98$, but t = 4.4 for $POP_{16(-1)}$) Sargan test $nR^2 = 28 < 31.41 = X^2_{(0.95,20)}$) (Strong Instrument)

$$\underset{(t=)}{\Delta C_{B2}} = 0.34\underset{(1.3)}{\Delta(Y - T_T)} + 0.61\underset{(1.8)}{\boldsymbol{\Delta}(\mathbf{T_T})} - 0.55\underset{(1.7)}{\boldsymbol{\Delta}(\mathbf{G_{T\&I}})}$$
$$- 22.89\underset{(-3.7)}{\Delta PR} - 1.62\underset{(-3.4)}{\Delta DJ_{-1}} + 24.06\underset{(2.8)}{\Delta XR_{AV}} + 102.23\underset{(0.1)}{\Delta POP_{16}}$$
$$+ 0.005\underset{(0.3)}{\Delta POP} + 0.12\underset{(0.1)}{\Delta ICC_{-1}} - 30.82\underset{(-0.9)}{\Delta M2_{AV}}$$
$$- 0.20\underset{(-1.7)}{\Delta(M2 - M1)_{Real}} - 18.54\underset{(-0.6)}{\boldsymbol{\Delta}\mathbf{UNEM}}$$
$$R^2 = 58.7\,\% \quad D.W. = 2.1 \; MSE = 103.40 \qquad (7.5.a.Alt)$$

And using the Alt2 strong instrument form:

Model 7.5.a.Alt2 2SLS estimates of borrowing, using unemployment rate as the business cycle control variable)

(Hausman tests indicate $G_{T\&I}$ and UNEM were endogenous. For $G_{T\&I}$: Wald $F = 3.3$, $t = 3.8$ for $M2_{AV}$; For UNEM (Wald $F = 13.6$, with $t > 3.3$ for PR_0 and Dep_{-2}. Sargan test: $nR^2 = 4.3 < X^2(95,15) = 25.0$) (Strong Instrument)

$$\underset{(t=)}{\Delta C_{B2}} = \underset{(0.7)}{0.34\Delta(Y - T_T)} + \underset{(1.8)}{0.72\mathbf{\Delta}(\mathbf{T}_T)} - \underset{(-1.5)}{1.78\mathbf{\Delta}(\mathbf{G}_{T\&I})}$$
$$- \underset{(-3.0)}{25.71\Delta PR} - \underset{(-3.9)}{1.91\Delta DJ_{-1}} + \underset{(3.0)}{24.38\Delta XR_{AV}} - \underset{(-0.5)}{562.25\Delta POP_{16}}$$
$$+ \underset{(0.8)}{0.027\Delta POP} + \underset{(0.5)}{1.48\Delta ICC_{-1}} + \underset{(0.4)}{28.06\Delta M2_{AV}}$$
$$- \underset{(-1.1)}{0.18\,\Delta(M2 - M1)_{Real}} + \underset{(0.3)}{33.54\,\mathbf{\Delta UNEM}}$$
$$R^2 = 48.4\ \%\quad D.W. = 2.2\ MSE = 117.06 \qquad (7.5.a.Alt2)$$

Here again, the OLS and one of the strong instrument 2SLS models yield about the same results; the statistically significant evidence is that both spending increase and tax cut deficits have about the same negative effect on consumer borrowing, but with the alternate strong instrument, the crowd out effect of spending deficits is more than twice as large. Again, we suspect the lower t statistics (compared to spending models) results from the model only explain 58.7 % of the variance in borrowing.

Finally, we estimate the effects of deficits on consumer borrowing without any control for the phase of the business cycle. Results are shown in Model 7.6 below.

Model 7.6 OLS estimates of borrowing, no business cycle control variable used

$$\underset{(t=)}{\Delta C_{B2}} = \underset{(1.7)}{0.42\Delta(Y - T_T)} + \underset{(2.5)}{0.69\mathbf{\Delta}(\mathbf{T}_T)} - \underset{(-2.3)}{0.54\mathbf{\Delta}(\mathbf{G}_{T\&I})}$$
$$- \underset{(-3.9)}{20.63\Delta PR} - \underset{(-3.5)}{1.60\,\Delta DJ_{-1}} + \underset{(2.9)}{21.79\,\Delta XR_{AV}} + \underset{(0.8)}{424.63\Delta POP_{16}}$$
$$- \underset{(-0.1)}{0.001\Delta POP} + \underset{(0.4)}{0.43\Delta ICC_{-1}} - \underset{(-1.0)}{34.31\Delta M2_{AV}}$$
$$- \underset{(-1.8)}{0.20\,\Delta(M2 - M1)_{Real}} \quad R^2 = 58.6\ \%$$
$$D.W. = 2.0\ MSE = 100.86 \qquad (7.6)$$

And, since both the exchange rate and POP16 variables were found Hausman-endogenous, and need to be instrumented, we have 2SLS results, developed using the standard variables to construct the instruments (which unfortunately are Wald-weak instruments).

Model 7.6.a 2SLS estimates of borrowing, no business cycle control used (Hausman tests indicate XR_{AV} (Wald F= 2.23) and POP_{16} (Wald F= 1.00) variables endogenous and both weak inst. (Sargan test $NR^2 = 6.0 < X^2(95,17) = 27.59$).

$$\underset{(t=)}{\Delta C_{B2}} = \underset{(1.5)}{0.40\Delta(Y - T_T)} + \underset{(3.6)}{0.84\boldsymbol{\Delta}(\mathbf{T}_T)} + \underset{(0.2)}{0.11\boldsymbol{\Delta}(\mathbf{G}_{T\&I})}$$
$$- \underset{(-1.1)}{14.07\Delta PR} - \underset{(-1.8)}{1.02\,\Delta DJ_{-1}} + \underset{(3.5)}{35.50\,\Delta XR_{AV}} + \underset{(1.2)}{5542.49\Delta POP_{16}}$$
$$- \underset{(-0.5)}{0.010\Delta POP} - \underset{(-0.2)}{0.32\Delta ICC_{-1}} - \underset{(-0.4)}{25.04\Delta M2_{AV}}$$
$$- \underset{(-2.6)}{0.44\,\Delta(M2 - M1)_{Real}} \quad R^2 = 16.6\ \%$$
$$D.W. = 1.1\ MSE = 143.16 \tag{7.6.a}$$

Since the instruments developed for XR and POP_{16} were Wald-weak, substantially stronger instruments were developed adding $XR_{AV}(-1)$ and POP16(−1) to the standard variable group used to initially develop all instruments. Results are presented in the Alternate version 7.6.Alt. shown below

Model 7.6.a.Alt 2SLS estimates of borrowing, no business cycle control used

(Hausman tests indicate XR_{AV} (Wald $F = 10.33$, with $t = 8.3$ for $XR_{AV}(-1)$) and POP_{16} (Wald $F= 1.98$, but $t= 4.4$ for $POP_{16(-1)}$) variables endogenous with consumption) (Sargan test $NR^2 = 28.5 < X^2_{(95,19)}=30.14$) (Strong Instrument)

$$\underset{(t=)}{\Delta C_{B2}} = \underset{(1.5)}{0.39\Delta(Y - T_T)} + \underset{(2.5)}{0.68\boldsymbol{\Delta}(\mathbf{T}_T)} - \underset{(1.9)}{0.59\boldsymbol{\Delta}(\mathbf{G}_{T\&I})}$$
$$- \underset{(-3.9)}{20.78\Delta PR} - \underset{(-3.4)}{1.60\,\Delta DJ_{-1}} + \underset{(2.8)}{23.98\Delta XR_{AV}} + \underset{(0.1)}{137.42\Delta POP_{16}}$$
$$+ \underset{(0.1)}{0.001\Delta POP} + \underset{(0.4)}{0.39\Delta ICC_{-1}} \underset{(-0.9)}{-29.61\Delta M2_{AV}}$$
$$- \underset{(-1.7)}{0.20\,\Delta(M2 - M1)_{Real}} \quad R^2 = 58.4\ \%$$
$$D.W. = 2.0\ MSE = 102.40 \tag{7.6.a.Alt}$$

and the Alt2 form of strong instrument:

Model 7.6.Alt2 2SLS estimates of borrowing, using no business cycle control variable

(Hausman tests indicate $G_{T\&I}$ and $(\Upsilon - T_T)$ endogenous. For $G_{T\&I}$: Wald $F= 4.1$, but $t > 3.3$ for $M2_{AV}$ and DEP_{-2}. For $(\Upsilon - T_T)$ (Wald $F= 4.1$, but $t = 4.5$ for $M2_{AV}$. Sargan test $NR^2 = 5.9 < X^2_{(95,16)}{=}26.30$). (Strong Instrument)

$$\underset{(t=)}{\Delta C_{B2}} = \underset{(1.0)}{0.34\Delta(Y - T_T)} + \underset{(2.3)}{0.64\boldsymbol{\Delta}(\mathbf{T}_T)} - \underset{(1.6)}{1.17\boldsymbol{\Delta}(\mathbf{G}_{T\&I})} - \underset{(-3.8)}{25.90\Delta PR}$$
$$- \underset{(-4.2)}{1.78\,\Delta DJ_{-1}} + \underset{(2.8)}{23.15\Delta XR_{AV}} - \underset{(-0.2)}{131.60\Delta POP_{16}} + \underset{(0.6)}{0.017\Delta POP}$$
$$+ \underset{(0.6)}{0.77\Delta ICC_{-1}} - \underset{(-0.1)}{2.63\Delta M2_{AV}} - \underset{(-1.5)}{0.18\,\Delta(M2 - M1)_{Real}}$$
$$R^2 = 58.3\ \%\quad D.W. = 2.2\ MSE = 106.26 \qquad (7.6.a.Alt2)$$

Here again, except for the government spending results in the weak instrument 2SLS model, the statistically significant evidence is that both spending increase and tax cut deficits have a negative effect on consumer borrowing, with some evidence indicating that the effect of both types of deficits is the same, but some evidence indicating the crowd out effects of spending deficits on consumer borrowing is greater. The results also indicate a slightly stronger crowd out effect when the business cycle is not controlled for. This indicates there is also some correlation between deficits and consumer borrowing caused by the business cycle. But the evidence of crowd out, indicated by the crowd out variable's coefficient size and statistical significance, when controlling for business cycle effects, is also strong;

Table 7.2 2SLS consumer borrowing findings summarized, compared to OLS (two-variable deficit effects)

Model#	$\Delta(T_T)$ β (t-*stat.*)	Δ $(G_{T\&I})$ β (t-*stat.*)	*Bus. cycle control*	*Method*
7.4	0.68 (2.4)	−0.48 (−2.3)	$GDP_{Real(-3)}$	OLS
7.4.a	0.83 (3.1)	+0.11 (0.1)		2SLS (Weak Inst.)
7.4.a.Alt	0.61 (2.2)	−0.57 (−1.9)		2SLS (Strong Inst.)
7.4.a.Alt2	0.64 (2.2)	−1.04 (−1.7)		2SLS (Strong Inst.)
7.5	0.62 (1.8)	−0.49 (−2.0)	Unem. rate	OLS
7.5.a	0.79 (2.3)	+0.12 (0.2)		2SLS (Weak Inst.)
7.5.a.Alt	0.61 (1.8)	−0.55 (−1.7)		2SLS (Strong Inst.)
7.5.a.Alt2	0.72 (1.8)	−1.79 (−1.5)		2SLS (Strong Inst.)
7.6.a	0.84 (3.6)	+0.11 (0.2)	No Control	2SLS (Weak Inst.)
7.6.a.Alt	0.68 (2.5)	−0.59 (−1.9)		2SLS (Strong Inst.)
7.6.a.Alt2	0.64 (2.3)	−1.17 (−1.6)		2SLS (Strong Inst.)
Average (All)	0.70 (2.4)	−0.58 (−1.3)		(All)
Av. (OLS)	0.66 (2.2)	−0.50 (−2.2)		(OLS only)
Av. (2SLS)	0.65 (2.1)	−0.57 (−1.8)		(Strong Inst. only)

Table 7.3 Recap of findings of deficits and borrowing variable on consumer spending (two-variable deficit effects)

2SLS Spending Model Findings Summarized:

Model#	$\Delta(T_T)$ *β (t-stat.)*	$\Delta(G_{T\&I})$ *β (t-stat.)*	$\Delta(BOR)$ *β (t-stat.)*	*Bus. cycle control*	*Method*
7.1	0.55 (11.4)	−0.26 (−3.7)	0.12 (3.1)	GDP $_{Real(-3)}$	OLS Only (No End og.)
7.2	0.63 (12.2)	−0.31 (−4.5)	0.12 (3.6)	Unem. rate	OLS Only (No Endog.)
7.2.a	0.63 (14.4)	−0.28 (−3.7)	0.13 (2.6)		2SLS (Weak Inst.)
7.2.a.Alt.	0.64 (12.0)	−0.28 (−3.9)	0.11 (3.9)		2SLS (Strong Inst.)
7.3	0.55 (12.5)	−0.25 (−3.4)	0.11 (3.4)	(None)	OLS Only (No Endog.)
Average	0.59 (12.0)	−0.28 (−3.9)	0.12 (3.5)	(w/o weak instrument results)	
Average (All)	0.60 (12.5)	−0.28 (−3.8)	0.12 (3.3)		
Average (OLS)	0.58 (12.0)	−0.27 (−3.9)	0.12 (3.4)	48	

very strong for tax cut deficits, and at least marginally strong for spending deficits (ignoring weak instrument findings).

7.3 OLS and 2SLS Consumer Spending and Borrowing Findings Summarized

Table 7.2 summarizes the findings of the tests cited above as to crowd out's effect on consumer borrowing.

7.3.1 Recap of Findings of Deficits and Borrowing Variables on Consumer Spending

Recapped in Table 7.3 are Table 7.1 findings regarding crowd out effect on consumer spending, for ease of comparison with the borrowing findings above.

7.3.2 *Overall Consumption Conclusions (Two-Variable Deficit Effects):*

1. Consumers spending is greater when there is greater access to borrowing, ceteris paribus. Though about 88 % of all borrowing appears to be done to finance consumer spending decisions driven by the other standard determinants of consumer demand (income, interest rates, etc.), the remaining 12 % appears to be independent of this, and may relate to access to credit. Other studies have found that consumer credit is more curtailed than business credit in poor economic times, and grows faster in good economic times (see Heim 2011).
2. Highly statistically significant negative effects of deficits on consumer spending are found in all two-variable deficit spending tests for both tax cut deficits and deficits caused by government spending.
3. Negative effects of deficits on consumer spending appear about twice as great for tax cut deficits ($0.58 per dollar of deficit) versus $0.28 (if the deficit is caused by a government spending increase). This may be because the MPC of those receiving tax cuts is lower than that of those receiving aid from government spending program deficits. If the reduction in loanable funds reduces consumer spending dollar for dollar, then that negative effect partially offset by the positive MPC effects of the government spending program will result in a smaller crowd out effect ($1 - .72 = .28$) for spending deficits.
4. Effects of Deficits on Consumer Borrowing: Test results varied with the particular strong instruments used (Alt. vs. Alt2). In the Alt models, deficits appear to have roughly the same effect on consumer borrowing, regardless of whether the deficit is due to tax cuts or spending increases. Averages for all strong instrument tests were $0.65 per dollar of tax cuts; $0.57 per dollar of spending increase. Borrowing findings are consistent with the spending findings, in the sense that the logic of the theory of crowd out requires the deficit's effect on borrowing to be as great at least as the effect on spending.
5. The negative borrowing effects of tax cut deficits were strongly statistically significant. The borrowing effects of government spending deficits generally showing the same negative relationship, but were less statistically significant, that is, their confidence interval around their estimated effects was substantially larger. In weak instrument tests, their effects on consumption were statistically

insignificantly different from zero, but weak instrument tests are not good indicators of relationships.

6. Statistical Technique: Both OLS and Strong-Instrument 2SLS yield about the same results on spending and on consumer borrowing. Weak-instrument 2SLS yields the same results for tax cut deficits effects on spending, but indicate no effect on borrowing for spending deficits. The strong 2SLS estimates are the most preferred on methodological grounds, though it is discomforting to find that strong instruments with different components (Alt vs. Alt2 models) can affect parameter estimates.

CHAPTER 8

Test Results: Investment Spending and Borrowing Models (Two-Variable Deficit)

This section retests many of the same investment spending and borrowing models used in Chap. 6, except deficit components T_T and $G_{T\&I}$ are tested as separate variables to determine if tax and spending effects on investment crowd out differ. Though these two variables appear to measure total government revenues and spending, not deficits, recall that our regression coefficients on these variables indicate how any one of them affects investment spending holding the other constant, that is, by changing the deficit.

Tests are run using either GDP lagged three periods, the unemployment rate as business cycle control variables or no business cycle control variable at all. Earlier tests showed no relationship between current period GDP and deficit size, so that model is not tested here. Borrowing models are tested further below. OLS and 2SLS results for each model are presented together here. In Chap. 6, they were separated into different sections of the chapter.

Section 8.1 tests 16 OLS and 2SLS models of investment spending, each using the two-variable definition of crowd out. Section 8.1.1 summarizes the 16 test results and finds that in all 16, spending deficits had a significant negative effect on investment spending, and in 15 of 16, spending deficits had a statistically significant negative effect on investment spending. Spending deficits had twice as large a negative effect on investment as did tax cut deficits (just the opposite of Chap. 7 consumption findings, where tax cut deficit negative effects were twice as large as spending deficit effects).

Section 8.2 tests 9 OLS and 2SLS models of consumer borrowing, each using the two-variable definition of crowd out. In all of them, both tax cut-caused deficits and spending deficits have a significant negative effect on

J.J. Heim, *Crowding Out Fiscal Stimulus*,
DOI 10.1007/978-3-319-45967-7_8

investment borrowing. Spending and tax cut deficits had about the same-size effect on borrowing.

Detailed analysis of each of these tests is provided in the remainder of the chapter.

8.1 OLS and 2SLS Spending Models

The first model tested includes a borrowing variable as a possible determinant of spending, and uses the real GDP lagged three years as the business cycle control variable. OLS is the statistical technique used, followed by 2SLS for this model. ("a" versions of OLS spending models represent those using DJ_0 and $PROF_0$ lags as the Tobin's q and profits variables. See end of Section 6.0 for explanation.)

Model 8.1 OLS estimates of determinants of investment spending, using real GDP_{-3} as the business cycle control variable

$$\underset{(t=)}{\Delta I_T} = +\underset{(6.5)}{0.32\Delta(ACC)} + \underset{(4.2)}{0.31\boldsymbol{\Delta}(\mathbf{T_T})} - \underset{(-4.3)}{0.46\boldsymbol{\Delta}(\mathbf{G_{T\&I}})} + \underset{(2.8)}{1.12\Delta DEP}$$
$$+\underset{(1.6)}{4.45\Delta CAP_{-1}} - \underset{(-1.9)}{3.79\Delta PR_{-2}} - \underset{(-3.6)}{0.40\Delta DJ_{-2}} - \underset{(-0.6)}{0.05\Delta PROF_{-2}}$$
$$+\underset{(3.8)}{6.05\Delta XR_{AV}} + \underset{(1.3)}{0.005\Delta POP} + \underset{(1.5)}{0.08\boldsymbol{\Delta}(\mathbf{BOR})} + \underset{(1.3)}{0.07\,\boldsymbol{\Delta}\mathbf{GDP_{Real(-3)}}}$$
$$R^2 = 94.4\ \% \qquad D.W. = 1.8, \quad MSE = 29.90 \tag{8.1}$$

Model 8.1.a OLS estimates of determinants of investment spending, using real GDP_{-3} as the business cycle control variable

$$\underset{(t=)}{\Delta I_T} = +\underset{(5.6)}{0.33\Delta(ACC)} + \underset{(3.3)}{0.30\boldsymbol{\Delta}(\mathbf{T_T})} - \underset{(-3.7)}{0.43\boldsymbol{\Delta}(\mathbf{G_{T\&I}})} + \underset{(2.0))}{0.55\Delta DEP}$$
$$+\underset{(1.8)}{4.44\Delta CAP_{-1}} - \underset{(-1.1)}{2.33\Delta PR_{-2}} - \underset{(-0.1)}{0.02\Delta DJ_{-0}} + \underset{(2.1)}{0.14\Delta PROF_{-0}}$$
$$+\underset{(3.7)}{6.58\Delta XR_{AV}} + \underset{(1.4)}{0.006\Delta POP} + \underset{(2.2)}{0.13\,\boldsymbol{\Delta}(\mathbf{BOR})} + \underset{(1.5)}{0.07\,\boldsymbol{\Delta}\mathbf{GDP_{Real(-3)}}}$$
$$R^2 = 93.5\ \% \quad D.W. = 1.9 \quad MSE = 32.19 \tag{8.1.a}$$

Model 8.1.Alt 2SLS estimates of determinants of investment spending, using real GDP_{-3} as the business cycle control variable

(Hausman Tests Indicate DEP, $G_{T\&I}$, and POP endogenous with investment spending, so instrumented: DEP (Wald F = 12.06 and

$t > 4.0$ for ACC, T_T and $\Upsilon - T_T$ components of instrument), $G_{T\&I}$ (Wald $F = 3.40$, but $t = 4.9$ for $M2_{AV}$ Instrument Components), and POP (Wald $F = 4.49$, but $t > 3.3$ for BOR, DJ_{-2} and $\Upsilon - T_T$ components). Sargan test $NR^2 = 12.24 < X^2_{(95,17)} = 27.59$ Hence, This is a Strong Instrument Model)

$$\underset{(t=)}{\Delta I_T} = +\underset{(7.3)}{0.30\Delta(\text{ACC})} + \underset{(3.5)}{0.33\boldsymbol{\Delta}(\mathbf{T_T})} - \underset{(-5.8)}{0.68\boldsymbol{\Delta}(\mathbf{G_{T\&I}})} + \underset{(1.6))}{0.93\Delta\text{DEP}}$$

$$+ \underset{(1.4)}{3.73\Delta\text{CAP}_{-1}} - \underset{(-1.8)}{5.97\Delta\text{PR}_{-2}} - \underset{(-1.8)}{0.27\Delta\text{DJ}_{-2}} - \underset{(-0.8)}{0.09\Delta\text{PROF}_{-2}}$$

$$+ \underset{(4.2)}{9.15\Delta\text{XR}_{\text{AV}}} + \underset{(2.0)}{0.009\Delta\text{POP}} - \underset{(-1.9)}{0.16\,\boldsymbol{\Delta}(\mathbf{BOR})} + \underset{(0.5)}{0.03\,\boldsymbol{\Delta}\mathbf{GDP}_{\mathbf{Real}(-3)}}$$

$$R^2 = 86.5\ \% \quad \text{D.W.} = 2.1\ \text{MSE} = 34.20 \qquad (8.1.\text{Alt})$$

Model 8.1.Alt.a 2SLS estimates of determinants of investment spending, using real GDP_{-3} as the business cycle control variable

(Hausman tests indicate five variables endogenous with investment spending, so instrumented: ACC (Wald test $F = 7.5$, but CAP_{-1} $t = 4.2$), DEP (Wald $F = 13.0$), DJ_0 (Wald $F = 10.8$), $PROF_0$, (Wald Test $F = 7.5$, POP_{-1} $t = 3.4$ and $M2_{AV}$ $t = 3.4$), and POP (Wald $F = 10.73$. Sargan Test $NR^2 = 6.0 < X^2_{(95,18)} = 28.9$. Hence, this is a Strong Instrument Model)

$$\underset{(t=)}{\Delta I_T} = +\underset{(4.8)}{0.44\Delta(\text{ACC})} + \underset{(3.3)}{0.26\boldsymbol{\Delta}(\mathbf{T_T})} - \underset{(-3.6)}{0.54\boldsymbol{\Delta}(\mathbf{G_{T\&I}})} - \underset{(-0.0))}{0.02\Delta\text{DEP}}$$

$$+ \underset{(2.8)}{11.37\Delta\text{CAP}_{-1}} - \underset{(-1.4)}{0.78\Delta\text{PR}_{-2}} + \underset{(0.0)}{0.002\Delta\text{DJ}_{-0}} + \underset{(1.2)}{0.13\Delta\text{PROF}_{-2}}$$

$$+ \underset{(3.3)}{8.31\Delta\text{XR}_{\text{AV}}} + \underset{(1.5)}{0.01\Delta\text{POP}} + \underset{(1.4)}{0.08\,\boldsymbol{\Delta}(\mathbf{BOR}_{-1})} + \underset{(2.3)}{0.15\,\boldsymbol{\Delta}\mathbf{GDP}_{\mathbf{Real}(-3)}}$$

$$R^2 = 92.7\ \% \quad \text{D.W.} = 2.0\ \text{MSE} = 34.71 \qquad (8.1.\text{Alt.a})$$

And using the Alt.a2 form of strong instrument;

Model 8.1.Alt.a2 2SLS estimates of determinants of investment spending, using real GDP_{-3} as the business cycle control variable

(Hausman tests indicate three variables endogenous with investment spending, so instrumented: DEP (Wald test $F = 16.7$, DJ_0 (Wald $F = 9.7$, but $t = 4.7$ for T_T), $PROF_0$ (Wald Test $F = 5.2$, but $= 5.5$ t for DJ_{-2} and Sargan Test $NR^2 = 7.4 < X^2_{(95,16)} = 26.3$. Hence, This is a Strong Instrument Model)

$$\underset{(t=)}{\Delta I_T} = +\underset{(4.5)}{0.28\Delta(\text{ACC})} + \underset{(3.5)}{0.27\boldsymbol{\Delta}(\mathbf{T}_\text{T})} - \underset{(-3.5)}{0.48\boldsymbol{\Delta}(\mathbf{G}_{\text{T\&I}})} - \underset{(-0.7))}{0.44\Delta\text{DEP}}$$

$$+\underset{(2.0)}{6.48\Delta\text{CAP}_{-1}} + \underset{(0.3)}{1.14\Delta\text{PR}_{-2}} + \underset{(0.0)}{0.006\Delta\text{DJ}_{-0}} + \underset{(4.4)}{0.30\Delta\text{PROF}_{-2}}$$

$$+\underset{(3.0)}{8.37\Delta\text{XR}_\text{AV}} + \underset{(2.2)}{0.01\Delta\text{POP}} + \underset{(2.7)}{0.17\,\boldsymbol{\Delta}(\mathbf{BOR}_{-1})} + \underset{(2.2)}{0.13\,\boldsymbol{\Delta}\mathbf{GDP}_{\mathbf{Real}(-3)}}$$

$$R^2 = 92.4\ \%\quad \text{D.W.} = 1.9,\quad \text{MSE} = 35.29 \qquad (8.1.\text{Alt.a2})$$

Model 8.2 below is identical to 8.1 above, except that the unemployment rate is used as the business cycle control variable instead of lagged GDP.

Model 8.2 OLS Estimates Of Determinants Of Investment Spending, Using The Unemployment Rate As The Business Cycle Control Variable.

$$\underset{(t=)}{\Delta \text{I}_\text{T}} = +\underset{(6.6)}{.30\Delta(\text{ACC})} + \underset{(2.8)}{.24\boldsymbol{\Delta}(\mathbf{T}_\text{T})} - \underset{(-4.0)}{.41\boldsymbol{\Delta}(\mathbf{G}_{\text{T\&I}})} + \underset{(4.5))}{1.44\Delta\text{DEP}} + \underset{(0.8)}{1.76\Delta\text{CAP}_{-1}}$$

$$-\underset{(-1.4)}{3.01\Delta\text{PR}_{-2}} - \underset{(-3.5)}{.43\Delta\text{DJ}_{-2}} - \underset{(-1.0)}{.09\Delta\text{PROF}_{-2}} + \underset{(2.8)}{4.74\Delta\text{XR}_\text{AV}} + \underset{(2.2)}{.007\Delta\text{POP}}$$

$$+\underset{(1.1)}{.06\ \boldsymbol{\Delta}(\mathbf{BOR})} - \underset{(-2.4)}{16.54\ \boldsymbol{\Delta}\mathbf{UNEM}}$$

$$\mathbf{R}^2 = 94.7\%\quad \text{D.W.} = 1.7\ \text{MSE} = 29.10 \qquad (8.2)$$

Model 8.2.a OLS estimates of determinants of investment spending, using the unemployment rate as the business cycle control variable

$$\underset{(t=)}{\Delta I_\text{T}} = +\underset{(4.9)}{0.31\Delta(\text{ACC})} + \underset{(1.9)}{.21\boldsymbol{\Delta}(\mathbf{T}_\text{T})} - \underset{(-3.1)}{.38\boldsymbol{\Delta}(\mathbf{G}_{\text{T\&I}})} + \underset{(2.9))}{.82\Delta\text{DEP}} + \underset{(0.8)}{1.79\Delta\text{CAP}_{-1}}$$

$$-\underset{(-1.2)}{2.87\Delta\text{PR}_{-0}} + \underset{(0.4)}{0.11\Delta\text{DJ}_{-0}} + \underset{(1.8)}{0.13\Delta\text{PROF}_{-0}} + \underset{(2.2)}{5.49\Delta\text{XR}_\text{AV}}$$

$$+\underset{(2.3)}{0.009\Delta\text{POP}} + \underset{(1.5)}{0.08\ \boldsymbol{\Delta}(\mathbf{BOR})} - \underset{(-1.8)}{13.83\ \boldsymbol{\Delta}\mathbf{UNEM}}$$

$$\mathbf{R}^2 = 93.5\ \%\quad \text{D.W.} = 2.0\ \text{MSE} = 32.27 \qquad (\text{Eq.8.2a})$$

Model 8.2.Alt 2SLS estimates of determinants of investment spending, using the unemployment rate as the business cycle control variable

(Hausman tests indicate $G_{T\&I,}$ and pop endogenous with investment borrowing, so instrumented: ($G_{T\&I}$: Wald $F = 3.47$, But $t = 4.5$ For $M2_{AV}$ Instrument Component), And POP (Wald $F = 4.92$, But $t > 4.3$ For $Y - T_T$

component of instrument. Sargan test $NR^2 = 22.24 < X^2_{(95,18)} = 28.87$) 2SLS tests results below. These are strong instruments

$$\underset{(t=)}{\Delta I_T} = +0.32\underset{(6.7)}{\Delta(\text{ACC})} + 0.24\underset{(3.0)}{\boldsymbol{\Delta}(\mathbf{T_T})} - 0.58\underset{(-5.8)}{\boldsymbol{\Delta}(\mathbf{G_{T\&I}})} + 1.46\underset{(4.8)}{\Delta\text{DEP}}$$

$$+ 2.40\underset{(0.9)}{\Delta\text{CAP}_{-1}} - 2.55\underset{(-1.2)}{\Delta\text{PR}_{-2}} - 0.46\underset{(-4.1)}{\Delta\text{DJ}_{-2}} - 0.08\underset{(-0.9)}{\Delta\text{PROF}_{-2}}$$

$$+ 5.28\underset{(3.4)}{\Delta\text{XR}_{\text{AV}}} + 0.012\underset{(2.9)}{\Delta\text{POP}} + 0.02\underset{(0.3)}{\Delta\left(I_{B(-1)}\right)} - 15.15\underset{(-2.0)}{\boldsymbol{\Delta}\textbf{UNEM}}$$

$$R^2 = 94.3\ \% \quad \text{D.W.} = 1.8 \quad \text{MSE} = 30.30 \qquad (8.2.\text{Alt})$$

Model 8.2.Alt.a 2SLS estimates of determinants of investment spending, using UNEM as the business cycle control variable

(Hausman tests indicate five variables endogenous with investment spending, so instrumented: ACC (Wald test $F = 9.3$, but CAP_{-1} $t = 4.4$), DEP (Wald $F = 17.0$), DJ_0 (Wald $F = 13.0$), PROF_0 (Wald Test $F = 7.2$, but POP_0 $t = 3.3$), and XR_{AV} (Wald $F = 11.6$).

Sargan Test $NR^2 = 10.5 < X^2_{(95,18)} = 28.9$. Hence, this is a Strong Instrument Model.

$$\underset{(t=)}{\Delta I_T} = +.35\underset{(2.7)}{\Delta(\text{ACC})} + .17\underset{(1.7)}{\boldsymbol{\Delta}(\mathbf{T_T})} - .45\underset{(-2.8)}{\boldsymbol{\Delta}(\mathbf{G_{T\&I}})} + .42\underset{(0.7)}{\Delta\text{DEP}} + 5.19\underset{(1.1)}{\Delta\text{CAP}_{-1}}$$

$$- .53\underset{(-0.1)}{\Delta\text{PR}_{-2}} + .20\underset{(0.7)}{\Delta\text{DJ}_{-0}} + .18\underset{(2.4)}{\Delta\text{PROF}_{-0}} + 7.00\underset{(2.1)}{\Delta\text{XR}_{\text{AV}}} + .015\underset{(2.3)}{\Delta\text{POP}}$$

$$+ .06\underset{(0.9)}{\boldsymbol{\Delta}(\textbf{BOR}_{-1})} - 12.08\underset{(-1.0)}{\boldsymbol{\Delta}\textbf{UNEM}}$$

$$\text{R}^2 = 93.1\% \quad \text{D.W.} = 2.1 \quad \text{MSE} = 33.70 \qquad (8.2.\text{Alt.a})$$

And using the Alt2 form of strong instruments:

Model 8.2. Alt.a2 2SLS estimates of determinants of investment spending, using real GDP_{-3} as the business cycle control variable

(Hausman tests indicate three variables endogenous with investment spending, so instrumented: DEP (Wald test $F = 18.5$), DJ_0 (Wald $F = 12.8$, but $t > 3.3$ for T_T and DJ_{-2}), and PROF_0 (Wald Test $F = 5.3$, but $t = 4.9$ for DJ_{-2}) Sargan Test $NR^2 = 7.5 < X^2_{(95,16)} = 26.3$. Hence, this is a Strong Instrument Model)

$$\underset{(t=)}{\Delta I_T} = +\underset{(3.7)}{0.26\Delta(\text{ACC})} + \underset{(2.5)}{0.21\boldsymbol{\Delta}(\mathbf{T}_{\text{T}})} - \underset{(-3.1)}{0.40\boldsymbol{\Delta}(\mathbf{G}_{\text{T\&I}})} + \underset{(0.5)}{0.26\Delta\text{DEP}}$$

$$+\underset{(1.0)}{2.37\Delta\text{CAP}_{-1}} + \underset{(0.4)}{1.66\Delta\text{PR}_{-2}} - \underset{(-0.2)}{0.07\Delta\text{DJ}_{-0}} + \underset{(2.7)}{0.34\Delta\text{PROF}_{-0}}$$

$$+\underset{(2.3)}{6.61\Delta\text{XR}_{\text{AV}}} + \underset{(2.3)}{0.015\Delta\text{POP}} + \underset{(1.7)}{0.16\,\boldsymbol{\Delta}(\mathbf{BOR}_{-1})} - \underset{(-1.4)}{10.68\,\boldsymbol{\Delta}\mathbf{UNEM}}$$

$$R^2 = 92.0\% \quad \text{D.W.} = 1.9 \quad \text{MSE} = 36.09 \qquad (8.2.\text{Alt.a2})$$

The next model is the same as Eq. 8.2.Alt., except DJ_{-2} and $Prof_{-2}$ were restored to the instrument used, strengthening it, though they are not used in the structural model itself.

Model 8.2.Alt.b 2SLS estimates of determinants of investment spending, unemployment rate used as business cycle control, same as 8.2.Alt except twice-lagged DJ and profits variables used

$$\underset{(t=)}{\Delta I_T} = +\underset{(4.9)}{0.33\Delta(\text{ACC})} + \underset{(2.0)}{0.22\boldsymbol{\Delta}(\mathbf{T}_{\text{T}})} - \underset{(-3.4)}{0.53\boldsymbol{\Delta}(\mathbf{G}_{\text{T\&I}})} + \underset{(3.0)}{0.81\Delta\text{DEP}}$$

$$+\underset{(1.0)}{2.39\Delta\text{CAP}_{-1}} - \underset{(-0.9)}{2.29\Delta\text{PR}_{-2}} + \underset{(0.4)}{0.10\Delta\text{DJ}_{-0}} + \underset{(1.9)}{0.13\Delta\text{PROF}_{-0}}$$

$$+\underset{(2.4)}{5.87\Delta\text{XR}_{\text{AV}}} + \underset{(2.8)}{0.013\Delta\text{POP}} + \underset{(0.9)}{0.05\,\boldsymbol{\Delta}(\mathbf{BOR}_{-1})} - \underset{(-1.5)}{12.40\,\boldsymbol{\Delta}\mathbf{UNEM}}$$

$$R^2 = 93.1\ \% \quad \text{D.W.} = 2.0 \quad \text{MSE} = 33.05 \qquad (8.2.\text{Alt.b})$$

Equation 8.2.Alt.b Graphed: Actual Investment Versus Investment Explained by Model 8.2.Alt.b. 1960–2010

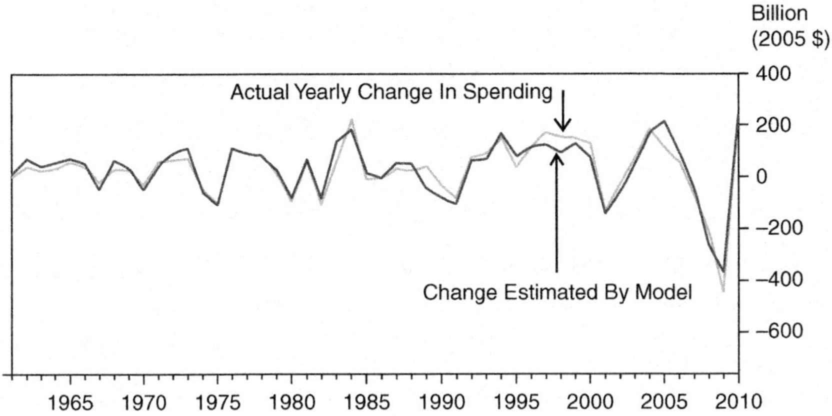

If no business cycle control variable is used, results are as follows:

Model 8.3 OLS Estimates of Determinants of Investment Spending, No Business Cycle Control Variable Used.

$$\underset{(t=)}{\Delta I_T} = +\underset{(6.4)}{0.33\Delta(\text{ACC})} + \underset{(3.8)}{0.30\boldsymbol{\Delta}(\mathbf{T}_\text{T})} - \underset{(-4.1)}{0.43\boldsymbol{\Delta}(\mathbf{G}_{\text{T\&I}})} + \underset{(3.9))}{1.41\Delta\text{DEP}}$$

$$+\underset{(1.4)}{3.26\Delta\text{CAP}_{-1}} - \underset{(-1.7)}{3.59\Delta\text{PR}_{-2}} - \underset{(-3.4)}{0.38\Delta\text{DJ}_{-2}} - \underset{(-1.0)}{0.08\Delta\text{PROF}_{-2}}$$

$$+\underset{(3.1)}{5.05\Delta\text{XR}_\text{AV}} + \underset{(1.9)}{0.007\Delta\text{POP}} + \underset{(1.5)}{0.08\,\boldsymbol{\Delta}(\mathbf{BOR}_{-1})}$$

$$\mathbf{R}^2 = 94.1\ \% \quad \text{D.W.} = 1.8 \quad \text{MSE} = 30.27 \qquad (8.3)$$

And the "a" version using current period values of the DJ and Prof variables is:

Model 8.3.a OLS estimates of determinants of investment spending, no business cycle control variable used

$$\underset{(t=)}{\Delta I_T} = +\underset{(5.4)}{0.33\Delta(\text{ACC})} + \underset{(3.1)}{0.29\boldsymbol{\Delta}(\mathbf{T}_\text{T})} - \underset{(-3.6)}{0.40\boldsymbol{\Delta}(\mathbf{G}_{\text{T\&I}})} + \underset{(2.7)}{0.88\Delta\text{DEP}}$$

$$+ \underset{(1.5)}{2.95\Delta\text{CAP}_{-1}} - \underset{(-1.7)}{2.74\Delta\text{PR}_{-0}} - \underset{(-0.0)}{0.003\Delta\text{DJ}_{-0}} + \underset{(2.0)}{0.14\Delta\text{PROF}_{-0}}$$

$$+ \underset{(2.3)}{5.71\Delta\text{XR}_{\text{AV}}} + \underset{(2.1)}{0.008\Delta\text{POP}} + \underset{(1.9)}{0.11\ \boldsymbol{\Delta}(\mathbf{BOR}_{-1})}$$

$$\mathbf{R}^2 = 93.2\ \% \quad \text{D.W.} = 1.9 \quad \text{MSE} = 32.70 \qquad (8.3.\text{a})$$

Model 8.3.Alt 2SLS estimates of determinants of investment spending, using real GDP_{-3} as the business cycle control variable

(Hausman tests indicate $G_{T\&I,}$ and POP endogenous with investment borrowing, so instrumented: $G_{T\&I}$ (Wald $F = 3.47$, but $t = 4.5$ for M2_{AV} Instrument Component), and POP (Wald $F = 4.92$, but $t = 4.3$ for $Y - T_T$ component. Sargan Test $\text{NR}^2 = 25.50 < X^2_{(95,18)} = 28.87$) 2SLS Tests Results Below. These Are Strong Instruments

$$\underset{(t=)}{\Delta I_T} = +\underset{(6.7)}{0.34\Delta(\text{ACC})} + \underset{(5.1)}{0.30\boldsymbol{\Delta}(\mathbf{T}_\text{T})} - \underset{(-5.6)}{0.63\boldsymbol{\Delta}(\mathbf{G}_{\text{T\&I}})} + \underset{(4.2))}{1.45\Delta\text{DEP}}$$

$$+ \underset{(1.5)}{3.84\Delta\text{CAP}_{-1}} - \underset{(-1.5)}{3.05\Delta\text{PR}_{-2}} - \underset{(-4.0)}{0.41\Delta\text{DJ}_{-2}} - \underset{(-0.9)}{0.07\Delta\text{PROF}_{-2}}$$

$$+ \underset{(3.5)}{5.62\Delta\text{XR}_{\text{AV}}} + \underset{(2.9)}{0.011\Delta\text{POP}} + \underset{(0.6)}{0.03\ \boldsymbol{\Delta}(\mathbf{BOR} - 1)}$$

$$\mathbf{R}^2 = 93.6\% \quad \text{D.W.} = 1.8 \quad \text{MSE} = 31.62 \qquad (8.3.\text{Alt})$$

And testing the alternate current period forms of Tobin's q and profits yields:

Model 8.3. Alt.a 2SLS estimates of determinants of investment spending, using no business cycle control variable

(Hausman tests indicate four variables endogenous with investment spending, so instrumented: ACC (Wald test $F = 11.5$), DJ_0 (Wald $F = 11.8$), $PROF_0$ (Wald Test $F = 6.0$, but DJ_{-2} $t = 3.9$) and POP (Wald $F = 13.1$). Sargan Test $NR^2 = 4.0 < X^2_{(95,14)} = 23.7$. Hence, Strong Instrument Model)

$$\underset{(t=)}{\Delta I_T} = +\underset{(2.8)}{0.36\Delta(ACC)} + \underset{(2.4)}{0.21\mathbf{\Delta}(\mathbf{T}_T)} - \underset{(-3.2)}{0.45\mathbf{\Delta}(\mathbf{G}_{T\&I})} + \underset{(1.2))}{0.86\Delta DEP}$$

$$+ \underset{(1.6)}{5.91\Delta CAP_{-1}} - \underset{(-0.1)}{0.23\Delta PR_{-2}} + \underset{(0.2)}{0.07\Delta DJ_{-0}} + \underset{(2.8)}{0.26\Delta PROF_{-0}}$$

$$+ \underset{(2.6)}{6.95\Delta XR_{AV}} + \underset{(1.5)}{0.01\Delta POP} + \underset{(1.5)}{0.09\ \mathbf{\Delta}(\mathbf{BOR}_{-1})}$$

$$R^2 = 92.6\ \% \quad D.W. = 2.1 \quad MSE = 34.51 \qquad (Eq.8.3.Alt.a)$$

Using the Alt.a2 form of strong instrument, we have

Model 8.3.Alt.a2 2SLS estimates of determinants of investment spending, using no business cycle control variable

(Hausman tests indicate two variables endogenous with investment spending, so instrumented: DJ_0 (Wald $F = 10.3$, but $t > 3.3$ for T_T Instrument for $Prof_0$: Wald Test $F= 5.7$, but $t=4.8$ for DJ_{-2} Sargan Test $NR^2=7.0 < X^2_{(95,15)} = 25.0$. Hence, Strong Instrument Model)

$$\underset{(t=)}{\Delta I_T} = +\underset{(2.8)}{0.28\Delta(ACC)} + \underset{(3.4)}{0.25\mathbf{\Delta}(\mathbf{T}_T)} - \underset{(-4.1)}{0.40\mathbf{\Delta}(\mathbf{G}_{T\&I})} + \underset{(1.7)}{0.71\Delta DEP}$$

$$+ \underset{(0.5)}{2.88\Delta CAP_{-1}} + \underset{(0.4)}{1.41\Delta PR_{-2}} - \underset{(-0.4)}{0.14\Delta DJ_{-0}} + \underset{(2.5)}{0.38\Delta PROF_{-0}}$$

$$+ \underset{(2.8)}{6.81\Delta XR_{AV}} + \underset{(2.0)}{0.01\Delta POP} + \underset{(1.4)}{0.18\ \mathbf{\Delta}(\mathbf{BOR}_{-1})}$$

$$R^2 = 92.6\ \% \quad D.W. = 2.1 \quad MSE = 34.51 \qquad (8.3.Alt.a2)$$

Table 8.1 2SLS investment spending findings summarized, compared to OLS (two-variable deficit effects)

Two-Variable OLS and 2SLS Investment Spending Model Findings Summarized

Model#	$\Delta (T_T)$ β (*t-stat.*)	$\Delta (G_{T\&I})$ β (*t-stat.*)	$\Delta (BOR_{-1})$ (*t-stat.*)	*Bus. Cycle Control*	*Method*
8.1	0.31 (4.2)	−0.46 (−4.3)	0.08 (1.5)	GDP $_{Real(-3)}$	OLS
8.1.a	0.30 (3.3)	−0.43 (−3.7)	0.13 (2.2)	GDP $_{Real(-3)}$	OLS
8.1.Alt	0.33 (3.5)	−0.68 (−5.8)	−0.16 (−1.9)		2SLS (Strong Inst.Alt)
8.1.Alt.a	0.26 (3.3)	−0.54 (−3.6)	0.08 (1.4)		2SLS (Str.Inst. Alt.a)
8.1.Alt.a2	0.27 (3.5)	−0.48 (−3.5)	0.17 (2.7)		2SLS (Str.Inst. Alt.a2)
8.2	0.24 (2.8)	−0.41 (−4.0)	0.06 (1.1)	Unem. Rate	OLS
8.2a	0.21 (1.9)	−0.38 (−3.1)	0.08 (1.5)	Unem. Rate	OLS
8.2.Alt	0.24 (3.0)	−0.58 (−5.8)	0.02 (0.3)		2SLS (Strong Inst.) "
8.2.Alt.a	0.17 (1.7)	−0.45 (−2.8)	0.06 (0.9)		2SLS (Str.Inst. Alt.a)
8.2.Alt.a2	0.21 (2.5)	−0.40 (−3.1)	0.16 (1.7)		2SLS (Str.Inst. Alt.a2)
8.2.Alt.b	0.22 (2.0)	−0.53 (−3.4)	0.05 (0.9)		2SLS (Str.Inst. Alt.b)
8.3	0.30 (3.8)	−0.43 (−4.1)	0.08 (1.5)	None	OLS
8.3.a	0.29 (3.1)	−0.40 (−3.6)	0.11 (1.9)	None	OLS
8.3.Alt	0.30 (5.1)	−0.63 (−5.6)	0.03 (0.6)		2SLS (Strong Inst.)
8.3.Alt.a	0.21 (2.4)	−0.45 (−3.2)	0.09 (1.5)		2SLS (Str. Inst. Alt. a)
8.3.Alt.a2	0.25 (3.4)	−0.40 (−4.1)	0.18 (1.4)		2SLS (Str.Inst. Alt.a2)
Average (All)	0.26 (3.2)	−0.47 (−4.0)	0.08 (1.2)		
Av.(OLS Only)	0.28 (3.6)	−0.43 (−4.1)	0.07 (1.4)	w/ DJ_{-2}, $PROF_{-2}$ models only (8.1,2&3)	
Av.(OLS Only)	0.27 (2.8)	−0.40 (−3.5)	0.10 (1.9)	w/ DJ_0, $PROF_0$ models only (8.1a,2a&3a)	
Av.(2SLS Only)	0.29 (3.9)	−0.63 (−5.7)	−0.04 (−0.3)	w/ DJ_{-2}, $PROF_{-2}$ models only (8.1,2,3.Alt)	
Av.(2SLS Only)	0.23 (2.8)	−0.45 (−3.4)	0.12 (1.6)	w/ DJ_0, $PROF_0$ mod. only(8.1-3.Alt a,a2)	

Alt = 2SLS; Strong Instrument
a = DJ_0 and $Prof_0$ Used instead of DJ_2 and $Prof_2$;
a2 = Instruments include "suspect" endogenous variables not found endogenous

8.1.1 2SLS Business Spending Findings Summarized, Compared to OLS

Table 8.1 below summarizes the findings of 2SLS tests on investment spending and compares them to the results obtained using OLS.

Comparing the subgroup averages, the effects of tax deficits are similar for OLS and 2SLS models, suggesting that for the OLS estimates, every dollar of tax deficit is associated with about \$0.27–\$0.28 decline in investment spending. For the 2SLS estimates, the decline in investment was \$0.23–\$0.29. For deficits caused by government spending increases, the OLS results suggest about a \$0.40–\$0.41 decline in investment spending per dollar increase in the deficit, but the 2SLS results suggest a larger decline: \$0.45–\$0.61 per dollar of deficit. Because the 2SLS estimates better control for the endogeneity problem, we consider these to be the more accurate estimates. Unlike the findings for consumption, access to borrowing does not seem to trigger any systematic increase in spending, independent of that caused by the other explanatory variables in the model.

8.2 OLS and 2SLS Borrowing Models

Unlike the spending model, there is good reason for the relationship between the Dow Jones composite average and business borrowing to be negative. Growth in equity assets should reduce the need to borrow. Hence, though we changed the profits variable from the two-period lag to zero-period lag in the "a" models below, we left the DJ average variable lagged one period. Using DJ_0 gave a consistently positive (but not significant) relationship with current borrowing, and reduced somewhat, the measured negative effect of crowd out on borrowing, but had no significant effect on the other variables in the model. While one can see why growing stock values might reduce crowd out's effects by reducing borrowing needs, it is hard to see why crowd out effects would decline if growing stock market prices increased demand for borrowed funds, as the positive correlation between DJ_0 and borrowing suggests. Hence, it seemed more plausible to stay with DJ_{-1}, which was found negatively related to current year borrowing, and therefore, more theoretically plausible, but left crowd out estimates slightly smaller, but closer to those obtained using the $PROF_{-2}$ models.

Model 8.4 OLS estimates of determinants of business borrowing, using real GDP_{-3} as the business cycle control, DJ_{-1} and $PROF_0$ used

$$\underset{(t=)}{\Delta I_B} = -\underset{(-0.3)}{.11\Delta(ACC)} + \underset{(2.4)}{.87\boldsymbol{\Delta}(\mathbf{T}_T)} - \underset{(-3.5)}{.88\boldsymbol{\Delta}(\mathbf{G}_{T\&I})} - \underset{(-0.4)}{.68\Delta DEP} - \underset{(-2.3)}{23.48\Delta CAP_{-1}}$$
$$- \underset{(-1.7)}{10.93\Delta PR_{-2}} - \underset{(-2.7)}{2.11\,\Delta DJ_{-1}} + \underset{(3.2)}{1.23\Delta PROF_{-2}} + \underset{(2.4)}{20.10\,\Delta XR_{AV}}$$
$$+ \underset{(3.0)}{.038\Delta POP} - \underset{(-1.0)}{.15\,\Delta(M2 - M1)_{Real}} - \underset{(-1.0)}{.17\,\boldsymbol{\Delta}\mathbf{GDP}_{\mathbf{Real}(-3)}}$$
$$R^2 = 59.6\% \quad D.W. = 1.9 \quad MSE = 119.82 \qquad (8.4)$$

Model 8.4.a OLS estimates of determinants of business borrowing, using real GDP_{-3} as the business cycle control variable, DJ_{-1} and $PROF_0$ used

$$\underset{(t=)}{\Delta I_B} = -\underset{(-0.7)}{0.19\Delta(ACC)} + \underset{(1.9)}{0.50\boldsymbol{\Delta}(\mathbf{T}_T)} - \underset{(-2.4)}{0.72\boldsymbol{\Delta}(\mathbf{G}_{T\&I})} - \underset{(-0.7)}{1.24\Delta DEP}$$
$$- \underset{(-1.8)}{15.32\Delta CAP_{-1}}\ \underset{(1.4)}{10.96\Delta PR_{-2}} - \underset{(-0.7)}{0.41\Delta DJ_{-1}} + \underset{(4.1)}{0.96\Delta PROF_0}$$
$$+ \underset{(2.1)}{14.24\,\Delta XR_{AV}} + \underset{(2.4)}{0.045\Delta POP} - \underset{(-0.4)}{0.07\,\Delta(M2 - M1)_{Real}}$$
$$- \underset{(-2.1)}{0.29\,\boldsymbol{\Delta}\mathbf{GDP}_{\mathbf{Real}(-3)}}$$
$$R^2 = 57.5\% \quad D.W. = 2.0 \quad MSE = 122.89 \qquad (8.4.a)$$

Model 8.4.Alt 2SLS Estimates Of Determinants Of Business Borrowing, Using Real GDP_{-3} As The Business Cycle Control Variable

(Hausman tests indicate DEP endogenous with investment borrowing, so instrumented (Wald $F = 13.4$, several instrument components $t \geq 3.3$) 2SLS tests results below. Sargan test $NR^2=23.00 < X^2_{(95,19)} = 30.14$) (Strong Instrument Model)

$$\underset{(t=)}{\Delta I_B} = -\underset{(-0.5)}{0.14\Delta(ACC)} + \underset{(2.5)}{0.96\boldsymbol{\Delta}(\mathbf{T}_T)} - \underset{(-3.6)}{0.89\boldsymbol{\Delta}(\mathbf{G}_{T\&I})} - \underset{(-1.1)}{2.12\Delta DEP}$$
$$- \underset{(-2.2)}{23.05\Delta CAP_{-1}} - \underset{(-1.7)}{11.47\Delta PR_{-2}} - \underset{(-2.6)}{2.00\,\Delta DJ_{-1}} + \underset{(3.7)}{1.30\Delta PROF_{-2}}$$
$$+ \underset{(2.4)}{20.97\,\Delta XR_{AV}} + \underset{(3.3)}{0.043\Delta POP} - \underset{(-0.7)}{0.09\,\Delta(M2 - M1)_{Real}}$$
$$- \underset{(-0.5)}{0.09\,\boldsymbol{\Delta}\mathbf{GDP}_{\mathbf{Real}(-3)}} \quad R^2 = 58.8\ \% \quad D.W. = 1.9 \quad MSE = 121.04$$

(8.4.Alt)

And the same model using the unemployment rate as the business cycle control variable, yields the following results:

Model 8.5 OLS estimates of determinants of business borrowing, using the unemployment rate as the business cycle control variable

$$\underset{(t=)}{\Delta I_B} = -\underset{(-0.1)}{0.03\Delta(\mathrm{ACC})} + \underset{(2.5)}{1.09\boldsymbol{\Delta}(\mathbf{T}_{\mathrm{T}})} - \underset{(-4.4)}{1.03\boldsymbol{\Delta}(\mathbf{G}_{\mathrm{T\&I}})} - \underset{(-1.0)}{1.63\Delta\mathrm{DEP}}$$
$$-\underset{(-2.0)}{16.48\Delta\mathrm{CAP}_{-1}} - \underset{(-1.7)}{13.93\Delta\mathrm{PR}_{-2}} - \underset{(-2.8)}{2.00\Delta\mathrm{DJ}_{-1}} + \underset{(3.4)}{1.32\Delta\mathrm{PROF}_{-2}}$$
$$+\underset{(3.1)}{23.42\Delta\mathrm{XR}_{\mathrm{AV}}} + \underset{(2.1)}{0.031\Delta\mathrm{POP}} - \underset{(-0.6)}{0.10\,\Delta(\mathrm{M2}-\mathrm{M1})_{\mathrm{Real}}}$$
$$+\underset{(1.4)}{40.19\,\boldsymbol{\Delta}\mathbf{UNEM}} \quad \mathrm{R}^2 = 60.2\ \% \quad \mathrm{D.W.} = 1.9 \quad \mathrm{MSE} = 118.90 \tag{8.5}$$

Model 8.5.a OLS estimates of determinants of business borrowing, using the unemployment rate as the business cycle control variable

$$\underset{(t=)}{\Delta I_B} = -\underset{(-0.4)}{0.11\Delta(\mathrm{ACC})} + \underset{(2.2)}{0.70\boldsymbol{\Delta}(\mathbf{T}_{\mathrm{T}})} - \underset{(-3.4)}{0.91\boldsymbol{\Delta}(\mathbf{G}_{\mathrm{T\&I}})} - \underset{(-1.2)}{2.58\Delta\mathrm{DEP}}$$
$$-\underset{(-0.7)}{5.51\Delta\mathrm{CAP}_{-1}} + \underset{(1.0)}{9.91\Delta\mathrm{PR}_{-2}} - \underset{(-0.4)}{0.224\Delta\mathrm{DJ}_{-1}} + \underset{(4.0)}{0.98\Delta\mathrm{PROF}_{0}}$$
$$+\underset{(2.8)}{18.53\Delta\mathrm{XR}_{\mathrm{AV}}} + \underset{(1.9)}{0.035\Delta\mathrm{POP}} - \underset{(-0.2)}{0.05\,\Delta(\mathrm{M2}-\mathrm{M1})_{\mathrm{Real}}}$$
$$+\underset{(1.4)}{34.38\,\boldsymbol{\Delta}\mathbf{UNEM}} \quad R^2 = 56.1\ \% \quad \mathrm{D.W.} = 1.90 \quad \mathrm{MSE} = 124.96 \tag{8.5.a}$$

Model 8.5.Alt 2SLS estimates of determinants of business borrowing, using the unemployment rate as the business cycle control variable

(Hausman tests indicate DEP endogenous with investment borrowing, so instrumented (Wald $F = 13.4$, several instrument components $t \geq 5.0$) 2SLS tests results below. Sargan test $\mathrm{NR}^2 = 21.42 < X^2_{(95,19)} = 30.14$) (Strong Instrument)

$$\underset{(t=)}{\Delta I_B} = -\underset{(-0.3)}{0.08\Delta(\text{ACC})} + \underset{(2.4)}{1.21\boldsymbol{\Delta}(\mathbf{T}_\text{T})} - \underset{(-4.1)}{1.02\boldsymbol{\Delta}(\mathbf{G}_{\text{T\&I}})} - \underset{(-1.7)}{3.11\Delta\text{DEP}}$$
$$-\underset{(-2.2)}{17.20\Delta\text{CAP}_{-1}} - \underset{(-1.9)}{14.79\Delta\text{PR}_{-2}} - \underset{(-2.6)}{1.85\Delta\text{DJ}_{-1}} + \underset{(3.8)}{1.38\Delta\text{PROF}_{-2}}$$
$$+\underset{(2.9)}{23.07\Delta\text{XR}_\text{AV}} + \underset{(2.6)}{0.039\Delta\text{POP}} - \underset{(-0.0)}{.01\,\Delta(\text{M2}-\text{M1})_\text{Real}}$$
$$+\underset{(1.4)}{45.69\,\boldsymbol{\Delta}\mathbf{UNEM}} \quad R^2 = 59.2\,\% \quad \text{D.W.} = 1.9 \quad \text{MSE} = 120.40 \tag{8.5.Alt}$$

And the same model without any business cycle control variable yields the following results:

Model 8.6 OLS estimates of determinants of business borrowing, using no business cycle control variable

$$\underset{(t=)}{\Delta I_B} = -\underset{(-0.3)}{0.09\Delta(\text{ACC})} + \underset{(2.5)}{.90\boldsymbol{\Delta}(\mathbf{T}_\text{T})} - \underset{(-4.4)}{.95\boldsymbol{\Delta}(\mathbf{G}_{\text{T\&I}})} - \underset{(-0.8)}{1.34\Delta\text{DEP}}$$
$$-\underset{(-2.3)}{20.30\Delta\text{CAP}_{-1}} - \underset{(-1.6)}{11.25\Delta\text{PR}_{-2}} - \underset{(-2.8)}{2.12\Delta\text{DJ}_{-1}} + \underset{(3.6)}{1.29\Delta\text{PROF}_{-2}}$$
$$+\underset{(3.1)}{22.81\Delta\text{XR}_\text{AV}} + \underset{(2.6)}{.034\Delta\text{POP}} - \underset{(-1.2)}{0.17\,\Delta(\text{M2}-\text{M1})_\text{Real}}$$
$$R^2 = 58.8\,\% \quad \text{D.W.} = 2.0 \quad \text{MSE} = 119.50 \tag{8.6}$$

Model 8.6.a OLS estimates of determinants of business borrowing, using no business cycle control variable

$$\underset{(t=)}{\Delta I_B} = -\underset{(-0.6)}{.16\Delta(\text{ACC})} + \underset{(2.2)}{.54\boldsymbol{\Delta}(\mathbf{T}_\text{T})} - \underset{(-3.4)}{.85\boldsymbol{\Delta}(\mathbf{G}_{T\&I})} - \underset{(-1.2)}{2.33\Delta\text{DEP}}$$
$$-\underset{(-1.2)}{9.00\Delta\text{CAP}_{-1}}\ \underset{(1.2)}{11.80\Delta\text{PR}_{-2}} - \underset{(-0.7)}{0.35\Delta\text{DJ}_{-1}} + \underset{(3.8)}{0.97\Delta\text{PROF}_0}$$
$$+\underset{(2.7)}{18.15\Delta\text{XR}_\text{AV}} + \underset{(2.2)}{0.040\Delta\text{POP}} - \underset{(-0.6)}{0.10\,\Delta(\text{M2}-\text{M1})_\text{Real}}$$
$$R^2 = 55.0\,\% \quad \text{D.W.} = 2.0 \quad \text{MSE} = 124.86 \tag{8.6.a}$$

Model 8.6.Alt 2SLS estimates of determinants of business borrowing, using no business cycle control variable.

(Hausman Tests Indicate DEP Endogenous With Investment Borrowing, So Instrumented (Wald $F = 13.4$, Several Instrument Components $t \geq 5.0$)

2SLS Tests Results Below. Sargan Test $NR^2 = 23.00 < X^2_{(95,19)} = 30.14$)
(Strong Instrument Model)

$$\underset{(t=)}{\Delta I_B} = -\underset{(-0.5)}{0.14\Delta(\mathrm{ACC})} + \underset{(2.6)}{.99\boldsymbol{\Delta}(\mathbf{T}_\mathrm{T})} - \underset{(-4.4)}{.93\boldsymbol{\Delta}(\mathbf{G}_{\mathrm{T\&I}})} - \underset{(-1.8)}{2.66\Delta\mathrm{DEP}}$$

$$-\underset{(-2.5)}{21.43\Delta\mathrm{CAP}_{-1}} - \underset{(-1.7)}{11.69\Delta\mathrm{PR}_{-2}} - \underset{(-2.6)}{1.99\Delta\mathrm{DJ}_{-1}} + \underset{(4.0)}{1.34\Delta\mathrm{PROF}_{-2}}$$

$$+\underset{(2.9)}{22.41\Delta\mathrm{XR}_{\mathrm{AV}}} + \underset{(3.2)}{0.042\Delta\mathrm{POP}} - \underset{(-0.7)}{0.09\,\Delta(\mathrm{M2}-\mathrm{M1})_{\mathrm{Real}}}$$

$$R^2 = 58.0\ \% \quad \mathrm{D.W.} = 2.0 \quad \mathrm{MSE} = 120.68 \qquad (8.6.\mathrm{Alt})$$

Note: Testing the (a) model form, which uses current period profits as a determinant of borrowing, not two-period lagged values as done in the models above, failed to show any explanatory variables Hausman-endogenous with business borrowing in any of the three business cycle models tested (GDP_{-3} UNEM and no control). The GDP_0 control model was not tested, since it had not been found highly correlated with the deficit in prior testing. Since the purpose of using the control was to see if controlling for the business cycle explained the tendency of the deficit and borrowing to move together due to the effects on both of the business cycles, GDP_0 did not seem to warrant further testing.

8.3 OLS and 2SLS Spending and Borrowing Findings Summarized

The two-variable formulation of the deficit was used in 24 tests of the investment spending or borrowing relationship to deficits. The effects of deficits caused by tax cuts and those caused by increases in government spending were separately tested to determine how they affected investment borrowing and spending. Results are summarized in this section.

Table 8.2 below summarizes the study's 2SLS findings regarding crowd out's effect on business borrowing, and compares them to its OLS findings.

Estimates generally indicate there is approximately a dollar reduction in business borrowing for each dollar increase in the deficit, regardless of whether the deficit is caused by tax cuts or spending increases, and estimates are all statistically significant, though the negative effects of spending deficits are the most significant. Hence, these nine borrowing model tests strongly support the crowd out hypothesis. Results using the same models, except current period profits are substituted for two-year lagged profits, also corroborate the crowd out hypothesis, though showing only \$0.61–\$0.83

reduced borrowing for each dollar of deficit. However, this may be because current period profits can proxy to some extent for business cycle effects. There is virtually no difference between the OLS and 2SLS estimates when using the two-year lagged version of the profits variable.

By comparison, findings presented earlier for the effects of deficits on *consumer* borrowing indicate each dollar of tax deficits was associated with a \$0.65 ($t = 2.1$) drop in consumer borrowing, and a dollar of spending deficit associated with a \$0.57 ($t = 1.9$) drop in consumer borrowing (average of OLS and 2SLS strong instrument findings from Table 7.2). So we conclude the effect of deficits on consumer borrowing is smaller than the effect on investment borrowing, but still substantial.

A point estimate of the total decline in consumer and business *borrowing* associated with each dollar of deficit is:

Hence, the estimates of the total effect on consumer and investment borrowing of tax cut and spending deficits is essentially the same: \$1.48–\$1.54 less borrowing per dollar of deficit.

Table 8.2 2SLS business borrowing conclusions summarized, compared to OLS (two-variable deficit effects)

Two-Variable OLS and 2SLS Business Borrowing Model Findings Summarized:

Model#	*$\Delta(T_T)$ β (t-stat.)*	*$\Delta(G_{T\&I})$ β (t-stat.)*	*Bus. Cycle Control*	*Method*
8.4	.87 (2.4)	- **.88 (−3.6)**	GDP $_{Real(-3)}$	OLS (Used)
8.4.Alt	.96 (2.5)	- .89 (−3.6)		2SLS(DJ$_{-1}$,PROF$_{-2}$,Strong Inst.)
8.4.a	.50 (1.9)	- .72 (−2.4)		OLS (DJ$_{-1}$, PROF$_0$ used)“
8.5	1.09 (2.5)	-**1.03 (−4.4)**	Unem. Rate	OLS
8.5.Alt	1.21 (2.4)	-1.02 (−4.1)		2SLS (DJ$_{-1}$,PROF$_{-2}$,Strong Inst.)
8.5.a	.70 (2.1)	- .91 (−3.4)		OLS (DJ$_{-1}$, PROF$_0$ used)
8.6	.90 (2.5)	- **.95 (−4.4)**	None	OLS
8.6.Alt	.99 (2.6)	- .93 (−4.4)		2SLS (DJ$_{-1}$,PROF$_{-2}$,Strong Inst.)
8.6.a	.54 (2.2)	- .85 (−3.4)		OLS (DJ$_{-1}$, PROF$_0$ used)
Average	1.00 (2.5)	−0.95 (−4.1)		OLS -All ex. “a”
Average	1.05 (2.5)	−0.95 (−4.0)		2SLS Strong Inst.
Average	.61 (2.1)	−0.83 (−3.1)		OLS “a” only
Average	.89 (2.4)	−0.91 (−3.7)		All Models Tested

Deficits are associated with even larger reductions in borrowing by consumers and businesses than reductions associated with the decline in spending. This is shown when these borrowing results are compared with spending results from Table 8.1 repeated in Table 8.3 below. The finding that borrowing decreased more than spending in the same period is consistent with the crowd out argument. It may suggest consumers and businesses are able to substitute savings or new income from the deficit-financed stimulus programs for borrowing they would do in the absence of these sources. (If spending reductions had been larger than borrowing reductions, it would have suggested that some other mechanism beside the crowd out effect (which acts only through reduced borrowing's implications for reduced spending) was contributing to the negative deficit/spending relationship.)

This finding that the borrowing results support the crowd out hypothesis holds for models that control for business cycle effects and those that do not. For the sample period shown, when business cycle effects are controlled for, estimates of the crowd out effect are about 10 % smaller, but still highly statistically significant. The 10 % difference is not statistically significant. This finding contradicts the (Krugman, et.al.) hypothesis that changes in the business cycle are what is responsible for the observed negative relationship between private spending and government deficits, not the crowd out effects of government stimulus programs.

That said, it is not clear why the decline in private borrowing is found to exceed the increase in the deficit. Crowd out theory does not currently

Table 8.3 Declines in borrowing per dollar of deficit*

Tax Cut Deficits:	
Δ(C&I Borrowing)	= Δ (tax cut deficit's effect on both consumption and investment) = ($0.65 average consumption effect + $0.89 average investment effect) Δ T_T = $ 1.54 decline in private borrowing per dollar of tax cut deficit.
Spending Increase Deficits:	
Δ(C&I Borrowing)	= Δ (spending increase deficits effect on consumption and investment) = ($0.57 average consumption effect + $0.91 average investment effect) Δ $G_{T\&I}$ = $ 1.48 decline in private borrowing per dollar of spending deficit.

*Taken from Tables 7.2 and 8.2

provide a theoretical answer to this question, nor does it seem to be addressed empirically in the professional literature. There are several reasons why this may occur:

1. If the government borrows (say) $1000, it may cut private borrowing by a larger amount because borrowing is lumpy. If you need a $10000 loan to finance a new car, and the bank can only give you $9000 (because it recently lent the government $1000 to finance a deficit), you may borrow nothing.
2. Borrowing models in this study only explain about 60 % of the variance. This suggests other factors that systematically affect borrowing, and should be controlled for, may be missing from the models tested. If the left-out variables are determinants of borrowing and are correlated with the deficit variables, the deficit's regression coefficients may be also picking up the left-out variables' effect.
3. The borrowing model combines determinants for both supply and demand of loanable funds, possibly resulting in parameter estimates that entangle both effects.
4. Borrowing data for businesses includes borrowing not only for investment but for other purposes such as cash flow as well. Our dollar for dollar estimates of deficit increases and borrowing declines may not all represent declines in investment borrowing.

In addition, we find spending declines less than private borrowing as deficits increase. Likely reasons why include:

1. Consumer savings or business-retained earnings/equity financing) may be used to fill part of the gap in financing consumer or business spending plans originally intended to be financed by borrowing, thereby diminishing the effect of reduced borrowing on spending.
2. *A dollar deficit may cause an initial dollar decrease in private borrowing due to crowd out. In addition, if the income windfall resulting from the tax cut or government spending stimulus program is used to buy things that consumers or businesses were planning to buy anyway, but finance by borrowing, this would further reduce private borrowing. Theoretically, the decline associated with each $1.00 deficit may be as much as $2.00, even though the decline in private spending directly due to financing the deficit (crowd out) is only $1.00. For example, a $1.00*

decline in private borrowing due to government borrowing to fund the deficit, and a second dollar decline in borrowing because people use the tax cut (or their additional income from the increased government spending) to make expenditures they had previously built into their spending plans, but had originally planned on financing with borrowed money.

A practical example might be an unemployed person who intended to pay for needed food or clothing by credit card borrowing, but due to increased unemployment insurance payments, or because that person became employed on a government stimulus project, now has income to pay for anything needed.

All of these hypotheses warrant further testing.

Table 8.4 below recaps our investment spending results originally presented in Table 8.1.

The 16 tests all indicate a highly statistically significant negative relationship between deficits and investment spending, and the magnitude of the estimated effect is essentially the same regardless of whether business cycle effects are controlled for or not, suggesting the crowd out problem exists in both good and bad economic times. This holds true for both tax cut-induced deficits and deficits caused by increased government spending.

Like the borrowing findings, the spending findings indicate more than a dollar's crowd out effect for each dollar of deficit incurred, though the differences are not as large. For the two-variable results, using Tables 7.1 and 8.1. strong instrument averages, and the negative effect on borrowing per dollar of deficit from of $1.52 for tax cuts, $1.48 for spending deficits (taken from Table 8.3), we get

Variable	*Tax Cut Deficit Effect*	*Spending Deficit Effect*	*Borrowing Variable Effect Tax Cut Deficit ·*	*Spending deficit*
ΔI_T	$0.23\ \Delta T_T$	$-0.45\ \Delta G_{T\&I}$	$0.12\times(0.89$ or $0.91)$	ΔBOR
ΔC_T	$0.59\ \Delta T_T$	$-0.28\ \Delta G_{T\&I}$	$0.12\times(0.65$ or $0.57)$	ΔBOR
$\Delta(I_T{+}C_T)$	$0.82\ \Delta T_T$	$-0.73\ \Delta G_{T\&I}$	$0.24\times(1.54$ or $1.48)$	ΔBOR

This suggests the crowd out effect for tax cuts in two-variable deficit models is $(0.82 + 0.24 \times 1.54 = 1.01)$.

Table 8.4 Recap of findings of deficits and borrowing variable on investment spending (two-variable deficit effects)

Two-Variable OLS and 2SLS Investment Spending Model Findings Summarized

Model#	$\Delta(T_T)$ β (*t-stat.*)	Δ ($G_{T\&I}$) β (*t-stat.*)	Δ (*BOR*) β (*t-stat.*)	*Bus. cycle Control*	*Method*
8.1	0.31 (4.2)	−0.46 (−4.3)	0.08 (1.5)	GDP $_{Real(-3)}$	OLS
8.1.a	0.30 (3.3)	−0.43 (−3.7)	0.13 (2.2)	GDP $_{Real(-3)}$	OLS
8.1.Alt	0.31 (4.6)	−0.77 (−6.3)	−0.08 (−0.9)		2SLS (Strong Inst.Alt)
8.1.Alt.a	0.26 (3.3)	−0.54 (−3.6)	0.08 (1.4)		2SLS (Str.Inst. Alt.a)
8.1.Alt.a2	0.26 (3.5)	−0.48 (−3.5)	0.17 (2.7)		2SLS (Str.Inst. Alt.a2)
8.2	0.24 (2.8)	−0.41 (−4.0)	0.06 (1.1)	Unem. Rate	OLS
8.2a	0.21 (1.9)	−0.38 (−3.1)	0.08 (1.5)	Unem. Rate	OLS
8.2.Alt	0.27 (3.6)	−0.63 (−5.5)	−0.06 (−0.8)		2SLS (Strong Inst.)
8.2.Alt.a	0.16 (1.7)	−0.45 (−2.8)	+.06 (0.9)		2SLS (Str.Inst. Alt.a)
8.2.Alt.b	0.22 (2.0)	−0.53 (−3.4)	0.05 (0.9)		2SLS (Str.Inst. Alt.b)
8.3	0.30 (3.8)	−0.43 (−4.1)	0.08 (1.5)	None	OLS
8.3.a	0.29 (3.1)	−0.40 (−3.6)	0.11 (1.9)	None	OLS
8.3.Alt	0.32 (4.7)	−0.66 (−5.1)	−0.01 (−0.2)		2SLS (Strong Inst.)
8.3.Alt.a	0.21 (2.4)	−0.45 (−3.2)	0.09 (1.5)		2SLS (Str.Inst. Alt.a)
8.3.Alt.a2	0.25 (3.4)	−0.40 (−4.1)	0.18 (1.4)		2SLS (Str.Inst. Alt.a2)
Average (All)	0.29 (4.0)	−0.56 (−4.9)	0.07 (0.4)	(w/ DJ_{-2}, $PROF_{-2}$ models only)	
Av.(OLS Only)	0.28 (3.6)	−0.43 (−4.1)	0.07 (1.4)	(w/ DJ_{-2}, $PROF_{-2}$ models only)	
Av.(OLS Only)	0.27 (2.8)	−0.40 (−3.5)	0.11 (1.9)	(w/ DJ_0, $PROF_0$ models only)	
Av.(2SLS Only)	0.30 (4.3)	−0.69 (−5.6)	−0.05 (−0.6)	(w/ DJ_{-2}, $PROF_{-2}$ models only)	
Av.(2SLS Only)	0.23 (2.9)	−0.47 (−4.1)	+.12 (1.6)	(w/ DJ_0, $PROF_0$ models only(Alta+b)	

And $(0.73 + 0.24 \times 1.48 = 1.09)$ for spending deficits, that is, \$1.09 – \$1.19 crowd out effect for each dollar of deficit. The results indicate the decline in private spending due to crowd out effects are approximately equal to the size of the deficit itself.

Do these results, which indicate deficits completely crowd out the positive effects of stimulus programs imply that deficit-driven Keynesian-type fiscal stimulus programs will always have no effect or negative effects? Based on the methods used above, which represent the best science that can be brought to bear on the issue, the answer appears to be yes, *if the deficits are financed by domestic borrowing*. These findings are not only statistically significant, but appear relatively robust to a wide range of periods sampled, and models tested.

However, there are two alternative ways a deficit can be financed without causing crowd out:

1. One way of financing stimulus programs not subject to crowd out effects, government deficits might be financed by foreign instead of domestic borrowing. At least from the domestic country's perspective, may not create a crowd out problem if it leaves the pool of domestically available loanable funds undisturbed, that is, if it is not done at the expense of less foreign lending that would ordinarily go to domestic consumers or businesses anyway, again creating a crowd out problem. However, even if the crowd out problem is avoided, if continued year after year, the growing national debt, and the nation's ability to pay it back, may cause problems, as it has in several European countries recently.
2. A second way of financing stimulus programs not subject to crowd out effects is financing the deficit by increasing the money supply. This might avoid the crowd out problem, but at the potential cost of increased inflation. In addition, this study was unable to find that the M1 money supply, or its lagged values, was a significant determinant of consumer or investment spending. This may be because the mechanism commonly used to increase M1 (open Market Operations) results in investors trading in securities to the Fed for M1, only, in the main, to use this M1 to buy other securities, not consumer and investment real goods and services.

   Both of these options to domestic borrowing are examined in more detail in Chap. 10.

CHAPTER 9

Are Findings Of One- and Two-Variable Deficit Models Consistent?

Adding the effects of deficits on consumption and investment together, we get total effect of deficits on spending in one-variable deficit models, reported earlier in this volume. (See Tables 5.7 and 6.5 average results for strong instrument models). These results for the one-variable model are recapped here for the variable and borrowing variables as determinants of consumer and investment spending.

Variable	*Tax-cut deficit effect*	*Spending deficit effect*	*Borrowing variable effect*
ΔI_T	$0.33\ \Delta T_T$	$-0.33\ \Delta G_{T\&I}$	0.13 ΔBOR
ΔC_T	$0.46\ \Delta T_T$	$-0.46\ \Delta G_{T\&I}$	0.12 ΔBOR
$\Delta(I_T + C_T)$	$0.79\ \Delta T_T$	$-0.79\ \Delta G_{T\&I}$	0.25

Tables 5.6 and 6.6 show that each dollar of deficit, whether caused by tax cuts or spending, results in \$1.92 decline in private borrowing; therefore, the one-variable deficit results suggests ($0.79 + 0.25 \times 1.92 = \$1.04$) of the stimulus effect of deficits on spending is offset by crowd out, that is, the net effect is small negative.

The two-variable results, using Tables 7.1 and 8.1. 2SLS averages, and the negative effect on borrowing per dollar of deficit of \$1.54 for tax cuts, \$1.48 for spending deficits (taken from Table 8.3), we get

J.J. Heim, *Crowding Out Fiscal Stimulus*,
DOI 10.1007/978-3-319-45967-7_9

Variable	*Tax-cut deficit effect*	*Spending deficit effect*	*Borrowing variable effect*
ΔI_T	0.23 ΔT_T	−0.45 $\Delta G_{T\&I}$	0.12×(0.89 or 0.91) ΔBOR
ΔC_T	0.59 ΔT_T	−0.28 $\Delta G_{T\&I}$	0.12×(0.63 or 0.57) ΔBOR
$\Delta(I_T + C_T)$	0.82 ΔT_T	−0.73 $\Delta G_{T\&I}$	0.24×(1.52 or 1.48) ΔBOR

This suggests the crowd out effect for tax cuts in two-variable deficit models is (0.82 + 0.24 × 1.52 = 1.19).

And (0.73 + 0.24 × 1.48 = 1.09) for spending deficits, that is, \$1.09–\$1.19 crowd out effect for each dollar of deficit. The results indicate the decline in private spending due to crowd out effects are \$0.09–0.19 larger than the size of the deficit itself, indicating net effects are very small or negative and noticeably larger than the net negative effect of one-variable deficit estimates.

To evaluate precise effects on GDP, we have to explicitly compare these crowd out effects to estimated stimulus effects of the deficit. This is done in Chap. 10.

CHAPTER 10

Effects of Stimulus Programs on GDP, Net of Crowd Out Effects

This chapter examines the effect of crowd out on GDP. Recall that Chaps. 5, 6, 7, and 8 examined only the consumption or investment components of GDP.

Chapter 10 (Sect. 10.1) estimates the Keynesian IS curve from this study's regression results. It uses the estimated results to calculate the effects of crowd out on the GDP. Two methods are used. The first calculates IS curve coefficients from consumption and investment curve coefficients previously estimated. The second method directly estimates all IS curve coefficients from one IS curve regression. The estimated effects on GDP of an increase in government spending were negative: one method yielding $ −0.35 per dollar increase in deficit spending, the other indicating $ −0.57. Estimates of the effects of tax cut deficits on GDP were also negative: one estimate was $ −0.47 per dollar of deficit, the other was $ −0.89.

Chapter 10 (Sect. 10.2) uses the Chap. 10 (Sect. 10.1) estimated effects of stimulus programs on the GDP, net of crowd out and earlier results to refute four arguments made by Krugman and others suggesting that under certain circumstances, fiscal stimulus programs will work, and that there are no real crowd out effects. Krugman's arguments are as follows:

(1) The observed negative relationship between private spending and deficits is caused by the business cycle, not crowd out (1/17/13).
(2) Stimulus programs will not have a net positive effect if they are too small (8/20/11), (also CNBC televised interview, 3/20/09).

J.J. Heim, *Crowding Out Fiscal Stimulus*,
DOI 10.1007/978-3-319-45967-7_10

(3) Crowd out can't occur in recessions because private borrowing declines, allowing government to borrow excess loanable funds to fund stimulus programs without causing crowd out (4/28/13).
(4) Because investment is already low in recessions, deficit-financed stimulus programs result in "crowding in", not "crowding out" of investment. This occurs because the stimulus program raises the GDP, which restores business confidence, resulting in increased investment (9/28/09).

The statistical findings obtained earlier which refute each of these arguments are examined in detail in Chap. 10 (Sect. 10.2).

Chapter 10 (Sect. 10.3) revisits Gale and Orszag's (2004) arguments that federal tax cuts and transfer spending increases can successfully stimulate the GDP, though others won't. This assertion was first tested for its effects on consumption and investment in Chap. 5, and found wanting. Here, it is retested using the full IS curve, and again, we could find no support for the argument.

Chapter 10 (Sect. 10.4) calculates the extent to which crowd out, though its negative effects on GDP, raises the unemployment rate. Had the Obama stimulus package been implemented all in one year, we estimate it would have increased unemployment between 1.4 % and 2.6 % for that year. If implemented over two years, the same total effect on unemployment would be half in each of the two years.

The remainder of this chapter provides the detailed analysis used to arrive at the conclusions above.

Two separate methods are used to estimate the net effect of deficits on the GDP, and they produce very similar results:

Method #1: The stimulus and crowd out effects of taxes and government spending deficits are analyzed using the coefficients found in earlier consumption and investment regressions. Adding C and I equation regression coefficients for stimulus and crowd out effects, adjusted for multiplier and accelerator effect estimates from those same equations, allows us to deduce the net stimulus effects of tax and government spending changes. For example, if our C and I regression results show

$\Delta C = 0.50\ \Delta T - 0.60\Delta G + 0.50\Delta\ (Y - T) \ldots + \ldots$ (Other C Determinants' Effects)

$\Delta I = 0.50\ \Delta T - 0.60\Delta G + 0.25\Delta ACC \ldots + \ldots$ (Other I Determinants' Effects)

then, using the implied multiplier/accelerator coefficient of $1/(1 - 0.50 - 0.25) = 4$, the deduced IS Curve coefficients for T, G are

$\Delta Y = 2.00\ \Delta T - 0.80 \Delta G \ldots + \ldots$ (Other C + I determinant Effects, and Net Exports)

Method #2: GDP is directly regressed on its IS curve determinants to obtain regression estimates of these tax and spending net effects.

10.1 Method #1: Effects Inferred from C and I Model Test Results

If we combine the best of our findings for the two-variable deficit models for consumption, (Eq. 7.1. OLS), and investment (Eq. 8.2.Alt.B Strong instrument, 2SLS), both of which include the borrowing variable and business cycle control variable (the unemployment rate or 3-lag GDP), we have the following estimates of marginal effects of deficits, shown below. They are slightly different than results used in similar examples at the end of Section 8 and in Section 9. This is because results from individual equations are used here; the earlier examples used average results from a number of equations tested, which included the specific equations used here.

Effects of Tax and Spending Deficits on Spending—Method 1

	Tax	*Spending*	*Borrowing (Also Affected by Deficits)*		
ΔC_T	$0.55 \Delta T_T$	$-0.26\ \Delta G_{T\&I}$	$+0.12\ \Delta C_{B2}$	MPC=0.50	(Eq. 7.1)
ΔI_T	$0.22 \Delta T_T$	$-\underline{0.53}\ \Delta G_{T\&I}$	$+\underline{0.05}\ \Delta I_{B2(-1)}$	ACC=0.33	(Eq. 8.2.Alt.B)
Total	$0.77 \Delta T_T$	$-0.79\ \Delta G_{T\&I}$	$+0.17\ (\Delta C_{B2} + \Delta I_{B2(-1)})$		

Adding the consumer and investment spending effects together, we get total crowd out effect of tax cuts or spending increases on consumer and investment spending. However, the coefficients on the tax and government spending variables are per dollar of deficit incurred, whereas the coefficient on the borrowing variable's effect on spending is given in dollars of borrowing, which need to be converted to dollars of deficit. Estimates of the effects of the deficit variables on consumer and business borrowing developed earlier are repeated below:

Effects of Tax and Spending Deficits on Spending—Method 1

	Tax	*Spending*	
$\Delta C_B =$	$0.61\ \Delta T_T$	$-0.55\ \Delta G_{T\&I}$	(Eq. 7.5.Alt)
$\Delta I_B =$	$\underline{1.21}\ \Delta T_T$	$-\underline{1.02}\ \Delta G_{T\&I}$	(Eq. 8.5.Alt)
Total	$1.82\ \Delta T_T$	$-1.57\ \Delta G_{T\&I}$	

These estimates indicate that, per dollar of deficit, that private C and I borrowing is reduced by more than one dollar ($1.82 for tax deficits, $1.57 for spending deficits). Results were highly statistically significant. One reason this may occur is because of discontinuities in the dollar magnitude of the borrowing process.

For example, if your company normally borrows enough each year to buy a new $5.00 ($ 5 million) machine, but only $4.00 is available this year because the government borrowed $1.00, you may not borrow any at all, since $4.00 won't pay for the machine. The net effect is that total private borrowing drops considerably more than what's needed to fund the deficit.

Consumer and business spending (and therefore the GDP) may also decline more than the amount of the deficit for the same reason. In addition, consumption and investment models in Section 8 indicate deficits have two effects on spending:

(1) The direct effects of the deficit on spending are given by the coefficients on the tax and government spending variables.
(2) They also reduce the amount people can borrow, and this is independently related to private spending. The amount of spending people do, given their income, interest rates, wealth, and so on, is also independently affected by how their access to borrowing given by the coefficient on the borrowing variable. Equations presented earlier indicate that for consumption, spending declines $0.12 per dollar of reduced borrowing that occurs due to deficits. This is in addition to the direct crowd out effects (measured by the tax and government spending variable coefficients) which cause private borrowing to decline. Here again, this may have to do with discontinuities. Borrowing is usually done to finance "big ticket" items. Reductions in loanable funds of $1.00 may cause deferral of spending on the whole item, perhaps worth $5.00. Conceptually, the deficit variables pick up the direct effect of lost borrowing access, the borrowing variable picks up the rest. There is some evidence of this in previously tested models which were identical except for inclusion of the borrowing variable. This is seen most clearly, for example, in equations 5.5.a and 5.6., which are exactly the same except that 5.6 does not include a borrowing variable. There, when the borrowing variable was dropped, the deficit variable's estimated

effect increased by exactly as much as indicated by the borrowing variable coefficient in Eq. 5.51.a. Comparisons of Eq. 5.15.a and Eq. 5.16-5.16.a show similar results. However, not all model variations show this effect, and there may be other reasons for the observed effect of borrowing declining more than dollar-for-dollar when deficits rise.

There are also other reasons beside discontinuities why net spending effects of deficits may be negative, particularly if stimulus payments made are used to maintain previous spending levels rather than increase them. For example, assume the government borrows a dollar that otherwise would have been borrowed by a new car buyer, and that this dollar is used to pay unemployment insurance to someone newly unemployed.

- Consumer purchases of new cars declines by $1.00 due to government borrowing of $1.00 to pay additional unemployment insurance.
- The new unemployment insurance income may be used to buy $1.00 of food bought last year out of employment income.
- Net observed effect: deficit increases $1.00, consumer spending drops one dollar compared to prior year, hence, the net negative stimulus effect observed.
- GDP also drops as deficit increases, reflecting the decline in consumption spending.
- Theoretically, accommodating monetary policy could increase the loanable funds pool by as much as government borrowing has drawn it down. This would allow the new car purchase to continue. The net effect would be that the deficit increases $1.00, consumer spending (and GDP) increase $1.00 from prior period, that is, a net stimulus effect of the deficit spending would be observed. This is what theory tells us should happen. (Increasing the available funds pool by foreign borrowing could achieve the same result. See Section 12.B for empirical evidence of this occurring during the 1981–83 recession period.) We were not able to find empirical evidence to support the theoretical effects of accommodating monetary policy, that is, changing the M1 money supply could also expand the loanable funds pool, have the same effect on consumption and GDP. When adding the M1 variable to our models, we consistently found it statistically insignificant. Though it is not clear

why, we suspect that one reason may be that most increases of M1 resulting from open market operations result from investors selling their securities to the Fed, and then using the M1 received to purchase other (mainly previously issued) securities, not real goods and services. Hence, increasing M1 the way the USA does it, may increase the bond market index, but probably not the GDP, at least not by much.

- Hence, the net effect of increasing deficits on the GDP theoretically could be positive (accommodating monetary policy works) or negative (accommodating monetary policy isn't attempted, doesn't work, or the new M1 gets channeled mainly into the securities market, not into demand for goods and services).
- Examining similar examples using tax cuts show the same results. For example, people who become unemployed during the current year still have some tax liability for the months they worked. A tax cut would reduce that, increasing disposable income. If the increased disposable income is used to buy food previously bought from employment income, then no net change in spending from the prior period occurs except the reduced purchase of new cars resulting from borrowing done to finance the deficit (using the prior example). Hence, the net observed effect is again that deficit increases are associated with a net decline in consumer spending and GDP.

Tax Cut Deficits (Method #1):

Δ(C & I Spending) = tax cut deficits' effect on consumption and investment

= \$− 0.77 decline in private spending per dollar of tax cut deficit (−0.55 consumption effect−\$0.22 investment effect).
\$− 0.31 additional decline due to reduced borrowing (\$0.17×\$1.82)
\$+0.50 Portion of tax cut saved, which offsets part of \$1.00 loss in loanable funds used to finance deficit
\$+ 0.50 stimulus effect (MPC).
\$−0.08 net initial negative effect on GDP per dollar of tax cut deficit.
X 5.88 multiplier/accelerator effects 1/(1−.50−.33) = 1/.17\$−0.47.
Total decrease in GDP associated with a \$1.00 tax cut stimulus.

Government Spending Deficits (Method #1):

Δ(C&I Spending) = spending deficits' effect on consumption and investment

$-0.79 decline in private spending per dollar of increased deficit spending ($-0.26 consumption effect +$-0.53 investment effect).
$-0.27 additional decline due to reduced borrowing ($0.17×($1.57)).
$+1.00 stimulus effect (Coefficient On G variable in IS function)
$-0.06 net initial negative effect on GDP of a tax cut deficit.
X 5.88 multiplier/accelerator effects 1/(1−.50−.33) = 1/.17
$-0.35. Total decrease in GDP associated with a $1.00 government spending stimulus.

Hence, the estimated net negative effect on the GDP per dollar of deficit is $0.47 for tax cut deficits and $0.35. for spending deficits,

Summarizing our Method#1 estimates of the effect of tax cut or government spending stimulus programs:

$$\Delta Y = 0.47\Delta T_T - 0.35\Delta G_{T\&I} \text{ (where } T_T \text{ is the size of the tax cut deficit and } G_{T\&I} \text{ is the size of the spending deficit)} \quad (10.1)$$

Hence, using Method #1, we conclude that attempts to stimulate the economy with deficits financed by borrowing, generated by either tax cuts or spending increases, are likely to be offset more than totally, by crowd out effects. Their net effect on the GDP is negative. This estimate includes the negative effect on spending of the decline in borrowing associated with shifting the method of finance of some planned spending from borrowing to stimulus income. This may provide the best (scientific) explanation available as to why the Obama stimulus program, which was about ½ tax cuts and ½ spending increases, did not seem to create a noticeable, if any, improvement in the economic situation, and based on our simulation results, probably made it worse. This may help explain why it has taken so long for the economy to rebound.

These results were obtained controlling for the effect of fluctuations in the business cycle on the deficit. The results do not support the hypothesis of Krugman (and many others) that observed simultaneous increases in the deficit and declining private spending are simply (accidental) correlates of an underlying economic decline which drags spending down and pushes deficits up. It is not that this doesn't happen, it is just that this explains only a part of the negative relationship. Most of our estimates suggest only a small part.

Our tests generally indicate crowd out effects of deficits occur at about the same magnitude, at all phases of the business cycle, that is, a separate business cycle variable was often found to be a statistically insignificant factor, given the other variables in the model. Further, its inclusion did not eliminate the statistical significance of the crowd out variable(s). Based on analysis of the other large postwar recession period (1981–83), the robustness of the crowd out effect when controlling for changes in the business cycle is associated with the fact that domestic loanable funds (savings) appears to decline in recessions more than the decline in loan demand (Section 12.B). Hence, any government borrowing from the pool of loanable funds in recessions has as much of a crowd out effect. The evidence indicates deficits incurred in recessions crowd out private borrowing and spending as much or more than they do in good economic times.

A second argument made in favor of stimulus programs is that without them, the economy would just fall further, that is, that government stimulus programs during a downward economic spiral have a net positive effect which offset what would have been further decline. This study's findings indicate that all deficit-financed stimulus programs have a negative, not a positive, effect on GDP. Hence, this study's findings suggest any deficit-financed stimulus program exacerbates downward spirals, not counters them.

A third argument made is that stimulus programs have to be very large to work. But our results indicate that whatever their size, their net effect is negative, not positive.

Method #2: From Direct Estimation of IS Curve Coefficients

In testing the full IS curve all at once to obtain estimates deficit and borrowing variable effects, controlling for all determinant of consumption and investment, plus government spending and net exports, 2SLS was used. Instruments were developed for variables found Hausman-endogenous, the Wald test was used to ensure the instruments used were not weak instruments, and Sargan tests were used to ensure the instruments replacing endogenous variables were not themselves endogenous with the dependent variable (Y). Borrowing and business cycle variables were included in the tests. The Partial Autocorrelations method of determining the order of autocorrelation present in the data was used. (Griffiths, Hill and Judge 1993, p.652) and indicated AR (2) and AR (7) controls were needed. The method basically involves testing t-statistics on p-order partial autocorrelation coefficients for statistical significance. If the t-statistic on the pth order coefficient was significant at the ~5 % level (test criteria t=2.00), an autocorrelation control of the pth order was included in the model. Use of these controls raised the Durbin–Watson statistic from 1.4 to 2.1, indicating the autocorrelation problem had been resolved.

Model 10.2 IS curve, W/O distinguishing between types of tax and government spending

$$\begin{aligned}
\underset{(t=)}{\Delta Y_T} &= \underset{(4.8)}{0.36\boldsymbol{\Delta}(\mathbf{T_T})} - \underset{(-0.6)}{0.11\boldsymbol{\Delta}(\mathbf{G_{T\&I}})} - \underset{(-2.0)}{8.21\Delta PR} - \underset{(-2.1)}{0.35\,\Delta DJ_{-0}} \\
&+ \underset{(4.7)}{1.04\,\Delta DJ_{-2}} - \underset{(-1.3)}{1.96\,\Delta XR_{AV}} + \underset{(1.0)}{209.06\Delta POP_{16}} + \underset{(3.2)}{0.04\Delta POP} \\
&+ \underset{(1.1)}{0.72\Delta ICC_{-1}} + \underset{(3.7)}{70.19\Delta M2_{AV}} + \underset{(9.0)}{.54\,\Delta ACC} + \underset{(3.8)}{1.65\Delta DEP} \\
&+ \underset{(2.2)}{7.23\Delta CAP_{-1}} + \underset{(2.1)}{6.77\Delta PR_{-2}} + \underset{(1.0)}{.09\Delta PROF} + \underset{(6.2)}{0.29\,\boldsymbol{\Delta}\left(\mathbf{C_{B2}} + \mathbf{I_{B(-1)}}\right)} \\
&+ \underset{(1.6)}{0.12\,\boldsymbol{\Delta}\mathbf{GDP_{Real(-3)}}} - \underset{(-0.3)}{0.06\Delta X} - \underset{(-4.2)}{0.63\,AR(2)} + \underset{(4.2)}{0.68\,AR(7)} \\
R^2 &= 97.2\ \%\quad D.W. = 2.1\quad MSE = 38.24 \qquad (10.2)
\end{aligned}$$

Hence, our Method #2 findings as to the net stimulus effects of changes in taxes or government spending are:

$$\Delta Y = \underset{(4.8)}{0.36\Delta T_T} - \underset{(-0.6)}{0.11\Delta G_{T\&I}} + \underset{(6.2)}{0.29\,\Delta\left(C_{B2}\&I_{B(-1)}\right)} \ldots \text{Etc} \ldots$$

$$R^2\ 97.2\ \%;\quad DW = 2.1\ (\text{From Eq. } 10.2)$$

Recall from Method 1 that we need to convert the borrowing coefficient from \$0.29 per dollar of reduced borrowing to (\$0.29 × 1.82 = \$0.53) for tax deficits or (\$0.29 × 1.57 = \$0.46) for spending deficits to convert the regression coefficient to a comparable figure per dollar of deficit. This leaves our estimated effects of deficit-creating tax cuts or government spending increases at

$$\Delta Y = \underset{(7.8)}{0.89\Delta T_T} - \underset{(3.0)}{0.57\Delta G_{T\&I}}\ (\text{From Eq. } 10.2)$$

- The findings indicate Tax Cuts Have A Substantial Negative, Statistically Significant Effect On GDP (Crowd Out Significantly Overwhelms Stimulus Effects: The Net Effect Is \$0.89 Per Dollar Of Deficit). Assuming The Covariance Of The Standard Errors Of The Tax (.075) And Borrowing Variables (0.047) Is Zero, The Standard Error On The Estimate Of \$0.89 Is SE = $\sqrt{[(0.075)^2 + (1.82)^2 (0.047)^2]} = 0.114$, Implying The *t*-Statistic is 7.8, Which Is Highly Significant)

- Spending Deficits Also Have A Negative, Impact On GDP Of $0.57 Per Dollar Of Deficit. Assuming The Covariance Of The Standard Errors Of The Spending (-.183) and Borrowing Variables (.047) Is Zero, The Standard Error On The Estimate Of $0.57 Is Se $= \sqrt{} \, [(-0.183)^2 + (1.57)^2(0.047)^2] = 0.196$, Implying The t-Statistic is 2.91, Which Is Significant at 1 % level)

The Method #1 results also indicated negative effects, but less severe. The estimates were:

$$\Delta Y = 0.47\Delta T_T - .35\Delta G_{T\&I} \tag{10.1}$$

10.2 Testing the Krugman Hypotheses

What we previously referred to as the "Krugman Hypothesis" are actually four different hypotheses. Two offer theories identifying variables other than crowd out that cause the negative relationship between deficit size and private spending to occur. And the other two argue that there are times (recessions) when crowd out, even if it exists generally, can't be a problem. Each is stated here in the form of an assertion, and the findings of this study relative to the assertion summarized. Dates cited refer to dates when Krugman discussed these issues in his New York Times (NYT) column or elsewhere. The four assertions are:

1. The observed negative relationship between private spending and deficits is caused by the business cycle, not crowd out (1/17/13).
2. Stimulus programs will not have a net positive effect if they are too small (8/20/11), (also CNBC televised interview, 3/20/09).
3. Crowd out can't occur in recessions because private borrowing declines, allowing government to borrow excess loanable funds to fund stimulus programs without causing crowd out (4/28/13).
4. Because investment is already low in recessions, deficit-financed stimulus programs result in "crowding in", not "crowding out" of investment. This occurs because the stimulus program raises the GDP, which restores business confidence, resulting in increased investment (9/28/09).

Assertion #1:

Even controlling for business cycle effects in the IS equation above, crowd out more than offsets stimulus effects of tax cut deficits, and spending deficits. If there is any merit to the Krugman hypothesis, ***dropping*** our business cycle control variable from the model should *increase* our estimates of the net negative effect of deficits, not for causal reasons, but simply because deficit growth and private spending declines, driven by economic decline, are accidentally correlated.

As before, 2SLS was used. Instruments were developed for variables found Hausman-endogenous, and they passed both Wald and Sargan tests. The borrowing variable was included, but not the business Cycle control variable. Autocorrelation was present and tests (cited earlier) indicated AR (1), AR (5) and AR (7) controls were needed. Use of these controls raised the Durbin–Watson statistic from 1.2 to 1.9.

Model 10.3 IS curve estimates government spending and taxes, net of crowd out

$$\underset{(t=)}{\Delta Y_T} = \underset{(7.0)}{0.54\mathbf{\Delta}(\mathbf{T_T})} - \underset{(-4.0)}{0.80\mathbf{\Delta}(\mathbf{G_{T\&I}})} - \underset{(-2.1)}{6.61\Delta PR} - \underset{(-2.2)}{0.41\,\Delta DJ_{-0}} - \underset{(-0.6)}{0.20\,\Delta DJ_{-2}}$$
$$+ \underset{(0.2)}{0.60\,\Delta XR_{AV}} + \underset{(2.0)}{916.86\Delta POP_{16}} + \underset{(6.4)}{0.08\Delta POP} + \underset{(4.6)}{1.71\Delta ICC_{-1}}$$
$$+ \underset{(3.7)}{127.59\Delta M2_{AV}} + \underset{(9.4)}{.65\,\Delta ACC} + \underset{(3.4)}{1.94\Delta DEP} + \underset{(3.2)}{12.02\Delta CAP_{-1}}$$
$$+ \underset{(3.1)}{9.88\Delta PR_{-2}} - \underset{(-2.3}{0.38\Delta PROF} + \underset{(1.6)}{0.09\,\mathbf{\Delta}(\mathbf{C_{B2}} + \mathbf{I_{B2(-1)}})}$$
$$+ \underset{(-1.4)}{-0.38\Delta X} - \underset{(-0.6)}{0.10\,AR(1)} + \underset{(3.3)}{0.48\,AR(5)} + \underset{(2.4)}{0.28\,AR(7)}$$
$$R^2 = 97.0\ \%\quad D.W. = 1.9\quad MSE = 39.15 \qquad (10.3)$$

Hence, our Method #2 findings as to the net stimulus effects of changes in taxes or government spending without controlling for business cycle effects are:

$$\Delta Y_{(t=)} = \underset{(7.0)}{0.54\Delta T_T} - \underset{(-4.0)}{0.80\Delta G_{T\&I}} + \underset{(1.6)}{0.09\Delta(C_{B2}\&I_{B(-1)})} \ldots \text{etc.} \quad \text{(From Eq. 10.3)}$$

Where again the borrowing effect (0.09) is multiplied by either 1.82 or 1.57 to convert the coefficient to cents per dollar of deficit, giving the following total effect estimates for tax and spending deficits

$$\underset{(t=)}{\Delta Y} = 0.70\underset{(5.5)}{\Delta T_T} - 0.94\underset{(-4.3.)}{\Delta G_{T\&I}} \quad \text{(From Eq. 10.3)}$$

Where the t-statistics are computed by the same method used in (Eq. 10.1.1a), the model with business cycle controls: Assuming the Covariance of the Standard Errors of the Tax (0.077) and Borrowing Variables (0.077) Is Zero, the Standard Error on the Estimate of \$0.70 Is SE = $\sqrt{[(0.077)^2 + (1.82)^2(0.056)^2]} = 0.1275$, Implying the t-Statistic Is 5.5, Which Is Highly Significantly Significant

For government spending, where the t-statistics are computed by the same method used in 10.1.1a), the model with business cycle controls: Assuming the Covariance of the Standard Errors of the spending (0.04) and Borrowing Variables (0.0031) Is Zero, the Standard Error on the Estimate of \$0.94 Is SE = $\sqrt{[(0.04)^2 + (1.57)^2(0.056)^2]} = 0.218$, Implying the t-Statistic is 4.3, Which Is Highly Significant

By comparison, controlling for business cycle effects we found crowd out had the following effect:

$$\Delta Y = 0.89\underset{(7.8)}{\Delta T_T} - 0.57\underset{(-2.9)}{\Delta G_{T\&I}} + \ldots \quad \text{(From Eq. 10.2)}$$

By <u>not</u> controlling for Krugman business cycle effects, our estimates of the negative relationship of tax cuts to GDP actually declines, contrary to expectations, but increase for government spending estimates, consistent with the Krugman effect. In both cases, the Krugman effect is smaller than the crowd out effect, and the crowd out effect is statistically significant and independent of it.

Controlling for the state of the economy, we can also see that borrowing as well as spending is negatively related to deficits. Holding the state of the economy constant, alternative tests regressing consumer and business borrowing on the deficit, indicated declines in consumer and business borrowing of \$1.13-\$1.27 per dollar increase in the deficit, as shown in Eq. 10.4–10.5 below:

$$\Delta \text{Borrowing}_{C\&B} = 1.13\underset{(2.4)}{\Delta (T_T - G_{T\&I})} + \underset{(1.5)}{0.14}\,\text{GDP} + $$

$$- \underset{(-4.0)}{0.51}\,\text{AR}(4) \quad \ldots \quad R^2 = 0.33$$

$$\text{DW} = 2.0 \qquad (10.4)$$

$$\Delta \text{Borrowing}_{\text{C\&B}} = \underset{(3.0)}{1.27} \Delta (T_T - G_{T\&I}) + \underset{(1.4)}{0.13} \text{ GDP}_{-3} + \\ - \underset{(-3.8)}{0.54} \text{ AR}(4) \quad \ldots \quad R^2 = 0.31 \\ \text{DW} = 2.0 \qquad (10.5)$$

Hence, we see that controlling for Krugman effects, there is still a somewhat greater than one-to-one relationship between increased public borrowing (deficits) and decreased private borrowing

Assertion #2

Another variant of the Krugman hypothesis is that stimulus programs work, but only if they are large enough. It is sometimes argued that the Obama stimulus program was not large enough, and that is why it did not have a major positive impact. However, our results above indicate that regardless of size, stimulus programs all have a net negative effect on the economy.

(A related argument is also based on the assumption that stimulus programs have a positive effect. The argument is that if things don't get better after a stimulus program is enacted, it is because the economy was still falling when it was enacted. The stimulus' expected positive effect on the economy was absorbed just bringing the decline to a halt, or reducing the rate of decline. This argument takes as a given the assumption stimulus programs work. Evidence from the exhaustively large number of empirical tests in this study indicates they do not. Instead of stopping a decline, they would likely exacerbate it.)

Assertion #3

A third variant of the Krugman hypothesis is that even if crowd out exists, it is not a problem in recessions because consumers and businesses don't want to borrow as much, so unborrowed funds are available for government to borrow without crowding out private borrowing and spending. Chapter 12 below shows Flow of Funds data indicate that during recessions, the pool of loanable funds drops as much or more than the demand for loans by consumers and businesses. So, during recessions, any attempt by government to borrow would cause a crowd out problem as real as in normal economic times.

Assertion#4

A fourth variant of the Krugman hypothesis is that in recessions, private investment is already low. Government deficits stimulate the economy, raising the GDP, and this restores business willingness to invest, that is, the deficit results in "crowding in" of investment, not "crowding out". But the empirical evidence discussed above indicates crowd out occurs in recessions as well as non-recession periods. This suggests deficit-financed stimulus programs don't work any better in recessions than they do in normal economic times. In both periods, (measurable) crowd out effects overwhelm stimulus effects. The result is deficit-financed stimulus programs have a net negative effect on the economy, the opposite of what is required for the "crowding in" hypothesis to work.

10.3 The Gale and Orszag Issue: Are some Types of Taxes and Spending Immune to Crowd Out Effects? Test Results

Gale and Orszag (2004) argued that federal tax cuts, but not state and local tax cuts, have a positive stimulus effect on consumption, and that government spending on transfers, but not government spending on goods and services, also has a positive net stimulus effect on consumption (and therefore, the economy). It was noted earlier that we could not replicate their findings within the context of the general consumption and investment models used in this study.

Below, we try to replicate their findings using the full IS curve model from above, where we have divided government receipts into two separate variables for federal receipts and for state and local tax receipts. We have also divided government spending into a spending on transfer payments variable, and a separate variable for all other government spending (most of which is spending on goods and services, that is, the government bureaucracy, its supplies and materials). Results are shown below in Model 10.6, using lagged GDP as the business cycle control and employing the standard Hausman, Wald, Sargan and autocorrelation tests cited above.

Model 10.6 2SLS estimates of GDP from IS curve, lagged GDP used as business cycle control

$$\underset{(t=)}{\Delta Y_T} = \underset{(1.5)}{.24\boldsymbol{\Delta}(\mathbf{T_F})} + \underset{(2.2)}{94\boldsymbol{\Delta}(\mathbf{T_{S\&L}})} - \underset{(-0.4)}{0.11\boldsymbol{\Delta}(\mathbf{G_{TR}})} - \underset{(-0.4)}{0.10\boldsymbol{\Delta}(\mathbf{G_{OTHER}})}$$

$$- \underset{(-1.0)}{5.61\Delta PR} - \underset{(-2.0)}{0.34\,\Delta DJ_{-0}} + \underset{(4.7)}{1.06\,\Delta DJ_{-2}} - \underset{(-1.4)}{2.32\,\Delta XR_{AV}}$$

$$+ \underset{(0.6)}{189.75\Delta POP_{16}} + \underset{(2.5)}{0.033\Delta POP} + \underset{(1.6)}{0.95\Delta ICC_{-1}} + \underset{(2.5)}{57.26\Delta M2_{AV}}$$

$$+ \underset{(8.5)}{.655\,\Delta ACC} + \underset{(3.6)}{1.97\Delta DEP} + \underset{(2.1)}{6.63\Delta CAP_{-1}} + \underset{(1.3)}{5.15\Delta PR_{-2}}$$

$$+ \underset{(1.5)}{0.16\Delta PROF} + \underset{(4.5)}{0.25\,\boldsymbol{\Delta}(\mathbf{C_{B2}} + \mathbf{I_{B2(-1)}})} + \underset{(-0.7)}{0.15\Delta X} - \underset{(1.5)}{0.11\Delta\, GDP_{-3}}$$

$$- \underset{(-3.3)}{0.64AR(5)} + \underset{(3.6)}{0.72\,AR(7)}$$

$$R^2 = 97.2\ \% \quad D.W. = 2.0 \quad MSE = 39.71 \qquad (10.6)$$

The results indicate deficits resulting from federal tax cuts have a negative effect on GDP, but it is only marginally statistically significant, but that deficits resulting from state and local tax cuts have a negative effect on GDP that is highly statistically significant. By comparison, Eq. 10.1.3 tells us government spending deficits of any type have a slightly negative, but insignificantly different from zero effect on the GDP. For spending deficits, crowd out effects just offset stimulus effects, leaving no net impact.

Using the current year unemployment rate as the business cycle control yields about the same results, as shown below in Model. 10.7:

Model 10.7 2SLS estimates of GDP from IS curve, current unemployment rate used as business cycle control

$$
\begin{aligned}
\underset{(t=)}{\Delta Y_T} = {} & \underset{(0.6)}{0.05\boldsymbol{\Delta}(\mathbf{T_F})} + \underset{(2.3)}{94\boldsymbol{\Delta}(\mathbf{T_{S\&L}})} + \underset{(0.7)}{0.\ 13\boldsymbol{\Delta}(\mathbf{G_{TR}})} - \underset{(-0.7)}{0.20\boldsymbol{\Delta}(\mathbf{G_{OTHER}})} \\
& - \underset{(-1.5)}{5.39\Delta \mathrm{PR}} + \underset{(0.9)}{13\ \Delta \mathrm{DJ}_{-0}} + \underset{(1..2)}{0\ .46\ \Delta \mathrm{DJ}_{-2}} + \underset{(0.5)}{2.32\ \Delta \mathrm{XR}_{\mathrm{AV}}} \\
& - \underset{(-1.8)}{341.32\Delta \mathrm{POP}_{16}} + \underset{(4.3)}{0\ .028\Delta \mathrm{POP}} + \underset{(1.7)}{.75\Delta \mathrm{ICC}_{-1}} + \underset{(2.2)}{40.16\Delta \mathrm{M2}_{\mathrm{AV}}} \\
& + \underset{(12.0)}{.50\ \Delta \mathrm{ACC}} + \underset{(8.3)}{3.47\Delta \mathrm{DEP}} + \underset{(0.7)}{2.54\Delta \mathrm{CAP}_{-1}} - \underset{(-0.8)}{3.64\Delta \mathrm{PR}_{-2}} \\
& + \underset{(1.7)}{.14\Delta \mathrm{PROF}} + \underset{(0.8)}{.08\ \boldsymbol{\Delta}(\mathbf{C_{B2}} + \mathbf{I_{B2(-1)}})} + \underset{(-0.8)}{0.12\Delta \mathrm{X}} - \underset{(-3.8)}{46.02\Delta\ \mathrm{UNEM}} \\
& + \underset{(4.2)}{0\ .62\mathrm{AR}(1)} - \underset{(-3.0)}{0.67\ AR(2)} \\
& R^2 = 97.6\ \%\quad \mathrm{D.W.} = 2.0\quad \mathrm{MSE} = 33.72
\end{aligned}
\qquad (10.7)
$$

And finally, Eq. 10.8 below repeats the same model, but with no business cycle control allowing for any additional negative correlation of deficits and GDP growth due to the business cycle to be added to our net crowd out effect. Adding these two effects together leaves both tax cut and spending deficits having a strongly significant negative effect on GDP. (A reminder: the tax variables' coefficients show the effects of tax changes holding government spending constant, that is, a change in the deficit caused by tax cuts. Similarly, the government spending variables show the effect of a change in government spending holding taxes constant, that is, a change in the deficit caused by changes in government spending.)

Model 10.8 2SLS estimates of GDP from IS Curve, no business cycle control used

$$\underset{(t=)}{\Delta Y_T} = \underset{(2.8)}{.38\boldsymbol{\Delta}(\mathbf{T_F})} + \underset{(2.9)}{1.38(\mathbf{T_{S\&L}})} - \underset{(-2.2)}{.72\boldsymbol{\Delta}(\mathbf{G_{TR}})} - \underset{(-2.5)}{.70\boldsymbol{\Delta}(\mathbf{G_{OTHER}})} - \underset{(-2.5)}{.70\Delta PR}$$

$$+ \underset{(0.1)}{.49\,\Delta DJ_{-0}} \quad - \underset{(-0.6)}{.21\,\Delta DJ_{-2}} + \underset{(0.4)}{1.58\,\Delta XR_{AV}} + \underset{(1.3)}{621.47\Delta POP_{16}}$$

$$+ \underset{(5.0)}{.071\Delta POP} + \underset{(3.2)}{1.58\Delta ICC_{-1}} + \underset{(6.9)}{106.61\Delta M2_{AV}} + \underset{(8.7)}{.68\,\Delta ACC}$$

$$+ \underset{(5.0)}{2.62\Delta DEP} + \underset{(2.5)}{11.50\Delta CAP_{-1}} + \underset{(1.0)}{5.70\Delta PR_{-2}} - \underset{(-1.1)}{.26\Delta PROF}$$

$$+ \underset{(0.0)}{.00\,\boldsymbol{\Delta}\left(\mathbf{C_{B2}} + \mathbf{I_{B2(-1)}}\right)} - . - \underset{(-1.5)}{.50\Delta X} + \underset{(.92)}{.21\,AR(1)}$$

$$+ \underset{(3.8)}{.70\,AR(5)} - \underset{(-0.6)}{.10\,AR(8)}$$

$$R^2 = 97.1\% \quad D.W. = 2.2 \quad MSE = 41.89 \qquad (10.8)$$

Summarizing the crowd out variable results in the three Orszag effect models, we get

Notice that without the business cycle control, we allow for Krugman effects to be confounded with crowd out effects. As a result, all types of tax cuts and spending increases appear to have a negative and statistically significant effect on the GDP. However, this large negative effect is actually the sum of smaller net crowd out effects and business cycle effects, the latter correlated with, but causally unrelated to crowd out effects.

If we control for business cycle effects, as done in the first two lines of the table 9.1 above, results only indicate the extent to which crowd out reduces or eliminates the stimulus effects of government deficits. The net stimulus effect appears to be insignificantly different from zero, statistically, except for state and local tax cuts, which appear to have a statistically significant negative effect.

In the third line of the Table 10.1, by not including the business cycle control, we allow the tax and government spending variables to also pick business cycle effects causing a negative relationship of deficits and GDP to occur, not caused by crowd out. This increases the estimated negative effects and statistical significance of both tax cuts and government spending on the GDP, but for reasons that are not causal in nature, but are simply driven by correlative effects of business cycles on both deficits and the GDP. Business cycle effects create deficits whose funding causes crowd out. But these deficits don't intentionally occur because someone is trying to stimulate the economy as a matter of economic policy. By combining the two

Table 10.1 Findings for three Orszag effect models

Bus. Cycle	*Deficit Created By*			
Control Used	Fed Tax Cut	S&L Tax Cut	Transfer Spending Incr.	Other G Spending Increases
GDP_{-3}	0.23 (1.5)	0.94 (2.2)	−0.11 (−0.5)	−0.10 (−0.5)
Unem. Rate	0.05 (0.6)	0.94 (2.3)	0.13 (0.7)	0.20 (−0.7)
None Used	0.38 (2.8)	1.38 (2.9)	−0.72 (−2.2)	-0.70 (−2.5)

types our measured deficit effects are found to be larger and more significant than we get measuring just crowd out effects alone (by using a variable to control for business cycle effects).

Controlling for business cycle effects, we find crowd out fully offsets the stimulus effects of deficits for both types of spending deficits, and also for federal tax cuts, that is, statistically, their estimated effects are not different from zero. Hence, such stimulus programs seem to have no net effect on the GDP one way or the other. For state and local tax cuts, however, crowd out effects seem to more than offset stimulus effects, resulting in such tax cuts having a net, statistically significant negative effect on GDP.

Even controlling for business cycle effects, crowd out still appears to offset stimulus effects fully (or more). This contradicts the Krugman hypothesis that what appears to be crowd out is really just a normal negative business cycle relationship between private spending and government deficits.

10.4 Effect of Changes in GDP On The Unemployment Rate

The relationship between changes in the GDP and changes in the unemployment rate for the1955–2010 period were estimated using both a linear and non-linear model as follows:

$$\underset{(t=)}{\Delta \text{Unem Rate}} = \underset{(6.8)}{1.031} - \underset{(-13.0)}{0.005\,\Delta \text{GDP}} \quad R^2 = 0.55;\ \text{DW} = 1.5; \qquad (10.9)$$

$$\underset{(t=)}{\Delta \text{Unem Rate}} = \underset{(11.8)}{1.359} - \underset{(-13.0)}{0.56\ 0.69\,\Delta \text{GDP}^{.17}} \quad \text{R}^2 = 0.75;\ \text{DW} = 2.0; \qquad (10.10)$$

Using the curvilinear fit increases explained variance 20 percentage points from 55 % to 75 %, and comports well with the notion that over time, technological progress allows for given increases in GDP to be produced by smaller increases in the labor force.

The regression relationship implies an additional $100 billion increase in the GDP in 2010 would have reduced the unemployment rate by 56.69 ($\$13{,}348.7B^{.17}$-$\$13{,}248.7^{.17}$) = 0.36 %, or about ¼ of the 1.359 % increase that would have prevailed if GDP had not changed at all, simply from population growth, represented by the constant term in Eq. 10.10

10.4.1 Obama Stimulus Program Effects On Unemployment Rate

The Obama stimulus program was $830 billion, ½ spending increases, ½ tax cuts.

From above, we know this implies a negative impact on GDP of

$$\Delta GDP = \$-605.9B = \underset{0.89\,(\$-415B)}{0.89\,(\Delta\text{ Total Taxes})} \underset{-0.57\,(\$+415B)}{-0.57\,(\Delta\text{ Total G Spending})}$$

(From Eq. 10.2)

Or about $0.73 decline in GDP per dollar of balanced stimulus (50 % tax cut, 50 %spending increase).

Based on the unemployment rate/GDP relationship indicated in the regression (Eq. 10.9) above, subtracting $605.9 billion from the actual 2010 real GDP ($13,248.7) billion to account for stimulus effects implies the unemployment rate would increase

$$\begin{aligned}\Delta \text{Unem.Rate} &= 1.359 - 56.69\left(\$12{,}642.8^{.17} - \$13{,}248.7^{.17}\right)\\ &= 1.359 - 56.69(-0.0398) = +3.62\%(\text{for one year!})\end{aligned}$$

In the absence of any growth or decline in the GDP, our model indicates we should expect unemployment to grow 1.359 % in a given year. The relatively negative estimated impact of the Obama stimulus on GDP would increase this to 3.62 %, ceteris paribus, or 2.26 percentage points. If the tax cuts and spending increases were allowed to lapse at the end of the year, allowing taxes and government spending to return to pre-stimulus levels, unemployment would drop by 2.26 %, *ceteris paribus*.

In 2010 unemployment rate of 9.6 % might have increased to 13.2 % in 2011, and then dropped to 12.3 % (13.2-2.25+1.359) in 2012 as the Obama stimulus ended, offsetting most of the natural yearly growth of 1.359 % expected in any year (ceteris paribus).

If we used estimates from method #1, our estimate of the effect of the Obama stimulus on GDP would be

$$\Delta \text{GDP} = \$ - 340.3B \;\; = \underset{0.47\ (\$-415\text{B})}{0\ .47\ (\Delta\ \text{Total Taxes})} - \underset{-0.35\ (\$+415\text{B})}{0\ .35\ (\Delta\ \text{Total G Spending})}$$

(From Eq. 10.1.)

Or about \$0.41 decline in GDP per dollar of balanced stimulus (50 % tax cut, 50 %spending increase).

Based on the unemployment rate/GDP relationship indicated in the regression (Eq. 10.2) above, subtracting \$340.3 billion from the actual 2010 real GDP (\$13,248.7) billion to account for stimulus effects implies the unemployment rate would increase:

$$\begin{aligned}\Delta \text{Unem.Rate} &= 1.359 - 56.69\left(\$12,908.4^{\cdot 17} - \$13,248.7^{\cdot 17}\right)\\ &= 1.359 - 56.69(-.02216) = +2.62\%(\text{for one year})\end{aligned}$$

In the absence of any growth or decline in the GDP, our model indicates we should expect unemployment to grow 1.359 % in a given year. The relatively negative estimated impact of the Obama stimulus on GDP would increase this to 2.62 %, ceteris paribus, or 1.26 percentage points. If the tax cuts and spending increases were allowed to lapse at the end of the year, allowing taxes and government spending to return to pre-stimulus levels, the unemployment rate would drop by 1.26 %, *ceteris paribus.*

In 2010, unemployment rate of 9.6 % might have increased to 12.2 % in 2011, and then nearly stabilized at 12.3 % (12.2-1.26+1.359) in 2012 as the Obama stimulus ended, offsetting most of the natural yearly growth of 1.359 % expected in any year (ceteris paribus).

The Bureau of Labor Statistics (BLS) reports that unemployment rates the years before and after the Obama stimulus were:

2002	5.8	2005	5.1	2008	5.8	2011	9.0
2003	6.0	2006	4.6	2009	9.3	2012	8.1
2004	5.5	2007	4.6	2010	9.6		

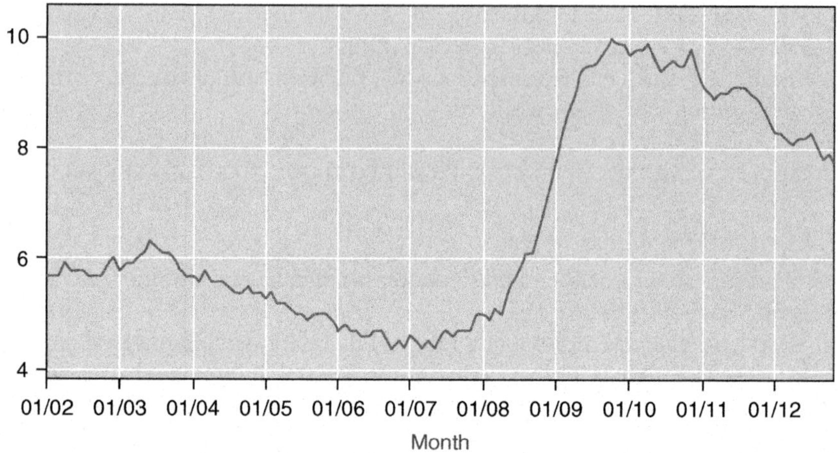

To return the 2010 rate of 9.6 % to the 4.6 % rates, just before the US economic slump in 2006 and 2007, would require a five percentage point drop in the unemployment rate. A 5 % reduction in the unemployment rate in 2010 would have required a $1.850 trillion further increase in the 2010 GDP. If an attempt was made to restore pre-2008 unemployment rates, a balanced package of tax increases and government spending cuts that would reduce the deficit sufficiently to do this (ceteris paribus) would be, using Eq. 10.2 again:

$$\Delta \text{GDP} = \$ + 1850.0\text{B} \quad = 0\ .89\ (\Delta\ \text{Total Taxes})$$
$$0.89\ (\$+1267.1\text{B})$$
$$-\ 0\ .57\ (\Delta\ \text{Total G Spending})$$
$$-0.57\ (\$-1{,}267.1\text{B})$$

(From Eq. 10.2)

which would take the 2010 budget deficit of ($3387.6 billion total taxes-$4960.75 total G spending) = $ −1573.14) and drive it to ($4654.7 total taxes − $3693.7 total G spending = $ +961.1B surplus), that is, total tax collections would, increase by 37 % over current levels, and total government spending would have to be cut by 26 %, eliminating the deficit and creating a $961.1 billion surplus.

Clearly, though this study finds a budget deficit to be a drag on the economy, using deficit reduction as the only tool to stimulate the economy sufficiently to lower the unemployment rate 5 % may not be practical. It would require a shift from a deficit of $ −1573.14B to a surplus of $961. This would constitute a major increase in national savings, and the positive effect on the GDP and the lower unemployment rate resulting from the increased national savings would certainly be consistent with standard Solow growth theory models. Nonetheless, it seems to be difficult on political and practical grounds to do so. We should be cautious in interpreting our econometric projections as well. The simulation stretches the projections of the model for deficit effects far beyond the range of deficit data in the model. We cannot be sure the observed deficit/GDP relationships still hold that far beyond the variation actually observed from 1960–2010.

One might argue that short-run forecasts of the effects of a change in stimulus policy should assume technological progress constant, since it does not change much in the short run. This suggests a more linear model of the effects of a change in GDP on unemployment would better simulate likely effects. The linear function results, repeated from above, are shown below, estimated from 1955–2010 US data. To keep the projection a function of the most recent past, the linear function for the five-year period 1996–2010 was also examined and showed a slight increase in the regression coefficient from −0.0048 to −0.0051, and explained considerably more variance (R^2 = 0.94), but at the price of extreme serial correlation.(DW = 0.79), making the coefficients estimated unreliable. AR(1) corrections improved the serial correlation partially (DW = 1.24), but returned the coefficient to (−0.0048). Adding AR(2) and AR(3) corrections did not help. Hence, our linear estimates of the effects of GDP on the unemployment rate are derived from the 1955–2010 data:

$$\underset{(t=)}{\Delta \text{Unem.Rate}} = \underset{(6.8)}{1.03} - \underset{(-6.5)}{0.0048\,\Delta(\text{GDP})}$$

$$R^2 = 0.55; \text{DW} = 1.5; \text{MSE} = 0.7\ \%$$

(From 10.9)

As noted, above, The Obama stimulus program was $830 billion, ½ spending increases, ½ tax cuts.

From above, we know this implies an increase in GDP of

$$\Delta GDP = \$-605.9B \;=\; \underset{.89\ (\$-415B)}{.89\ (\Delta\ \text{Total Taxes})} - \underset{-.57\ (\$+415B)}{.57\ (\Delta\ \text{Total G Spending})}$$

(From Eq. 10.2)

Subtracting $605.9 billion from the actual 2010 real GDP ($13,248.7) billion implies the unemployment rate will increase

$$\begin{aligned}\Delta \text{Unem.Rate} &= 1.03 - 0.0048\ (\$12,642.8 - \$13,248.7)\\ &= 1.03 - 0.0048(-605.9) = +3.94\%(\text{for one year})\end{aligned}$$

an increase in the unemployment rate of 2.94 % over what it would have been without the stimulus program. Our earlier result, which assumed technological progress, suggested a rise in unemployment from 1.36 to 3.62 % due to the same stimulus, ceteris paribus, an increase of 2.25 % (the smaller change due to the stimulus resulting from the larger intercept value in the technological progress non-linear model).

In the absence of any growth or decline in the GDP, our (short) long-run unemployment model indicates we should expect unemployment to grow (1.03 %) 1.359 % in a given year. The relatively small, but negative, estimated impact of the Obama stimulus would increase this to (3.94 %) 3.62 %, ceteris paribus, or about (2.25) 2.94 percentage points, a sizable amount. If the tax cuts and spending increases were allowed to lapse at the end of the year, allowing taxes and government spending to return to pre-stimulus levels, unemployment would drop by the same percentages, ceteris paribus.

Using the *short term* no technological progress model, to achieve a full 5 % drop in the unemployment rate would require a change in GDP of

$$\begin{aligned}-5\ \% = \Delta \text{Unem.Rate} &= 1.03 - 0.0048\ (\Delta GDP)\ \ \text{where the } \Delta GDP\\ &= \$1.256T\end{aligned}$$

This is considerably less than the $1.850 trillion change suggested by the *long-term* GDP/unemployment rate relationship model.

A balanced package of tax increases and government spending cuts that would reduce the deficit sufficiently to do this (ceteris paribus) would be, using Eq. 10.2 again:

$$\Delta GDP = \$ + 1256.0B \quad = \underset{0.89\ (\$+860.3B)}{0.89\ (\Delta \text{ Total Taxes})} \quad - \underset{-0.57\ (\$-860.3.B)}{0.57\ (\Delta \text{ Total G Spending})}$$

(From Eq. 10.2)

Which would take the 2010 budget deficit of (Total Taxes – Total G spending) = (\$3387.6B – \$4960.75 = \$–1573.14) and drive it down to (\$+4247.9 total taxes – \$4100.45 total G spending = \$ –147.45 deficit). The deficit would be nearly eliminated, but at markedly reduced public spending and increased taxing levels. Here again, though the tax increases and spending cuts are smaller than before, the practicality of using only this approach to reduce the unemployment rate 5 % remains problematic since it involves increasing taxes 25 % and reducing government spending 17 % in total for both federal and state and local governments. In addition, on technical grounds, we cannot be sure the technical coefficients of the model would remain accurate with experience so far outside the range of deficit changes in the model, though the general finding of positive effects of deficit reduction should not change. The spread in the deficit (Total T-Total G, including transfers) between low and high over the 50 years covered by this study was \$1.5 trillion, and that big a spread occurred only twice. Swings required to bring the unemployment rate down 5 % are nearly the same. Hence, the projection is based on swings not heavily weighed in calculating the model's coefficients.

CHAPTER 11

Dynamic Effects

There are two kinds of dynamic effects that could occur from a change in an explanatory variable in the model, such as the government deficit.

1. Short-run dynamic effects such as those obtained from this paper's IS curve tests, in which we measure dynamic effects (such as multiplier effects) during the current period sufficiently to show the total current period effects of a current period shock to the system, for example, a change in the deficit.
2. Long-run dynamic effects, covering multiple periods. Here we have two choices: (a) use a long-run model, like Solow's growth model to assess the long-term effects of a decline in investment due to a government deficit crowding out private borrowing, or (b) use a short-run model, like the ones used in this study and iteratively calculate the effects in both current and future years, until some stable equilibrium is achieved, of a current period shock to the system.

11.1 Incorporating Dynamic Effects in the IS Curve Model

We can estimate the dynamic effects of a one-time deficit-driven change in the GDP of $1050 billion from the standard Keynesian IS curve formulation using two of the study's best consumption and investment spending

J.J. Heim, *Crowding Out Fiscal Stimulus*,
DOI 10.1007/978-3-319-45967-7_11

functions (Eq. 7.2.Alt and 8.2.Alt), and substituting them into the GDP identity:

$$\Delta Y = \Delta C + \Delta I + \Delta G + \Delta(X - M)$$

Actually doing so is a bit beyond the scope of this paper. However, we can demonstrate how this would work with some simplifying assumptions (e.g.):

(1) that government spending and taxes after the initial stimulus return to their earlier levels after a specified period or periods, and
(2) variables whose current values are driven in part by current or past values of the GDP are specified in tests using only their initial exogenous part, augmented by the effect of the current or lagged values of the GDP appropriate for that variable through the multiplier effect. For example, If our GDP determination model implying

$$Y = 0.50\,(Y - T) + 0.30\text{ ACC} + G + (X - M) + 0.10\text{ DJ} \quad (\text{where DJ} = \text{DJ}_{\text{EXOG}} + 0.20\,Y)$$

we can easily show that

$$Y = [1/(1 - 0.50 - 0.30 - 0.02)]\,[-0.50T - 0.30Y_{-1} + 0.10\text{ DJ}_{\text{EXOG}} + G + (X - M)\,]$$

that is, the "everything is a function of everything else" problem reduces to simply a change in multiplier/accelerator effect when one uses the exogenous portion of variables so affected. We would then iterate through the model as many times as necessary to incorporate any lagged effects of explanatory variables.

Such a model would be a dynamic model in the sense that it allows for several iterations of interactive effects in the same period. But it does not show the dynamic path of multiplier/accelerator effects iteration by iteration during the current period. It shows only the initial change in the current period in some explanatory variable (like the government deficit), and its total change by the end of the current period on the variables of interest, *C*, *I* and *Y*. Put another way, this study has been done in comparative statics, showing only the before and after effects in one period only of a current period shock on *C*, *I* and *Υ*.

We can also show future period effects of the current period change in an explanatory variable by calculating the current year effect of a shock on GDP (i.e., *Υ*), making some assumptions about initial conditions in the year the shock occurs: that is, what the initial values of *T*, Y_{-1}, DJ_{EXOG}, *G*, and *X*–*M* were), and estimating the current year values of GDP with and without the shock.

Having done this, we will have obtained the current year effects of the shock. To obtain estimates of the current period shock on future years GDP, assuming that except for lagged changes of the current period shock, occurring in a future year, everything else is constant at current year values. We would then just iteratively calculate additional future year changes as needed until the system reaches an equilibrium.

A simple example will show how easy it is to do this with the type of short-run model used in this paper, since the long-run is nothing more than the sum of future year (short-run) changes. Assume the IS curve for GDP determination is as follows:

$$Y_0 = f_c(Y_0 - T_0,\ DJ_{-2}) + f_i(ACC)_0 + G_0 + (X - M)_0$$

Where f_c is the consumption function, and the determinants of consumption are disposable income ($Y_0 - T_0$) and a stock market index of financial wealth (DJ_0); f_i is the investment function, and the only determinant of investment is the accelerator ($ACC = Y_0 - Y_{-1}$); G_0 is government expenditures and $(X - M)_0$ is net exports. Suppose further that last year's GDP was $1200. If we also hypothesize that

$$C_0 = 0.50\ (Y - T)_0 + (1.0\ DJ_{EXOG} + 0.15\ Y_{-2})$$

$$DJ_0 = (1.0\ DJ_{EXOG} + 0.20\ Y_{-2})$$

$$I_0 = 0.15\ (Y_0 - Y_{-1})$$

$$T = \$200$$

$G \& (X - M) = \$700$ (before stimulus of $\Delta G = 10$, which continues in each future year as well)

$$DJ_{EXOG} = 10$$
$$Y_{-1\text{Initial}} = 1200$$
$$Y_{-2\text{Initial}} = 1000$$

Then our initial conditions IS curve models with and without the shock to government spending are

$$\begin{aligned} Y_{0(\text{w/o shock})} &= \left(2.86_{\text{multiplier}}\right)\left(-0.5 \times 200 - 0.15 \times 1200 + 700 + 10 \right. \\ &\quad \left. + 0.15 \times 1000\right. \\ &= 1658.8 \end{aligned}$$

$$\begin{aligned} Y_{0(\text{w/shock})} &= \left(2.86_{\text{multiplier}}\right)\left(-0.5 \times 200 - 0.15 \times 200 + 710 + 10 \right. \\ &\quad \left. + 0.20 \times 1000\right. \\ &= 1687.4 \end{aligned}$$

And assuming all variables in the model stay constant at year 0 values, except for those affected by lags, we can iteratively calculate our way toward the new long-run equilibrium resulting from the current period change in government spending (+10):

In this simple three-variable model of the economy, the GDP, which had been $1658.8 (billion) before the change in government spending, rising to $1687.4(billion) the year of the change (the change in G times the multiplier/accelerator), continues growing until it reaches a new long-term equilibrium of $1771. The dynamic path upward toward the new equilibrium oscillates back and forth in ever smaller amounts, something like a damped Bessel function, until after 60 iterations, the new equilibrium of the GDP, $1773, is reached.

In the larger IS model of GDP determination presented in Chap. 10, the net effects in the current year of both deficit-raising tax cuts and government spending increases were found to be negative (unlike the simplified example above). This is the short-run, or current-period, equilibrium. While it can capture multiplier or other iterative effects occurring in the current period, it does not pick up any part of this year's changes whose effect is lagged one period or more. In the example above, the interplay of the lagged effects moved the GDP even further in the same direction as the initial period effect.

While it would be desirable to know the dynamic path the change in GDP takes in subsequent periods because of the lagged effects of this year's changes on other variables, it is beyond the scope of this study for two reasons:

1. the size of the models used (the full IS curve has 18 variables, some of whose current year values affect GDP only after a lag), and
2. some of these 18 explanatory variables in the model are driven, at least in part, by lagged changes in the GDP. Hence, before dynamic modeling can take place, additional testing of variables is needed so we can separate their endogenous and exogenous parts, as we did with our stock market variable (DJ) above. Dynamic modeling would then incorporate the endogenous, current period GDP-driven, part of an explanatory variable into an expanded multiplier/accelerator term, and use the exogenous part as the explanatory variable. Some lagged variables may include both lagged effects of GDP and exogenous parts.

Clearly, however, once those regressions are estimated, the full long-term effects of a policy change, like a change in the government deficit, is feasible, and the process of iterating forward, a simple spreadsheet exercise.

11.2 Consistency with Solow Growth Model Estimates of Effects of Declining Savings on Investment

Our econometric testing indicates that reduction of the pool of loanable funds, principally composed of domestic savings, to pay for government deficits, will have negative consequences. It reduces the amount available for borrowing by consumers and for investment. The decline can lead to a net decrease in capital per worker, and capital per worker is a major determinant of worker productivity. Declining worker productivity leads to a decline in GDP and per capita GDP.

This short-run current period result is strongly supported by our exhaustive econometric testing. Solow (1956) found the same thing holds in the long run: ceteris paribus, reducing saving available to fund investment is to reduce investment; reducing investment is to reduce GDP and living standards.

More broadly, Solow argued that savings (investment), population growth and technological progress were the key determinants of long-run economic growth, and that consumption is determined by current income and the marginal propensity to consume (the mpc). In our model, current income is also the principal determinant of consumption. Savings is given in a very Keynesian fashion as (1-mpc). Declines in saving cause declines in investment per worker and GDP per worker in the Solow model.

In this study's model, population growth is held constant and technological progress is assumed constant (year-to-year change in GDP is treated as due to the 18 explanatory variables in the model, which is true in the short run, but in the long run, technological progress is key). The model examines the pool of savings available for private use, and how that pool contracts if part of it must be diverted to pay for government deficits. The effects of diversion of funds from this pool on both GDP and investment are found to be negative. This is exactly what the Solow (1956) growth model predicts for the long run as well.

Hence, to the extent deficits reduce the pool of saving, the long-term effects of government deficits is the same as the short-term effects: deficits reduce funds available for private investment, reducing growth in GDP and the standard of living.

11.3 Dynamic Effects of Changes in Consumer and Business Confidence

Not all effects of deficits on the economy may be related in some standard mechanical way to economic variable. In the midst of a recession, the level of consumer confidence may be positively affected by government willingness to do something to try and help, that is, to undertake a deficit-financed stimulus program, even though stimulus programs may have a zero or negative direct effect on GDP. Some economists (and most politicians) would argue the effect of the stimulus program on consumer confidence may itself stimulate consumer spending, which would raise the GDP.

We would like to test that hypothesis. We will use the Conference Board's Index of Consumer Confidence (ICC) as our measure of how consumer confidence goes up or down as deficits grow or diminish in size. Some economists would also argue stimulus programs may also positively affect investor confidence. We would also like to test that assertion. We will take the ups and downs of the stock market as a measure of investor confidence. The measure of the stock market used will be the NYSE composite index.

Regressing next year's ICC, and separately current year ICC, on the current year deficit using the GDP as a control for all other things that can affect ICC, we obtained the following results:

1. Regressing Next Year's ICC on the Current Year Deficit

$$\underset{(t=)}{\Delta \mathrm{ICC}_{+1}} = \underset{(-4.8)}{-14.52} \underset{(-0.9)}{-0.01\,\Delta(T-G)_0} + \underset{(5.7)}{0.06\,\Delta \mathrm{GDP}_{+1}} \quad R^2 = 0.38;\ \mathrm{D.W.} = 1.7$$

2. Regressing Current Year ICC on the Current Year Deficit

$$\underset{(t=)}{\Delta \mathrm{ICC}_0} = \underset{(-2.2)}{-7.72} + \underset{(3.1)}{0.04\,\Delta(T-G)_0} + \underset{(2.5)}{0.04\,\Delta \mathrm{GDP}_0} \quad R^2 = 0.42;\ \mathrm{D.W.} = 2.0$$

Unfortunately, the data did not support the hypothesis that initiating a deficit improved consumer confidence. Model 1 results indicate no statistically significant relationship between this year's deficit and future (next year's) ICC levels, controlling for the state of next year's economy. Model 2 results comparing changes in this year's deficit with changes in this year's ICC, were somewhat unexpected. They indicate that controlling for the state of this year's economy, the more the deficit grows the lower consumer confidence gets. A rising deficit is associated with a declining ICC index. Consumers may interpret the introduction of stimulus programs as indicating the government thinks things are really looking bad for the future.

The data did not support the hypothesis that initiating a deficit improved investor confidence either. Regressing the current and next year's NYSE Composite Index on this year's deficit, using the GDP as a control for all other things that can affect investor confidence, we obtained the following results:

3. Regressing Next Year's ICC on the Current Year Deficit

$$\underset{(t=)}{\Delta \text{NYSE}_{+1}} = \underset{(-2.0)}{-30.59} + \underset{(1.2)}{0.06\, \Delta(T-G)_0} + \underset{(3.2)}{0.22\, \Delta \text{GDP}_{+1}} \quad R^2 = 0.48; \text{D.W.} = 1.7$$

4. Regressing Current Year ICC on the Current Year Deficit

$$\underset{(t=)}{\Delta \text{NYSE}_0} = \underset{(-0.6)}{-5.04} + \underset{(4.2)}{0.19\, \Delta(T-G)_0} + \underset{(2.4)}{0.11\, \Delta \text{GDP}_0} \quad R^2 = 0.57; \text{D.W.} = 1.9$$

Model 3 shows no significant relationship between what the deficit is this year and what NYSE becomes next year. In Model 4, the relationship between this year's deficit and this year's NYSE, controlling for the general state of the economy, indicates the NYSE Index goes up as the deficit comes down, not the other way around. Put the other way, this somewhat unexpected result indicates a rising deficit is associated with a decline in the stock market index. Whatever the actual state of the economy, enacting a deficit may negatively affect investor confidence.

Hence, we conclude that neither of the two variables we use to capture the state of mind of consumers or investors and their confidence in the economy appears to improve when deficits increase. The hypothesized positive effect on consumer or investor confidence associated with the announcement of a deficit-financed government stimulus program may not really exist; in fact, the opposite may be the case.

Testing Recession Effects Separately

Though, in general, stimulus programs do not appear to raise consumer or investor confidence, they may do so in recessions, when it is most important: when consumer and investor confidence is already depressed, and needs boosting. Using NBER data on when recessions occurred, we defined a recession year as one in which two or more quarters were designated recession periods by NBER. Models 5–8 below are identical to Models 1–4 above, except that the deficit variable is divided into two variables: deficits incurred in recessions and deficits incurred in non-recession periods. To obtain separate deficit variables, the complete deficit data set is multiplied by a dummy variable having a value of one in recessions, and zero otherwise. This provides the recession deficit variable. Multiplying the complete deficit data set by (1-recession dummy) provides the deficit variable for non-recession periods.

Even testing separately for effects in recession $[\Delta(T-G)_{0(R)}]$ and non-recession $[\Delta(T-G)_{0(NR)}]$ periods, the data did not support the hypothesis that initiating a deficit improved consumer confidence. Regressing the current and next year's ICC on the current year deficit using the GDP as a control for all other things that can affect ICC, we obtained the following results:

5. Regressing Next Year's ICC on the Current Year Deficit

$$\underset{(t=)}{\Delta \mathrm{ICC}_{+1}} = \underset{(-4.5)}{-14.76} \underset{(-1.0)}{-0.01\,\Delta(\mathrm{T}-\mathrm{G})_{0(R)}} - \underset{(-0.4)}{0.01\,\Delta(T-G)_{0(NR)}} + \underset{(5.3)}{0.06\,\Delta \mathrm{GDP}_{+1}} \quad R^2 = 0.38;\ \mathrm{D.W.} = 1.7$$

6. Regressing Current Year ICC on the Current Year Deficit

$$\underset{(t=)}{\Delta \mathrm{ICC}_{0}} = \underset{(-1.9)}{-7.66} + \underset{(1.7)}{0.04\,\Delta(T-G)_{0(R)}} + \underset{(1.8)}{0.04\,\Delta(T-G)_{0(NR)}} + \underset{(2.3)}{0.04\,\Delta \mathrm{GDP}_{0}} \quad R^2 = 0.42;\ \mathrm{D.W.} = 2.0$$

Model 5 indicates no statistically significant relationship between this year's deficit and future (next year's) ICC levels, controlling for the state of next year's economy. This holds true for both recession and non-recession periods. Model 6 results comparing changes in this year's deficit with changes in this year's ICC, were somewhat unexpected. They indicate that controlling for the state of this year's economy, the more the deficit grows the lower consumer confidence gets. A rising deficit in both recessions and non-recessions is associated with a declining ICC index.

To measure the effect on investor confidence, we regressed the current and next year's NYSE Composite Index on the current year deficits in recessions and non-recessions, using the GDP as a control for all other things that can affect ICC. We obtained the following results:

7. Regressing Next Year's ICC on the Current Year Deficit

$$\underset{(t=)}{\Delta \text{NYSE}_{+1}} = \underset{(-3.3)}{-32.43} + \underset{(0.4)}{0.02\, \Delta(T-G)_{0(\text{R})}} + \underset{(1.7)}{0.10\, \Delta(T-G)_{0(\text{NR})}} + \underset{(6.0)}{0.22\, \Delta \text{GDP}_{+1}} \quad R^2 = 0.49;\ \text{D.W.} = 1.7$$

8. Regressing Current Year ICC on the Current Year Deficit

$$\underset{(t=)}{\Delta \text{NYSE}_{0}} = \underset{(0.1)}{1.67} + \underset{(4.2)}{0.27\, \Delta(T-G)_{0(\text{R})}} + \underset{(2.1)}{0.12\, \Delta(T-G)_{0(\text{NR})}} + \underset{(2.1)}{0.09\, \Delta \text{GDP}_{0}} \quad R^2 = 0.61;\ \text{D.W.} = 1.7$$

Here again we see no significant relationship between this year's deficit and the NYSE Composite Index next year (Model 7), regardless of whether the deficit is incurred in a recession or non-recession year. The relationship between this year's deficit and this year's NYSE (Model 8), controlling for the general state of the economy, was again somewhat unexpected: It indicated that controlling for the state of this year's economy, the more the deficit grows the lower investor confidence gets. A rising deficit in both recessions and non-recessions is associated with a declining NYSE index. Here again, this may mean investors take the government's announcement of stimulus programs as an indicator the economy is in worse shape than they thought.

Hence, we conclude that neither of the two variables we use to capture the state of mind of consumers and investors and their confidence in the economy, the Consumer Confidence Index or the NYSE Composite Index, appears to improve when deficits increase, and this is as true in recessions as non-recession periods. This suggests that the commonly hypothesized positive psychological effect that may accompany the announcement of a deficit-financed government stimulus program may not be really exist; in fact, the opposite may be the case.

CHAPTER 12

Alternatives to Financing Stimulus Programs with Domestic Borrowing

The chapter also shows that reductions in the pool of loanable funds can be replenished by foreign borrowing, alleviating crowd out effects.

Do the above results, which indicate complete crowd out, imply deficit-driven stimulus programs will always have negative, or negligible different from zero results? The science this study was able to bring to bear on the question, suggests the answer is yes, *if the deficits are financed by domestic borrowing*. But there may be alternative ways of financing budget deficits that avoid crowd out.

12.1 Increasing the Money Supply; Foreign Borrowing

There are two alternatives to domestic borrowing for financing stimulus programs: (1) print money or (2) borrow from other countries' saving pool rather than the domestic pool. Either option would leave the pool of domestic funds available for consumer and business borrowing unchanged when the government borrows to finance a deficit.

- Print Money
  This study had no success showing changes in the M1 money supply, either nominal or real, as a determinant of private spending, or as something that offsets crowd out effects causing the negative relationship of deficits and private borrowing. As noted earlier, this may be because the mechanism commonly used to increase M1 (open market operations) results in investors selling securities to the Fed for M1,

J.J. Heim, *Crowding Out Fiscal Stimulus*,
DOI 10.1007/978-3-319-45967-7_12

only to use the M1 to buy more securities, not real goods and services. This would occur if a major reason investors sell securities is portfolio rebalance: to obtain funds to invest in other securities which seem likely to be more profitable going forward. Hence, the real GDP may be unaffected by an increase in M1 (but bond prices are likely to rise).
- Foreign Borrowing
  Borrowing from foreign nations indeed allows more domestic spending and can replace losses in the domestic loanable funds pool caused by borrowing-financed deficits. However, this option may be viewed as a "beggar thy neighbor" approach. European sources who examined earlier versions of this paper noted foreign borrowing may be problematic as a policy, in light of some European countries' recent problems with chronic deficits made possible by easy access to borrowing from other European nations.

We have shown that government deficits are associated with decreased private borrowing. Results for the one-variable deficit models of crowd out effects on borrowing were similar to the two-variable deficit model's findings (1.82 for tax cuts and 1.57 for spending deficits). The 2SLS strong instrument findings for the one-variable model from earlier in the paper are repeated below.

For one-variable deficit borrowing models we have from Tables 5.7 and 6.6

$$\begin{array}{lll} \Delta I_B & 1.11\,(t=4.5)\,\Delta T_T & -1.11\,(t=4.5)\,\Delta G_{T\&I} \\ \underline{\Delta C_B} & \underline{0.81\,(t=5.5)\,\Delta T_T} & \underline{-0.81\,(t=5.5)\,\Delta G_{T\&I}} \\ \Delta(I_T+C_T) & 1.92\,\Delta T_T & -1.92\,\Delta G_{T\&I} \end{array}$$

Hence, a dollar deficit is associated with a nearly \$2.00 decline in private borrowing (ceteris paribus). We noted earlier that drops in private borrowing larger than the deficit itself are to be expected if borrowing is "lumpy", that is, done in discrete chunks to pay for specific items. The inability of a bank to lend <u>all</u> that is needed to buy a specific item, for example, a car, because <u>part</u> has been loaned to the government to finance a deficit, may mean <u>none</u> of what is required to buy the car gets borrowed. This problem was previously discussed in Chaps. 8 (Sect. 8.3) and 10 (Sect. 10.1).

The importance of the deficit (crowd out), relative to other variables, as an influence on borrowing was shown in Heim (2011). Stepwise regression showed the deficit to be either the most important factor explaining variance in business borrowing over the 1960–2000 period in the USA, explaining 10–25 % of all the variance depending on whether the first out or first in method was used. Five variables were tested, including the deficit, the accelerator, the exchange rate, interest rate and the DJ composite average (as a proxy for Tobin's *q*). For consumption borrowing, it was the third most important after disposable income and the exchange rate (first in), or fourth most important, after those two variables and the Dow Jones composite index (first out), out of nine variables tested. Contributing lesser amounts to the variance in consumer borrowing were the interest rate, population size, ratio of young to old in the population, consumer confidence and the M2 average.

12.2 A Further Note on Avoiding Crowd Out Effects by Borrowing from Foreign Sources

There is no crowd out problem to hamper the effects of stimulus programs if borrowing is done from loanable funds available from foreign sources of saving, rather than domestic, presuming the funds do not reduce other intended foreign lending to the domestic country. However, some may view this as a "beggar thy neighbor" strategy for growing one's own domestic economy by using another's saving, or as a way of enabling profligate government spending by some countries, through chronic and, perhaps, unsustainable levels of borrowing from another.

That said, there are potential benefits to borrowing countries attempting to stimulate an economy during a recession by deficit-financed stimulus programs. The potential usefulness of foreign borrowing can be seen by examining the other post-World War II recession of comparable scale to the 2008 recession in the USA (Heim, 2011, pp. 16–18). In that recession period, domestic savings dropped by $30.5 billion, and private investment dropped as well, though not by as much—$8.1 billion. (See Table 12.1 below.) But total public and private investments were able to rise 7.9 billion, thanks to the US's ability to borrow $38.4 billion in foreign funds, $30.5 billion to offset the drop in domestic savings, and $7.9 billion to fund the increase in total investment. See Table 12.1 below.

Technical Note: Total investment should equal total domestic savings, and foreign savings lent to the domestic country. It does not in the Flow of Funds data. The statistical discrepancy shows the extent to which total

Table 12.1 1981–83 savings and investment (billions of current dollars)

Year	*Total gross dom. saving*	*Personal savings*	*Business savings*	*Gov't. savings*	*Depreciation allowance savings*	
1981	$646.1	$236.7	$ 65.2	$ −49.2	$ 393.3	
1983	602.4	226.9	95.7	−171.4	451.1	
Change	$ −43.7	$ −9.8	$+30.5	$ −122.2	$ +57.8	
Year	*Total gross investment*	*Private domestic I investment*	*Gov't. Acct. Trans.*	*Net capital lending*	*Net Foreign. (-Bor.)*	*Statistical discrepancy (Investment>Savings)*
1981	$ 682.6	$572.4	$106.9	$0.1	$ 3.2	$ 36.6
1983	652.1	564.3	122.9	0.1	−35.2	49.7
Change	$ −30.5	$ −8.1	$+16.0	$0.0	$ −38.4	$ +13.1

Source: Flow of Funds Data cited in *Economic Report of the President, 2010, Table B-32*)

investment exceeds total domestic saving. This may result from either over counting investment or under counting total saving available for investment, (which would include foreign borrowing, and accounts for the bulk of the "statistical discrepancy"). Subtracting the discrepancy from 1981 and 1983 investment leaves the changes in investment and saving equal at \$ −43.7 billion; adding the discrepancy to savings in those years leaves investment equal to saving at \$ −30.5 billion. That is what we have done. Basically, the change in investment and saving relevant to the crowd out issue is

$$\$-8.1\Delta(\text{Bus Inv.})+16.0\ \Delta(\text{G Inv.})=+38.4\ \Delta(\text{Increased Foreign Borrowing})-30.5\Delta(\text{Domestic Saving})$$

$$\$+7.9 \text{ net investment} = \$+7.9 \text{ net increase in available savings} \quad (12.1)$$

Or

$$\$-8.1\ (\Delta\text{Business Investment}) = \$\ 7.9\ (\text{Net increase in available saving}) -16.0\ (\text{Increase Gov't. Investment}) \quad (12.2)$$

As an accounting identity, the flow of funds data say that for a given level of available saving, if government investment goes up, private investment must go down. However, there are behavioral relationships involved. If increased government investment demand results in increased interest rates, this should generate more savings. By doing so, at least part of the (otherwise, dollar for dollar) reduction in the other types of investment may be avoided. The econometric analysis shown earlier in this paper shows a systematic negative relationship between deficits (government borrowing) and private borrowing over the 1960–2010 period. It also shows changes in total private spending virtually identical to changes in the deficit.

Access to foreign borrowing may increase total savings (from all sources) available for investment, but whatever total is available, it must be divided between private and government investment; if one goes up, the other must go down, as both the flow of funds accounts indicate, and the econometric findings confirm. In this sense, the flow of funds data and the behavioral data of this study on spending/deficit relationships are in full agreement.

Alternatively, if foreign borrowing remained at $38.4 billion, but borrowing to finance government investment has been $16 billion less (reducing the deficit a similar amount), $16 billion in savings would have been freed up for private use. Business investment may not have declined at all, and may have grown (again, an empirical question, since we do not know the effect on interest rates). Hence, interpreting the effect of the actual decline in savings on private investment crowd out is difficult to do simply by inspecting the available Flow of Funds data. Better information is probably provided by the behavioral econometric models of earlier sections, which do indicate crowd out is a problem.

Without a deficit in 1981–83, that is, without government borrowing, if no foreign borrowing had been available to compensate for the $30.5 billion decline in domestic saving, private investment would have had to decline by a comparable amount.

CHAPTER 13

A Note on the Disposable Income Variable Used in Consumption Models

It was noted in the literature review section that the variable used to represent disposable income consumption functions in this study was (GDP−Total Government Revenue, or $Y-T_T$), and that this was similar to the National Income variable used by Kuznets in his pathbreaking 1940s and 1950s studies of the consumption/income relationship. More commonly these days, disposable personal income is used as the income variable in consumption studies. This chapter adds two additional equations to this study, allowing comparison of the after-tax income variable we use with the more traditional disposable personal income variable.

Below we show that the variable we use captures the effects of changing after-tax income on consumption better than the disposable personal income variable more commonly used today. This is because it recognizes businesses, out of business income, as well as individuals, out of their disposable income purchase consumer goods and services, for example, coffee and bagels from a local supermarket for a staff meeting. By including such business income-driven purchases, our after-tax income variable captures more of the actual variation in consumption that occurs than the traditional disposable personal income variable alone captures, as we see from the R^2s in the comparison below.

To show the similarity of results using disposable personal income, we have one of the best models of consumption used in this study, the model given in Eq. 7.1. It was estimated using OLS because our standard Hausman test method indicated no endogeneity. Disposable Personal

J.J. Heim, *Crowding Out Fiscal Stimulus*,
DOI 10.1007/978-3-319-45967-7_13

Income differs from the ($\Upsilon - T_T$) variable used in this study in the following way:

Disposable Personal Income = Personal Income – (Total Taxes – CIT – ½ FICA Taxes). This leaves "personal" income taxes defined as the total of Personal Income Tax (PIT), ½ Federal Insurance Contributions Act (FICA), Sales and Misc. taxes. These added to the corporate income taxes (CIT) and the other half of FICA taxes, equal total government revenue. (See Economic Report of the president, 2012, Table 83 for government revenue, Table 27 for personal income.)

Results are repeated below for the consumption model given by Model 7.1, which used the ($\Upsilon - T_T$) definition, and for the same model using disposable personal income, labeled Model 7.1a, also calculated using OLS since the standard method for calculating Hausman endogeneity indicated no statistically significant level of endogeneity was present among the right hand side variables. Very similar results were obtained using the alternative method for testing for Hausman endogeneity described earlier in Chap. 5 (Sect. 5.5), labeled below as Model 7.1.b.

Model 7.1 Consumption function (using $\Upsilon - T_T$):

$$\begin{aligned}
\underset{(t=)}{\Delta C_T} = {} & \underset{(11.4)}{0.50\Delta(Y - T_T)} + \underset{(11.4)}{0.55\boldsymbol{\Delta}(\mathbf{T}_{\mathrm{T}})} - \underset{(-3.7)}{0.26\boldsymbol{\Delta}(\mathbf{G}_{\mathrm{T\&I}})} \\
& - \underset{(-5.1)}{11.81\Delta \mathrm{PR}} + \underset{(5.3)}{0.42\,\Delta \mathrm{DJ}_{-2}} + \underset{(2.3)}{3.42\,\Delta \mathrm{XR}_{\mathrm{AV}}} - \underset{(-1.3)}{336.65\Delta \mathrm{POP}_{16}} \\
& + \underset{(2.6)}{0.012\Delta \mathrm{POP}} + \underset{(1.3)}{0.36\Delta \mathrm{ICC}_{-1}} + \underset{(3.8)}{40.86\Delta \mathrm{M2}_{\mathrm{AV}}} \\
& + \underset{(3.1)}{0.12\,\boldsymbol{\Delta}\mathbf{C}_{\mathrm{B2}}} + \underset{(1.1)}{0.04\,\Delta \mathrm{GDP}_{\mathrm{Real}(-3)}} \quad \mathbf{R}^2 = 94.9\ \%\quad \mathrm{D.W.} = 1.8 \\
\mathrm{MSE} = {} & 25.45 \qquad (7.1)
\end{aligned}$$

Model Eq. 7.1.a Same Model as 7.1, except disposable personal income used (OLS)

$$\begin{aligned}
\underset{(t=)}{\Delta C_T} = {} & \underset{(6.2)}{0.38\Delta(Y_P - T_P)} + \underset{(9.2)}{0.45\boldsymbol{\Delta}(\mathbf{T}_{\mathrm{T}})} - \underset{(-2.5)}{0.33\boldsymbol{\Delta}(\mathbf{G}_{\mathrm{T\&I}})} \\
& - \underset{(-4.2)}{9.35\Delta \mathrm{PR}} + \underset{(3.0)}{0.47\,\Delta \mathrm{DJ}_{-2}} + \underset{(2.2)}{3.56\,\Delta \mathrm{XR}_{\mathrm{AV}}} - \underset{(-1.6)}{446.88\Delta \mathrm{POP}_{16}} \\
& + \underset{(3.0)}{0.02\Delta \mathrm{POP}} + \underset{(0.3)}{0.13\Delta \mathrm{ICC}_{-1}} + \underset{(4.2)}{65.46\Delta \mathrm{M2}_{\mathrm{AV}}} + \underset{(5.3)}{0.25\,\boldsymbol{\Delta}\mathbf{C}_{\mathrm{B2}}} \\
& + \underset{(1.2)}{0.05\,\Delta \mathrm{GDP}_{\mathrm{Real}(-3)}} \quad \mathbf{R}^2 = 90.1\ \%\quad \mathrm{D.W.} = 2.4\ \mathrm{MSE} = 35.49 \qquad (7.1.a)
\end{aligned}$$

Model Eq. 7.1.b Same Model as 7.1, except disposable personal income used (2SLS Strong Instrument)

$$\underset{(t=)}{\Delta C_T} = \underset{(2.4)}{0.35\Delta(Y_P - T_P)} + \underset{(6.2)}{0.53\boldsymbol{\Delta}(\mathbf{T}_\mathrm{T})} - \underset{(-2.1)}{0.87\boldsymbol{\Delta}(\mathbf{G}_{\mathrm{T\&I}})}$$
$$- \underset{(-3.0)}{15.04\Delta\mathrm{PR}} + \underset{(3.3)}{0.55\ \Delta\mathrm{DJ}_{-2}} + \underset{(1.8)}{5.60\ \Delta\mathrm{XR}_{\mathrm{AV}}} - \underset{(-1.5)}{743.80\Delta\mathrm{POP}_{16}}$$
$$+ \underset{(2.5)}{0.028\Delta\mathrm{POP}} - \underset{(-0.4)}{0.24\Delta\mathrm{ICC}_{-1}} + \underset{(3.0)}{97.89\Delta\mathrm{M2}_{\mathrm{AV}}}$$
$$+ \underset{(3.1)}{0.20\ \boldsymbol{\Delta}\mathbf{C}_{\mathbf{B}2}} + \underset{(0.9)}{0.05\ \Delta\mathrm{GDP}_{\mathrm{Real}(-3)}} \quad \mathbf{R}^2 = 85.3\ \%\quad \mathrm{D.W.} = 2.4$$
$$\mathrm{MSE} = 43.21 \qquad (7.1.\mathrm{b})$$

Conclusions regarding crowd out remain the same; both components of the deficit have statistically significant coefficients indicating they are negatively related to consumer spending. Results for other variables in the model are roughly the same as before.

R^2 drops 4.8 % points when substituting personal income for $(Y - T_T)$. This may be because not all spending on consumer goods and services recorded by government statisticians may be out of consumer income. Some may be out of business income (profits). Profits, when added to Eq. 7.1.a as separate income variables were found to be statistically significant determinants of spending on consumer goods, in addition to personal income.

On the other hand, when the typical income variable used in this study $(Y - T_T)$ is substituted for personal income, profits are not found statistically significant as a second income variable. This suggests the profits variable may be behind the drop in explanatory power when using personal income.

Using personal income also reduces the multiplier effect inferred by the new model. If the consumption function is:

$$\begin{aligned} C &= \alpha_1 \quad \alpha_1(Y_P - T_P) + \beta_1 T_T \quad + \ldots.\mathrm{etc} \ldots..\beta_1 \\ &= \alpha_1 \quad \alpha_1(\gamma_1 Y_T - \gamma_2 T_T) + \beta_1 T_T \quad + \ldots.\mathrm{etc} \\ &= \alpha_1 \quad \alpha_1\gamma_1 Y_T + (-\alpha_1\gamma_2 + \beta_1)T_T \quad + \ldots.\mathrm{etc} \end{aligned}$$

So, in an IS equation, this becomes

$$Y = 1/(1 - \alpha_1\gamma_1)[(-\alpha_1\gamma_2 + \beta_1)T_T + \ldots \text{etc} \ldots]$$

Since γ_1 and γ_2 are both less than one, $\alpha_1\gamma_1$ will be less than α_1, and hence, the multiplier will be smaller. Further, since $\alpha_1\gamma_2$ is also less than one, pre-multiplier initial effect of a tax cut, given by—$\alpha_1\gamma_2$, will also be smaller than it would be otherwise, reducing the extent to which it can offset the crowd out effect of a tax cut, $+\beta_1$.

The finding of a smaller multiplier when using disposable income (vs. $T_T - G_{T\&I}$) is consistent with our finding in Eq. 7.1a.Alt of a smaller observed effect of disposable personal income's impact on consumption, compared to $(T_T - G_{T\&I})$.

Finally, no adjustments have to be made to the investment disposable income variable. It already has the employer half of FICA and CIT subtracted to get the profit figures used.

CHAPTER 14

Do Crowd Out Effects Differ in Recession and Non-recession Periods?

One variant of the Krugman argument notes that the demand for loans by consumers and businesses declines during recessions. It is argued this allows governments to borrow additional funds to finance stimulus programs without crowding out private investment, since some funds in the existing pool of loanable funds are no longer being used by private borrowers. And this occurs at the very time when stimulus programs are needed most (recessions). Countering that, our examination of the 1981–83 recession period (see Chap. 12 (Sect 12.2)) indicated that, *the supply of domestic savings* (i.e., the pool of loanable funds available from domestic sources) dropped more than the *demand for borrowed money dropped.* If the pool declines more than private demand, government attempts to borrow these funds to finance stimulus programs would create at least as severe a crowd out problem in recessions as in non-recession periods. By comparison, borrowing from foreign sources of loanable funds is not likely to cause a crowd out problem as long as there has not been a previous domestic private sector demand for the same foreign funds.

Section 14.1 discusses the methodology used to compare crowd out effects in recession and non-recession periods. Section 14.2 tests eight consumption and four investment models that compare crowd out effects in both recessions and non-recessions. Out of 38 different crowd out variables in these 12 models (tax deficits in recessions, tax deficits in non-recession periods, spending deficits in recessions, spending deficits in non-recession periods, changes in deficit regardless of cause, etc.), 36 had statistically significant regression coefficients showing deficits had a negative

J.J. Heim, *Crowding Out Fiscal Stimulus*,
DOI 10.1007/978-3-319-45967-7_14

effect on consumer or investment spending, and that this held for recessions as well as non-recession periods. Two (of six) tests of spending deficits in recessions showed no significant effect on consumption.

Section 14.3 develops a single-regression IS curve that tests both spending and tax-cut crowd out effects separately for recession and non-recession periods. Findings indicate tax-cut deficits have larger crowd out than stimulus effects, creating a net negative effect on the GDP. Spending deficits were found to have stimulus effects about equal to their crowd out effects, leaving no significant net effect on the GDP.

14.1 Methodology

We wish to more systematically examine the issue of recession effects on crowd out over the full 1960–2010 period covered by this study. To do so, we have retested two of our key (most completely specified) models: the consumption function model (Eq. 7.1) and the investment function models (Eq. 8.Alt.b). These retested structural models are the same models tested before, except that two groups of government tax and spending deficit measures are included in each model. One deficit variable $(T_T - G_{T\&I})_R$ for years in which the NBER has indicated two or more quarters of the year were in recession, and one for which only one or no quarters were recession periods $(T_T - G_{T\&I})_{NR}$. The four new deficit components of these two deficit measures were tested for stationarity using the augmented Dickey–Fuller test. The standard Hausman, Wald and Sargan tests described earlier were used to discover and correct for endogeneity in the consumption and investment models. When testing for endogeneity, all variables in the two models were tested using the following exogenous and lagged variables as first stage Hausman test regressors.

DJ_{-2}	Y_{-3}	ICC_{-1}
Pop_{16}	$\dot{C}ap_{-1}$	$I_{B(-1)}$
Pop	PR_{-2}	$M2_{AV}$

All other variables were considered suspect of endogeneity with either consumer spending or investment spending, and were Hausman-tested. Those found endogenous were replaced with Wald-tested non-weak instruments, and the instruments were tested for endogeneity using Sargan tests. Augmented Dickey–Fuller tests on all four deficit variables showed them to be stationary, as was the case for all other variables, except three which were cointegrated (see Section 3: Methodology). The one-variable definition of the deficit was found stationary for non-recession periods, and marginally non-stationary for recession periods. Models are tested in first differences to help reduce serial correlation and multicollinearity problems.

1960–2010 data from the *Economic Report of the President* (2011and 2002) and the *Flow of Funds Accounts* of the Federal Reserve (2011) were used. The effects of a wide range of variables on consumption and investment spending and borrowing were estimated. The variables tested include the following, repeated from Chaps. 5 and 6 for easy reference when examining test results:

Consumption	*Investment*
Disposable Income ($Y_T - T_T$)	Samuelson's Accelerator (ACC)
Deficit Variables ($T_T - G_{T\&I}$)	Deficit Variables ($T_T - G_{T\&I}$)
Wealth (DJAV)	Depreciation Allowances (DEP)
Interest rates (PR or r)	Interest Rates
Exchange rates (XR_{AV})	Tobin's q (DJ)
Consumer Confidence (ICC)	Profits (PROF)
Population Size (POP)	Exchange rates (XR_{AV})
Population Age Composition (POP_{16})	Population Size (POP)
Money supply (M1 or M2)	
Consumer borrowing ($C_{B \text{ or } B2}$)	Business Borrowing ($I_{B(-1)}$)

A substantial review of the economic literature found these variables, or representatives of them cited as the major determinants of consumer or investment demand. Therefore, these variables were included in the regression models tested.

Statistical significance levels for all tests in Chap. 14 are as follows:

2.7 = 1 % Significance Level	1.8 = 7 % Significance Level
2.3 = 3 % Significance Level	1.7 = 10 % Significance Level
2.0 = 5 % Significance Level	1.6 = 11 % Significance Level
	1.5 = 15 % Significance Level

14.2 Test Results

14.2.1 Consumption Function Findings

Model 14.1 OLS test of consumption using separate recession and non-recession deficit variables

(Using 1 variable formulation of deficit)

$$\underset{(t=)}{\Delta C_T} = \underset{(7.8)}{0.47\Delta(Y_T - T_T)} + \underset{(6.8)}{0.46\boldsymbol{\Delta}(\mathbf{T}_\mathrm{T} - \mathbf{G}_{\mathrm{T\&I}})_\mathbf{R}}$$
$$+ \underset{(6.8)}{0.48\boldsymbol{\Delta}(\mathbf{T}_\mathrm{T} - \mathbf{G}_{\mathrm{T\&I}})_\mathbf{NR}} - \underset{(-4.9)}{12.37\Delta\mathrm{PR}} + \underset{(3.5)}{0.38\ \Delta\mathrm{DJ}_{-2}}$$
$$+ \underset{(2.7)}{3.73\ \Delta\mathrm{XR}_{\mathrm{AV}}} - \underset{(-2.0)}{544.98\Delta\mathrm{POP}_{16}} + \underset{(4.3)}{0.018\Delta\mathrm{POP}}$$
$$+ \underset{(1.5)}{0.51\Delta\mathrm{ICC}_{-1}} + \underset{(5.0)}{52.63\Delta\mathrm{M2}_{\mathrm{AV}}} + \underset{(3.3)}{0.14\ \Delta C_{\mathrm{B2}}}$$
$$+ \underset{(1.2)}{0.05\ \Delta\mathrm{GDP}_{\mathrm{Real}(-3)}} \quad R^2 = 94.1\%$$
$$\mathrm{D.W.} = 1.9\ \mathrm{MSE} = 27.34 \tag{14.1}$$

Variable definitions are as noted above. The OLS results show crowd out having virtually the same effect in both recessions (.46 $\Delta(T_T{-}\mathrm{G}_{\mathrm{T\&I}})_{\mathrm{R}}$) as in non-recession periods (0.48 $\Delta(T_T{-}G_{T\&I})_{\mathrm{NR}}$). This finding is consistent with the implication of the Chap. 12 B case study's finding for the 1981–83 recessionary period, which was that crowd out is a potential problem in recession periods as well as more normal economic times. Endogeneity tests showed the deficit variable in recessions was endogenous with consumption, indicating 2SLS would be a better means of testing. Strong instruments for these variables were developed and used in 2SLS tests and are presented in Eq. 14.2 below (Strong instrument development method discussed in Methodology, Section 4):

Model 14.2 2SLS test of consumption using separate recession and non-recession deficit variables

(one variable formulation of deficit).

($T_T{-}G_{T\&I}$) Only Endogenous Var.; Wald test of Instrument: $F = 10.1$, C_{B2} $t = 4.8$, $I_{B(-1)} = 5.8$.

(Strong Instrument)

$$\underset{(t=)}{\Delta C_T} = \underset{(5.6)}{0.42\Delta(\mathrm{Y_T} - \mathrm{T_T})} + \underset{(6.1)}{0.65\boldsymbol{\Delta}(\mathbf{T_T} - \mathbf{G_{T\&I}})_{\mathbf{R}}}$$
$$+ \underset{(7.3)}{0.53\boldsymbol{\Delta}(\mathbf{T_T} - \mathbf{G_{T\&I}})_{\mathbf{NR}}} - \underset{(-4.6)}{14.35\Delta \mathrm{PR}} + \underset{(4.6)}{0.54\,\Delta \mathrm{DJ}_{-2}}$$
$$+ \underset{(2.8)}{5.20\,\Delta \mathrm{XR_{AV}}} - \underset{(-1.7)}{583.14\Delta \mathrm{POP}_{16}} + \underset{(4.2)}{0.020\Delta \mathrm{POP}}$$
$$+ \underset{(0.4)}{0.18\Delta \mathrm{ICC}_{-1}} + \underset{(4.4)}{65.89\Delta \mathrm{M2_{AV}}} + \underset{(1.9)}{0.08\,\Delta \mathrm{C_{B2}}}$$
$$+ \underset{(1.1)}{0.04\,\Delta \mathrm{GDP_{Real(-3)}}} \quad R^2 = 92.7\ \%$$
$$\mathrm{D.W.} = 1.9\ \mathrm{MSE} = 30.51 \qquad (14.2)$$

The 2SLS results show a tendency for crowd out to be a slightly bigger problem in recessions than in non-recession periods, but the difference is not statistically significant. We conclude both the OLS and 2SLS one-variable deficit tests show crowd out to have statistically significant negative effects of the same magnitude in both recession and non-recession periods.

Equation 14.3 below tests the separate effects of each of the deficit variables, taxes and government spending, in both recessions and non-recession periods. We wish to see if tax cut deficits differ from spending deficits in their effects on consumption:

Model 14.3 OLS test of consumption using separate recession and non-recession deficit variables

(Two-variable formulation of deficit)

$$\underset{(t=)}{\Delta C_T} = \underset{(9.5)}{0.52\Delta(Y_T - T_T)} + \underset{(4.8)}{0.65\boldsymbol{\Delta}(\mathbf{T_T})_{\mathbf{R}}} - \underset{(1.5)}{0.13\boldsymbol{\Delta}(\mathbf{G_{T\&I}})_{\mathbf{R}}}$$
$$+ \underset{(8.5)}{0.55\boldsymbol{\Delta}(\mathbf{T_T})_{\mathbf{NR}}} - \underset{(-3.2)}{0.30\boldsymbol{\Delta}(\mathbf{G_{T\&I}})_{\mathbf{NR}}} - \underset{(4.7)}{12.78\Delta \mathrm{PR}}$$
$$+ \underset{(4.1)}{0.45\,\Delta \mathrm{DJ}_{-2}} + \underset{(2.2)}{3.24\,\Delta \mathrm{XR_{AV}}} - \underset{(1.2)}{323.78\Delta \mathrm{POP}_{16}}$$
$$+ \underset{(1.9)}{0.010\Delta \mathrm{POP}} + \underset{(1.3)}{0.39\Delta \mathrm{ICC}_{-1}} + \underset{(3.6)}{44.42\Delta \mathrm{M2_{AV}}}$$
$$+ \underset{(3.0)}{0.11\,\Delta \mathrm{C_{B2}}} + \underset{(0.8)}{0.03\,\Delta \mathrm{GDP_{Real(-3)}}} \quad \mathrm{R}^2 = 95.1\%$$
$$\mathrm{D.W.} = 1.8\ \mathrm{MSE} = 25.60 \qquad (14.3)$$

However, there was a very high level of multicollinearity between $(T_T)_R$ and $(G_{T\&I})_R$ (r=0.69), 20 points higher than between any other variables.

This appears to have had a distorting effect on the coefficient and *t*-statistic for $(G_{T\&I})_{\mathrm{R}}$. Hence, our finding in Eq. 14.3 of little crowd out effect of spending deficits in recessions is suspect. Eliminating the $T_{T\,\mathrm{R}}$ variable and retesting strengthens the coefficient and raises its statistical significance markedly, clear evidence of the multicollinearity problem as shown in 14.3.1 below.

Model 14.3.1 OLS test of consumption using separate recession and non-recession deficit variables

(Two-variable formulation of deficit)

(Same as 14.3. except $\mathrm{T_{TR}}$ Omitted to test for multicollinearity effects on $\mathrm{G_{T\&I(R)}}$.)

$$\begin{aligned}
\underset{(t=)}{\Delta C_T} = {} & \underset{(6.1)}{0.46\Delta(Y_T - T_T)} + \underset{(\mathbf{N.A.})}{(\mathbf{.N.A.})\boldsymbol{\Delta}(\mathbf{T_T})_{\mathbf{R}}} \\
& - \underset{(2.5)}{0.57\boldsymbol{\Delta}(\mathbf{G_{T\&I}})_{\mathbf{R}}} + \underset{(4.9)}{0.47\boldsymbol{\Delta}(\mathbf{T_T})_{\mathbf{NR}}} - \underset{(-2.7)}{0.27\boldsymbol{\Delta}(\mathbf{G_{T\&I}})_{\mathbf{NR}}} \\
& - \underset{(2.6)}{7.92\Delta \mathrm{PR}} + \underset{(1.1)}{0.17\,\Delta \mathrm{DJ}_{-2}} + \underset{(1.3)}{2.79\,\Delta \mathrm{XR_{AV}}} - \underset{(1.9)}{440.54\Delta \mathrm{POP_{16}}} \\
& + \underset{(4.0)}{0.018\Delta \mathrm{POP}} + \underset{(1.4)}{0.61\Delta \mathrm{ICC}_{-1}} + \underset{(1.8)}{24.66\Delta \mathrm{M2_{AV}}} \\
& + \underset{(3.4)}{0.21\,\Delta C_{B2}} + \underset{(1.5)}{0.07\,\Delta \mathrm{GDP_{Real(-3)}}} \quad \mathrm{R}^2 = 90.9\% \\
& \mathrm{D.W.} = 1.8 \ \mathrm{MSE} = 34.49
\end{aligned} \tag{14.3.1}$$

That said, we do need an estimate of the crowd out effects of tax cut deficits in recessions, so we must restore the variable in a form that allows it to show the effect of tax cuts during recessions while reducing the severe multicollinearity of this variable in recessions with government spending. We do this in equation 14.3.2 below by treating the average tax deficit for the recession year and the year before as the recession year deficit. This reduces the multicollinearity to ($r = 0.52$), and strengthens the coefficient and statistical significance of the government spending variable effect during recessions noticeably.

Model 14.3.2 OLS test of consumption using separate recession and non-recession deficit variables (two-variable formulation of deficit)

(Same as 14.3. except $\mathrm{T_{TR}}$ in recession years replaced by average taxes for the recession year and the year preceding it to reduce multicollinearity effects on of $T_{T(\mathrm{R})}$ on $G_{T\&I(\mathrm{R})}$)

$$\underset{(t=)}{\Delta C_T} = \underset{(7.0)}{0.47\Delta(Y_T - T_T)} + \underset{(6.1)}{0.29\boldsymbol{\Delta}(\mathbf{T}_\mathrm{T})_\mathbf{R}} - \underset{(3.4)}{0.36\boldsymbol{\Delta}(\mathbf{G}_{\mathrm{T\&I}})_\mathbf{R}}$$
$$+ \underset{(6.4)}{0.55\boldsymbol{\Delta}(\mathbf{T}_\mathrm{T})_\mathbf{NR}} - \underset{(-2.3)}{0.22\boldsymbol{\Delta}(\mathbf{G}_{\mathrm{T\&I}})_\mathbf{NR}} - \underset{(3.2)}{7.87\Delta \mathrm{PR}}$$
$$+ \underset{(3.6)}{0.47\,\Delta \mathrm{DJ}_{-2}} + \underset{(1.6)}{2.39\,\Delta \mathrm{XR}_{\mathrm{AV}}} - \underset{(1.3)}{313.21\Delta \mathrm{POP}_{16}}$$
$$+ \underset{(2.2)}{0.011\Delta \mathrm{POP}} - \underset{(-0.1)}{0.05\Delta \mathrm{ICC}_{-1}} + \underset{(3.5)}{38.94\Delta \mathrm{M2}_{\mathrm{AV}}}$$
$$+ \underset{(3.5)}{0.17\,\Delta \mathrm{C}_{\mathrm{B2}}} + \underset{(1.2)}{0.04\,\Delta \mathrm{GDP}_{\mathrm{Real}(-3)}} \quad \mathrm{R}^2 = 94.0\%$$
$$\mathrm{D.W.} = 2.1 \ \mathrm{MSE} = 28.44 \qquad (14.3.2)$$

Now the OLS results clearly indicate a statistically significant crowd out effect for both the tax and the government spending variables, and indicate these are as likely to occur in recessions as in non-recessions. The coefficient on the recession tax variable is noticeably smaller due to averaging; in essence, we have created an "errors in variables" problem with its expected downward in regression estimates. Taken together, the OLS and 2SLS results overall obtained by separating the deficit variables seem to indicate a negative effect of crowd out on consumption for tax cut deficits compared to spending deficits. One possible explanation for this may be that tax cut stimulus income is more likely to be used, at least in part, for investment, compared to income received from government spending stimulus programs, since tax cuts are more likely to accrue to companies or wealthier income individuals. We commented earlier (Chap. 12 (Sect. 12.1)) on the adverse effects on goods and services that might result if money demand is diverted from them to securities.

We conclude that OLS tests show that

(1) Both tax and spending deficits are significant in recessions as well as non-recession periods.
(2) Tax deficits have a more negative effect on consumption than spending deficits.

That said, 2SLS proved to be the most appropriate tool for examining this issue, since both components of the deficit, $(T_T)_R$ and $(G_{T\&I})_R$ were found Hausman-endogenous. They were replaced by strong instruments in Equation 14.4 below.

Model 14.4 2SLS test of consumption using separate recession and non-recession deficit variables (two-variable formulation of deficit)

(Endogenous: $T_{(R)}$ (Wald $t = 5.6$ for C_{B2}, 4.9 for $I_{B(-1)}$; $F = 10.5$) and $G_{T\&I(R)}$ (Wald $t = 4.6$ for $I_{B(-1)}$; $G_{T\&I(NR)} = 4.3$; $F = 7.9$). Strong Instrument. Sargan test: $nR^2 = 1.5 < X^2_{(.95,15)} = 25.0$

$$\begin{aligned}
\underset{(t=)}{\Delta C_T} = {} & \underset{(6.4)}{0.48\Delta(Y_T - T_T)} + \underset{(4.7)}{0.95\mathbf{\Delta(T_T)_R}} - \underset{(-0.8)}{0.21\mathbf{\Delta(G_{T\&I})_R}} \\
& + \underset{(9.7)}{0.55\mathbf{\Delta(T_T)_{NR}}} - \underset{(-3.2)}{0.46\mathbf{\Delta(G_{T\&I})_{NR}}} - \underset{(4.5)}{15.52\Delta PR} \\
& + \underset{(5.9)}{0.61\,\Delta DJ_{-2}} + \underset{(2.7)}{4.63\,\Delta XR_{AV}} - \underset{(1.2)}{462.86\Delta POP_{16}} \\
& + \underset{(1.9)}{0.015\Delta POP} + \underset{(0.8)}{0.31\Delta ICC_{-1}} + \underset{(3.8)}{67.96\Delta M2_{AV}} \\
& + \underset{(1.4)}{0.05\,\Delta C_{B2}} + \underset{(0.2)}{0.01\,\Delta GDP_{Real(-3)}} \quad R^2 = 93.8\% \\
& D.W. = 1.7 \; MSE = 28.97
\end{aligned} \tag{14.4}$$

Here again, the degree of multicollinearity was high between the two recession period deficit components ($r = 0.69$), and there was a concern this may be distorting the results in 14.4. The distortive effects of the multicollinearity can be seen in Eq. 14.4.1 below, where the tax variable for recession periods is omitted: the government spending variable's magnitude and statistical significance increase enormously, as we would expect if multicollinearity with the omitted variable were affecting it substantially.

Model 14.4.1 2SLS test of consumption using separate recession and non-recession deficit variables (two-variable formulation of deficit)

(Using same instruments as 14.1, but leaving (TT)R out to test for multicollinearity effects on government spending deficits during recessions)

$$\begin{aligned}
\underset{(t=)}{\Delta C_T} = {} & \underset{(2.4)}{0.32\Delta(Y_T - T_T)} + \underset{(\mathbf{N.A.})}{(\mathbf{N.A.})\mathbf{\Delta(T_T)_R}} - \underset{(-2.7)}{1.15\mathbf{\Delta(G_{T\&I})_R}} \\
& + \underset{(4.2)}{.41\mathbf{\Delta(T_T)_{NR}}} - \underset{(-2.8)}{.55\mathbf{\Delta(G_{T\&I})_{NR}}} - \underset{(2.4)}{9.57\Delta PR} \\
& + \underset{(1.5)}{.27\,\Delta DJ_{-2}} + \underset{(1.8)}{5.13\,\Delta XR_{AV}} - \underset{(1.9)}{776.64\Delta POP_{16}} \\
& + \underset{(3.2)}{.030\Delta POP} + \underset{(0.7)}{.46\Delta ICC_{-1}} + \underset{(2.2)}{51.69\Delta M2_{AV}} \\
& + \underset{(2.8)}{.18\,\Delta C_{B2}} + \underset{(1.5)}{.09\,\Delta GDP_{Real(-3)}} \quad R^2 = 87.6\% \\
& D.W. = 2.1 \; MSE = 40.40
\end{aligned} \tag{14.4.1}$$

As before, we do need an estimate of the crowd out effects of tax cut deficits in recessions, so we must restore the variable in a form that allows it to show the effect of tax cuts during recessions while reducing the severe multicollinearity of this variable in recessions with government spending. We do this in Eq. 14.4.2 below by treating the average tax deficit for the recession year and the year before as the recession year deficit. This reduces the multicollinearity to ($r = 0.52$), and strengthens the coefficient and statistical significance of the government spending variable effect during recessions noticeably. Here again, government spending and this tax variable were found Hausman-endogenous, and were replaced by strong instruments.

Model 14.4.2 2SLS test of consumption using separate recession and non-recession deficit variables (two-variable formulation of deficit)

(Endogenous: T_{TR} (Wald $t = 4.3$ for DJ_{-2}, 3.9 for $I_{B(-1)}$; 4.0 for Y_{-2}, $F = 7.0$) and $G_{T\&I(R)}$(Wald $t = 4.6$ for $I_{B(-1)}$; $G_{T\&I(NR)} = 4.3$; $F = 7.9$). Strong Instrument. Sargan test: $nR^2 = 1.5 < X^2_{(.95,15)} = 25.0$

$$\begin{aligned}
\underset{(t=)}{\Delta C_T} = {} & \underset{(4.6)}{0.41\Delta(Y_T - T_T)} + \underset{(4.5)}{0.90\boldsymbol{\Delta}(\mathbf{T}_{\mathrm{TAV}})_{\mathbf{R}}} - \underset{(-2.1)}{0.55\boldsymbol{\Delta}(\mathbf{G}_{\mathrm{T\&I}})_{\mathbf{R}}} \\
& + \underset{(8.2)}{0.56\boldsymbol{\Delta}(\mathbf{T}_{\mathrm{T}})_{\mathbf{NR}}} - \underset{(-2.0)}{0.33\boldsymbol{\Delta}(\mathbf{G}_{\mathrm{T\&I}})_{\mathbf{NR}}} - \underset{(3.2)}{8.68\Delta \mathrm{PR}} \\
& + \underset{(5.4)}{0.68\,\Delta \mathrm{DJ}_{-2}} + \underset{(2.1)}{3.33\,\Delta \mathrm{XR}_{\mathrm{AV}}} - \underset{(1.3)}{411.33\Delta \mathrm{POP}_{16}} \\
& + \underset{(1.9)}{0.014\Delta \mathrm{POP}} - \underset{(1.0)}{0.47\Delta \mathrm{ICC}_{-1}} + \underset{(3.6)}{59.91\Delta \mathrm{M2}_{\mathrm{AV}}} \\
& + \underset{(2.7)}{0.14\,\Delta C_{B2}} + \underset{(0.8)}{0.03\,\Delta \mathrm{GDP}_{\mathrm{Real}(-3)}} \quad R^2 = 92.2\% \\
& \mathrm{D.W.} = 2.1 \ \mathrm{MSE} = 32.27
\end{aligned} \tag{14.4.2}$$

With this adjustment, we find both types of deficits having sizable statistically significant crowd out effects in recessions as well as non-recession periods. Both types of deficits also have larger crowd out effects in recessions than in non-recession periods. Using the average of the current year and prior year's taxes as a proxy for this year's to reduce multicollinearity effects achieved its objective: the simple correlation between this tax variable and government spending in recession periods from 0.69 to 0.52.

Had we used taxes of two years before in the average with current year taxes, our regression t statistics would have been even more markedly strengthened, but these results are not presented on the grounds that the average of taxes for the current and immediate past period is a better proxy for current year tax effects than the average of current year taxes and those from two years ago, and the results less likely to be a statistical aberration.

When current and prior year averages for both the tax and government spending variables are used, results are nearly identical to those shown in 14.4.2.

Hence, our 2SLS conclusions regarding crowd out's effect on consumption remain the same as our OLS conclusions:

(1) Both tax and spending deficits have significant negative effects on consumption in recessions as well as non-recession periods.
(2) Tax deficits have a more negative effect on consumption than spending deficits.

14.2.2 *Investment Function Findings*

Equation 14.5 below presents the OLS form of the investment equation used earlier in Section 8.1. except that it includes the deficit variable ($T_T - G_{T\&I}$) twice, each multiplied by a dummy variable to provide separate estimates for recession ($\mathbf{\Delta(T_T - G_{T\&I})_R}$) and non-recession ($\mathbf{\Delta(T_T - G_{T\&I})_{NR}}$) effects:

Model 14.5 OLS test of investment using separate recession and non-recession deficit variables (one-variable formulation of deficit)

$$
\begin{aligned}
\underset{(t=)}{\Delta I_T} = {} & +\underset{(5.8)}{.29\Delta(ACC)} + \underset{(5.6)}{.42\mathbf{\Delta(T_T - G_{T\&I})_R}} \\
& + \underset{(3.8)}{.31\mathbf{\Delta(T_T - G_{T\&I})_{NR}}} + \underset{(2.1)}{.66\Delta DEP} + \underset{(1.5)}{2.85\Delta CAP_{-1}} \\
& - \underset{(-2.0)}{3.97\Delta PR_{-2}} - \underset{(-0.4)}{.09\Delta DJ_{-0}} + \underset{(2.1)}{.13\Delta PROF_{-2}} \\
& + \underset{(2.9)}{6.05\Delta XR_{AV}} + \underset{(1.0)}{.004\Delta POP} + \underset{(2.1)}{.12\,\Delta(BOR_{-1})} \\
& + \underset{(1.1)}{.06\,\Delta GDP_{Real(-3)}} \quad R^2 = 93.7\% \\
& D.W. = 2.0 \; MSE = 31.86
\end{aligned} \qquad (14.5)
$$

The OLS results indicate statistically significant crowd out effects in both recession and non-recession periods, and that the crowd out effect of deficits may be greater in recession periods (as was the case with consumption).

However, four variables in the model were found endogenous with investment spending. These variables were replaced by Wald-strong instruments, using 2SLS. Results are presented in Equation 14.6 below.

Model 14.6 2SLS estimates of determinants of investment spending, using one-variable deficit, and using real GDP_{-3} as the business cycle control variable

(Hausman Tests Indicate 4 Variables Endogenous With Investment Spending, So Instrumented: DJ_0 (Wald test $F = 7.1$, but $(I_{B(-1)})$ $t = 3.9$), DEP (Wald $F = 22.1$ and $t = 5.0$ for DEP_{-1}), $PROF_0$ (Wald Test $F = 4.5$, but $DJ_{-1\&-2AV}$ $t = -3.6$ and ACC $t = 3.4$). Sargan Test $NR^2 = 3.4 < X^2_{(95,15)} = 25.0$. This is a Strong Instrument Model)

$$\begin{aligned}
\underset{(t=)}{\Delta I_T} = &+ \underset{(2.6)}{.20\Delta(ACC)} + \underset{(3.2)}{.69\boldsymbol{\Delta}(\mathbf{T}_T - \mathbf{G}_{T\&I})} + \underset{(-4.0)}{.40\boldsymbol{\Delta}(\mathbf{T}_T - \mathbf{G}_{T\&I})} \\
&+ \underset{(0.7)}{.36\Delta DEP} + \underset{(0.8)}{2.20\Delta CAP_{-1}} + \underset{(0.2)}{1.12\Delta PR_{-2}} - \underset{(-1.3)}{.70\Delta DJ_{-0}} \\
&+ \underset{(1.8)}{.45\Delta PROF_{-2}} + \underset{(3.3)}{7.96\Delta XR_{AV}} + \underset{(2.0)}{.008\Delta POP} \\
&+ \underset{(1.0)}{.17\,\Delta(BOR_{-1})} + \underset{(1.3)}{.10\,\Delta GDP_{Real(-3)}} \quad R^2 = 88.8\% \\
&D.W. = 1.9 \; MSE = 43.00
\end{aligned} \tag{14.6}$$

Here again, the findings indicate crowd out has a more negative effect on investment spending in recessions, though the differences are not statistically significant, nor are they significantly different from the OLS crowd out results. That said, though technically a strong instrument, substituting the instrument for the endogenous variables resulted in a 4.9 percentage point drop in explained variance, and reduced significance levels for several variables. An even stronger instrument would probably reduce these differences between OLS and 2SLS results.

Models 14.7 and 14.8 retest the same investment model, but provide separate estimates of the effects of the tax cut and spending deficits:

Model 14.7 OLS test of investment using separate recession and non-recession deficit variables (two-variable formulation of deficit)

$$\underset{(t=)}{\Delta I_T} = +\underset{(5.4)}{0.31\Delta(\text{ACC})} + \underset{(3.4)}{0.41\boldsymbol{\Delta}(\mathbf{T}_{\text{T}})_{\mathbf{R}-}} - \underset{(-2.3)}{0.42\boldsymbol{\Delta}(\mathbf{G}_{\text{T\&I}})_{\mathbf{R}}}$$
$$+\underset{(3.3)}{0.28\boldsymbol{\Delta}(\mathbf{T}_{\text{T}})_{\mathbf{NR}-}} - \underset{(-3.1)}{0.37\boldsymbol{\Delta}(\mathbf{G}_{\text{T\&I}})_{\mathbf{NR}}} + \underset{(2.2)}{0.67\Delta\text{DEP}}$$
$$+\underset{(1.5)}{3.68\Delta\text{CAP}_{-1}} - \underset{(-1.7)}{3.49\Delta\text{PR}_{-2}} - \underset{(0.3)}{0.07\Delta\text{DJ}_{-0}}$$
$$+\underset{(1.9)}{0.13\Delta\text{PROF}_0} + \underset{(2.6)}{6.22\Delta\text{XR}_{\text{AV}}} + \underset{(1.2)}{0.005\Delta\text{POP}}$$
$$+\underset{(2.0)}{0.12\,\Delta(\text{BOR}_{-1})} + \underset{(1.3)}{0.07\,\Delta\text{GDP}_{\text{Real}(-3)}} \quad R^2 = 93.8\ \%$$
$$\text{D.W.} = 2.0 \text{ MSE} = 32.51 \tag{14.7}$$

Both tax cut and spending deficits are found to have statistically significant crowd out effects. This is true for both recessions and non-recession periods, and results suggest slightly larger crowd out effects of deficits in recessions, but the difference is not statistically significant. Endogeneity issues suggest 2SLS may be an even more appropriate statistical tool for analysis, since the DEP, DJ_0 and PROF were all found Hausman-endogenous and were replaced by strong instruments. Results are shown in Model 14.8 below.

Model 14.8 2SLS Estimates of determinants of investment spending, using two-variable deficit, and using real GDP_{-3} as the business cycle control variable

(Hausman Tests Indicate ThreeVariables Endogenous With Investment Spending. These Variables Have Been Instrumented: DJ_0 (Wald test $F = 9.2$, but $(T_T)_{\text{R}}$ $t = 3.4$), DEP (Wald $F = 13.9$ and $t = 7.1$ for DEP_{-1}), PROF_0 (Wald Test $F = 3.8$, but $\text{DJ}_{-1\&-2\text{AV}}$ $t = 4.5$. Sargan Test $\text{NR}^2 = 3.0 < X^2_{(95,16)} = 26.3$. This is a Strong Instrument Model)

$$\underset{(t=)}{\Delta I_T} = +\underset{(5.2)}{0.29\Delta(\text{ACC})} + \underset{(2.9)}{0.39\boldsymbol{\Delta}(\mathbf{T}_{\text{T}})_{\mathbf{R}-}} - \underset{(-2.2)}{0.44\boldsymbol{\Delta}(\mathbf{G}_{\text{T\&I}})_{\mathbf{R}}}$$
$$+\underset{(2.9)}{0.29\boldsymbol{\Delta}(\mathbf{T}_{\text{T}})_{\mathbf{NR}-}} - \underset{(-3.3)}{0.46\boldsymbol{\Delta}(\mathbf{G}_{\text{T\&I}})_{\mathbf{NR}}} - \underset{(0.6)}{0.39\Delta\text{DEP}}$$
$$+\underset{(2.0)}{6.33\Delta\text{CAP}_{-1}} - \underset{(-0.1)}{0.61\Delta\text{PR}_{-2}} - \underset{(-0.1)}{0.04\Delta\text{DJ}_{-0}}$$
$$+\underset{(1.0)}{0.21\Delta\text{PROF}_0} + \underset{(3.0)}{7.79\Delta\text{XR}_{\text{AV}}} + \underset{(2.1)}{0.012\Delta\text{POP}}$$
$$+\underset{(1.4)}{0.16\,\Delta(\text{BOR}_{-1})} + \underset{(2.1)}{0.14\,\Delta\text{GDP}_{\text{Real}(-3)}} \quad R^2 = 93.2\ \%$$
$$\text{D.W.} = 2.0 \text{ MSE} = 34.40 \tag{14.8}$$

Again, both types of deficits are found significantly related to reduced investment spending, and the effect appears to be about the same in recessions. In non-recession periods, spending deficits have a more negative effect than tax cut deficits.

14.3 Effects of Deficits on GDP in Recession/ Non-recession Periods

14.3.1 Implicit IS Curve Net Effects of Both Stimulus and Crowd Out Effects of Deficits

From discussion of crowd out theory in Chap. 2, we know that the form of the IS Curve incorporating both stimulus and crowd out effects of stimulus programs takes the form

$$\text{GDP} = \text{Y} = \left(\frac{1}{1-\beta}\right)[(-\beta + \lambda_1 + \lambda_2)\,T + (1 - \lambda_1 - \lambda_2)\,G - \theta\,r \\ + \gamma\,\text{ACC} + (X - M)\ldots + \ldots\text{etc.}] \qquad \text{(From Eq. (2.10))}$$

Where β is the marginal propensity to consume, λ_1 is the crowd out effect of deficits on consumer spending and λ_2 is the effect of deficits on investment spending. But this does not account for differences in recession and non-recession periods. To show this, we need to revise this to allow for different effects in recession and non-recession periods, as done in Eq. 14.9 below:

$$\begin{aligned}\text{GDP} = Y = \left(\frac{1}{1-\beta}\right)[&\left(-\beta + \lambda_{1(R)} + \lambda_{2(R)}\right) T + \left(1 - \lambda_{1(R)} - \lambda_{2(R)}\right) G \\ &+ \left(-\beta + \lambda_{1(NR)} + \lambda_{2(NR)}\right) T + \left(1 - \lambda_{1(NR)} - \lambda_{2(NR)}\right) G \\ &- \theta\, r + \gamma\, ACC + (X - M)\ldots + \ldots\text{etc}\ldots.\end{aligned} \qquad (14.9)$$

Or, using coefficient estimates from consumption Eq. 14.4.2 and investment Eq. 14.8.

$$
\begin{aligned}
GDP = Y = \left(\frac{1}{1-\beta}\right) & \left[\left(-0.41 + 0.90 + 0.39 - 0.59^{*}\right) T + (1 - 0.55 - 45)\, G \right. \\
& + \left(-0.41 + 0.56 + 0.29 - 0.59^{*}\right) T + (1 - 0.33 - 0.46)\, G \\
& \left. + 0.14\, C_{B2} + 0.16\, I_{B(-1)} \cdots + \ldots \text{etc} \ldots \right] \qquad (14.10)
\end{aligned}
$$

*The (−0.59) factor reflects the fact that a proportion of the tax cut is not spent (i.e., the mps). It is returned to the savings pool, reducing the loss of funds available for private borrowing due to government crowd out borrowing to finance the deficit. (0.59 = 1-mpc) represents the upper limit of how much is returned to the pool of loanable funds for further use buying goods and services. Part may be diverted to purchases of stocks and bonds from traders who then use the money to purchase other securities, and so on. See discussion in Chap. 12 (Sect 12.1) and after Eq. 14.4.2.

To calculate the impact of deficits on the borrowing variables, recall the following relationships of deficits to borrowing given in Chap. 10 (Sect. 10.1), using the same method of inferring from consumption and investment regression results.

Spending effects of deficits due to crowd out in part act through the borrowing variable in each spending model. The effects, estimated in Eqs.7.5.Alt and 8.5.Alt, and used in Method #1 IS curve calculations earlier when recession/non-recession effects were not individually calculated (Section 10.1.1.) are shown below:

Effects of deficits on borrowing—used in Method 1

Tax cut deficit	Spending deficit	
$\Delta C_B = 0.61\ \Delta T_T$	$-0.55\ \Delta G_{T\&I}$	(Eq. 7.5.Alt)
$\Delta I_B = 1.21\ \Delta T_T$	$-1.02\ \Delta G_{T\&I}$	(Eq. 8.5.Alt)
Total 1.82 ΔT_T	$-1.57\ \Delta G_{T\&I}$	

Estimates from the borrowing models indicate that, per dollar of deficit incurred, statistically significant findings indicate that private C and I borrowing is reduced by more than one dollar ($1.82 for tax deficits, $1.57 for spending deficits). As noted in earlier (Chap. 8 (Sect 8.3)), this larger than one-for-one reduction in borrowing associated with a dollar increase in the deficit may occur because a dollar deficit used to (e.g.,) increase unemployment benefits, has two effects on borrowing:

- Money available for private borrowing is reduced by \$1, to finance the government deficit. If borrowing is "lumpy" borrowing may decline by more than \$1.00.
- Part or all of the new transfer income may not be used by stimulus recipients to increase their spending, but merely to substitute the new stimulus income for additional borrowing they would otherwise have to do to finance normal spending on essentials, (e.g., using a credit card to purchase food), this would show up as a further decline in borrowing associated with deficits. Hence, total borrowing would decline more than a dollar, for each dollar of deficit incurred.

Since the effects of tax and spending deficits on borrowing were not calculated separately for recession and non-recession periods, we shall use the estimated effects for the whole 50-year sample period shown above. These suggest the total effect on C and I spending of the borrowing effect is

$$0.14\ \Delta C_B = (0.14)(0.61)\ \Delta T_T - (0.14)(0.55)\ \Delta G_{T\&I}$$
$$0.16\ \Delta I_B = (0.16)(1.21)\ \Delta T_T - (0.16)(1.02)\ \Delta G_{T\&I}$$
$$\text{Total } (0.28)\ \Delta T_T - (0.24)\ \Delta G_{T\&I}$$

Where Eqs. 14.4.2 and 14.8 indicate that in addition to crowd out effects measured directly through the deficit variables, there is a \$0.14 change in consumer spending for each dollar change in consumer borrowing induced by the deficit, and a \$0.16 change in investment spending related to a dollar decline in investment borrowing.

Hence, Eq. 14.10 becomes

$$\text{that is, } Y = \left(\frac{1}{1-\beta}\right)[+0.29_R T + 0.00_R$$
$$-0.15_{NR}T + 0.21_{NR}G \ldots + 0.28T - 0.24G) \quad \text{(Eq. 14.10.1)}$$

$$\text{or} \quad Y = \left(\frac{1}{1-\beta}\right)[+0.57_R T - 0.24_R G\,] \quad \text{in recessions} \ldots$$

$$Y = \left(\frac{1}{1-\beta}\right)[+0.13_{NR}T - 0.03_{\mathrm{NR}}G\,] \quad \text{in nonrecessions}$$

The results indicate that in both recessions and non-recessions, tax cut and spending deficit stimulus programs have a net negative impact on the GDP.

These results compare to the deficit effect for the whole 50-year period sampled (representing the average of recession and non-recession periods) given in Chap. 10 (Sect 10.1.1) using this same method: a decline in GDP of $0.35 per dollar of tax cut deficit and $0.47 per dollar of spending deficit.

Reasons for the net zero or negative effect of deficit stimulus programs on the GDP were explained earlier in the paper. (See Chap. 10 (Sect. 10.1). In short, borrowing model evidence reviewed earlier indicates borrowing declines more than $1.00 for each dollar of deficit incurred. The first dollar reduction can be attributed to crowd out of private borrowing required to finance the tax cut or government spending increase out of the current pool of loanable funds. The additional drop in borrowing may occur because people use their new stimulus income to buy goods they would have bought anyway, but out of borrowed money, for example, a new car purchased out of an increase in disposable income due to a tax cut. Since one (typically) borrows to buy what one's disposable income will not cover, stimulus income may directly reduce borrowing without increasing intended spending. A one-dollar tax cut, even if all of it is spent, may be spent on items that the consumer would otherwise have borrowed for, such as the new car. Hence, tax cut stimulus results in a zero increase in spending, but at the price of a dollar's reduction in spending by those from whom the government borrowed money to finance the tax cut. This leaves tax cuts having a net negative effect on the GDP.

An even more intuitive example is the government borrowing $1.00 from a bank to increase unemployment benefits. This cuts any spending the bank's traditional borrowers had planned to do out of money borrowed from that bank by $1.00. But stimulus spending programs are often geared toward the unemployed, rather than typical bank borrowers. The unemployed person receiving the new dollar in income will probably spend it on food or other necessities they otherwise would have had to borrow for (perhaps by charging their credit card). This again leads to a net negative stimulus effect of government spending on private spending.

Method #2 from Section 10.1.2 was used to directly estimate all coefficients in the IS curve in one regression equation, using the same model used there except for dividing the single tax and government spending variables into recession and non-recession variables. The following results were obtained using OLS:

Model 14.11 OLS single regression model used to simultaneously estimate all IS curve parameters

$$\underset{(t=)}{\Delta Y_T} = \underset{(4.2)}{.72\boldsymbol{\Delta}(\mathbf{T_T})_\mathbf{R}} + \underset{(0.4)}{.08\boldsymbol{\Delta}(\mathbf{G_{T\&I}})_\mathbf{R}} + \underset{(4.6)}{.37\boldsymbol{\Delta}(\mathbf{T_T})_\mathbf{NR}}$$
$$- \underset{(-0.6)}{.16\boldsymbol{\Delta}(\mathbf{G_{T\&I}})_\mathbf{NR}} - \underset{(2.0)}{8.58\Delta PR} - \underset{(-3.0)}{.41\,\Delta DJ_{-0}} + \underset{(5.0)}{1.17\,\Delta DJ_{-2}}$$
$$- \underset{(-1.1)}{1.64\,\Delta XR_{AV}} + \underset{(1.7)}{478.51\Delta POP_{16}} + \underset{(3.6)}{.04\Delta POP}$$
$$+ \underset{(1.8)}{1.12\Delta ICC_{-1}} + \underset{(5.0)}{85.39\Delta M2_{AV}} + \underset{(9.5)}{.53\,\Delta ACC}$$
$$+ \underset{(2.5)}{1.47\Delta DEP} + \underset{(2.1)}{6.07\Delta CAP_{-1}} + \underset{(1.6)}{6.70\Delta PR_{-2}}$$
$$+ \underset{(0.7)}{0.07\Delta PROF} + \underset{(6.5)}{0.27\,\boldsymbol{\Delta}\left(\mathbf{C_{B2}} + \mathbf{I_{B(-1)}}\right)} + \underset{(1.9)}{0.06\,\Delta GDP_{Real(-3)}}$$
$$+ \underset{(0.6)}{0.11\Delta X} - \underset{(-4.6)}{0.66\,AR(2)} + \underset{(5.4)}{0.80\,AR(7)}$$
$$R^2 = 97.7\ \%\quad D.W. = 2.4\quad MSE = 36.26 \tag{14.11}$$

Hence, our Method #2 findings as to the net stimulus effects of changes in taxes or government spending are:

$$\underset{(t=)}{\Delta Y} = \underset{(4.2)}{0.72\Delta(T_T)_R} + \underset{(0.4)}{0.08\Delta(G_{T\&I})_R} + \underset{(4.6)}{0.37\Delta(T_T)_{NR}} - \underset{(-0.6)}{0.16\Delta(G_{T\&I})_{NR}}$$
$$+ \underset{(6.5)}{0.27\,\Delta\left(C_{B2}\&I_{B(-1)}\right)} \ldots + \ldots \text{etc} \qquad \text{(From Eq. 14.11)}$$

Recall from Method 1 that we need to convert the borrowing coefficient from \$0.27 per dollar of reduced borrowing to (\$0.27 × 1.82 = \$0.49) for tax deficits or (\$0.27 × 1.57 = \$0.42) for spending deficits to convert the regression coefficient to a comparable figure per dollar of deficit. This leaves our estimated effects of deficit-creating tax cuts or government spending increases at

$$\underset{(t=)}{\Delta Y} = \underset{(5.4)}{0.99\Delta(T_T)_R} - \underset{(-0.9)}{0.19\Delta(G_{T\&I})_R} + \underset{(5.8)}{0.64\Delta(T_T)_{NR}} - \underset{(-1.6)}{0.43\Delta(G_{T\&I})_{NR}}$$
$$\text{(From Eq. 14.12)}$$

The IS curve estimates of effects on the GDP of stimulus programs in recession and non-recession periods can be stated as follows:

- The findings indicate tax cuts have a substantial negative effect on GDP in recessions (crowd out significantly overwhelms stimulus effects: the net effect is \$0.99 per dollar of deficit). Assuming the covariance of the standard errors of the tax variable (0.17) and borrowing variables (0.04) is zero, the standard error on the estimate of \$0.99 is S.E. = $\sqrt{[(0.17)^2 + (1.82)^2(0.04)^2]} = 0.185$, implying the *t*-statistic is 5.4, which is highly statistically significant

- The findings also indicate tax cuts also have a substantial negative effect on GDP in non-recession periods (crowd out significantly overwhelms stimulus effects: the net effect is \$0.64 per dollar of deficit). Assuming the covariance of the standard errors of the tax variable (0.08) and borrowing variables (0.04) is zero, the standard error on the estimate of \$0.37 is S.E. = $\sqrt{[(0.08)^2 + (1.82)^2(0.04)^2]} = 0.11$, implying the *t*-statistic is 5.8, which is highly statistically significant.
- Spending deficits also have a negative impact on GDP in recessions of \$−0.19 per dollar of deficit. Assuming the covariance of the standard errors of the spending variable (0.20) and borrowing variables (0.04) is zero, the standard error on the estimate of \$−0.19 is se = $\sqrt{[(-0.20)^2 + (1.57)^2(0.04)^2]} = 0.209$, implying the *t*-statistic is 0.9, which indicates the coefficient, though having a negative sign, is not significantly different from zero, that is, no net effect, positive or negative.
- Spending deficits were also found to have a negative impact on GDP in non-recession periods of \$−0.16 per dollar of deficit. Assuming the covariance of the standard errors of the spending variable (0.27) and borrowing variables (0.04) is zero, the standard error on the estimate of \$−0.43 is S.E. = $\sqrt{[(-0.27)^2 + (1.57)^2(0.04)^2]} = 0.277$, implying the *t*-statistic is 1.6, which indicates the coefficient, though having a negative sign, is not significantly different from zero, that is, no net effect, positive or negative.

Hence, our Method #2 overall conclusion is that tax cut stimulus programs financed by deficits have a net negative effect on the GDP, that the negative effect may actually be greater in recessions. Our overall conclusion regarding spending deficits is that they have a net zero effect on the GDP after crowd out effects are taken into consideration, and that this holds for both recessions and non-recessions. Method 1 results were similar, but are difficult to compare precisely since standard errors were not calculated. These results were obtained by incorporating crowd out variables into a standard Keynesian deficit-driven stimulus model, and subjecting it to econometric testing.

By comparison, our Chap. 10 (Sect. 10.1) results, which gave average results for both recession and non-recession periods in the whole 50 years sampled were

$$\Delta Y = \underset{(7.8)}{0.89\Delta T_T} \underset{(3.0)}{-0.57\Delta G_{T\&I}} \qquad \text{(From Eq. 10.2)}$$

that is, the average for the whole sample period was estimated to be between the recession and non-recession effect for tax cuts. For government spending programs, the estimated average effect for the whole period had the same negative sign, and was statistically significant, but was noticeably higher than either the recession or non-recession estimates calculated above, but the difference is within two standard deviations of the estimate obtained testing for the average effect for the whole period.

We conclude the results for models with and without recession/ non-recession controls are very consistent for tax cut deficits and roughly consistent for spending deficits, though Method #2 shows noticeably higher negative effects for spending deficits than Method #1.

CHAPTER 15

Does the Gale and Orszag Hypothesis Explain Tax and Spending Effects Better in Recessions Than Non-recession Periods?

In earlier tests (Section 10.3), we were unable to corroborate Orszag and Gale's findings that Federal tax cuts and transfer spending programs have net simulative effects, while other types of spending and tax cuts do not. However, these earlier tests did not involve testing recession and non-recession periods separately. Hence, we will now separately test the Gale and Orszag hypothesis for both recession and non-recession periods. We will retest the standard IS curve model given in Section 10.1.2, except for dividing government receipts into two parts, federal receipts (T_F) and state and local government receipts ($T_{S\&L}$), and dividing government spending variables into two parts: spending on transfer programs (G_T) and non-transfer spending (G_{NonT}). Separate estimates will be obtained for each of these four variables for recession and non-recession periods.

Ten IS curve models were tested. In recessions, most tests showed negative effects on GDP of state and local government tax cuts, and for any type of government spending (except transfers). All negative findings were statistically significant. Most tests of federal tax cuts or increases in transfer payments showed no statistically significant effect on GDP in either direction.

In non-recession periods, generally all four types of deficits were found to have no net effect on GDP. Coefficients were insignificant on 34 out of 40 tests. The occasional significant findings did not concentrate on any one type of deficit.

To remove autocorrelation in the models, the partial autocorrelation method described in connection with tests on Eq. 10.1.1 was used,

J.J. Heim, *Crowding Out Fiscal Stimulus*,
DOI 10.1007/978-3-319-45967-7_15

indicating an AR(9) control was needed. OLS results using the Υ_{-3} business cycle control are given in Eq. 15.1 below.

Model 15.1 OLS test of Orszag hypothesis for differential effects of tax and spending deficits on GDP in recession and non-recession periods

$$\begin{aligned}
\underset{(t=)}{\Delta Y_{T}} =& -\underset{(-0.8)}{0.48\boldsymbol{\Delta}(\mathbf{T_F})_{\mathbf{R}}} + \underset{(4.0)}{12.50\boldsymbol{\Delta}(\mathbf{T_{S\&L}})_{\mathbf{R}}} + \underset{(1.1)}{1.26(\mathbf{G_T})_{\mathbf{R}}} - \underset{(-3.9)}{5.10\boldsymbol{\Delta}(\mathbf{G_{NonT}})_{\mathbf{R}}} \\
&+ \underset{(1.7)}{0.42\boldsymbol{\Delta}(\mathbf{T_F})_{\mathbf{NR}}} + \underset{(2..1)}{1.99\boldsymbol{\Delta}(\mathbf{T_{S\&L}})_{\mathbf{NR}}} - \underset{(-2.5)}{1.02\boldsymbol{\Delta}(\mathbf{G_T})_{\mathbf{NR}}} - \underset{(-1.0)}{0.68\boldsymbol{\Delta}(\mathbf{G_{NonT}})_{\mathbf{NR}}} \\
&+ \underset{(0.8)}{7.80\Delta \mathrm{PR}} - \underset{(-2.7)}{1.24\,\Delta \mathrm{DJ}_{-0}} - \underset{(-1.3)}{0.71\,\Delta \mathrm{DJ}_{-2}} + \underset{(2.5)}{15.67\,\Delta \mathrm{XR}_{\mathrm{AV}}} - \underset{(-0.4)}{239.88\Delta \mathrm{POP}_{16}} \\
&+ \underset{(4.2)}{0.07\Delta \mathrm{POP}} + \underset{(0.2)}{0.26\Delta \mathrm{ICC}_{-1}} + \underset{(1.2)}{49.89\Delta \mathrm{M2}_{\mathrm{AV}}} + \underset{(3.9)}{0.62\,\Delta \mathrm{ACC}} + \underset{(2.8)}{4.31\Delta \mathrm{DEP}} \\
&+ \underset{(1.8)}{18.19\Delta \mathrm{CAP}_{-1}} - \underset{(-0.1)}{1.73\Delta \mathrm{PR}_{-2}} - \underset{(-0.6)}{0.16\Delta \mathrm{PROF}} - \underset{(-2.2)}{0.23\,\Delta\left(C_{B2} + I_{B(-1)}\right)} \\
&+ \underset{(1.7)}{0.12\,\boldsymbol{\Delta}\mathbf{GDP}_{\mathbf{Real}(-3)}} + \underset{(1.2)}{0.45\Delta \mathrm{X}} + \underset{(5.3)}{0.87\,\mathrm{AR}(9)} \\
& \underset{\mathrm{MSE}=48.64}{R^2 = 96.9\%, \mathrm{D.W.} = 2.2}
\end{aligned} \tag{15.1}$$

Results indicate that during recessions, state and local government tax cuts and all spending increases except transfer programs have a net negative effect on GDP, whereas federal tax cuts and transfer spending increases have no statistically significant net effect on the GDP either way. In this sense, the findings do provide support for the argument that there are differential effects, but <u>not</u> for the argument that federal tax cuts and spending on transfers have a positive effect. Rather, the data indicate negative effects for both types of tax cuts and for non-transfer spending, but a zero net effect on the GDP for transfer spending. In non-recession periods, both types of tax cuts and transfer spending had a negative relationship to GDP. Non-transfer government spending was not found to have any effect.

Since we are already controlling for recession/non-recession effects on crowd out, the use of lagged GDP or other business cycle controls may be pointless. Repeating the above test without $GDP_{Real(-3)}$ yields nearly identical results, confirming the adequacy of using separate recession and non-recession spending and tax variables.

The negative sign on the Federal tax variable for recessions was unexpected; virtually all previous tests have shown strongly significant positive signs on tax variables. Unusually strong intercorrelation between two explanatory variables can distort estimates to the point of changing signs from that more accurately representing the underlying relationship. A check for that indicated that the simple correlation coefficient (0.85) between yearly changes in federal taxes and state and local taxes, and of (−0.79) between the federal tax variable and transfer spending variable in recessions were far higher than any other correlations in the data set. Replacing the federal tax variable for recessions with its average value for the current and prior year, unfortunately, as was done earlier to address a similar problem, actually raised the multicollinearity levels to (0.92) and (0.81), respectively. Instead, we substituted the one-year lagged values for the current values, which brought the correlation with state and local taxes in recessions down to (0.79) and the correlation with transfer spending down to (−0.62). Retesting the model using the lagged tax variable markedly improved statistical significance of many variables and restored the expected positive sign and statistical significance of the federal tax variable. Results are shown in Eq. 15.2 below.

Model 15.2 OLS test of Orszag hypothesis for differential effects on GDP in recession and non-recession periods

(Using one-year lagged values of $\Delta(T_F)_R$ to remove distortive effects of severe multicollinearity. Otherwise, test is the same as 15.1. above.

$$\begin{aligned}
\underset{(t=)}{\Delta Y_T} = \; & +\underset{(4.1)}{1.04\boldsymbol{\Delta}(\mathbf{T_F})_\mathbf{R}} + \underset{(3.5)}{6.61\boldsymbol{\Delta}(\mathbf{T_{S\&L}})_\mathbf{R}} + \underset{(1.4)}{1.03(\mathbf{G_T})_\mathbf{R}} - \underset{(-4.1)}{3.88\boldsymbol{\Delta}(\mathbf{G_{NT}})_\mathbf{R}} \\
& + \underset{(2.2)}{0.46\boldsymbol{\Delta}(\mathbf{T_F})_\mathbf{NR}} + \underset{(1.5)}{1.17\boldsymbol{\Delta}(\mathbf{T_{S\&L}})_\mathbf{NR}} - \underset{(-1.8)}{0.89\boldsymbol{\Delta}(\mathbf{G_T})_\mathbf{NR}} \\
& - \underset{(-1.2)}{0.69\boldsymbol{\Delta}(\mathbf{G_{NT}})_\mathbf{NR}} - \underset{(-0.2)}{1.57\Delta \mathrm{PR}} - \underset{(-2.3)}{0.85\,\Delta \mathrm{DJ}_{-0}} - \underset{(-0.1)}{0.06\,\Delta \mathrm{DJ}_{-2}} \\
& + \underset{(1.9)}{12.41\,\Delta \mathrm{XR_{AV}}} \quad \underset{(0.3)}{221.31\Delta \mathrm{POP}_{16}} + \underset{(4.8)}{0.06\Delta \mathrm{POP}} \\
& + \underset{(0.7)}{1.00\Delta \mathrm{ICC}_{-1}} + \underset{(2.4)}{72.44\Delta \mathrm{M2_{AV}}} + \underset{(5.3)}{0.77\,\Delta \mathrm{ACC}} + \underset{(2.1)}{2.47\Delta \mathrm{DEP}} \\
& + \underset{(2.1)}{21.99\Delta \mathrm{CAP}_{-1}} + \underset{(0.4)}{3.34\Delta \mathrm{PR}_{-2}} - \underset{(-0.4)}{0.12\Delta \mathrm{PROF}} \\
& - \underset{(-0.9)}{0.12\,\boldsymbol{\Delta}\left(\mathbf{C_{B2}} + \mathbf{I_{B(-1)}}\right)} + \underset{(1.2)}{0.12\,\Delta \mathrm{GDP_{Real(-3)}}} \\
& + \underset{(0.5)}{0.15\Delta X} + \underset{(2.4)}{0.58\,\mathrm{AR}(9)} \quad \underset{\mathrm{MSE}=44.45}{R^2 = 97.4\%, \mathrm{D.W.} = 2.3}
\end{aligned} \tag{15.2}$$

Here, in recessions, deficits caused by either type of tax cut or by increasing spending on non-transfer items has a negative effect on GDP, consistent with most earlier findings. Increased spending on transfers has no statistically significant effect one way or the other. In non-recession periods, only federal tax cuts have a net negative effect; state and local tax cuts, and both kinds of spending increases have no significant net effect on GDP in either direction. In short, again we find no support for the Gale and Orszag hypothesis. As was the case with 15.1, dropping the business cycle control leaves the results essentially unchanged (though this result is not shown here).

Eq. 15.3 below shows results when the current unemployment rate is used as the business cycle control.

Model 15.3 OLS test of Orszag hypothesis for differential effects on GDP in recession and non-recession periods

(Using one-year lagged values of $\Delta(T_F)_R$ to remove distortive effects of severe multicollinearity, and using the current year unemployment rate as the business cycle control. Otherwise, test is the same as 15.1. above.

$$
\begin{aligned}
\underset{(t=)}{\Delta Y_T} = \; & +\underset{(0.6)}{0.15\boldsymbol{\Delta}(\mathbf{T_F})_{\mathbf{R}}} + \underset{(4.2)}{4.09\boldsymbol{\Delta}(\mathbf{T_{S\&L}})_{\mathbf{R}}} + \underset{(2.8)}{1.24(\mathbf{G_T})_{\mathbf{R}}} - \underset{(-2.2)}{1.83\boldsymbol{\Delta}(\mathbf{G_{NT}})_{\mathbf{R}}} \\
& +\underset{(0.6)}{0.08\boldsymbol{\Delta}(\mathbf{T_F})_{\mathbf{NR}}} + \underset{(1.3)}{0.84\boldsymbol{\Delta}(\mathbf{T_{S\&L}})_{\mathbf{NR}}} + \underset{(0.3)}{0.09\boldsymbol{\Delta}(\mathbf{G_T})_{\mathbf{NR}}} \\
& -\underset{(-0.5)}{0.20\boldsymbol{\Delta}(\mathbf{G_{NT}})_{\mathbf{NR}}} - \underset{(-2.8)}{12.04\Delta PR} - \underset{(-1.5)}{0.31\,\Delta DJ_{-0}} - \underset{(-0.6)}{0.21\,\Delta DJ_{-2}} \\
& +\underset{(1.5)}{7.66\,\Delta XR_{AV}} \quad \underset{(1.4)}{1210.31\Delta POP_{16}} + \underset{(4.8)}{0.05\Delta POP} \\
& +\underset{(0.9)}{0.69\Delta ICC_{-1}} + \underset{(2.4)}{44.76\Delta M2_{AV}} + \underset{(6.7)}{0.57\,\Delta ACC} + \underset{(5.8)}{3.15\Delta DEP} \\
& +\underset{(3.5)}{13.57\Delta CAP_{-1}} + \underset{(0.4)}{1.66\Delta PR_{-2}} - \underset{(-1.1)}{0.12\Delta PROF} \\
& -\underset{(-0.8)}{0.06\,\Delta\left(C_{B2} + I_{B(-1)}\right)} - 0.82 \quad \underset{(-5.9)}{0.35\,\Delta UNEM} \qquad (15.3) \\
& +\underset{(1.5)}{0.25\Delta X} + \underset{(0.7)}{0.13\ AR(9)} \quad \underset{MSE=33.38}{R^2 = 98.5\%, D.W. = 1.9}
\end{aligned}
$$

With this model, controlling for business cycle effects with the unemployment rate markedly changes results for transfer spending in recessions. Now in recessions, federal tax cuts have no significant effect, state and local tax cuts still have a negative effect. Increased government spending on transfers does have a statistically significant positive impact on GDP, though other types of spending increases appear to have no effect either way. The findings also indicate that in non-recession years, no type of tax cut or spending increase has any significant net effect on GDP, either positive or negative. Clearly, the big news here is that increased transfer spending in recessions, unlike other spending, can have a positive effect on the GDP. The estimated effect is $1.24 per dollar of increased transfer spending (offset slightly perhaps by adverse effects of increased borrowing).

However, here again there is a substantial multicollinearity problem which appears to be affecting the Eq. 15.3 results. State and local taxes are correlated −0.73 with government transfer spending, and transfer spending +0.61 with the unemployment rate. (Earlier, we had also found multicollinearity problem in the unemployment rate affected its sign in some tests. See Eq. 7.2.Alt.) This combination of intercorrelations appears to be distorting the estimate for transfer payments compared to all our earlier results. The correlation between transfer spending and the previous business cycle control variable, lagged GDP (Υ_{-3}), was only +0.21. As Carl Fox has shown, intercorrelation among explanatory variables distorts regression estimates (Fox, 1961, pp. 257, 452). Replacing current period state and local tax receipts with the average of current and prior year receipts markedly reduces the correlations and restores the estimated effect of transfer spending to comparability with 15.1 and 15.2, without markedly changing estimates obtained for other key variables, as shown in 15.4 below.

Model 15.4 Same test as 15.3. Above, but with the current year recession period state and local tax variable replaced by the average of its current year and prior year values.

$$
\begin{aligned}
\underset{(t=)}{\Delta Y_T} = {} & \underset{(0.8)}{+0.24\boldsymbol{\Delta}(\mathbf{T_F})_{\mathbf{R}}} \underset{(2.8)}{+3.55\boldsymbol{\Delta}\left(\mathbf{T_{S\&L(AV)}}\right)_{\mathbf{R}}} \underset{(1.6)}{+0.81(\mathbf{G_T})_{\mathbf{R}}} \underset{(-3.2)}{-1.83\boldsymbol{\Delta}(\mathbf{G_{NT}})_{\mathbf{R}}} \\
& \underset{(0.7)}{+0.09\boldsymbol{\Delta}(\mathbf{T_F})_{\mathbf{NR}}} \quad \underset{(1.4)}{+0.91\boldsymbol{\Delta}(\mathbf{T_{S\&L}})_{\mathbf{NR}}} \underset{(0.8)}{+0.22\boldsymbol{\Delta}(\mathbf{G_T})_{\mathbf{NR}}} \underset{(-0.3)}{-0.14\boldsymbol{\Delta}(\mathbf{G_{NT}})_{\mathbf{NR}}} \\
& \underset{(-1.44)}{-8.34\Delta \mathrm{PR}} \underset{(-0.8)}{-0.17\,\Delta \mathrm{DJ}_{-0}} \underset{(-0.8)}{-0.23\,\Delta \mathrm{DJ}_{-2}} \underset{(1.5)}{+8.12\,\Delta \mathrm{XR}_{\mathrm{AV}}} \quad \underset{(0.7)}{624.95\Delta \mathrm{POP}_{16}} \\
& \underset{(4.2)}{+0.044\Delta \mathrm{POP}} \underset{(1.1)}{+1.02\Delta \mathrm{ICC}_{-1}} \underset{(1.6)}{+34.34\Delta \mathrm{M2}_{\mathrm{AV}}} \underset{(7.8)}{+0.56\,\Delta \mathrm{ACC}} \underset{(5.2)}{+3.50\Delta \mathrm{DEP}} \\
& \underset{(2.5)}{+9.53\Delta \mathrm{CAP}_{-1}} \underset{(-0.3)}{-1.77\Delta \mathrm{PR}_{-2}} \quad \underset{(-0.6)}{-0.08\Delta \mathrm{PROF}} \underset{(-1.3)}{-0.10\,\Delta\left(C_{B2}+I_{B(-1)}\right)} \\
& -0.71 \quad \underset{(-6.1)}{0.47\,\Delta \mathrm{UNEM}} \underset{(0.1)}{-0.02\Delta \mathrm{X}} \underset{(1.1)}{+0.30\,\mathrm{AR}(9)} \\
& \underset{\mathrm{MSE}=33.61}{R^2 = 98.5\%, \mathrm{D.W.} = 1.9}
\end{aligned} \tag{15.4}
$$

As was the case with 15.1 and 15.2 where the less multicollinearity ridden variable Υ_{-3} was used as the business cycle control variable, transfer spending is now found statistically insignificant in recessions. All types of tax and spending change have a zero net effect on GDP except two: state and local tax cuts, and non-transfer spending in recessions. Both have a negative effect. (To avoid a previous multicollinearity problem between the two tax types during recessions, we had replaced the current period federal tax variable with its value lagged one period in 15.2. We now return it to current year values to avoid the same problem, since we are using a lagged value of state and local taxes. Hence, the federal tax variable in recessions returns to the statistically insignificant state it held in Eq. 15.1.)

2SLS Tests

To deal with endogeneity between GDP and most contemporaneous explanatory variables, the current period explanatory variables were replaced by instruments. Wald tests were undertaken to determine, for each variable replaced, whether the instrument was strong or weak. Testing indicated the instrument was a strong instrument for all the contemporary period variables, except for transfer spending in non-recession periods and the non-transfer government spending variable in recessionary periods, for which the instrument is a weak instrument. We were unable to find one instrument that would serve as a strong instrument for them and the other variables at the same time. Results are shown in 15.5 below (which uses the current period variant of the $(T_F)_R$ variable).

Model 15.5 2SLS test of Orszag hypothesis for differential effects on GDP in recession and non-recession periods

(Strong Instrument used for all current period RHS variables except $(T_{\text{TR}})_{\text{NR}}$ and $(T_{\text{NT}})_R$ Sargan test $nR^2 = 4.9 < X^2_{(.95,\ 14)} = 23.7$)

$$
\begin{aligned}
\underset{(t=)}{\Delta Y_T} = \; & \underset{(-0.2)}{-0.16\boldsymbol{\Delta}(\mathbf{T_F})_\mathbf{R}} + \underset{(1.7)}{5.63\boldsymbol{\Delta}(\mathbf{T_{S\&L}})_\mathbf{R}} + \underset{(1.4)}{0.96(\mathbf{G_T})_\mathbf{R}} - \underset{(-2.2)}{2.69\boldsymbol{\Delta}(\mathbf{G_{NT}})_\mathbf{R}} \\
& + \underset{(0.9)}{0.30\boldsymbol{\Delta}(\mathbf{T_F})_\mathbf{NR}} + \underset{(0.5)}{0.52\boldsymbol{\Delta}(\mathbf{T_{S\&L}})_\mathbf{NR}} - \underset{(-2.4)}{1.35\boldsymbol{\Delta}(\mathbf{G_T})_\mathbf{NR}} \\
& - \underset{(-1.3)}{0.62\boldsymbol{\Delta}(\mathbf{G_{NT}})_\mathbf{NR}} - \underset{(-1.0)}{12.03\Delta\text{PR}} - \underset{(-2.1)}{0.65\,\Delta\text{DJ}_{-0}} + \underset{(0.3)}{0.16\,\Delta\text{DJ}_{-2}} \\
& + \underset{(1.0)}{4.73\,\Delta\text{XR}_{\text{AV}}} + \underset{(0.6)}{818.60\Delta\text{POP}_{16}} + \underset{(4.2)}{0.07\Delta\text{POP}} \\
& + \underset{(0.7)}{0.67\Delta\text{ICC}_{-1}} + \underset{(3.2)}{85.11\Delta\text{M2}_{\text{AV}}} + \underset{(5.8)}{0.81\,\Delta\text{ACC}} + \underset{(0.6)}{0.89\Delta\text{DEP}} \\
& + \underset{(3.1)}{28.32\Delta\text{CAP}_{-1}} + \underset{(2.4)}{15.21\Delta\text{PR}_{-2}} - \underset{(-1.0)}{0.20\Delta\text{PROF}} \\
& + \underset{(1.4)}{0.19\,\Delta\left(C_{B2} + I_{B(-1)}\right)} + \underset{(2.1)}{0.21\,\Delta\text{GDP}_{\text{Real}(-3)}} \\
& + \underset{(1.0)}{0.29\Delta\text{X}} + \underset{(1.3)}{0.23\,\text{AR}(9)} \quad \underset{\text{MSE}=52.57}{R^2 = 96.3\%, \text{D.W.} = 2.5}
\end{aligned}
\tag{15.5}
$$

Results indicate no net effect on GDP for any of the tax variables or for transfer spending, whether in recessions or non-recession periods. Government spending on non-transfer programs has a net significant negative effect on GDP in recessions but is insignificant in non-recession periods. Transfer spending is just the opposite: insignificant in recessions, negatively significant in non-recessions.

Model 15.6 below tests the same model except for replacing the recession federal tax variable with its one-year lagged value, as was done with the OLS tests Eqs. 15.2 and 15.3 above.

Model 15.6 2SLS test of Orszag hypothesis for differential effects on GDP in recession and non-recession periods

(Strong Instrument used for all current period RHS variables except $(T_{TR})_{NR}$ and $(T_{NT})_{R}$; $(T_F)_R$ lagged one year. Sargan test $nR^2 = 5.1 < X^2_{(.95,\ 14)} = 23.7$)

$$\begin{aligned}
\underset{(t=)}{\Delta Y_T} = \; & \underset{(2.3)}{+0.66\boldsymbol{\Delta}(\mathbf{T_F})_{\mathbf{R}}} \underset{(4.3)}{+5.16\boldsymbol{\Delta}(\mathbf{T_{S\&L}})_{\mathbf{R}}} \underset{(1.3)}{+0.97(\mathbf{G_T})_{\mathbf{R}}} \underset{(-4.5)}{-3.44\boldsymbol{\Delta}(\mathbf{G_{NT}})_{\mathbf{R}}} \\
& \underset{(1.6)}{+0.40\boldsymbol{\Delta}(\mathbf{T_F})_{\mathbf{NR}}} \underset{(0.4)}{+0.34\boldsymbol{\Delta}(\mathbf{T_{S\&L}})_{\mathbf{NR}}} \underset{(-2.7)}{-1.36\boldsymbol{\Delta}(\mathbf{G_T})_{\mathbf{NR}}} \\
& \underset{(-1.4)}{-0.77\boldsymbol{\Delta}(\mathbf{G_{NT}})_{\mathbf{NR}}} \underset{(-1.4)}{-12.38\Delta \mathrm{PR}} \underset{(-2.4)}{-0.69\,\Delta \mathrm{DJ}_{-0}} \underset{(0.4)}{+0.13\,\Delta \mathrm{DJ}_{-2}} \\
& \underset{(1.3)}{+8.36\,\Delta \mathrm{XR}_{AV}} \underset{(0.4)}{+430.40\Delta \mathrm{POP}_{16}} \underset{(4.6)}{+0.07\Delta \mathrm{POP}} \\
& \underset{(0.8)}{+1.00\Delta \mathrm{ICC}_{-1}} \underset{(3.9)}{+90.10\Delta \mathrm{M2}_{AV}} \underset{(7.1)}{+0.88\,\Delta \mathrm{ACC}} \underset{(1.1)}{+1.27\Delta \mathrm{DEP}} \\
& \underset{(3.8)}{+29.95\Delta \mathrm{CAP}_{-1}} \underset{(2.4)}{+12.01\Delta \mathrm{PR}_{-2}} \underset{(-0.8)}{-0.17\Delta \mathrm{PROF}} \\
& \underset{(0.3)}{+0.06\,\Delta\left(C_{B2} + I_{B(-1)}\right)} \underset{(1.6)}{+0.19\,\Delta \mathrm{GDP}_{\mathrm{Real}(-3)}} \\
& \underset{(0.6)}{+0.16\Delta \mathrm{X}} \underset{(1.6)}{+0.31\ \mathrm{AR}(9)} \quad \underset{\mathrm{MSE}=42.23}{R^2 = 96.9\%, \mathrm{D.W.} = 2.7}
\end{aligned} \tag{15.6}$$

These findings suggest that the crowd out problem is worse for both types of tax cuts and non-transfer spending during recessions. During recession the transfer spending effect is positive, but statistically insignificant. In non-recession periods, generally, no type of tax cut or spending appears to have a statistically significant effect, except non-transfer spending's negative effect.

In Eq. 15.7, we rerun the Eq. 15.6 model, except substituting the unemployment rate for Υ_{-3} as the business cycle control variable.

Model 15.7 2SLS test of Orszag hypothesis for differential effects on GDP in recession and non-recession periods, unemployment rate used as business cycle control variable

(Strong Instrument used for all current period RHS variables except $(T_{TR})_{NR}$ and $(T_{NT})_R$; $(T_F)_R$ lagged one year. Sargan test $nR^2 = 8.3 < X^2_{(.95,\ 14)} = 23.7$)

$$
\begin{aligned}
\underset{(t=)}{\Delta Y_T} = \; & +\underset{(0.8)}{.25\boldsymbol{\Delta}(\mathbf{T_F})_{\mathbf{R}}} + \underset{(5.6)}{4.48\boldsymbol{\Delta}(\mathbf{T_{S\&L}})_{\mathbf{R}}} + \underset{(3.4)}{1.71(\mathbf{G_T})_{\mathbf{R}}} - \underset{(-2.3)}{2.05\boldsymbol{\Delta}(\mathbf{G_{NT}})_{\mathbf{R}}} \\
& + \underset{(0.1)}{.02\boldsymbol{\Delta}(\mathbf{T_F})_{\mathbf{NR}}} + \underset{(1.2)}{.81\boldsymbol{\Delta}(\mathbf{T_{S\&L}})_{\mathbf{NR}}} - \underset{(-0.1)}{.02\boldsymbol{\Delta}(\mathbf{G_T})_{\mathbf{NR}}} \\
& - \underset{(-0.6)}{.26\boldsymbol{\Delta}(\mathbf{G_{NT}})_{\mathbf{NR}}} - \underset{(-3.4)}{13.15\Delta PR} - \underset{(-0.8)}{.26\,\Delta DJ_{-0}} - \underset{(-0.3)}{.11\,\Delta DJ_{-2}} \\
& + \underset{(1.6)}{7.64\,\Delta XR_{AV}} \quad \underset{(1.2)}{1164.17\Delta POP_{16}} + \underset{(4.2)}{.05\Delta POP} + \underset{(0.5)}{.42\Delta ICC_{-1}} \\
& + \underset{(2.7)}{48.23\Delta M2_{AV}} + \underset{(6.6)}{.61\,\Delta ACC} + \underset{(5.7)}{3.02\Delta DEP} + \underset{(4.3)}{15.33\Delta CAP_{-1}} \\
& + \underset{(0.9)}{3.26\Delta PR_{-2}} - \underset{(-1.8)}{.15\Delta PROF} - \underset{(-0.6)}{.05\,\Delta\left(C_{B2} + I_{B(-1)}\right)} \\
& - \underset{(-6.4)}{.87.00\,\Delta UNEM} + \underset{(1.7)}{.38\Delta X} + \underset{(0.3)}{.05\,AR(9)} \\
& R^2 = \underset{MSE=34.99}{98.4\%, D.W. = 2.2}
\end{aligned}
\qquad (15.7)
$$

As was the case with the same model, when tested using OLS, this model shows a statistically significant, positive relationship between spending on transfers in recession and the GDP. Other government spending and state and local tax cuts are found significantly negatively related to the GDP; federal tax changes have no statistically significant effect one way or the other. In non-recession periods, no form of tax or spending change—up or down—seems significantly related to the GDP.

Here again, the multicollinearity issue raised in connection with using the unemployment rate variable in Eqs. 15.3 and 15.4, was addressed by replacing the current year state and local tax variable used in recession periods with its current and prior year average, and the federal tax variable in recessions restored to current year values. The unemployment rate was not found Hausman-endogenous, and therefore, was added to the instrument list used in Eq. 15.5, 15.6, and 15.7. Results are shown in 15.8 below, and were virtually identical to the OLS results presented earlier (Eq. 15.4) for the same model; (Sargan test: $nR^2 = 8.9 < X^2_{(.95,15)} = 25.0$.)

Model 15.8 Same as Model 15.7, except two-year average of $T_{S\&L}$ used, current value of T_F in recessions restored

$$\underset{(t=)}{\Delta Y_T} = +\underset{(0.8)}{.24\boldsymbol{\Delta}(\mathbf{T_F})_{\mathbf{R}}} + \underset{(2.8)}{3.55\boldsymbol{\Delta}\left(\mathbf{T_{S\&L(AV)}}\right)_{\mathbf{R}}} + \underset{(1.7)}{.81(\mathbf{G_T})_{\mathbf{R}}} - \underset{(-3.2)}{1.84\boldsymbol{\Delta}(\mathbf{G_{NT}})_{\mathbf{R}}}$$

$$+\underset{(0.7)}{.09\boldsymbol{\Delta}(\mathbf{T_F})_{\mathbf{NR}}} + \underset{(1.4)}{.91\boldsymbol{\Delta}(\mathbf{T_{S\&L}})_{\mathbf{NR}}} + \underset{(0.8)}{.22\boldsymbol{\Delta}(\mathbf{G_T})_{\mathbf{NR}}} - \underset{(-0.3)}{.14\boldsymbol{\Delta}(\mathbf{G_{NT}})_{\mathbf{NR}}}$$

$$-\underset{(-1.4)}{8.34\Delta PR} - \underset{(-0.8)}{.17\,\Delta DJ_{-0}} - \underset{(-0.8)}{.23\,\Delta DJ_{-2}} + \underset{(1.5)}{8.12\,\Delta XR_{AV}} \quad \underset{(0.7)}{624.90\Delta POP_{16}}$$

$$+\underset{(4.2)}{.044\Delta POP} + \underset{(1.1)}{1.02\Delta ICC_{-1}} + \underset{(1.6)}{34.34\Delta M2_{AV}} + \underset{(7.8)}{.56\,\Delta ACC} + \underset{(5.2)}{3.50\Delta DEP}$$

$$+\underset{(2.5)}{9.53\Delta CAP_{-1}} \quad -\underset{(-0.3)}{1.77\Delta PR_{-2}} \quad -\underset{(-0.6)}{.08\Delta PROF} \quad -\underset{(-1.3)}{.10\,\Delta\left(C_{B2} + I_{B(-1)}\right)}$$

$$-\underset{(-6.1)}{.71.47\,\Delta UNEM} - \underset{(0.1)}{.02\Delta X} \quad + \underset{(1.1)}{.30\,AR(9)}$$

$$R^2 = 98.5\%, D.W. = 1.9 \qquad (15.8)$$
$$MSE=33.61$$

Table 15.1 summarizes the findings of Eqs. 15.1, 15.2, 15.3, 15.4, 15.5, 15.6, 15.7, 15.8 for the magnitude and significance of the deficit variables, in the IS model for GDP determination.

Overall, the Gale and Orszag test findings indicate that during recessions:

(1) The crowd out problem is actually worse for both types of tax cuts and spending increases.
(2) Non-transfer spending and both federal and state and local tax cuts have a negative effect on GDP during recessions; transfer spending effect is positive, but statistically insignificant.

The Gale and Orszag test findings indicate that during non-recession periods no type of tax cut or spending increase appears to have a statistically significant effect of GDP in either direction.

Hence, we conclude that the best we can say about federal versus state and local tax cuts is that federal cuts have no significant effect on the GDP, while state and local tax cuts have a negative effect in recessions, and no net effect in normal times.

Table 15.1. Summary of Orszag hypothesis tests calculated separately for recession/non-recession periods

	$T_{F(R)}$	$T_{S\&L(R)}$	$G_{T(R)}$	$G_{NT(R)}$	$T_{F(NR)}$	$T_{S\&L(NR)}$	$G_{T(NR)}$	$G_{NT(NR)}$
Model#	*B (t)*	*B (t)*	*B (t)*	*B (t)*	*B (t)*	*B (t)*	*B (t)*	*B (t)*
15.1	−0.49	12.50	1.26	−5.10	0.42	1.99	−1.02	−0.68
	(0.7)	(4.0)	(1.1)	(3.9)	(1.7)	(2.1)	(2.5)	(1.0)
15.1a	−0.36	11.98	0.90	−4.75	0.37	1.96	−0.86	−0.79
	(0.6)	(3.7)	(0.7)	(3.2)	(1.5)	(2.1)	(1.8)	(1.1)
15.2	1.04	6.61	1.03	−3.87	0.46	1.17	−0.89	−0.69
	(4.1)	(3.5)	(1.4)	(4.1)	(2.4)	(1.5)	(1.8)	(1.2)
15.3	0.15	4.09	1.24	−1.83	0.08	0.84	0.09	−0.20
	(0.6)	(4.2)	(2.8)	(2.2)	(0.6)	(1.3)	(0.3)	(0.5)
15.4	0.24	3.55	0.81	−1.84	0.09	0.91	0.22	−0.14
	(.8)	(2.8)	(1.6)	(3.2)	(0.7)	(1.4)	(0.8)	(0.3)
15.5	−0.16	5.63	0.96	−2.69	0.30	0.52	−1.35	−0.62
	(0.2)	(1.7)	(1.4)	(2.2)	(0.9)	(0.5)	(2.4)	(1.3)
15.5a	0.07	5.53	0.62	−2.53	0.22	0.28	−1.33	−1.02
	(0.1)	(1.9)	(0.8)	(1.7)	(0.7)	(0.2)	(1.6)	(1.5)
15.6	0.66	5.17	0.97	−3.44	0.40	0.34	−1.36	0.77
	(2.3)	(4.3)	(1.3)	(4.5)	(1.6)	(0.4)	(2.7)	(1.4)
15.7	0.25	4.48	1.71	−2.05	0.02	0.81	−0.02	−0.26
	(0.8)	(5.6)	(3.4)	(2.3)	(0.1)	(1.2)	(0.1)	(0.6)
15.8	0.24	3.55	0.81	−1.84	0.09	0.91	0.22	−0.14
	(0.8)	(2.8)	(1.6)	(3.2)	(0.7)	(1.4)	(0.8)	(0.3)
Model Averages:								
All	0.16	6.31	1.03	−2.99	0.25	0.97	−0.63	−0.53
	(1.1)	(3.5)	(1.6)	(3.1)	(1.1)	(1.2)	(1.5)	(0.9)
OLS	0.06	7.75	1.05	−3.48	0.28	1.37	−0.49	−0.50
	(1.4)	(3.6)	(1.5)	(3.3)	(1.4)	(1.7)	(1.4)	(0.8)
2SLS	0.21	4.87	1.05	−2.51	0.21	0.57	−0.77	−0.25
	(0.8)	(3.3)	(1.7)	(2.7)	(0.8)	(0.7)	(1.5)	(0.8)

For transfer spending, the best we can say is there appears to be no significant net effect of either in either recessions or non-recessions. For non-transfer spending, the effect on GDP is negative in recessions, but it has no effect in non-recession periods.

Adding the effects of deficits on the borrowing variable to the direct effects changes the coefficients of the estimated effect, but does not appear to change the statistical significance. By comparison, in Chap. 14, where recession and non-recession effects of only total taxes and total government spending were tested for differences in recession and non-recession effects, we found the following:

$$\underset{(t=)}{\Delta Y} = \underset{(5.4)}{0.99\Delta(T_T)_R} + \underset{(5.8)}{0.64\Delta(T_T)_{\text{NR}}} - \underset{(-0.9)}{0.19\Delta(G_{T\&I})_R} - \underset{(-1.6)}{0.43\Delta(G_{T\&I})_{\text{NR}}} \quad \text{((15.12), Repeated)}$$

that is, there are negative effects of deficit-financed tax cuts on the GDP in both recession and non-recession periods, and no statistically significant net effect on the GDP of deficit-financed government spending programs, regardless of the state of the economy. By comparison, the Gale and Orszag type-models showed everything having no net effect except for negative effects in recessions of state and local tax cuts or non-transfer government spending.

CHAPTER 16

Summary of Findings and Conclusions

More than 30 years ago, Otto Eckstein, one of the world's most distinguished econometricians, noted the extent to which crowd out offsets the effectiveness of fiscal stimulus programs, was "still" unresolved:

> Does fiscal policy work? Or does the financing of deficits "crowd out" private activity? This has been one of the more durable controversies in macroeconomic theory. (Eckstein 1983, p. 35)

Unfortunately, this question, perhaps the most important question macroeconomists are asked to address, remains unresolved today. The failure to resolve this issue can only be an embarrassment to the macroeconomics profession.

In an attempt to resolve this issue once and for all, this study undertakes statistical tests of 228 separate models of stimulus programs and their crowd out effects. Thousands of regression coefficients and their statistical significance levels are calculated. The study uses the best science available to control for the large number of factors that affect consumption and investment that could leave results about crowd out's effect ambiguous, were they not controlled for. After first results were obtained, key models were then retested a second time on data from different time periods to ensure results were reliable. They were then retested again a third time using different statistical techniques, this time to ensure the results were not an artifact of the regression technique used, or at least to identify any differences that might occur, and determine if their causes were technical or substantive.

J.J. Heim, *Crowding Out Fiscal Stimulus*,
DOI 10.1007/978-3-319-45967-7_16

They were then retested a fourth time to see if effects differed in recession and non-recession periods. Finally, they were retested yet again, a fifth time, to see if results that held in general for tax and spending deficits, held for different types of tax cuts and government spending increases.

In short, the testing was exhaustive and designed to cover every conceivable variant of fiscal stimulus programs that might possibly provide a successful means for stimulating the economy. If some variant was missed, it was by accident, not intent.

All this was done in hopes that the quality of the science undertaken would be so strong that the findings could not be brushed aside as "just another study". Based on the work done here, hopefully the issue of how much stimulus programs are affected by crowd out effects can be put to rest.

It is easy to understand why standard deficit-driven Keynesian stimulus theory is attractive. It is appealing theoretically and has been the "go to" option for policy makers in both political parties for many decades. This is particularly true in recession periods, when both policy analysts and politicians are desperate for ideas on how to end the crisis.

However, Keynesian stimulus theory has been plagued with empirical problems. If deficits work to stimulate the economy, econometric testing of standard Keynesian "IS Curve" formulations should yield a negative sign on the tax variable and a positive sign on the government spending variable (See Chap. 2 above). Yet econometric testing generally yields statistically significant results having the <u>wrong sign</u> for the effects of tax cut and spending stimulus programs. These empirical tests indicate tax cut stimulus programs actually reduce the GDP, not increase it. The same is often true for government spending stimulus effects, or at best, that they have no effect at all on the GDP.

The cause of this inconsistency of theory and empirical tests appears to be related to the long-observed negative correlation showing private spending declines as government deficits increase.

Two major theories have been advanced to explain why deficits may be negatively related to consumer and business spending:

- <u>The "Crowd Out" Theory</u>: Government borrowing to finance deficits reduces money available for consumers and businesses to borrow, forcing a reduction private spending (in a world in which spending is determined not only by income but also by access to borrowing for cars, houses, etc.). This offsets any stimulus effect resulting from tax cuts or increased public spending allowed by the deficit. This may leave no net stimulus effect, or even a negative effect.

- The Krugman (et al.) Hypothesis: Deficits naturally rise in bad economic times, as tax collections drop and government spending on things like unemployment insurance automatically increase. The same bad times cause consumer and business spending to drop, independent of what is going on with the deficit. It is the bad economic times that cause the observed correlation of rising deficits and declining private spending, not crowd out caused by government deficits.

Using the best science available, this study tested 228 sophisticated economic models of what determines consumer and business spending and borrowing, and the GDP. The intent was to see if government deficits and crowd out were factors affecting consumer and investor spending decisions. In most of these tests, the state of the economy was controlled for, so that Krugman effects (declining economy causing both rising deficits and declining private spending) could not be accidentally misconstrued as a crowd out effect. Chapter 3 provides details of the testing methodology used. Distinguished members of the econometric community have offered comments on it, which have been incorporated where appropriate.

When evaluating the effects of deficit-driven stimulus programs and crowd out, large numbers of other variables were controlled for. This was done to ensure that if these variables were correlated with government deficits, as well as consumer or investment spending, (e.g., stock market movement or company profits), their effects could not accidentally be counted as deficit effects, simply because they were not controlled for. Exhaustive controls are an ironclad requirement for good science. A list of these other control variables is provided at the beginning of Chaps. 5 and 6.

Chapters 5, 6, 7 and 8 present the tests and findings of this study for four main groups of tests undertaken. Results are presented showing both the direct and indirect effects of crowd out, per dollar of deficit incurred. The first effect is the direct reduction in private spending. In Table 5.5, repeated immediately below, the tests indicate a $1.00 growth in government deficits directly reduces consumer spending $0.45 on average (and the same deficit causes additional declines in investment spending).

The second, more indirect effect stems from the decline in borrowing, which itself causes a decline in spending. The indirect effect in this table indicates that consumer borrowing also declines due to crowd out, causing consumer spending to drop another $0.12 per dollar of reduced borrowing. There are a number of reasons for this:

Table 5.5 Effect of deficits on consumer spending

	(Per $ dollar of deficit)	*(Per dollar of borrowing)*
Spending tests	*Deficit effect*	*Add'l. Borrowing effect*
Average (All Tests):	$ 0.45 (6.2)	$ 0.12 (2.3)
Av.(2SLS Str.Inst.Only*)	$ 0.46 (5.5)	$ 0.12 (2.4)
Average (OLS**):	$ 0.46 (7.4)	$ 0.12 (3.2)

t-statistic in parentheses
*2 Stage least squares regression, strong instrument tests only
**Ordinary least squares regression

(1) Much borrowing is done to finance big ticket items; government borrowing to finance its deficit may reduce what the bank can lend you from (say) $5000 to 4000, but if you need the full $5000 to buy the item, a $1000 deficit may reduce your borrowing and spending by the full $5000, that is, the net stimulus effect of deficits is negative due to crowd out, not just zero, simply because borrowing is "lumpy".
(2) Suppose this year there is no deficit. Total borrowing might be (e.g.) $1000 by someone who wants to buy some furniture and an additional $1000 borrowed by an unemployed person to buy food (perhaps by credit card borrowing). Next year, suppose someone else wants to borrow $1000 to buy furniture. Suppose the government also borrows $1000 to provide unemployment benefits to the same unemployed person. The one dollar borrowed by the government cuts private borrowing needed to buy the furniture by a $1000 due to crowd out, and the new unemployment benefits income removes the need for the unemployed to borrow. Net result: deficit grows one dollar, private borrowing drops two.

These and other reasons why there are negative effects of deficits on private borrowing and spending, not just offsetting effects, are discussed in detail in Chaps. 8 (Section 8.3) and 10 (Section 10.1).

Chapter 5 presents tests on 118 consumer spending or borrowing models using a one-variable definition of the deficit ($T_T - G_{T\&I}$). Results from Chap. 5, Table 5.5 are summarized below and show a strong negative effect of deficits on consumer spending:

Table 7.1 Effect of deficits on consumer spending

	(Per dollar of deficit)		*(Per dollar of borrowing)*
Spending tests	*Tax Def.*	*Spend. Def.*	*Borrowing effect*
Average (All tests)***	\$ 0.60 (12.5)	−0.28 (−3.8)	0.12 (3.3)
Av.(2SLS Str.Inst.Only)	\$ 0.64 (12.0)	−0.28 (−3.9)	0.11 (3.9)
Average (OLS)	\$ 0.58 (12.0)	−0.27 (−3.9)	0.12 (3.4)

t-statistic in parentheses.
***OLS and Strong Instrument Models

Chapter 7 presents 17 additional tests on consumer spending or borrowing models using a two-variable definition of the deficit (to see if the effects of tax cut and spending deficits differed). Results from Table 7.1 are summarized below. They also show a strong negative effect of deficits on consumer spending. Notice the effects of tax deficits are stronger, and the effects of spending deficits weaker, than the average of the two effects given in Table 5.5, where only a single variable was used to represent both types of deficit:

Chapter 6 presents tests on 80 investment spending or borrowing models using a one-variable definition of the deficit ($T_T - G_{T\&I}$). Results from Table 6.6 are summarized below and show a strong negative effect of deficits on investment spending:

Chapter 8 presents 25 additional tests on investment spending or borrowing models using a two-variable definition of the deficit (to see if the effects of tax cut and spending deficits differed). Results from Table 8.4 are summarized below. They also show a strong negative effect of deficits on investment spending. Notice the spending effects are stronger, and the tax effects weaker than the average of the two effects given in Table 6.6.

Notice that the effects of tax and spending deficits are different in consumption and investment models, yet if we add them together (see last page of Chap. 8) they are roughly the same for total consumption and investment spending, for example, for all tests, tax deficits direct total crowd out effect is \$0.82 per dollar of deficit; spending deficits total crowd out effect is \$0.73. In both cases, there is another \$0.24 in secondary borrowing effects.

Virtually all tests found that government deficits are associated with reduced consumer and business borrowing and spending. This adverse effect was found when the general state of the economy was controlled

Table 6.6 Effect of deficits on investment spending

	(Per dollar of deficit)	*(Per dollar of borrowing)*
Spending tests	*Deficit Effect*	*Borrowing Effect*
Average (All Tests)	\$ 0.30 (3.6) to 0.35 (5.5)	0.09 (1.8) to 0.19 (1.7)
Av.(2SLS Str.Inst.Only)	\$ 0.30 (3.4) to 0.34 (3.9)	0.09 (1.8) to 0.19 (1.7)
Average (OLS)	\$ 0.30 (3.6) to 0.33 (5.5)	0.10 (1.9) to 0.13 (2.1)

t-statistic in parentheses

Table 8.4 Effect of deficits on investment spending

	(Per dollar of deficit)		*(Per dollar of borrowing)*
Spending tests	*Tax Def.*	*Spend. Def.*	*Borrowing effect*
Average (All tests)	\$0.29 (4.0)	−0.56 (−4.9)	0.07(0.4)
Av.(2SLS Str.Inst.Only)[1]	\$0.23 (2.9)	−0.47 (−4.1)	0.11(1.9)
Average (OLS)	\$0.27 (2.8)	−0.40 (3.5)	0.10 (1.9)

t-statistic in parentheses
[1]Models using $Prof_{-0}$, DJ_0

for, indicating crowd out's effect was not being confused with Krugman's noted business cycle effect, but was something that occurred separately. Detailed presentation of individual test statistics are provided and summarized at the end of Chaps. 5, 6, 7 and 8.

Chapter 9 compares the 1 and 2 variable deficit results and finds them very consistent for tax deficits, and roughly consistent for spending deficits. For two-variable deficits, estimates of the negative effects of spending deficits are noticeably greater.

Chapter 10 (Section 10.1) estimates the effects of government stimulus programs, net of crowd out, on the GDP, rather than just consumption or investment alone. Two different methods of testing are used. Both indicate deficits induced by tax cuts had a decidedly large, statistically significant net negative effect on the GDP (\$0.47–\$0.89 per dollar of deficit), and spending deficits had a smaller, but still net negative effect on the GDP (\$0.35–\$0.57 per dollar of deficit) over the past 50 years, but the spending effect was, statistically speaking, insignificantly different from zero. The more negative effect of tax cut deficits stems from their smaller initial stimulus effect, which acts initially through the marginal propensity to consume (less than 1.0 per dollar of tax cut), compared to the initial stimulus effect of government spending (1.0 per dollar of deficit). Both are later magnified through multiplier effects. Unlike stimulus effects, crowd out effects tend to be the same, more than offsetting initial smaller stimulus effects of tax cuts, just offsetting the larger stimulus effects of spending projects.

Chapter 10.2 evaluates the four Krugman hypotheses in light of these findings. The analysis concludes as follows:

(1) Crowd out, not changes in the business cycle, is the major cause of the observed decline in private consumer and investment spending when deficits rise.
(2) Tests indicate net stimulus program effects are always zero or negative, regardless of stimulus size. Hence, any observed failure of stimulus programs to work is not because they are too small, or because their positive effects were used up just stopping the economy's crash.
(3) The crowd out effect of deficits is as great in recessions as normal economic times. This is because savings (the pool of domestic loanable funds) drops as much as loan demand during recessions. This leaves the reduced pool just equal to the reduced loan demand. Hence, any government borrowing in recessions creates the same crowd out problem, leaving stimulus programs as ineffective. In some cases, the pool of loanable funds may drop faster than loan demand, causing an even worse situation.
(4) Deficit-financed stimulus programs do not stimulate investment during recessions by improving the economy, causing business confidence to increase, and "crowding in" to result. Test results indicated their effect on the economy is typically negative, creating just the opposite effect.

Chapter 10 (Sect. 10.3) tests for Gale and Orszag effects. A 2004 study by former federal budget director Peter Orszag and economist William Gale found that Federal tax cuts have a positive stimulus effect on the economy, though state and local tax cuts have a negative effect. They also found that government spending on transfer income programs had a net stimulus effect on the economy, though spending on all other government programs did not. The portions of the Gale and Orszag study dealing with state and local tax cuts and non-transfer government spending are consistent with this study. However, the findings regarding federal tax cuts and transfer spending are not. Unlike Gale and Orszag, we did not find positive stimulus effects for federal tax cuts or for transfer spending increases.

Using the same models this study previously tested in Chaps. 5, 6, 7, and 8, but dividing the two total tax and total government spending variables into Gale and Orszag's four types of taxes and government spending, and retesting, we obtained no evidence of the Gale and Orszag effect. We have noted earlier (See Section 2.3.2) that Orszag's testing gave a net effect of tax cuts on consumer spending only, and did not factor in investment crowd out effects (as our IS curve models do). This may be a cause of the difference in results.

Chapter 10 (Section 10.4) uses the estimates of both the stimulative and crowd out effects to estimate the effects of the $830 billion 2009 Obama stimulus program. The results indicated the program's impact on the GDP was negative ($−340.3 billion to $−605.4 billion), a drop associated with an <u>increase</u> in the unemployment rate of 1.26–2.26 %. The effect in 2010 would have been to raise the unemployment rate from 9.6 % to 12.2–13.2 %, had other factors that influence the GDP not been moving in a more positive direction and offsetting crowd out effects (exports, the exchange rate, profits, the effect of prior year declines in interest rates, etc. These positive effects can also be estimated from the tests enclosed).

On a more technical note, Chap. 11 shows that while this study is done using comparative statics models, the same models could be relatively easily converted to dynamic models for further testing.

Chapter 12 notes that the crowd out problem can be avoided if borrowing is done from foreign sources of funding, provided these funds are not already part of the pool of foreign funds commonly used by domestic private borrowers. Evidence from the US recession period of 1981–83, shows that the pool of loanable funds (savings) declined more than loan demand. Hence, any government borrowing to finance a stimulus program during this recessionary period should have created a crowd out problem. However, a large increase in foreign borrowing was able to avoid crowd out problems that would have otherwise occurred from the large growth in the government deficit during this period.

Chapter 13 also deals with a technical issue. It shows that the definition of disposable income used in this study's consumption functions ($Y - T$) is equivalent or better than the disposable personal income definition more commonly used in economic studies.

Chapter 14 tests 13 models to see if crowd out is as big a problem in recessions as in non-recession periods. It finds crowd out is as much of a problem in recessions as in normal economic times. This appears to be because the pool of loanable funds drops as much or more during recessions than loan demand, leaving any borrowing of part of it by government to fund a deficit as much a problem for private borrowers as during normal times. The pool drops because the decline in income in recessions causes savings to drop. This also was an important finding, since it is sometimes argued that even if crowd out is a problem normally, it is not in recessions because private borrowing declines, leaving funds available for government to borrow without hurting private borrowers. Overall, Chap. 14 indicates tax cut deficits have a negative effect on GDP in both recession and non-recession periods, and spending deficits have no effect on the GDP either way.

Chapter 15 extends the recession/non-recession effect analysis of Chap. 14 to test for Gale and Orszag effects separately in recession and non-recession periods, testing ten additional models. No evidence of Gale and Orszag effects was found in non-recession periods. In recessions, state and local tax cuts and non-transfer spending were found negatively related to the GDP, and federal tax cuts and transfer spending were found to have no net effect. Some initial evidence of positive transfer spending effects in recession periods was found, but was later evaluated as due to a statistical problem (multicollinearity), which when corrected, left no statistically significant evidence of a positive effect.

16.1 Concluding Observation

The models tested in this study hypothesize a demand-driven economy. Supply is assumed to be sufficiently elastic to meet changes in demand in relatively short periods of time, and consumer spending is assumed driven principally by current income (essentially a Keynesian economy), but other factors are important, too. Testing of these models (when crowd out is included) indicated they explain 90–97 % of the yearly changes in consumer and investment spending, and the GDP, over the past 50 years. Even without the crowd out variables, they explain much of the variation. Earlier studies, referenced in the literature review section, indicate crowd out adds 6.4–15 % to explanatory power. This is strong evidence that the hypotheses tested, and nitty-gritty details about their underlying structure, are reasonably accurate representations of how the economy operates.

That said, typical Keynesian models fail to show that deficit-financed "stimulus" programs are likely to have a zero or negative effect on the economy, or explain why that might happen. This results from errors of omission in the theory. Some effects of deficits are stimulative, as the Keynesian's point out (and our tests show them). However, there are some effects of deficits that can negatively influence the deficit's total effect, and these are omitted in most tests of the standard Keynesian system. These are the crowd out variables, the variables constituting the government deficit. Including them is necessary to ensure there are variables in empirical tests which can capture the negative effects of government borrowing on private spending.

In this study, our fix for the standard system is not to scrap it, but just to add crowd out variables to it and retest. The results are used to re-estimate the whole system, and the re-estimated parameters are checked to see if they are more consistent with observed reality. We conclude they are. Tests consistently indicate crowd out, along with disposable income and the investment accelerator, are the most important variables in the consumption and investment models. The expanded system, including the crowd out variable, explains virtually all of the variation in consumer and investment spending that has occurred the past 50 years, as shown in the consumption and investment graphs below.

Hence, we conclude that not only did we successfully test for crowd out's effect on stimulus programs, but we picked the best type of models to do so—those that were already very good at explaining what drives economic behavior.

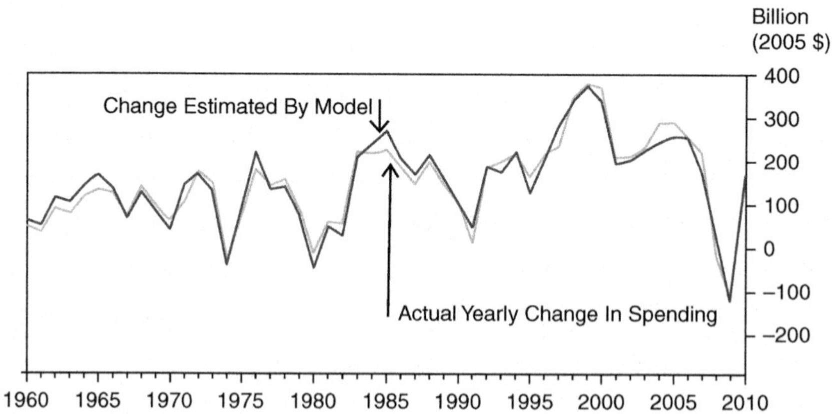

Consumption spending

Consumption Model Shown:

$$\underset{(t=)}{\Delta C_T} = \underset{(11.4)}{0.50\Delta(Y - T_T)} + \underset{(11.4)}{0.55\boldsymbol{\Delta}(\mathbf{T}_\mathrm{T})} - \underset{(-3.7)}{0.26\boldsymbol{\Delta}(\mathbf{G}_{T\&I})}$$

$$- \underset{(-5.1)}{11.81\Delta \mathrm{PR}} + \underset{(5.3)}{0.42\,\Delta \mathrm{DJ}_{-2}} + \underset{(2.3)}{3.42\,\Delta \mathrm{XR}_{\mathrm{AV}}} - \underset{(-1.3)}{336.65\Delta \mathrm{POP}_{16}}$$

$$+ \underset{(2.6)}{0.012\Delta \mathrm{POP}} + \underset{(1.3)}{0.36\Delta \mathrm{ICC}_{-1}} + \underset{(3.8)}{40.86\Delta \mathrm{M2}_{\mathrm{AV}}}$$

$$+ \underset{(3.1)}{0.12\,\boldsymbol{\Delta}\mathbf{C}_{\mathbf{B}2}} + \underset{(1.1)}{0.04\,\Delta \mathrm{GDP}_{\mathrm{Real}(-3)}}$$

$$R^2 = 94.9\ \%\quad \mathrm{D.W.} = 1.8\ \mathrm{MSE} = 25.45 \tag{7.1}$$

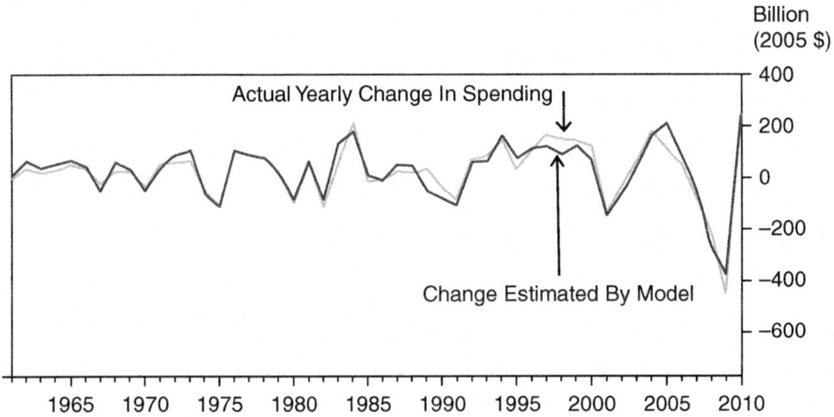

Investment spending

Investment Model Shown:

$$\underset{(t=)}{\Delta I_T} = + \underset{(4.9)}{0.33\Delta(\mathrm{ACC})} + \underset{(2.0)}{0.22\boldsymbol{\Delta}(\mathbf{T}_\mathrm{T})} - \underset{(-3.4)}{0.53\boldsymbol{\Delta}(\mathbf{G}_{T\&I})}$$

$$+ \underset{(3.0))}{0.81\Delta \mathrm{DEP}} + \underset{(1.0)}{2.39\Delta \mathrm{CAP}_{-1}} - \underset{(-0.9)}{2.29\Delta \mathrm{PR}_{-2}}$$

$$+ \underset{(0.4)}{0.10\Delta \mathrm{DJ}_{-0}} + \underset{(1.9)}{0.13\Delta \mathrm{PROF}_{-0}} + \underset{(2.4)}{5.87\Delta \mathrm{XR}_{\mathrm{AV}}}$$

$$+ \underset{(2.8)}{0.013\Delta \mathrm{POP}} + \underset{(0.9)}{0.05\,\boldsymbol{\Delta}(\mathbf{BOR}_{-1})} - \underset{(-1.5)}{12.40\,\Delta \mathrm{UNEM}}$$

$$R^2 = 93.1\ \%\quad \mathrm{D.W.} = 2.0\ \mathrm{MSE} = 33.05 \tag{8.2.Alt.b}$$

Bibliography

Barley, R. 2010. The Hidden Risks Governments Create by Delaying Cuts. *Wall Street Journal*, February 2, p.C14.

Barro, R.J., and C.J. Redlick. 2011. Macroeconomic Effects from Government Purchases and Taxes. *Quarterly Journal of Economics* 126(1): 51–102.

Blanchard, O., and R. Perotti. 2002. An Empirical Characterization of the Dynamic Effects of Changes in Government Spending and Taxes on Output. *The Quarterly Journal of Economics* 117(4): 1329–1368.

Chan, S. 2010. Group of 7's Finance Ministers Stand By Stimulus Programs. *NY Times*, February 2, p.A16.

Conference Board, The. 2003/2011. *Economic Report of the President, 2002 and 2010.* Washington, DC: U.S. Government Printing Office.

Conference Board, The. *The Conference Board's Index of Consumer Confidence.* The Conference Board, Inc. 845 Third Avenue, New York, NY, pp. 10022–6600.

Eckstein, O. 1983. *The DRI Model of the U.S. Economy.* New York: McGraw – Hill.

Ford, S. 1986. A Beginner's Guide To Vector Autoregression. Staff Paper P86-28, Institute of Agriculture, Forestry and Home Economics. University of Minnesota.

Fox, K. 1968. *Intermediate Economic Statistics.* New York: John Wiley and Sons.

Friedman, B. 1978. Crowding Out or Crowding In? Economic Consequences of Financing Government Deficits. *Brookings Papers on Economic Activity.* 1978(3): 593–641.

Furceri, D., and R. Sousa. 2009. The Impact of Government Spending on the Private Sector: Crowding Out versus Crowding In Effects. *NIPE WP 6/2009*, Nucleo De Investigaca Politicas Economicas, Universidade Do Minho, Portugal.

———. 2011. *Flow of Funds Accounts of the United States*, Data Series TODNS, TBSDODNS, CMDEBT, FGSDODNS, SLGSDODNS, AND DODFS.

J.J. Heim, *Crowding Out Fiscal Stimulus*,
DOI 10.1007/978-3-319-45967-7

Washington, DC. Board of Governors of the Federal Reserve System. March 11, Update. www.federalreserve.gov/releases/z1/current/

Gale, W.G., and P.R. Orszag. 2004. Budget Deficits, National Saving, and Interest Rates. *Brookings Papers on Economic Activity*. 2004(2): 101–187.

Granger, C.W.J. 1969. Investigating Causal Relations by Econometric Models and Cross-Spectral Methods. *Econometrica* 37: 424–438.

Hall, Robert. 1978. Stochastic Implications of the Life Cycle—Permanent income Hypothesis: Theory and Evidence. *Journal of Political Economy* 86(6): 971–987.

Heim, John J. 2007. How Much Does The Prime Interest Rate Affect U.S. Investment? *Journal of the Academy of Business and Economics*. 7(1): 143–149.

———. 2010. Do Government Deficits Crowd Out Consumer and Investment Spending? *Journal of the Academy of Business and Economics*. 10(3). Also available by the same title as Working Paper # 1005, *Department of Economics Working Paper Series*, Rensselaer Polytechnic Institute, Troy, N.Y., July 2010.

———. 2011. Is Crowd Out A Problem In Recessions? Working Paper # 1102, *Department of Economics Working Paper Series*. Troy, NY: Rensselaer Polytechnic Institute.

———. 2012a. Does Crowd Out Hamper Government Stimulus Programs In Recessions? *Journal of Applied Business and Economics* 13(2): 11–27.

———. 2012b. The Different Crowd Out Effects of tax Cut and Spending Deficits. *Applied Econometrics and International Development* 12(2): 105–122.

Jaeger, A. 1992. Does Consumption Take a Random Walk? *The Review of Economics and Statistics* 74(4): 607–614.

Kraay, A. 2012. How Large is the Government Spending Multiplier? Evidence From World Bank Lending. *Quarterly Journal of Economics* 127: 829–887.

Krugman, P. 2009. Crowding In. *New York Times*, September 28.

———. 2013. The Story of Our Time. *New York Times*, April 28.

Mankiw, G. 2006. The Macroeconomist as Scientist and Engineer. *Journal of Economic Perspectives* 20(4): 29–46.

Molena, H. 1991. The Time Series Consumption Function: Error Correction, Random Walk and the Steady-State. *The Economic Journal* 101(406): 382–403.

Mountford, A., and H. Uhlig. 2008. What Are The Effects Of Fiscal Policy Shocks? *NBER Working Paper # 14551*, December.

NBER. 2016. *S. Business Cycle Expansions and Contractions*. National Bureau of Economic Research, 1050 Massachusetts Avenue, Cambridge, MA, 02138.

Sims, C.A. 1972. Money, Income and Causality. *The American Economic Review* 62 (4): 540–552 (Sept. 11972).

———. 1977. Macro-economics and Reality. *Center for Economic Research Discussion Paper No. 77–91*. Department of Economics, University of Minnesota, Minneapolis, Minnesota.

Solow, R.M. 1956. A Contribution to the Theory of Economic Growth. *Quarterly Journal of Economics*, 70(1): 65–94.

———. 2010. Testimony to the Subcommittee on Oversight and Investigations of the Committee on Science and Technology, U.S. House of Representatives hearing on "Building a Science of Economics for the Real World".

Spencer, R.W., and W.P. Yohe. 1970. The Crowding Out of Private Expenditures by Fiscal Policy Actions. *Federal Reserve Bank of St. Louis Review*.

Triola, M. 2012. *Elementary Statistics*, 11 edn. Boston: Addison Wesley.

Uhlig, H. 2005. *Journal of Monetary Economics* 52: 381–419.

Woodford, M. 2011. Simple Analytics of the Government Expenditure Multiplier. *American Economic Journal: Macroeconomics* 3(1): 1–35.

Index

J.J. Heim, *Crowding Out Fiscal Stimulus*,
DOI 10.1007/978-3-319-45967-7

Printed by Printforce, the Netherlands